Making Nature Sacred

Making Nature Sacred

Literature, Religion, and Environment in America from the Puritans to the Present

JOHN GATTA

OXFORD
UNIVERSITY PRESS

2004

OXFORD

UNIVERSITY PRESS

Oxford   New York
Auckland   Bangkok   Buenos Aires   Cape Town   Chennai
Dar es Salaam   Delhi   Hong Kong   Istanbul   Karachi   Kolkata
Kuala Lumpur   Madrid   Melbourne   Mexico City   Mumbai   Nairobi
São Paulo   Shanghai   Taipei   Tokyo   Toronto

Copyright © 2004 by Oxford University Press, Inc.

Published by Oxford University Press, Inc.
198 Madison Avenue, New York, New York 10016

www.oup.com

Oxford is a registered trademark of Oxford University Press

Library of Congress Cataloging-in-Publication Data
Gatta, John.
Making nature sacred : literature, religion, and environment in
America from the Puritans to the present / John Gatta.
    p. cm.
Includes bibliographical references and index.
ISBN 978-0-19-516506-7
1. American literature—History and criticism.   2. Nature
in literature.   3. Religion and literature—United States.
4. Environmental protection in literature.   5. Natural history—
United States.   6. Nature—Religious aspects.   7. Holy, The, in literature.
8. Religion in literature.   9. Ecology in literature.   I. Title.
PS163 .G37 2004
810.9'36—dc22   2003026911

Printed in the United States of America
on acid-free paper

For Sam Pickering

Preface

Though I have spent the better part of my adult life pondering questions related both to religion and to the environmental imagination, this book represents my first extended effort to put the two together. In the past, my scholarly investigation of topics related to literature and faith rarely ventured out-of-doors. When I was growing up, in a typical American suburb after World War II, the environmental movement had yet to gain popular attention. But I always felt peculiarly drawn to the patch of field and woodland that I roamed as a child beside my home in Schenectady, New York. I suppose I never quite recovered from the shock of seeing this pleasantly enchanted, if not sacred, spot turn, some years ago, into a dreary strip mall. The local dairy farm, too, has long since been displaced by commercial development. So for me, as for countless others of my generation, the period that ended childhood's bucolic innocence happened to coincide with the beginning of decisive environmental and cultural changes. The postwar era saw development of a new interstate highway system, flourishing chemical and pesticide industries, limitless suburban sprawl, the decline of family farming, and the malling of America—but also, in time, new initiatives toward ecological restoration.

Like many others, too, I was moved when I first encountered Thoreau's *Walden* as an adolescent. This book, unlike any other I had read, awakened me not only to the beauty and surpassing worth of literature but also to the potentially religious—even sacramental— power of nature as reverenced by one committed to living deeply and deliberately. For me, this last awareness was reinforced by summer experiences at camp in the Adirondacks, a region that I still find sustaining during annual visits to Silver Bay on Lake George.

Although the churches have, by and large, been slow to integrate the newer promise of creation spirituality with the wisdom of classic Christianity, such a conjunction seems desperately needed at a time when we have gained unprecedented knowledge about the ways our environmental policies, particularly in the United States, affect the fate of this planet. Buddhist, Native American, and other traditions also have much to contribute to emerging conversation about the greening of religion. The current ecological crisis must be understood, I think, not just as an array of technical problems but as a genuine crisis of spirit and imagination. Since religion deals in ultimate questions, while our culture's literature embodies its deepest hopes and fears, an interfusion of both disciplines should cast light on this major issue of our time. Or so I came to feel, once I fastened on the idea of tracing the interplay between religion and environment across the full span of American literary history.

But this ambition did not take hold until I had already begun to teach offerings related to environmental literature, and had been writing about literature and religion for some time. One semester I found myself teaching an undergraduate course in "American Nature Writing" with my colleague Sam Pickering. We talked, argued, and occasionally sauntered along trails in our "Quiet Corner" of Connecticut. Sam's ebullient personality made this team-teaching assignment a treat for me. Himself an accomplished nature writer and author of familiar essays, Sam does not share my fascination with theology. Nonetheless, he insisted with typical generosity, at the close of one lecture session in the course, that I write a book about this idea of literature's involvement with numinous nature that had so plainly captivated my attention. The thought had never occurred to me before but struck me as obvious once he voiced it. So it is both fitting and satisfying for me to dedicate this book to Sam.

As the project began to take shape, I received intellectual stimulation from several quarters. I am grateful for the advice and support offered by fellow members of the Pew Foundation Working Group on Religion and American Literature, especially Lawrence Buell (who also helped me settle on a suitable title for the book), Harold Bush, Michael Colacurcio, Andrew Delbanco, James Dougherty, and Roger Lundin. My friend Ted Coolidge provided useful comments on an earlier draft of chapter 3. Other helpful recommendations came from two anonymous readers for Oxford University Press. Here at the University of Connecticut, I have benefited from suggestions offered by Donna Hollenberg, Michael Meyer, Jerry Phillips, and my lunchroom colleagues. But since none of these people saw the full manuscript before it went to press, the usual disclaimer about my sole responsibility for error applies all the more.

I have also learned pertinent things from my interactions with graduate students—including Chris Anderson, Bob Bitondi, Emily Cardinali, Pete Chidester, Bob Curry, Kurt Heidinger, and Karen Renner—who are pursuing their own ecocritical investigations. Karen Renner deserves special thanks for the technical assistance she provided while I was preparing the manuscript for publication. My former graduate student Ning Yu supplied two photo illustrations. My university provided the release time I needed to complete the project.

I benefited, too, from the crossdisciplinary intellectual stimulation afforded by Connecticut's Teale Lecture Series on Nature and Environment, ably lead by the biologist Greg Anderson. Over the years, this series has offered me the valuable opportunity of arranging visits to campus by several speakers relevant to the project—including Lawrence Buell, Peter Matthiessen, and Gary Snyder. Last year's campus visit by Bill McKibben, which Sam Pickering arranged, also fed this ongoing discussion.

As always, my wife, Julia, and daughter, Mary, contributed to my endeavor in more ways than I can say. I am grateful as well for the encouragement I received from Cynthia Read, executive editor at Oxford University Press, who has been unfailingly helpful and understanding at every stage of the book's production.

A portion of the commentary in chapter 8 has been adapted from my essay "Peter Matthiessen" in *American Writers, Supplement, 5*, ed. Jay Parini, Charles Scribner's Sons, copyright © 2000, pp. 199–217. That material is reprinted by permission of The Gale Group.

I also acknowledge with thanks permission granted me to cite the following.

"What Happened Here Before" (excerpt) by Gary Snyder, from *Turtle Island*, copyright ©1974 by Gary Snyder. "In Tonga" (excerpt) by Denise Levertov, from *A Door in the Hive*, copyright ©1989 by Denise Levertov. "A Hundred a Day" (excerpt) By Denise Levertov, from *This Great Unknowing: Late Poems*, copyright ©1968 by the Denise Levertov Literary Trust, Paul A. Lacey and Valerie Trueblood Rapport, Co-Trustees. "Tragic Error," "Settling," "Elusive," "Morning Mist," "Open Secret," Against Instrusion," and "Sojourns in the Parallel World" (excerpts) by Denise Levertov, from *The Life Around Us*, copyright ©1997 by New Directions Publishing Corp. Used by permission of New Directions Publishing Corporation. Citations from "Spring," "Nature," "The Ponds," and "Going to Walden," from *House of Light* by Mary Oliver, Copyright ©1990 by Mary Oliver. Reprinted by permission of the Molly Malone Cook Literary Agency. Citation from "Turtle," from *House of Light* by Mary Oliver, Copyright ©1990 by Mary Oliver. Reprinted by permission of Beacon Press, Boston. Excerpts from Annie Dillard's *Pilgrim at Tinker Creek*, © 1999, reprinted by permission of HarperCollins Publishers. Pattiann Rogers, *The Dream of the Marsh Wren: Writing as Reciprocal Creation*, edited by Scott Slovic (Minneapolis: Milkweed Editions, 1999); and "Fractal: Repetition of Form over a Variety of Scales" in *Song of the World Becoming: New and Collected Poems, 1981–2001* (Minneapolis: Milkweed Editions, 2001). Copyright © 1999, 2001 by Pattiann Rogers. Used with permission from Milkweed Editions. Excerpts from *Arctic Dreams: Imagination and Desire in a Northern Landscape*, © 1986 by Barry Lopez, reprinted by permission of Sterling Lord Literistic, Inc. Excerpts from *A Timbered Choir*, © 1998 by Wendell Berry and excerpts from *Mountains and Rivers Without End*, © Gary Snyder, both reprinted by permission of Counterpoint Press, a member of Perseus Books, LLC.

Biblical citations throughout are ordinarily taken from the Authorized (King James) Version since this translation was favored by most of the writers discussed here.

Contents

Making Nature Sacred

Introduction

"It's sort of what we have instead of God." This classic remark by Brett Ashley, a character in Hemingway's novel *The Sun Also Rises* (1926), epitomizes both the modern crisis of faith and our inescapable need to embrace either religion or some proxy vehicle of commitment to values beyond ourselves. In Ashley's case, the substitution amounts to a negatively phrased moral resolution. Her decision "not to be a bitch" is what she has instead, and what enables her to "feel rather good," if not sanctified.[1] Particularly since the Victorian era, other forms of surrogate religion—including literature, science, psychotherapy, and social reformation—have also competed for favor throughout Western culture. In America, though, no path for pursuing self-transcendence has seemed more enduringly accessible than the one leading nature devotees into the continent's own forests, fields, river valleys, and mountains.

By the nineteenth century, this preoccupation with American nature might be cynically regarded as a surrogate not only for organized religion but also for the contrasting wealth of material artifacts and prestige of high artistic culture attributed to Europe. Thus, Hawthorne complained in the preface to his final romance, *The Marble Faun* (1860), set in Italy, that his native land with its "commonplace prosperity" had no civilized ruins, "no antiquity, no mystery" comparable to Europe's and conducive to imaginative inspiration.[2] Nonetheless, what many Americans of Hawthorne's era thought they still had to believe in and venerate "instead of" all these things was American Nature, God's own plenty of undeveloped land on a scale of beauty and majesty unsurpassed in the known world. "I must tell you that there is something in the proximity of the woods which is very singular,"[3] the French emigré writer J. Hector St. John de Crèvecoeur confided to readers in his *Letters from an American Farmer* (1782); and this singular proximity began to mark the American soul (though not always for the good, in Crèvecoeur's view) even in its pre-Columbian youth. As everyone recalls from F. Scott Fitzgerald's evocation of landscape in *The Great Gatsby*, early European encounters with the "fresh green breast of the New World" provoked impressions of wonder bordering on worship.

Belief in the numinous, regenerative force of American landscapes has permeated the visual arts as well. Such conviction is unmistakable in works by nineteenth-century artists associated with the Hudson River school of painting. Figures such as Thomas Cole, Frederic Church, and Albert Bierstadt loved to paint uplifting images of waterfalls, rugged hills, and other picturesque scenes. Thomas Cole, in his "Essay on American Scenery" (1835), explained that since the "scenes of solitude" available in sublime wilderness came undefiled from the hand of God, they readily inspired contemplation of "eternal things" and the divine creator. Observing that biblical episodes of numinous experience had commonly taken place in remote landscapes, Cole insisted that "the wilderness is YET a fitting place to speak of God."[4] Nor was Cole alone in seeing God's glory shine from the presumably unsullied face of nature.

The term "nature" is notoriously elusive,[5] but belief in the rejuvenating and spiritually sustaining capacities of outdoor experience has remained an article of faith in the United States long after belief in pastoral idealism should have expired. Incredibly, belief in the more-than-material "strangeness"[6] of material nature has somehow managed to survive this country's transformation by industrialization, the demise of noncommercial agrarianism, the intellectual triumph of empirical science, and the latter-day emergence of a postindustrial consumer society wedded to technology. Within popular culture, hints of this survival can be seen in the proliferation of campgrounds, conservation organizations, and outdoor programs of all sorts marketed today across the land. Both literature and American literary scholarship have plentifully embodied it, too, in ways worth considering in some detail. The imaginative testimony of authorial and fictive characters ranging from Natty Bumppo and Huck Finn to Emily Dickinson, Henry Thoreau, Black Elk, Rachel Carson, and Annie Dillard includes many encounters with the ineffable spirits of nature. At the level of gross generalization, that much is clear. Much harder to outline, however, are the theologies and spiritualities of nature variously reflected in such testimonies. If there can be no such thing, in post-Enlightenment culture, as animistic faith that gods or spirits dwell directly "in" the tree, precisely what kind of religious responses to the nonhuman world *have* remained viable in American life and letters? That is the main question I was drawn to pursue in the pages that follow.

What makes this inquiry all the more problematic, by way of what Henry James would call a "beautiful difficulty," is the peculiar character of American religiosity. As Alexis de Tocqueville and other social commentators have observed, America resisted the full-scale secularization of society longer and usually more vigorously than Europe. Despite the major impact of secular skepticism, organized religion is still practiced today by appreciable numbers of

Americans, particularly in some sections of the country. Or as Jake Barnes, the American narrator of Hemingway's novel, replies to Lady Brett Ashley's confession of doubt, "Some people have God. . . . Quite a Lot." Even those fiercely independent American writers who have mostly rejected the forms of institutional religion they inherited, and do not "have God" in any conventional sense, often confirm in their most fertile imaginings that such forms retain a certain hold on *them*. Thus, nature spirituality frequently presents itself in American literary culture as a supplement rather than a surrogate for revealed religion. What might a selective survey of the nation's "nature writing" show us about the ways experiential faith in a numinous nature can coexist, albeit at times uneasily, with the belief-systems of organized religion? Here was another large question I wanted to address.

A few critical developments in the history of literary scholarship have prepared the way for this investigation. One, of course, is the twentieth-century emergence of American literature as a field of academic study. A good deal of early critical attention then focused on the mode of symbolic romance, which commonly features individualized confrontations with elemental nature in place of the denser social interaction prevalent in the realistic novel. It is telling that Perry Miller, our most distinguished intellectual historian of the last century, underscored the confidence of nineteenth-century Christian citizens that "God speaks to us" with peculiar force "in the sublimity of Nature" and that "America, beyond all nations, is in perpetual touch with Nature." Themes related to "Nature," "pastoralism," or "wilderness" figured prominently in critical studies of American literature and culture published after World War II.[7] But with the rise of the environmental movement after 1970, the topic developed a new tone and urgency—leading toward the still more recent emphasis on "ecocriticism" as an important new way of approaching literary culture in colleges and universities across the United States.

Like any other new way of reading, ecocriticism has not always been practiced or understood the same way by all who claim involvement in it. For the most part, though, it describes an angle of ethical attention rather than a fixed methodology or discrete body of texts. Cheryll Glotfelty has usefully defined it as a critical approach to literature that examines "the relations between writers, texts, and the world" but regards the world as "the entire ecosphere" rather than simply "the social sphere." Ecocriticism is an "earth-centered approach to literary studies" that probes "the relationship between literature and the physical environment." For the critic William Howarth, "ecocriticism seeks to redirect humanistic ideology, not spurning the natural sciences but using their ideas to sustain viable readings."[8]

A crucial statement of ecocriticism appeared when Lawrence Buell published his book *The Environmental Imagination* in 1995.[9] Focusing on nonfiction, Buell discussed the ways that an authentically "ecocentric" understanding of literature involves full attentiveness to the nonhuman world, a conscious mediation between actual and imaginary frames of perception. In environmental texts, according to Buell, the nonhuman environment is regarded as a substantial presence—not merely as a backdrop or setting. Thus, ecocriticism encourages readers to look beyond conventionally defined nature themes to adopt a renewed perspective on texts and the world. In a subsequent, much-discussed article appearing in the *New York Times Magazine*, critic Jay Parini observed the rapid emergence of new course offerings in environmental studies that include literary texts and that bridge the chasm between science and humanities.[10]

Within this larger enterprise, which is grounded in the historicism of American Studies, my aim here is to traverse another gap, that which ordinarily divides ecocriticism from the theological concerns of religious studies. In fact, the religious import of American environmental literature has yet to be fully recognized or understood, even though the sense of an unseen, transcendental or sacred Presence within the natural world has persisted within North American literature and culture from the beginnings of English settlement to the present day. Significantly, American writers who share little else by way of personal disposition or beliefs have often perceived in nature something beyond itself—and beyond themselves. To this extent, Frederic Jackson Turner's classic frontier hypothesis remains viable: the cultural proclivity to regard unsettled or less settled landscapes as sacred space must be deemed characteristically, if not uniquely, American.

Although this penchant for sacralizing the nonhuman environment is most obviously revealed in the Transcendentalist writers associated with nineteenth-century Romanticism, it also appears variously in earlier Puritan and non-Christian figures (including the neo-pagan Thomas Morton and the deist Thomas Jefferson) as well as in present-day authors. It may be informed by pantheistic or by more orthodox religious assumptions—or by amalgams of both. Native American mythologies reveal yet another form of the conviction that the material world should be venerated as sacred space. Beliefs in a numinous nature may be implicated in worldly politics—in the territorial ambition of nineteenth-century Manifest Destiny, for example, or other forms of exceptionalism. Or they may be tied to more global conceptions of citizenship, as in the modern case of Peter Matthiessen's book *The Snow Leopard*, an American journey to distant lands that challenges nationalistic assumptions.

In Catherine L. Albanese's illuminating book-length study, the spirituality inherent in American cultural constructions of the environment is discussed as an analytically discrete though protean "cluster of beliefs, behaviors, and values" called "nature religion."[11] My approach in what follows is somewhat different. Instead of positing any distinct religion of nature in America, I investigate the ways in which representative nature-minded writers nurtured within the Christian tradition, or within certain other established religious traditions, have tried to envision the New World environment. I consider how the perspectives developed within these more orthodox, nonnative traditions have been modified by encounter with other spiritualities—and with the land itself. In sum, my concern is not with "nature religion" as such, but with the imaginative chronicle of those who have variously endeavored to couple the symbolic assumptions of historically based, established religions with palpable experience of America's woods, fields, seascapes, and open air. I aim to describe not a religion of nature but the diverse theologies of Creation that have arisen and found figurative expression within the primary context of Western religion.

Among the major traditions of world religion, Christianity, not surprisingly, has most deeply affected the ecological outlook of English-speaking North Americans. More particularly, subcultures shaped religiously by Protestant Christianity have dominated imaginative expression in this sphere until the last half-century or so, when more eclectically Christian and Catholic versions of ecospirituality have also gained prominence in writers such as Annie Dillard, Barry Lopez, Wendell Berry, and Kathleen Norris. Less predictable, though, in demographic terms is the substantial influence that Buddhism— rather than Judaism or Islam—has had on modern American nature writing, as reflected in the varied production of figures such as Jack Kerouac, Gary Snyder, and Peter Matthiessen. By contrast, the strongly urban orientation of most Jewish-American writers helps explain the limited involvement with the nonhuman world displayed in this literature.[12] Native American attitudes toward the physical world deserve special notice in assessments of the continent's religious history. Deferring to the fuller treatments offered elsewhere by anthropologically trained specialists, I consider only one facet of this heritage in chapter 7, which includes a reading of Black Elk. African-American literature, too, commonly evokes a spirituality mediated through the nonhuman world, as evidenced in fiction by Zora Neale Hurston and Toni Morrison. And yet, because the urge to escape degrading conditions in the rural South has been so central to African-American experience and self-expression, this literature often bears a problematic relation to conventional notions of nature writing. At the start of chapter 8, my assessment of a little-discussed novel by W.E.B. Du Bois, and of the religiosity nurtured within southern black "maroon communities," is again meant to serve only as a suggestive, rather than exhaustive, treatment of the pertinent racial issues.

It is perhaps needless to add that, even within the limits just indicated, my survey of religious environmental literature is scarcely comprehensive. Among the many other figures who warrant attention in a full survey of this field are Emily Dickinson, John Burroughs, Mark Twain, Willa Cather, Robert Frost, John Steinbeck, Robinson Jeffers, Wallace Stegner, Norman Maclean, Leslie Silko, Kathleen Norris, Terry Tempest Williams, and Chet Raymo. I am consoled, however, by the confidence that "of making many books there is no end" (Ecclesiastes 12:12) and that ecospiritual accounts of such writers either have appeared or will appear in other books. If anything, one might wonder if this grand tour covers too much ground. The itinerary stretches across several periods of literary and intellectual history; it covers an uneven terrain marked by multiple genres—both poetry and fiction, in addition to the expected bulk of nonfictional prose. Some sweep is required, though, to trace the developmental history of this broadly religious tendency to regard the visible biosphere as a source of invisible meaning and inspiration. Moreover, I hope this literary panorama of numinous nature in America, a vista that stretches across generic and chronological boundaries, allows the views of individual writers to emerge in clearer perspective.

Accordingly, sections devoted to close textual reading alternate with broader summaries; and chapters focused specifically on Jonathan Edwards and Henry Thoreau have been interposed between chapters addressing multiple authors and topics. The Edwards chapter, situated in eighteenth-century discourse, includes a time-fracturing detour that leads the argument briefly through Aldo Leopold's twentieth-century "land ethic." Because the project's sweeping inquiry demands a reconsideration of classic nineteenth-century naturalists such as Thoreau and Emerson, I regard the sixth chapter on Thoreau as a centerpiece of the study. The two other chapters (4 and 5) devoted to literary expressions of Romantic religion also include sections on Bryant, Cooper, Whitman, Hawthorne, and Melville. Margaret Fuller and Celia Thaxter receive some attention here, too, though women writers become most prominently identified with the spiritualization of nature in the next century, when ecofeminist criticism emerges as well. Before then, as Buell and others have observed, the hero of the wilderness quest-romance in classic American literature is usually cast as a solitary male.

So the book's plan is to proceed in most cases chronologically, offering critical commentary on representative writers by way of tracing pivotal phases in the cultural narrative. I have tried to situate readings of primary texts within the extended context of intellectual, social, and religious history. Some of the texts are relatively unfamiliar, at least to those who customarily read and teach literature; others, such as Hawthorne's "The Old Manse" and Melville's *Moby-Dick*, are thoroughly canonical but rarely associated with "nature writing."

My first three chapters on early literature highlight writers of colonial New England because I share the longstanding conviction that this terrain provides a seminal and symbolically rich—if no longer inevitable—point of departure for inquiry across broad expanses of American cultural and religious history. Early American figures treated here include well-known Puritans such as Anne Bradstreet, William Bradford, Edward Taylor, Cotton Mather, and Jonathan Edwards as well as the eccentric Anglican adventurer Thomas Morton, and the Quakers John Woolman and William Bartram. My opening chapter explores the ambivalent response of early English colonists to New England's wilderness. For seventeenth-century Puritans, untamed nature was at once a challenge, a force to be mastered by human industry, and a revelatory field of divine Creation. The second chapter includes a novel attempt to read Anne Bradstreet's "Contemplations" ecocritically, so as to admit the poet's reliance on European traditions of "meditating on the creatures" while exploring her interest in local American scenes.

In approaching figures such as Edwards and Woolman in chapters 2 and 3, I wanted to affirm the ecological value of texts that lack direct visualization of landscapes and organisms. The chief environmental import of Edwards's work, for example, lies in the realm of religious and philosophical ethics rather than in the naturalist's re-creation of life in the field. Particularly in his earlier years, Edwards could respond almost viscerally to the material realities of trees, mountains, flowers, and insects encountered on his home grounds in the Connecticut River Valley. Yet his commitment to interpreting the world in theological and philosophic terms meant that he apprehended nature largely, as Clyde A. Holbrook puts it, "at second hand."[13] Nor does the Quaker John Woolman qualify as a nature writer in the usual sense, insofar as little of his extant writing is devoted to landscape description or travel narrative. Yet his ethical theology of compassion, as expounded in the *Journal*, clearly includes the notion of human responsibility toward the nonhuman world and raises telling questions about the nature of animal life. Woolman's account of his youthful mistreatment of birds, like Bartram's confession of complicity in the slaughter of a bear and her cub, offers a striking illustration of human connection with the "brute creation."

To be sure, it is unwise to dwell too much in ethical or philosophic abstractions at the expense of renewing acquaintance with the physical immediacy of nature. As Jay Parini points out, humanists disenchanted with the abstract, "solipsistic tendencies" of poststructuralist theory—as well as with narrow views of departmental specialization—may find ecocriticism appealing precisely because it "marks a re-engagement with realism, with the actual universe of rocks, trees and rivers that lies behind the wilderness of signs" (52). Such recovery of actuality is often prominent in the writing of scientifically disposed naturalists, including several examined in this book, who do not regard their own expression primarily or exclusively in literary terms. At the same time, speculative thought and critical theory can help recall us to another crucial realism: the recognition that beyond study of individual organisms and ecosystems, "nature" itself exists not as empirical fact so much as linguistic sign. "Nature" points toward a protean, elusive, highly subjective phenomenon that is inextricably wedded to cultural assumptions and human imaginings. If the nonhuman world has indeed, in Coleridge's phrase and according to deep ecology, "a life of its own" distinct from human culture and civilization, that life must nonetheless be interpreted by human beings mostly in human terms.

Nature writing, then, can never describe a purely autonomous realm but must perforce say something about humanity's perceived *relation* to nonhuman creatures or biospheric systems. Wordsworth's reminder that we "half create" what we perceive speaks also to American perceptions of nature. Emerson similarly acknowledged that the power by which we delight in "fields and woods" resides not "in nature, but in man, or in a harmony of both."[14] It has come to seem increasingly naive to locate "nature" only in roadless wilderness areas, in those presumably pristine sites from which humankind has been evacuated. Still, modern naturalist writers such as Aldo Leopold and Edwin Way Teale have sustained Thoreau's zeal for discovering residual "wildness" in the undomesticated small animals and plants that abound even in settled bioregions.

Although virtually nothing we encounter on the planet can now be regarded as outside the sphere of human influence, one can at least identify organisms and processes that seem relatively "wild"—that is, beyond immediate human control. The sacred, too, traditionally names a reality apart from workaday culture, a category of existence outside the bounds of human control and rationalization. Hence one can observe in several of the witnesses considered here a persistent, religiously significant tendency to associate wildness with a sense of the sacred. Even Melville, despite his intensely skeptical interrogation of natural theology and providentialism, evokes impressions in *Moby-Dick* of a divinely unknowable mystery coursing beneath the "great shroud of the sea."

I think it most fruitful, then, to imagine "nature" as something both authentically discovered, or discoverable, *and* humanly constructed. The same is true of our reaction to nature as divine Creation. This paradoxical perception has been aptly described by Belden C. Lane, who develops a phenomenological approach to the matter informed by Paul Ricoeur's hermeneutics. On the one hand, Lane points out that a strictly "constructivist" understanding cannot honor the sense of intensified presence that has always attached itself to individual or communal experiences of hallowed places. On the other hand, a purely "essentialist" approach risks embracing a naively magical worldview. It posits credence in sacred places with a potency detached from the stories that humanity interlaces with geography. To move past these polarities, one must acknowledge the richly dialectical interplay between Nature and Culture. In Ricoeur's terms, this would mean learning to pass beyond the uncritical enthusiasm of a first naiveté, through a dis-illusioning hermeneutics of suspicion, to that renewed capacity for wonder and reengagement with mythic landscapes characteristic of a second naiveté. "This second naivete," Ricoeur explains, "aims to be the postcritical equivalent of the precritical hierophany."[15]

Belden Lane's axiom that "sacred place is ordinary place, ritually made extraordinary"[16] thus describes an understanding crucial to my argument. Making nature sacred is a cocreative act that humans can and do perform, through ritual and imagination—at least up to a point. Beyond that point, those who wait upon earth's unseen mysteries may encounter something they know is *not* them or theirs, though it beckons to the soul. They sense God's immanence in the world. Naturalistic testimonies to some such experience of numinous presence crowd the history of American letters. To speak, then, of "making nature sacred" need not imply disenchanted skepticism about all prospects of transcendence. When John Muir first entered Yosemite, for instance, he was seized by assurance that the place's "divine landscape-countenance" revealed a dynamic Creation surpassing every human artifice. Muir says he gazed, "awe-stricken," at scenes hallowed with the glory of "Beauty beyond thought everywhere, beneath, above, made and being made forever."[17]

Admittedly, through the decades following Muir's death in 1914, the problem of defining Nature in contradistinction to Culture has been complicated immeasurably, to the point where there is reason to fear that the ideological "end of nature" has already been sealed by present-day developments in biotechnology and genetic engineering.[18] The eclipse of nature is also, inevitably, a function of contemporary postmodern philosophy. That the challenge of seeing nature is at base a hermeneutical problem of interpreting the visible world as text was nonetheless already implicit in nineteenth-century figures such as Emerson and Thoreau. As I argue in chapter 6, for example, Thoreau's writing reflects a distinctive self-consciousness about the need to interpret or translate natural facts. In addition to reassessing Thoreau's nature mysticism, his complex relation both to traditional theism and to evolutionary theory, I have been particularly concerned to discover how Thoreau "read" the text of nature in the light of principles influenced by Coleridge's biblical hermeneutic. In religious terms, the faith embodied in *Walden* is notable as well by virtue of the author's commitment to reimagining the precincts of Walden reverentially as sacred space. Though often viewed as simple pantheism, Thoreau's spiritualization of nature incorporated elements of traditional Christian belief in a personal Creator and in the world as divine Creation. But for Thoreau, as for most writers representing American Romanticism, the essential challenge was to undo that dis-enchantment of the world precipitated by the European Enlightenment.

The challenge grew yet more formidable in the wake of Darwinism. This reputedly antireligious and pessimistic intellectual context is central to my inquiry in chapter 7, which includes treatment of recognized turn-of-the-century nature writers such as Mary Austin and John Muir. My reading of Muir, for example, aims to capture the sheer intensity of religious feeling—a piety at once unorthodox and mystical, yet biblically Protestant—that suffused this writer's naturalism. In this chapter, too, I discuss Rachel Carson's lifelong aspiration to blend scientific curiosity with a religiously indeterminate yet robust spirituality. Resisting strictly materialistic appraisals of nature, Carson was awed by the beauty of what she examined, the beauty of things seen as well as unseen in a nonhuman order whose marvels exceeded human boundaries. Carson's poetic praise of the world's inexhaustible wonder and mystery is most evident in her oceanic writings, which expose the contemplative spirituality that informed her larger vision of ecology. This accomplished empirical scientist found herself enchanted, above all, by the concealed beauty of tidal pools set in ocean caves. Carson's profound sense of "reverence for life" also generated moral passion, a prophetic imperative for change best displayed in the rhetoric of *Silent Spring*.

In the last three chapters, I extend my survey to a diverse sampling of present-day writers. One might well expect that in the modern era as scientific determinism and preoccupation with urban society replaced faith and mysticism, testimonies to the sacred nature of nature would begin to disappear. Some such tendency is indeed apparent in writers conventionally linked to scientific "naturalism"—Stephen Crane, Frank Norris, and Theodore Dreiser. Yet despite the profound effects of Darwinism and other materialist ideologies on the worldview of modern Americans, many post–World War II writers—including Rachel Carson, Loren Eiseley, and Annie Dillard—continued to confirm some version of Emerson's declaration that "particular natural facts are symbols of particular spiritual facts."

So I conclude the study with assessment of that counterintuitive development by which our era of postmodern skepticism has seen a resurgence of writing involved in the quest for a spiritual dimension or sacred presence in nature. Most ecocriticism published thus far presumes that nature writing must be interpreted in purely secular terms. Ironically, though, much of the primary literature it addresses displays a religious sense of wonder at nature's endlessly textured abundance, variability, and dynamism. Edward Hoagland, himself a prolific author, announces baldly that "nature writing, despite its basis in science, usually rings with rhapsody as well—a belief that nature is an expression of God." Modern and contemporary writers often eschew such explicitly theistic language. Yet many of them confirm Rachel Carson's belief that close inspection of the nonhuman world can deepen what Albert Schweitzer called "reverence for life," can stir assent to a spiritual ecology or to what Carson herself called "something that takes us out of ourselves."[19]

Much of the newer literature in this vein qualifies as environmental nonfiction, thus satisfying current inclinations to equate "nature writing" with nonfiction. In chapters 8 and 9, I analyze several relevant and celebrated works of creative nonfiction by Barry Lopez, Peter Matthiessen, Wendell Berry, and Annie Dillard. There is compelling fiction, too, as evidenced by John Cheever's *Oh What a Paradise It Seems* and Marilynne Robinson's *Housekeeping*, that deserves notice within this still-unidentified body of American expression I presume to call religious environmental literature. My account of literary exoticism in chapter 8 addresses both genres, since I include here readings of Lopez's *Arctic Dreams* and Matthiessen's *Snow Leopard* as well as of W.E.B. Du Bois's novel *The Quest of the Silver Fleece* and Matthiessen's fictional Watson trilogy. This chapter's excursion through exotic spaces ranges across several extreme, forbidding, or unsettled lands, from the Florida Everglades and swamps of Virginia and Alabama to Arctic tundra and remote Himalayan high country. But insofar as the works in question concern themselves not merely with physical adventure but with spiritual quest, they demonstrate that the appeal of exoticism is not always escapist. Barry Lopez, for example, dramatizes the notion that an invisible landscape coexists with each northern scene that meets his gaze. Not only remote lands but, in the light of imagination, any physical place harbors a richly enigmatic capacity "to transcend whatever we would make of it."[20]

By contrast with the far-roaming adventure tales that dominate chapter 8, the homewatching literatures discussed in chapter 9 raise the problem of how vitalizing contact with "nature" can be recovered or preserved within settled human communities. Interest in the character of daily life on a writer's home ground has become more prominent in postindustrial America, where the possibility of retreat to pristine wilderness seems less and less viable. This chapter's contemporary focus on "reclaiming the sacred commons" presumes, therefore, that human community should be considered an integral part of the ecological "household." How can human homes be developed in sustainable harmony with natural ecosystems? How might Americans learn to reinhabit the land so as to reverence its localized integrity of spirit, and to minimize the damage wrought by settlement? Such "bioregional" concerns are conspicuously addressed in Wendell Berry's prose writings. Having returned to inhabit the farm country of his ancestral origins in Henry County, Kentucky, Berry has for many years written essays communicating his broader hope for a spiritually integrated harmony between land and community. These writings manifest the distinctive conviction that land should be treated as a divine gift and sacrament.

In *A Pilgrim at Tinker Creek,* Annie Dillard likewise conducts her meditative interrogations of Creation in the setting of a relatively settled locale near Virginia's Blue Ridge. Dillard wanders far afield in her spiritual journeying, collecting ideas from several different religious traditions as well as from modern science in an effort to reconceive the relation between God's will and nature's freedom. But while her pursuit is theologically adventurous, taking her well along the contemplative path of unknowing, it remains geographically anchored at Tinker Creek. Dillard focuses her naturalistic inquiry quite deliberately on commonplace creatures such as trees, insects, and a neighborhood stream.

John Cheever's short novel takes place in territory even more familiar than Tinker Creek: a suburbanized settlement near New York City. Though superficially a tale deploring pollution of the town's pond, *Oh What a Paradise* ends up challenging assumptions that have traditionally sustained American pastoralism. It also expresses Cheever's ultimate renewal of faith in the holiness of Creation. Marilynne Robinson's *Housekeeping* is set in threatening mountain country of the Pacific Northwest rather than in safely settled civilization. Yet the novel concentrates attention on the problem of domesticity, on the question of how to find one's home within the wider world of nature. Significantly, Robinson's existential drama frames this question in religious terms. The two main characters become drifters, souls who make their peace with nature but also reflect biblical if not Calvinist doctrine in the way they know themselves to be pilgrims without a permanent home on earth.

My book concludes with a chapter devoted to contemporary poetry. One could name a fair number of present-day poets germane to assessing the religious dimensions of ecopoetry. I have elected to comment on five: Gary Snyder, Wendell Berry once again, Patiann Rogers, Denise Levertov, and Mary Oliver. Though they differ theologically and otherwise, all of these writers compose earth-centered poems expressing love for Creation and a spirituality thoroughly embedded in the material world. Their writing displays a common reverence toward animal life. It evokes awareness of nonhuman mysteries that are finally inaccessible to human understanding or control. And so these poets rarely call to mind moments of epiphany or divine illumination. They are more apt to imagine episodes that reveal what is *not* reliably known about creatures and landscapes. In an era of rational indeterminacy, this unknowing approach to reality, a disposition that recalls age-old traditions of apophatic or "negative way" mysticism, as well as Buddhist *sunyata,* has gained peculiar sway.

I argue, too, that ecopoetry is best suited to support meditation rather than direct persuasion. The meditative impulse suffuses this writing, which aims to integrate interiority with landscape by way of imagination. Both Wendell Berry's *Sabbath Poems* and Gary Snyder's *Mountains and Rivers without End* derive from meditative exercises their authors had pursued for decades. And when Denise Levertov lived in Seattle during the last years of her life, she composed a remarkable series of poems, steeped in mindfulness, that record her responses to the nearby presence of Mount Rainier.

Since the last third of the twentieth century, then, religious environmental literature of every genre has flourished in the United States, along with a few relevant film productions. The startling amplitude of such writing appearing in recent years suggests we may indeed be witnessing something of a spiritual renaissance in American letters. A book of this scale can only begin to recognize the existence of the subgenre and to suggest some of its implications both for reading selected texts and for interpreting the physical world. Though I hope to supply here a novel context for approaching one constellation of familiar and not-so-familiar texts, the space open to further exploration remains as big as all outdoors.

I

Landfall

The New World as New Creation

Hayle Holy-Land

Nowhere in literature of the American colonial period is the sheer excitement of landfall following the ordeal of oceanic passage better conveyed than in Thomas Tillam's verses "Uppon the First Sight of New-England June 29, 1638." Even before touching shore, the immigrant poet opens his lyric by saluting the coast of Massachusetts as "holy-land." Little is known about Tillam, or about why he soon returned to Europe from a place he had greeted with such zeal: "Hayle holy-land wherin our holy lord / Hath planted his most true and holy word."[1]

In any case, the apostrophe now seems to epitomize a vision of sacred ground in the New World that would remain in sight, through many different frames of perception and shifts in focus, to our own day. In the essay "Walking," for example, Thoreau later described his travels in Massachusetts as a sauntering, or "sort of crusade," toward a latter-day "Holy Land." Retreating from profane civilization, Thoreau is drawn to the darkest woods he can find or to thick swamp, which he enters "as a sacred place,—a *sanctum sanctorum*." And for seventeenth-century Algonkians, the elements and organisms of Southern New England had already been animated by nature persons, already permeated with the sacred presence of Manitou, before English settlers arrived.[2]

For most modern readers, though, the impression Thomas Tillam conveys of New England's holy land is terribly disappointing in the end, despite the rush of emotion with which he begins. We want to know how someone in his circumstance will react to the new look of this land—to its towering oaks, its huge flocks of passenger pigeons, its bear and strange moose. Or if the poet is still too far from shore to witness such things, we wonder what broader prospect of the place will first seize his imagination. Will he be struck initially by the granite ruggedness of the coastline, by the sandy expanses of Cape Cod, or by the blocks of dense forest? Yet Tillam's poem frustrates all these expectations. It tells us nothing, absolutely nothing, about the country's physical appearance. The land itself is invisible. All the poet "sees" are New England's visible saints. Ignoring the nonhuman environment, Tillam gazes exclusively on that heroic remnant of the faithful graced to possess the place:

> Hayle happye people who have dispossest
> Your selves of friends, and means, to find
> > some rest
> For your poore wearied soules, opprest of late.
> . . . .
> Methinks I heare the Lambe of God thus
> > speake
> Come my deare little flocke, who for my sake
> Have lefte your Country, dearest friends, and
> > goods
> And hazarded your lives o'th raginge floods
> Posses this Country; free from all anoye
> Heare I'le bee with you, heare you shall
> > Injoye
> My sabbaths, sacraments, my minestrye
> And ordinances in their puritye.

In his first glimpse of land, Tillam sees no native trees or open forest but only an imported enclave of gospel purity, a church walled against the disordering depredations of Satan. What he sees "planted" here is nothing biotic or green but God's Word embedded in the covenanted community. For Tillam, then, the sanctity of New England lies not in its land or *bios* but in its regenerated fellow colonizers. The place itself qualifies as "holy" only in the privative sense that it is "free from all anoye" of popish corruption and ungodly persecution.

Yet even Tillam's urge to erase the continent's physical landscape warrants attention for what it suggests about prevailing cultural assumptions, and in this regard his poem is a useful starting point for considering the relation between religion and nature writing in early New England. On the one hand, we can identify a fair body of descriptive, promotional writing—typified by William Wood's account in *New Englands Prospect* (1634)—that offers firsthand observation of the region's geography, climate, natural history, and ethnography. On the other hand, we face an intimidating abundance of religious writing preserved from Puritan New England. Yet a curious divide opens between these two forms of discourse. William Wood's genre of "experimentall description," which treats the actual "nature of the country,"[3] operates within an essentially secular frame of reference. Conversely, most of the Puritans' theological treatises and sermons focus intensively on the Book of Written Revelation, opened and applied to souls in New England society, rather than on what might be gleaned from the Book of Nature. Even a promotional but clerically authored work such as Francis Higginson's *New-Englands Plantation* enforces a clear separation between its treatment of practical matters relevant to settlement, its description of the land, and its appraisal of the Bay plantation's spiritual condition.

Thus, Nature and Religious Culture usually seem to occupy separate spheres in early New England writing. Only a few sustained, overt attempts to integrate human response to the natural environment with revealed religion can be found throughout Puritan American literature. Spiritualized nature writing of the sort practiced by Thoreau did not, of course, exist. For that matter, "nature" itself clearly meant something different for seventeenth-century New Englanders than it did for Thoreau or for us. Often, then, one must look beneath the "plain sense" of these writings, and beyond later conventions of nature writing, to understand more fully how colonists tried to reconcile their experience of North America's physical environment with their religious faith and imagination.

Particularly in the earliest stages of New England colonization, settlers were more eager to possess than to be possessed by the land. Sorely pressed to survive, they showed considerably more interest in mastering than in marveling over their new physical environment. Frost said it best: "The land was ours before we were the land's."[4]

In several respects, first-generation Puritans tried indeed to armor themselves against the wilderness, to wall out the untamed and ostensibly ungodly forces that surrounded them. Harriet Beecher Stowe once posed the teasing question whether Puritan theology would have fared differently if the New England founders had landed first in Florida rather than on Plymouth Rock.

However, one cannot assume that Puritans settling in Florida would have developed milder religious ideas, or formulated a radically different theology of nature.[5] Seventeenth-century colonizers of Massachusetts were, after all, more interested in fashioning these outlying plantations into a reformed England than they were in encountering a genuinely new land. Accordingly, the colonial conceit of remaking England in America could be surprisingly literalistic—as reflected most obviously in John Smith's "New England" nomenclature, but perhaps most strikingly in William Wood's fancy that the extreme temperature swings of America's northeastern climate simply replicated conditions that had once prevailed in England. Despite their anxiety to discern signs of personal conversion, religious-minded immigrants to New England were more interested in transplanting than in transforming English culture.[6]

From William Bradford's "Hideous and Desolate Wilderness"
to Cotton Mather's Sacred Geography

Probably the most frequently cited illustration of Puritan hostility toward the
New World environment is William Bradford's account of the Pilgrim landing
at Provincetown in his history *Of Plimoth Plantation*. Bradford had already
acknowledged the merits of planting a colony in the great expanse of "unpeopled" America. These lands beckoned as particularly "fruitful and fit for habitation" because he considered them "devoid of all civil inhabitants, where there
are only savage and brutish men which range up and down, little otherwise
than the wild beasts of the same." Lacking the particular temptations and social
distractions Bradford's group had experienced in Holland, New England offered religious-minded settlers not only plentiful land but also, as things turned
out, the chance to display heroic virtue in the face of privation. Seafaring emigrants reaching Cape Cod's shore in November would find nothing there by
way of worldly satisfaction to divert them from realizing their elemental de-
pendence on the Redeemer. "What could now sustain them but the Spirit of
God and His grace?"[7] Bradford exclaims. What else indeed. Not even manna,
which fed the Hebrews in their desert wilderness, is offered to sustain God's
people in this remote place.

Still, Governor Bradford celebrates the landfall episode as a visionary triumph. If the ideal of Puritan faith was to live solely upon the Word, New
Plymouth never came closer to fulfilling its vocation as a sanctified community
than at that first embrace of American soil. By then, the Mayflower band had
shared an almost sacramental ordeal of regeneration by water when they successfully "passed through a sea of troubles," but they had yet to face those more
dispiriting troubles and quarrels that would eventually dissolve the colony's
identity. Writing ten years after the fact, Bradford himself began the process
of mythologizing the founders; and doubtless he embellished his descriptive
rhetoric to heighten the contrast between a forbidding outer landscape and the
land of promise glimpsed inwardly at the summit of this community's faith.
Even in *Mourt's Relation* (1622), the other major record of these events, members of the Plymouth band admit taking comfort, when they first spy Cape
Cod, in "seeing so goodly a land, and wooded to the brink of the sea."[8] Yet
Bradford, as retrospective sacred chronicler, exults in the scene's bleakness and
renders thanks for a vision that, in view of the Cape's physical topography, had
to be entertained imaginatively without benefit of an actual holy mountain:

> And for the season it was winter, and they that know the winters of
> that country know them to be sharp and violent, and subject to cruel
> and fierce storms, dangerous to travel to known places, much more
> to search an unknown coast. Besides, what could they see but a hid-
> eous and desolate wilderness, full of wild beasts and wild men—and
> what multitudes there might be of them they knew not. Neither
> could they, as it were, go up to the top of Pisgah to view from this

wilderness a more goodly country to feed their hopes; for which way soever they turned their eyes (save upward to the heavens) they could have little solace or content in respect of any outward objects. For summer being done, all things stand upon them with a weather-beaten face, and the whole country, full of woods and thickets, represented a wild and savage hue. . . .

What could now sustain them but the Spirit of God and His grace? May not and ought not the children of these fathers rightly say, "Our fathers were Englishmen which came over this great ocean, and were ready to perish in this wilderness; but they cried unto the Lord, and He heard their voice and looked on their adversity." (62–63)

The profound distrust Bradford expresses toward the American environment must be understood, though, within the context of his history's peculiar genre, purpose, occasion, and audience. Today, for example, we are rightly disturbed by the cultural arrogance of English attitudes toward Native Americans. Though Bradford shows less inclination than saints of Massachusetts Bay to claim an exceptional status for his community, his rhetoric does dehumanize the land's inhabitants by conflating "wild beasts and wild men," ignoring existing settlements to categorize the place as elemental "wilderness." He later gloats over John Mason's destruction of the Pequots, including women and children burned in their homes at Mystic, Connecticut, in 1637, calling the mass slaughter a "sweet sacrifice." Moreover, the Pilgrim saints first manage to obtain seed they regard as essential for survival by pilfering baskets of corn the Indians had buried for their own use. The settlers rationalize their acquisition as a loan. Grateful to God's "special providence" for crucial assistance supplied by Squanto and Samoset, Bradford's people did manage for decades to preserve comparatively cordial relations with the indigenous peoples, especially with the Wampanoags, at least until the death of Massasoit. They understood the trade and security benefits of peaceful coexistence. By the last quarter of the seventeenth century, though, when Bradford was dead and King Philip's War erupted, the more environmentally disruptive agricultural practices of English colonizers stirred Indian resentment even against the Old Colony (Plymouth) but still more against leadership of the Massachusetts Bay Colony. No wonder a graduate student of mine caustically suggests revising the title of Frost's poem "The Gift Outright" to expose the land seizures and genocidal intrusion of English colonizers as "the theft outright."

The initially fearful reaction to New England's physical environment that Bradford describes is understandable enough, however, quite apart from Puritan theology or colonialist ideology. Recalling that Bradford's wife perished mysteriously while the ship still lay at anchor and that half the original *Mayflower* passengers were dead by the summer following the Provincetown landing, we should scarcely find it surprising that Bradford felt more threatened than inspired by the prospect of wintering on the Cape with meager provisions in a place rife with disease. No new arrival, Calvinist or not, would be inclined to extol the picturesque beauty of surroundings so immediately inhospitable to survival.

The forbidding image of America as a "howling wilderness" that suffuses English colonial writings of this period carries certain positive biblical connotations as well.[9] Thus, during their forty years of arduous confrontation with the Sinai's desert wilderness, wandering Hebrews endured trials that tested and strengthened them, eventually shaping them into a covenant people. As Bradford's writing attests, this biblical analogy was never far from the imaginative consciousness of literate saints throughout the New England colonies. At the same time, in polar juxtaposition to the wasteland epithet, both secular and religious promotional writing frequently imaged the New World as an earthly paradise of superabundant resources. Puritan representations of this trope emphasized the land's *potential* prosperity, when cultivated and improved by human labor. Thus, the minister John White believed such a place encouraged "piety and godliness" because it yielded "sufficiency with hard labour and industry."[10] New England could not be mistaken for a garden of tropical ease, and in that regard it is probably just as well that the *Mayflower* ended up planting the Separatist settlement even farther north than the Pilgrims had intended. Even so, Puritans and Pilgrims often marveled, once they had survived the first shock of transplantation, over the plentitude of natural wealth available in the region's timber, arable land, beaver furs, and fish off Cape Cod. From the standpoint of Reformed piety, such wealth appropriated in moderation was not merely an economic resource but a special providence, a sign of divine grace to which the faithful must respond with gratitude and cooperative effort. Thus, Bradford reports the Pilgrims' welcoming the arrival of "sweet and gentle showers" (131) to relieve a life-threatening drought in July as a deliberate token of divine mercy.

Bradford's main concern was to record the Pilgrim story faithfully for the benefit of future generations, interpreting its triumphs and misfortunes as a reflection of sacred, providential history when he could discern evidence of divine intent but wisely refraining from such exegesis when he could not.[11] Accordingly, the interest he displays in the region's natural features is wholly practical and incidental to his appraisal of the community's welfare. Certainly, though, Bradford is attentive to the environmental conditions affecting settlement, as when he describes the band's satisfaction at marching "into the land" selected for their habitation and finding there "divers cornfields and little running brooks, a place (as they supposed) fit for habitation" (72). Still more detail figures in the geophysical observations recorded in *Mourt's Relation*.

Even so, a pivotal question about religion and environmental history remains: to what extent did Puritan doctrine—or, for that matter, fundamental teachings of biblical Judaism and Christianity—feed the impulse of English colonizers to destroy "wilderness" and to achieve decisive mastery over nature? We can observe, to begin with, that religious rhetoric justifying active exploitation or "improvement" of the land abounds in colonial writing, though Bradford's history more often assumes than articulates these claims. Typically, Puritans defended their expansion into territories already inhabited by native peoples by invoking the Old Testament precedent of Hebrew advances into Canaan. They observed that New England's indigenous peoples never took formal title of their lands, never enclosed them or maintained livestock, and never established permanent dwellings in the English manner.[12] What justified land possession, they believed, was active cultivation or other "improvement" of the existing environment. The epidemic that decimated the Patuxets before their arrival was, they concluded, further evidence that God meant the English to resettle the tribe's newly evacuated territory. By one modern interpretation, Puritan urges to reform the landscape were simply an extension of the original Protestant passion for "reformation."[13]

Most predictably, apologists for the energetic colonization of American soils as well as peoples found their warrant in Genesis 1:28-29, universalizing this presumably prehistoric command to "subdue" and "have dominion" over the earth with all its creatures into a current moral imperative. Statements to this effect can be cited, for example, in writings by John Winthrop, Frances Higginson, and the Massachusetts Court.[14] Back in 1945, George F. Willison offered a flagrant illustration of how Holy Writ could be used to sanction territorial ambition:

> The English attitude toward the natives' rights was never more succinctly expressed than by a town meeting at Milford, Connecticut, in 1640: "Voted, that the earth is the Lord's and the fulness thereof; voted, that the earth is given to the Saints; voted, that we are the Saints."[15]

Of course, New England Puritans were hardly the only group to exercise the kind of self-serving logic evident in this syllogism. Some, in fact, have held the mainstream tradition of biblical Christianity chiefly responsible for the ecological harm wrought by Western culture. In 1967, the historian Lynn White, Jr., claimed in an immensely influential essay, entitled "The Historical Roots of Our Ecologic Crisis," that the Judeo-Christian doctrine of Creation has encouraged rapacious exploitation of the earth by setting God apart from nature and giving human beings license to subdue the earth to their will. Though it has also become usual in religious circles to counter such charges with reference to a theology of "stewardship" rather than stark domination of nature, White's essay remains more canonical than Scripture itself in present-day course anthologies and curricula pertaining to environmental studies. Other explanations of the developed world's ecological offenses fix primary blame on masculinist patriarchy, on imperialist capitalism, or on the despiritualizing and narrowly objectifying view of nature fostered by modern science—though Christian doctrine has also been selectively implicated with each of these influences.[16] It is doubtful, however, whether the complex of attitudes that define any culture, ancient or modern, can be retraced through some evolutionary path of intellectual and spiritual history to a single root.

Thus, one can easily locate religious *justifications* for environmental practices already favored by New England Puritans. It is much harder to prove that theological ideas uniquely *motivated* these English colonists to behave as they did toward the nonhuman world. In brief, anthropology goes further than theology toward explaining the gross differences that ecological history reveals between Puritan and Amerindian modes of inhabiting New England. William Cronon reminds us that New England's nature should not be viewed as pristine and static at the time of European contact. Southern New England tribes had by then shifted from an earlier phase of hunting and gathering to a mixed livelihood based on game pursuit as well as hoe agriculture. Their farming methods, which recognized the value of nitrogen-fixing legumes and seasonal migration, showed some advantages over those applied by Europeans; and they had long "managed" the forest environment for game and horticultural benefit through periodic burnings.[17] Contrasting English practices that featured land enclosure, livestock, plow and grain-based horticulture, and permanent settlements were plainly not determined by Puritanism as such. They reflected customs and attitudes that were similarly applied in non-Puritan colonies such as Jamestown. Again, the example of Providence Island, a New World Puritan colony that derived support from plantation slavery, suggests that theology may affect environmental practice less directly than climate, economics, and sociocultural circumstances.

For that matter, it remains unclear what practical ecological consequences can be traced to any society's religious beliefs. Buddhist teachings, for example, typically affirm the ethical standing of nonhuman creatures and the need for planetary compassion more explicitly than do Western doctrines of salvation and justification. Yet, well before the industrial era, parts of China and Japan had suffered severe deforestation and erosion—sometimes, in appreciable measure, because so much timber had been cut for the construction of large Buddhist temples. Today, we cannot predict that in regions of the world traditionally dominated by non-Abrahamic faiths, environmental practices wiser than Europe's will necessarily prevail, particularly in cultures that are developing industrial or postindustrial economies roughly comparable to ours.[18]

Once we grant the broader point that English practices and cultural attitudes toward inhabiting the land differed fundamentally from those exhibited by Native Americans, we may discover that Bradford's account idealizes a scripturally based ethic of land use that, in the setting of seventeenth-century colonialist ideology, seems fairly restrained. If theology had any distinctive influence on Plymouth's approach to land use, the biblical ground of this authority was not Genesis 1–2 but Acts 2:44: "And all that believed were together, and had all things common." Bradford saw a direct correlation between proper landholding and the ideal of holding together Plymouth's blessed fellowship. New Plymouth, he records, had briefly considered a strictly communistic approach to agriculture. Driven to exploit private initiative to increase their yield, the Pilgrims soon rejected this "common course and condition" as a practical concession to human nature. Yet they remained committed to curbing individual ambitions that would otherwise demand ever-expanding personal property and wealth. When permanent allotments of ground for raising corn were finally approved, apparently not before 1624, "to every person was given only

FIGURE I.I.   Historic reconstruction of dwelling and garden plot in Plimoth.
(Photo courtesy of Plimoth Plantation, Plymouth, Massachusetts.)

one acre of land, to them and theirs, as near the town as might be; and they
had no more till the seven years were expired" (145).

With an entire continent at their backs, settlers were urged to content
themselves with farming a single acre of property. Although immediate human
interests rather than ecocentric motives determined this policy of containment,
it promised more favorable environmental consequences than one usually associates with Puritan colonization.

Few of America's later abuses in land management can therefore be traced
to the example set at Plymouth. Bradford believed that, beyond its worldly
benefits, maintaining a cohesive and concentrated settlement fulfilled a spiritual requirement because only thus could New Plymouth recreate the primitive
ideal of Christian community set forth in the Acts of the Apostles. In other
Puritan colonies, too, some settlements adopted land policies that recalled practices in England of "the open-field system of strip-farming with its relatively
egalitarian land distribution and the communal requirements of collective
ploughing and harvesting."[19]

Such determined resistance to population sprawl could not be sustained
for long in Plymouth, however, to say nothing of America at large. After the
rise of larger settlements in Massachusetts Bay challenged the Separatist col-

ony's position in the region, economic conditions suddenly offered Pilgrims a lucrative market in surplus corn, grain, and livestock. Looking to expand their production of these cash commodities, plantation members also looked to expand their property. The resulting prosperity led inevitably to dispersion, with new settlements springing up soon at Duxbury and Marshfield, and thereafter at Nauset. To what extent these developments eroded Bradford's faith in the community's special destiny, or whether he ever posited such a singular mission for Plymouth, remain matters of dispute. Certainly, though, he was distressed to witness the division of "those that had lived so long together in Christian and comfortable fellowship." Nor did he welcome the new prosperity as a sign of grace. Instead he lamented it as the harbinger of an aggressively secular, acquisitive, and individualistic mindset soon to be recognized as the trademark of Yankee capitalism:

> For now as their stocks increased and the increase vendible, there was no longer any holding them together, but now they must of necessity go to their great lots. They could not otherwise keep their cattle, and having oxen grown they must have land for plowing and tillage. And no man now thought he could live except he had cattle and a great deal of ground to keep them, all striving to increase their stocks. By which means they were scattered all over the Bay quickly and the town in which they had lived compactly till now was left very thin and in a short time almost desolate. (253)

Bradford is disturbed to find that the community's center will not hold, that economic forces have undone Plymouth's uneasy compromise between group loyalty and private initiative. To judge from his sardonic phrasing, though, the plantation's geographic extension troubles him less than the boundless expansion of acquisitive desire he perceives in fellow church members. Bay Colony leaders such as William Hubbard and Increase Mather would also come to denounce land lust as a prime cause of conflict with Native Americans as well as of moral and social degeneration.[20]

Yet in time, as Puritan colonists advanced farther into the great woods and deepened their experience of the New World environment, the land itself also began to reshape their collective identity. For the most part, first-generation colonists considered themselves transplanted, reformed Britons who instinctively projected an English cultural identity and nomenclature onto the landscape.[21] By the third generation, the process of being possessed by a new land was well underway, even for a Bostonian like Cotton Mather. Despite the extravagant rhetorical style of *Magnalia Christi Americana* (1701), Mather indicates plainly enough that the place itself had now acquired retrospectively a status of sacred geography rarely attributed to it in earlier accounts. True, Francis Higginson could describe with relish "the new paradise of New England" he first glimpsed off Cape Ann in 1629, praising the region's "gay woods and high trees," its array of yellow flowers and "many fair green pastures." Likewise the Hebrew name that first-generation settlers conferred on Salem, a place originally identified in Psalm 76:2 as God's dwelling place, opened the potential for venerating American ground as sacred space.[22]

Not until Mather's time, though, did New Englanders often press the implications of a typology by which earlier writers had played with scriptural analogies to present-day events but that now revealed their country to be a blessed geophysical abode, a localized counterpart of Israel with millennialistic promise. In Mather's version of this mythos, God in his Providence had ordained "the *Concealing* of *America* for so long a time, as in the *Discovering* of it, when the fulness of Time was come for the Discovery." Hence the continent itself could be construed as a tabernacle, a peculiar concentration of God's ubiquitous presence. Compared with the old Jerusalem temple, though, the physical scope of this sanctuary seemed virtually unbounded: "*Geography* must now find work for a *Christiano-graphy* in Regions far enough beyond the Bounds wherein the *Church* of God had thro' all former Ages been circumscribed." One could now identify concretely on the ground, between forty and forty-eight northerly latitudes, "the Spot of *Earth*, which the God of Heaven *Spied out* for the Seat of such *Evangelical*, and *Ecclesiastical*, and very remarkable Transactions, as required to be made an *History*."[23]

Thus, despite the Puritans' general fear and suspicion of unsettled land, they were also disposed to regard the wild continent as uncorrupted space— and even, on occasion, as a sacred site of regeneration by contrast with the rejected Catholic emphasis on locally consecrated church edifices. The Puritans did *not*, of course, regard their own meetinghouses as sacred space, even though these buildings supplied the usual setting for common worship. As its name indicates, the meetinghouse was always considered a secular site, an unconsecrated structure in which the sacred activity of worship as well as the decidedly worldly and often contentious business of group governance could take place. In the Great Migration, reformers turned their backs on every form of church edifice that had been raised during centuries of European tradition. When Puritan emigrants first reached Boston in 1630, they found no church buildings or statues there that needed to be smashed in Cromwellian fashion; but they were scarcely about to erect such forms, either, or to approve the importation of popish rituals. The great-steepled gothic edifice of St. Botolph's Church, John Cotton's parish home in old Boston, was not to be replicated here.[24] Consistent with original New Testament usage, the "church" was henceforth to designate only a people, the living body of believers, rather than a place. In New England, though, the church's body came to understand its life as so organically and symbiotically extended *into* the place that Puritan rhetoricians like Mather began to confer on American geography, too, a measure of consecration. When the perennial human urge to designate sacred space affected the Puritan imagination, its compensatory force projected veneration onto land rather than buildings.[25]

The typological comparisons between Israel and New England that suffuse Puritan literature help to clarify this movement toward a spatially localized holiness. In first-generation writers figures such as Bradford, John Winthrop, and John Cotton, a loosely analogical rather than strictly typological rhetoric of nationhood prevails. Bradford suggests that the Pilgrim experience often resembles that of the ancient Israelites, but he perceives some striking contrasts as well. He never claims that his separatist community is God's uniquely chosen people in direct typological succession to Israel and the primitive Christian church. Nor does the author of the last portion of *Mourt's Relation*, Plymouth colonial agent Robert Cushman, suppose God had ordained by direct revelation that American territory was a sacred gift comparable to the consecration of Canaan for the Jews. No present-day territory qualifies as "legally holy and appropriated unto a holy people," the writer concedes, since "now there is no land of that sanctimony" once enjoyed by ancient Israel.[26]

Inevitably, though, the figure of Israel in America assumes new shades of meaning as it intersects with the actualities of life on New England soil. Cotton Mather's allusion to the "History of a New-English Israel" presents bold claims for the region's status, though that language still seems to apply more to people than to place. Yet as Mather piles up other place titles, including "the Garden of *New-England*" and "New Jerusalem," and particularly as he invokes the example of Abraham's journey to a new land to recall the saints' removal to America, we can sense his "Israel" figures reaching toward material incarnation: a *"Christiano-graphy."*[27] After all, the Abrahamic tradition preserved in ancient Israel (and, for that matter, in present-day Israel) underscored the relation between the people's religious faith and their rootedness in a specific geographic territory, a land construed as their divinely gifted inheritance. So it should not surprise us that an earthier, physically localized sense of "Israel" eventually found a place beside more ethereal perceptions in the religious consciousness of those inhabiting the "New English Israel."

Mather's own figurative writing does not show the completion of this shift from spiritualized antitypes to a fully materialized environment. As Cecelia Tichi points out, as early as 1650 the more literal-minded Edward Johnson better illustrates by anticipation New England's growing confidence that its saints would help God achieve millennialistic renewal as they rebuilt "the most glorious Edifice of Mount Zion" in Massachusetts Bay. "Know this is the place," Johnson declares, "where the Lord will create a new Heaven, and a new Earth in, new Churches, and a new Common-wealth together." Johnson's zeal to change the landscape by creating towns and mills, clearing woods and marshes, and mustering able soldiers scarcely looks like "environmental reform" in present-day terms. Yet for Johnson in *Wonder-Working Providence of Sions Saviour in New England* (1654), the "laborious worke" of colonizing assisted the emergence of God's New Creation. The New Israel of the endtime would, he thought, be constituted from the elect of every nation but was already being prepared as "forerunners of Christs Army" rose up from "these low Shrubs" planted in New England.[28]

Shades of biblical analogy between a material Israel and latter-day America eventually found a place even in the secular, unpuritan mind of Thomas Jefferson, a southerner whose comments on agrarianism argue yet another version of the case that the nation's democratic identity must be rooted in palpable soil. Reluctant to see America emulate Europe's trade in "manufactures," Jefferson avowed in his *Notes on the State of Virginia* that "those who labor in the earth are the chosen people of God, if ever he had a chosen people, whose breasts he has made his peculiar deposit for substantial and genuine virtue." If American farms were the heartland of Jefferson's New Israel, Europe's cities resembled the old Egypt of error and corruption. For Jefferson, populist land distribution within a largely agricultural economy was essential to preserving the "sacred fire" of individual liberty and integrity.[29]

Thomas Morton's Idol Experiment: Nature Religion in New Canaan

Though I have wandered a little from William Bradford's narrative, I must return to the neighborhood of Plymouth—in physical proximity, at least—to assess the ecospiritual significance of Thomas Morton's *New English Canaan* (1637), which demands to be read in conjunction with Bradford's testimony in *Of Plimoth Plantation*. Set against Bradford's Puritanism, Morton's outlook as a nominally Anglican, neopagan entrepreneur gives rise to a radically dissenting view of America as holy land. Ideological pluralism begins to define New England from the first. Yet this battle of books also exposes points of congruence between the contesting colonizers. The Puritan and anti-Puritan authors both attribute some kind of singular, sacred status to their settlements. And both presume that the raw facts of New World nature must be interpreted in the light of Old World texts and cultural traditions.

Thomas Morton's notorious trading settlement at Ma-re Mount (formerly Mount Wollaston), near present-day Quincy, lay too close to New Plymouth for the comfort of William Bradford's saints. In every other respect, though, Bradford's persona as righteous reformer seems far distant from that of Morton as flamboyant adventurer and scandalous bon vivant. Bradford portrays Morton as a dissolute fellow who threatens the godly community through his sponsorship of atheism, hedonism, and dissolution. Morton portrays the Pilgrims as obtuse prigs and busybodies whose intolerance threatens the glorious liberty presented to English colonizers in a land abounding in natural wealth. Just as Bradford makes Morton an archvillain of his narrative, so also Morton aims his sharpest satire at the Separatists—including the non-Puritan military leader Myles Standish, lampooned as "Captain Shrimp." Each writer perceives the other as villainous, a shadow contrary of himself. Bradford portrays Morton as a pernicious anarchist, while Morton represents the Separatists as bigoted fanatics who exceed their legal authority in expelling him repeatedly from the region and who neglect the opportunities afforded by an earthly paradise.

As any classroom instructor learns, the students' first ballot in a sympathy runoff between these contesting colonizers always favors Morton. After all, Bradford's famous account of the Maypole episode makes the governor look like a caricature of the humorless, repressive Puritan. He charges Morton with impiety and reckless endangerment of other colonists, with maintaining "(as it were) a School of Atheism" while trading guns and alcohol with the Indians. Most Puritanically, he castigates Morton for indulging in recreational frivolity. That renegade figure who designates himself "Mine Host" apparently loves to party; and the Mayday revelry he hosts at Merrymount includes not only drinking, dancing, and "frisking together like so many fairies, or furies, rather" but also "worse practices" doubtless allied with "lasciviousness" and with the group's having invited "the Indian women for their consorts" (*Of Plymouth Plantation*, 205–206). Bradford can scarcely contain his indignation at seeing his people's godly territory profaned by this "Lord of Misrule." In his mind, Morton's devotion to an "idle or idol maypole" epitomizes the offense presented by his bacchanalian, insolent, and undisciplined ways. From the undergraduate's point of view, Morton is bound to win the nod over Bradford in what looks like a contest between playboy and killjoy. Or as John Seelye once observed, "it is easy for us to love Thomas Morton, to regard him as a spirit of wilderness freedom, his Maypole a halfway mark between pagan monuments to priapic power and the liberty pole of later times." Even Hawthorne, whose fictional treatment reaches well below the surface conflict, recognizes that this case presents itself most immediately as one in which "jollity and gloom were contending for an empire."[30]

Morton's position looks appealing today for reasons surpassing his defense of festive recreation. One might applaud his egalitarian spirit in liberating from indentured servitude men who joined his trading enterprise at Merrymount after Captain Wollaston had arranged to sell off their associates in Virginia. One might also be impressed by Morton's appreciative, relatively detailed account of Native American practices and beliefs in the first book of *The New English Canaan*. Morton insists that by comparison with the "Christians" he has encountered in New England, these "Infidels" are, in fact, "most full of humanity." Affirming the "harmless Salvages" to be "his neighbors," he respects their mental powers as "very ingenious, and very subtle" people and praises their generosity in offering food to anyone in need. Unlike the Puritans, he welcomes the prospect of racial interaction and intermarriage.[31]

By the same token, Morton's response to New England's natural environment seems considerably more appreciative than that registered by Bradford. Instead of fearing or walling out "the natural endowments of the country" (55), he celebrates its beauty. He acknowledges, for the most part, that this land is already inhabited rather than a wholly unpeopled "wilderness." In the Second Book of *New English Canaan*, he offers a capacious naturalistic survey of the region's biological, mineral, and geophysical features. The varieties and uses of beech trees, the habits of muskrat, the presence of whetstone deposits—all of this and more receives notice in Morton's resource anatomy. From the first, Morton declares that his "survey of the country" has only enlarged his admiration for this New World paradise:

> The more I looked, the more I liked it. And when I had more seri-
> ously considered of the beauty of the place, with all her fair endow-

ments, I did not think that in all the known world it could be paralleled. . . . For in mine eye, 'twas Nature's Masterpiece: Her chiefest
Magazine of all, where lives Her store. If this land be not rich, then
is the whole world poor. (53–54)

Morton gives occasional hints that a religious sense affects the way he
ritualizes his zeal for the wild world. The clearest instance of his flirtation with
a neopagan "nature religion" appears in chapter 14 of book 3, "Of the Revels
of New Canaan." Unmistakably, Morton presents the Maypole erected from "a
goodly pine of 80 feet long" with "a pair of buck's horns" (134) as a phallic
emblem, a centerpiece of the erotic dance represented in his prose and poetic
account of Mayday at Merrymount. In conjunction with these suggestions, the
tree and its associated revelries recall as well the seasonal fertility rituals celebrated throughout the ancient Mediterranean and Near Eastern world. Such
connections are reinforced by Morton's penchant for Latinate vocabulary and
frequent if sometimes enigmatic allusions to classical mythology, as in his
mention of Maja (or Maia), the Roman goddess of spring also linked to learning
and agriculture. Morton conflates seasonal rituals recollected from the ancient
world with those still surviving in "the old English custom" of European folk-
ways and, in turn, with those he perceives in Native American revels and rites
honoring nonhuman life. If, as Morton surmised, native New Englanders were
actually descended from a scattered band of ancient Trojans, such syncretistic
blending made all the more sense. As a site of human engagement with multiple forms of nonhuman nature, this maypole ritual aptly combines invocation
of both sea (Latin *mare*) and "mount," of animal as well as vegetative orders of
life.

In defiance of the Separatists, Morton also claims his own Christian sanction for celebrating Mayday by pointing out that May 1 is "the festival day of
Philip and Iacob [James]" in the Anglican liturgical calendar. We might well
question the depth of Morton's religious commitment to Anglican Christianity
and doubt his claims to suffering harassment by virtue of devotion to the Book
of Common Prayer. Indeed, the Christian feastday of Saint Philip and Saint
James provides a comically slender pretext for the almost orgiastic festivities
that Morton describes. Still, Anglican religious practice in Old England had
preserved the Catholic observance of Rogation Days, seasonal prayer rituals
involving procession through cropland. One occasion on which "The Great
Litany," found in Anglicanism's *Book of Common Prayer*, would be used was
the major rogation, often observed April 25, on the verge of Mayday. "The Great
Litany" included a corporately recited petition "that it may please thee to give
and preserve to our use the kindly fruits of the earth, so as in due time we
may enjoy them."[32] Whether or not Morton remembered these precedents specifically, he insisted that New Canaan's revels represent the keeping of "holliday" (136). Morton certainly knew that the very idea of a (calendar-determined)
fixed, non-Sabbath holy day was repugnant to Puritans, as were most naming
rituals of the sort incorporated within Ma-re Mount's inaugural May "holliday."
Thus, the "precise Separatists" disdained Morton's putative Anglicanism as

virtually equivalent to paganism. For his part, Morton enjoyed satirizing their rejection of nature-based ritualism as symptomatic of their general inability to delight in the land's "natural endowments."

Inspecting the matter more closely, though, we might properly hesitate to canonize Thomas Morton as an ecological saint. His attitudes toward native inhabitants, for example, appear less uniformly enlightened once we recognize his main rhetorical intent to dramatize the cruelty of "Christian" Separatists by contrasting them ironically with humane and generous "savages." (Roger Williams, another outlaw in Puritan eyes, sometimes adopted the same rhetorical strategy.) Like other English colonizers, Morton expresses satisfaction that deadly epidemics have reduced the native population, thereby encouraging fresh European settlement. He mistakenly concludes that the Amerindians he observes have "no worship nor religion at all" (24). Here William Wood, whose account of New England Morton constantly derides, comes closer to the mark. Nor is Morton above exploiting native peoples, economically or sexually, to serve his own ends at Merrymount. His ribald address to indigenous women in "The Song"—"Lasses in beaver coats come away, / Ye shall be welcome to us night and day"—betrays predatory impulses linked to questionable views of ethnic and gender relations.

Although Morton's shady reputation prior to emigrating may have been the product of Puritan slander,[33] an unscrupulous will to dominate can likewise be read in the rhetoric of his responses to the physical environment. Morton opens his promotional and self-promotional essay by imagining that New Canaan lies before him "Like a fair virgin, longing to be sped / And meet her lover in a Nuptial bed" (7). He extends this familiar European, masculinist fantasy of America as virgin land[34] by suggesting that insofar as this untouched body has yet to be ravished by Europeans with their "art and industry," "her fruitful womb, / Not being enjoyed, is like a glorious tomb." The land itself *must* be colonialized—as a vitalizing obligation, but also as a deed of rightful pleasure. *The New English Canaan* demonstrates Morton's proto-American confidence that a man can, in the very act of fulfilling his own enjoyment and profit, ensure the propagation of new life for the country at large. If Morton liked what he saw in colonial New England, much of what he saw there was an open field of saleable commodities, a place ripe for economic exploitation by unfettered individuals.

In this light, Morton becomes the prototype not of wilderness-lovers like Thoreau or Muir but of free-market entrepreneurs like Franklin or Carnegie. His "idol" maypole becomes a pioneering trademark for America's worship of success—and, indeed, a brilliant promotional device advertising at long distance "how to find out the way to Mine Host of Mar-re Mount" (135). At least one plausible construction of Morton, who remains a teasingly protean figure, would identify his ultimate concerns as secular—centered on the pursuit of pleasure and material profit—rather than religious at all. It would define his actual religious orientation, such as it was, as that of a nominal Anglican whose flirtation with neopagan spirituality never reached consummation.

My point here in challenging Morton's standing as greenwood hero is not to reverse sympathies in the Bradford-Morton contest but to suggest that these two colonizers from Jacobean England shared a good deal more, by way of cultural attitudes and environmental assumptions, than their polemical statements may at first reveal. Both were committed to extending England's influence in the Western hemisphere, though they disagreed about strategies for colonization. Both assumed that colonists were obliged to intervene conspicuously in the processes of nature, though they differed on the forms of environmental restraint they believed settlers should exercise. Morton, for example, respected the limits of armed assault on Amerindian territory more than the Puritans did—and more than Bradford acknowledges in depicting him as a lawless Dionysian. On the level of material motives, both Plymouth and Merrymount were desperately interested in controlling the region's lucrative fur trade. Morton, who is more candid than Bradford about acknowledging this rivalry, is credible when he argues that the Pilgrims' envy of his success in marketing beaver pelts goes far toward explaining the ferociousness of their antipathy toward him.

Bradford and Morton agree, too, that whatever the Maypole confrontation means, it is an apex episode in the local narrative. They even agree, in surprising measure, about the symbolic import of the maypole. Interestingly, Morton never denies Pilgrim charges that Merrymount's pine tree functions as an "idol"—that is, as the focus of devotion to pre-Christian religions that sacralize natural forces and enact fertility rites. He may have realized that the pole was a fair replica of the ancient *asherah*, or cultic post of Canaanite religion, denounced by Old Testament prophets; and he must have known about the Hebrew Bible's related denunciation of worship in "high places," whether or not his own local prominence deserved the precise Philistine title of Mount Dagon conferred by his opponents. Yet he refuses to recognize his plantation's own cultic emblem as shameful, as a "lamentable spectacle." Thus, instead of denying the "idol" accusation, Morton ridicules it by extending and redefining the term. He knows that the Pilgrims have already denounced the Book of Common Prayer, too, as "an idol, and all that use it Idolaters" (187). Proud of his Renaissance learning, he delights in exposing his fascination with poetic beliefs embodied in ancient mythology but scorned by the Separatists. He will not apologize, in this land of diversity, for gathering around him manifold styles of religion and a demographically mixed multitude embracing what his prayer book describes as "all sorts and conditions of men." He will plead guilty, as charged, to toying with a version of goddess worship but complain with mock indignation that the Separatists have stupidly attributed Merrymount's patronage to the wrong goddess—to Flora rather than Maia. Apparently the "precise separatists" are embarrassingly imprecise about analyzing the varieties of religion lying outside their narrow mental and physical domain. Nor would Morton admit anything disgraceful about Bradford's claim of "idle" revelry or, for that matter, about enjoying the "idyll" of life at Merrymount plantation.

Starting with his title, Morton even shares with his Puritan opponents a fondness for invoking biblical analogies in which New England figures as a version of "the Israelites' Canaan." In conjunction with Edenic imagery, this typology expresses Morton's faith in the extraordinary material and immaterial promise of a country that is "nothing inferior to Canaan of Israel" (2, 13).[35] Instead of designating his own community as the New Israel, Morton situates *his* honorific Israel not in people but in place. And instead of stigmatizing the Amerindians as figurative Amalekites or Philistines who must die for Israel to be born, he implies that all who truly love the land's natural endowments, who relish this place whose bounty recalls that of Old Israel, deserve the gift of inhabiting "New English Canaan." By this standard, of course, Morton finds the Pilgrims lacking since they manifest too little love and enjoyment of their adopted land, as well as scant charity toward their human neighbors. Because the Pilgrims insist on reminding themselves that heaven is their only authentic home, they have yet to embrace Cape Cod as their material Israel. In Morton's view they remain insulated, perversely disengaged from their larger human and physical environment. When Morton calls them "Separatists" and "cruel Schismaticks" (198), he does so with an acerbic accent meant to persuade his readers that *they*, not he, are the oddball renegades who have removed themselves from the world and from fellowship with the Church of England.

A detail featured in Morton's account of the Maypole episode reveals another significant point about how his environmental perceptions coincide with, but also diverge from, those of Bradford. The author of *New English Canaan* discloses that in addition to cavorting in circles with fellow revelers, he took pains to fix to the pole an explanatory poem, the piece that begins "Rise, Oedipus." The poem seems to be something of a tease, an "enigmatically composed" riddle certain to befuddle Pilgrims who are enticed to puzzle over its meaning. Still, the very idea of attaching a text to the tree is revealing. The poem serves thereby as an interpretive gloss not only on Merrymount's name and justification but also on the maypole itself, which stands in turn as a synecdoche for the free-spirited green world. This detail of attaching text to tree, as well as the general gathering of classical and biblical references with naturalistic description throughout *New English Canaan*, confirms Morton's desire to "read" the New World's nature through texts drawing heavily on Old World traditions. For Morton, Greco-Roman mythology offered a suitable medium for perceiving and expressing his amorous relation to the land. He thus alludes to "Cytherea's [Aphoridite's] power, who points to land" by way of blessing Merrymount's festival; and similarly appealing to eroticism, he observes gleefully that one who "played Proteus (with the help of Priapus) put their [that is, the Separatists'] noses out of joint."

Yet despite their passionate dispute about what to make of the new world they chronicled, Bradford and Morton agree that humans must somehow *interpret* raw nature, preferably in the light of written texts, and that the meaning of nonhuman Creation is never self-evident. (Presumably the Amerindians, too, develop unwritten constructions of elemental nature, which Morton recognizes in cases such as their reading of constellations.) For Bradford, of course, the Bible is the crucial illuminative text, despite his frequent references to secular works throughout *Of Plymouth Plantation*. Whereas Morton's mythological imagination helps define his erotic embrace of "New English Canaan,"

Bradford's attachment to selected biblical texts promotes a measure of detachment from material habitations for those who "knew they were pilgrims" and
lifted their eyes "to the heavens, their dearest country" (*Of Plymouth Plantation*,
p. 47; see Hebrews 11:13–16). The Reformed exegete and reprobate critic differ
fundamentally in their readings of New England. These contesting colonizers
diverge also in the major pre-texts they select to configure their interpretations.
For both of them, however, European cultural values support a hermeneutical
conviction that the nonhuman world must be textualized, that humans are
perpetually drawn to reimagine and reembody nature in subjective writing. It
would remain for Thoreau, two centuries later, to develop a fully self-conscious
elaboration of this principle.

2

Meditating on the Creatures in Early American Life and Letters

Visible Wonders of the Invisible World

The Calvinist legacy of New England Puritanism confirmed the inaccessible, unknowable character of God's essence. At the same time, seventeenth-century Puritans affirmed that God had revealed in Scripture and the person of Christ all that elect humanity needed to know about the way to salvation. God's will touching proper organization of the church, God's provision for covenant relations with humankind, and God's expectations in the realm of moral law could likewise be discerned with confidence. Moreover, souls were urged to assume active roles in the quest for salvation by inwardly preparing themselves for saving grace and outwardly confirming their visible sanctity. Following Perry Miller, intellectual historians have commonly interpreted Puritan doctrines of "preparation" for conversion and participation in the covenant of grace as endorsing the capability of souls to influence their spiritual development despite predestination and the infirmity of the human will. From Saint Paul's dictum that "if any man be in Christ, he is a new creature" (2 Corinthians 5:17), it followed that saints were called to participate in God's consummation of the new Creation. The evangelical imperative of Reformation gave saints a dynamic vocation to advance God's kingdom in the world—to render them, by today's parlance, "cocreators" with God.

Puritans assumed that, beyond the definitive revelation of Scripture, signs in the phenomenal world also declared God's glory and will. I have already examined the case of William Bradford, a writer diligent about recording signs of God's intention in cloudbursts, earthquakes, and other natural occurrences. Attentiveness to natural wonders and portents also suffuses the writing of Edward Johnson, the Mathers, and other New England Puritans across several generations. God's ceaseless wonder-working could be perceived in human affairs as well as in outdoor fields and the skies overhead. Peculiar births and sudden deaths, blazing comets and violent storms—all could be understood as acts of special Providence. Moreover, as David D. Hall has demonstrated, this sense that seventeenth-century New Englanders sustained of living in "an enchanted universe" was not shaped exclusively by Christian theology. What Hall calls the age's "lore of wonders" resided instead in a popular culture developed from centuries of European tradition but already under attack by the middle of the seventeenth century. This extensive body of beliefs had been preserved from diverse sources but "was compounded out of four main systems of ideas—apocalypticism, astrology, natural history, and the meteorology of the Greeks."[1]

For New Englanders, popular beliefs and Christian theology converged in the conviction that visible facts of Creation were symbolically linked to the invisible realm of spirit. Though the Puritans rejected liturgical use of the Nicene Creed, they shared its twofold assurance that God had fashioned "all things visible and invisible." Hence it should not surprise us that Cotton Mather, who chronicled the wonders visibly evidenced by New England history in his *Magnalia Christi Americana* (1701), also endeavored to pursue *The Wonders of the Invisible World* (1693) in his notorious account of the Salem witchcraft controversy. Reformed Protestants typically claimed that the "plain sense" of Scripture was, or ought to be, understandable to any thoughtful believer. Yet interpreting the meaning of signs presented by earthly creatures, or in stellar terms by what Hawthorne called those "awful hieroglyphics" inscribed on "the cope of heaven," posed a tougher challenge.[2] The printed text of the Bible was physically bound, and contained a changeless canon, whereas the phenomenal world appeared to be limitless, perpetually in flux.

Accordingly, Puritans were often chastened from supposing that nature's meanings were self-evident, or that even saints could always decipher the signs reliably. It is true that figures such as John Winthrop and Edward Johnson exude confidence in their exegesis of natural providences. So does William Bradford in several notable episodes of his history. Sometimes life offered the Puritan easy illustrations of didactic purpose, with God's favor or punishment meted out according to predictably partisan standards of merit. Particularly in later portions of his history, though, Bradford reflects more indecision about how to understand God's activity in the world. Many passages in Puritan diaries and journals likewise reflect a personal struggle to comprehend, a reluctance to conclude too quickly what kind of moral or sacred significance might be disclosed by creaturely events.

Such hesitation was well founded. After all, the gospel age of miracles, of drastic interruptions in natural law amounting to immediate revelation, had ended. To suggest otherwise was, for the orthodox, to accept Anne Hutchinson's heretical views. Moreover, the gospels report that even most eyewitness observers of Jesus' miracles had failed to comprehend them or, by the idiom of Saint John's gospel, had remained blind to the spiritual meaning of the signs. So, in the current dispensation, faithful souls were usually left to ponder the import of "wonders" or "providences" rather than full-scale "miracles." Wondrous events were not wholly transparent but translucent moments, occasions when one might look through the visible world to glimpse something of the unseen. To achieve this discernment often required experience in the *discernment* spiritual discipline of meditation.

Edward Taylor and Anne Bradstreet, recognized today as colonial New England's two leading poets, offer pertinent examples of how Puritan spirituality managed to incorporate both Protestant and pre-Reformation traditions of "meditation on the creatures." In Taylor's case, we have first to admit that we are dealing with a meditative imagination more characteristically engaged in the world of Scripture than in material Creation. Inevitably, Taylor's best-known writing in his collection of 217 poems titled *Preparatory Meditations* includes many natural figures associated with fields such as astronomy, botany, and mineral geology. Yet they remain figures, with little direct connection to nature in the field, to impressions of the American landscape, or to recognizable views of Taylor's frontier environment in Westfield, Massachusetts.

In his extensive body of prose writings, however, the poet openly displays his fascination with natural science and his attentiveness to remarkable providences. As town physician, he maintained a lively interest in what passed at the time for medicine and chemistry. He was well versed in alchemy, while his knowledge of herbalism offered practical benefits for healing as well as horticulture. Such concerns are evident in several bound volumes of manuscript prose, including material copied from other sources in his "Dispensatory," "Metallographia," and "Commonplace Book." Taylor's botanical curiosity about trees, plants, gardens, and cuttings informs imagery used in several of the *Preparatory Meditations* as well as in the personal lyric "Upon Wedlock, and Death of Children."

Taylor had himself supplied examples of natural curiosities for Increase Mather's *Essay for the Recording of Illustrious Providences* (1684). And in his fragmentary poetic musing about "The Great Bones Dug Up at Claverack" he considers an amazing find from New York state reported in July 1705. Taylor believes that rational analysis confirms the bones to be remains of a giant creature, presumably human, who stood seventy feet tall and lived some two centuries earlier, as described in legends preserved by the Sopos Indians. For Taylor this discovery, like other marvels in which "Nature exceeds itselfe," inspires wonder and admiration for the "Glorious One" who planted "the Tree of Nature."[3] Yet because he believes God has endowed nature's tree with a life of its own, he fixes his attention on the observable paleontological evidence instead of pursuing biblical analogies, as we might expect of the Puritan divine. As scientifically incredible as the Claverack episode must look to us today, it does show Taylor's eagerness to assess "wonders" in the light of naturalistic inquiry and empirical observation.[4]

Taylor also manifests a response to actualities of the creaturely world in the eight "occurants," or occasional poems that he finished composing sometime before 1689. More emblematic or allegorical than genuinely symbolic, these lyrics stop short of interpreting nature as a second source of revelation. Still, pieces such as "Upon a Spider Catching a Fly" and "Upon a Wasp Child with Cold" do reflect the poet's close observations of entomological life. Though weighted toward didacticism, they present subtler theological teachings than are customarily attached to insect fables. Moreover, these fruits of "extemporall" rather than "deliberate" meditation, as the modes are differentiated by Joseph Hall in his influential *Arte of Divine Meditation* (1606), stand within a long-established Christian tradition of meditation on the creatures.[5] Supported by Ignatian as well as Protestant schools of meditation, this tradition stretched as far back as Saint Bonaventure, whose spirituality aimed to recover "traces" of God scattered throughout Creation, or indeed to the Psalmist, who was moved to "consider" (Psalm 8:3) with holy wonder the multitude of God's creatures spanning earth and sky.

Taylor's reaction to natural disturbance in his poem "Upon the Sweeping Flood" aptly represents the practice of "extemporall" or occasional meditation on the creatures. Unlike the bookish and methodically ordered lyrics in the *Preparatory Meditations*, this piece responds to the spectacle of an actual flash flood. Its full manuscript title even dates the event precisely: August 13–14, 1683. When the Woronoco and Connecticut rivers overflowed, the waters damaged homes, plantings, and at least one mill in Westfield, as Taylor mentions in his "Church Records."[6]

For Taylor, the first and most obvious meaning of the event was conventionally moralistic. Like other Puritans, he believed that natural calamities often embodied divine punishment for sin. This interpretation would be strengthened by biblical precedent. In the poem's first stanza, Taylor shows us how the "liquid drops" that temporarily "drown" his corner of New England, like those that flooded Noah's world, come as chastening for human sin. He identifies this sin as "our Carnall love." The disastrous flood begins, ironically enough, when "our cheeks were dry and eyes refusde to weep," with the compensating result that "Tears bursting out ran down the skies darke Cheek."

But how should we understand the precipitating offense of "Carnall love"? Rather than a private sexual transgression, this sin of which "wee" stand convicted must refer generically to the human race or, in narrowest terms, to the New England congregational race in some phase of its ongoing controversy with God. And at least one name for the sin that, in the second and final stanza, sorely provokes God's excremental wrath to fall upon "our lofty heads" must be pride, the original fault leading toward the primal deluge. So "Carnall love" amounts to a complacent love of self that obstructs communion with all other creatures and with the broader love of God. Pictured here in the graphic imagery of dry and constipated affections, it also infects the whole of nature, as Saint Paul had observed in Romans 8:22. The wordplay in Taylor's poem confirms that even the aerial reaches of Creation are indeed "fallen."

Faced with the obstinacy of self-love, the poem releases a torrent of sacred sarcasm in its second stanza to dramatize the perversity of supposing that human willfulness could ever supply the proper enema to cure Creation:

> Were th' Heavens sick? must wee their Doctors bee
> And physick them with pills, our sin?
> To make them purg and Vomit, see,
>   And Excrements out fling?
> We've griev'd them by such Physick that they shed
> Their Excrements upon our lofty heads.[7]

Taylor's graphic imagery anticipates later visions of environmental apocalypse in which human misdeeds precipitate ills that are more globally catastrophic than a flash flood. Even when the culture no longer perceives "acts as of God" as divinely ordered retribution or correction for sin, a conviction persists in many quarters that environmental offenses issue naturally and inevitably in suitable "punishment" for at least a portion of humanity. Thus, a literalized update of Taylor's poem gives surprising credence to the notion that human selfishness, evidenced in the profligate release of combustion gasses from domestic and industrial sources, ends up raining toxic acidity and other atmospheric ills "upon our lofty heads." Even in Taylor's own preenvironmentalist consciousness, "Carnall love" cannot be wholly disassociated from the grasping, self-serving impulse to monopolize local water rights that a certain Thomas Dewey is charged with displaying in the same paragraph of Westfield's Church Records wherein the poet mentions the "great Flood" of 1683.

Taylor's poem also conveys subtler views of humankind's relation to Creation than are exposed by its central formula of retribution for sin. The evocative image of tears running "down the skies darke Cheek" highlights "our" contrasting refusal to repent, to feel any grief for our fault. Taylor's conceit of a weeping world also suggests that humans are not the only creatures who bear inexplicable sorrow. Saint Paul had testified, in the same well-known chapter where he indicts the "carnally minded," that "the whole creation groaneth and travaileth in pain together until now" (Romans 8:22). Taylor's image thus recalls the broadly orthodox teaching that nature, too, can be expected to suffer birthpangs of bringing forth the new Creation, even as it shares in the consequences of sin.

Ultimately, then, the poet of "Upon the Sweeping Flood" admits ambiguity in the meanings presented by natural signs. Though assured that God acts through meteorological processes, Taylor perceives this presence to be something of a two-edged sword. The storm's divinely mediated punishment also yields a purgative catharsis leading to hope of repentance. The lightning "flame" of God's charity becomes a piercing, regenerative force that can supplant the passions of carnal love. If "acts of God" like the sweeping flood are aptly viewed as punishment for sin, fit judgments on humanity's dungish ways, they can also be understood as nature's outpouring of regenerative compassion, vicariously on our behalf from the bowels of God. Toward the close of *Walden*, Henry Thoreau, too, confesses faith in the strangely creative potential of an excremental vision. And like the flood that engulfed Noah, the stream of vomit and excrement dispensed in Taylor's poem can be read as yet another line in the incarnational message that the poet elsewhere describes as God's "rich Love Letter to us from above."[8]

Anne Bradstreet's Meditation on the Creatures

On the basis of a single work titled "Contemplations," Anne Bradstreet warrants recognition as the first poet to record a sustained, appreciative response to outdoor experience in British North America. By 1650, Bradstreet had already made history as the first colonist to publish a volume of poetry, *The Tenth Muse Lately Sprung Up in America*. She composed "Contemplations" sometime thereafter, probably in the 1660s. It appeared first in a second volume of her poems published posthumously in 1678. More than three decades earlier Bradstreet had moved, with her husband Simon Bradstreet and four of the eight children she would eventually bear, from Ipswich, Massachusetts, to the still more remote inland settlement of North Andover. Before ending up in North Andover, Bradstreet had endured other momentous changes of life. When she was only eighteen, having already married and survived major illness, she faced the shock of leaving a cultured environment in Lincolnshire to accompany the 1630 Great Migration of Puritans to the Bay Colony. There she confronted rude living conditions and unfamiliar requirements for church membership. Although she testified that at first "my heart rose" against something in the "new world and new manners" of this country, she soon accepted her American estate as God's will.[9] In subsequent years, she would also have to accept the disorientation of moving her household repeatedly from first landing in Charlestown (Boston) to Newtown (Cambridge), Ipswich, and North Andover. Once she had settled in Andover, though, she was apparently able to find refreshment from her domestic duties by taking solitary walks in the woods. To judge from "Contemplations," she was more impressed by the land's beauty than its dangers. The speaker of her poem delights in sauntering through the autumnal splendors of forest and riverbank on the North Shore. At times, this pastoral enthusiasm can delude us into feeling that the poem's voice sounds more proto-Romantic than Puritan.[10]

Still, "Contemplations" has never seemed to invite ecocritical analysis. Readers often wonder, in fact, if the poet really *sees* the New England scene she purports to describe. Far from specifying naturalistic details or identifying species with distinctive relation to an American landscape, Bradstreet usually settles for generically vague references to fish, trees, sun, and "a goodly river's side." She offers no place names, no markers of distance or direction. Moreover, she evidently reads the visible world through lenses supplied by at least three nonnative traditions of textual perception. Thus, under the abstracting influence of classical mythology, her sun appears as "Phoebus," the river flows toward "Thetis' house," a songbird bears the name "Philomel." Another layer of interpretive precedent for Bradstreet's musings derives from later European conventions, particularly those involving folk culture and literary representations of pastoral. When the poet writes of sitting on verdant riverbanks and enjoying the company of a "merry grasshopper," with predators wholly out of sight and mind, one must wonder if she is really facing New England's wilds or strolling in an Old English garden. A third layer of her interpretive imagination is, of course, biblical. She not only glosses her account of natural phenomena with scriptural allusions but interrupts her personal report with seven stanzas of biblical commentary (stanzas 11–17) that seem an odd digression from the main course of meditation on the natural world. Does the poem, then, allow any sight of an actual America through all of these imported lenses?

Within the limits of its primary purpose as religious meditation rather than naturalistic description, I believe it does. Bradstreet makes no claim, of course, to possessing field training in Old World science, to say nothing of mastering the unstable nomenclature she would need for empirical delineation of New World organisms. Nor does she claim any interest in examining nature for its own sake. After granting those limits, and the force of Bradstreet's cultural preconceptions, we can read "Contemplations" as a certain type of nature poem: a meditation on the creatures founded in Christian tradition but stirred by encounter with the New World. This encounter was geographically rooted in what Bradstreet must have observed in woods near her home on the North Shore. Though she never specifies the locale of her sauntering, internal suggestions and biographical data point to North Andover, earlier named Andover or Merrimack, as the most likely setting. So I think it profitable to attempt an ecocritical reading of "Contemplations" that probes not only the spirituality of the world that Bradstreet sets forth in this work but also the discretely material spirit of place that helped inspire her reflections.

Bradstreet's opening stanzas offer several suggestions about the setting of "Contemplations." Told explicitly that we are approaching sunset in autumn, we are also presented with brilliantly colored foliage more typical of New England than of the British scenes Bradstreet knew in her previous life. The deciduous trees, so "richly clad" in the fading sun that they "seemed painted," enchant the eye with tones "Of green, of red, of yellow, mixed hue." No wonder the poet finds her senses "rapt . . . at this delectable view." Yet her reason recalls that such glory in the created "under world" only reflects the surpassing "excellence" of a Creator who "dwells on high" (204–205). Bradstreet is struck by the beauty of the world, witnessed at the dying hour of a dying season, and this mixed impression of transience and transcendence becomes a major theme of the poem. The poet's attention fixes ultimately on the peculiar paradox of human existence. Humans are creatures destined by nature for death but drawn by the spirit toward eternal life. Thus, their position within the divine scheme of Creation is oddly amphibious: they inhabit both temporal and timeless realms of being.

In the poet's view, humankind lives at once within, yet apart from, the community of animal Creation. We belong and do not belong to "nature." By the end of her poem Bradstreet illustrates, again paradoxically, how our unique position as existential amphibians is mirrored ecologically in the double lives of certain nonhuman organisms, amphibians of another sort.

Bradstreet reaches her conclusions not through methodical reasoning, however, but through an ambulatory, meandering style of meditation. This more spontaneous pattern of meditation, which typically begins with a "composition of place" but wanders freely thereafter in the spirit, has been described as Augustinian or Protestant in contrast to stricter Ignatian procedures.[11] In Bradstreet's day, Reformed sanction for the idea that meditating on the creatures could elevate the soul and senses had been widely articulated, most notably by Richard Baxter in *The Saints' Everlasting Rest*. Because all meditation required strict solitude, Baxter also supposed that outdoor settings encouraged inward reflection and that "Isaac's example, in going out to meditate in the field, will, I believe, best suit with most."[12] There is no reason to doubt that the movements of inner reflection recorded in Bradstreet's poem were accompanied by actual physical motion, so that "Contemplations" amounts to a walking meditation. And once again, the relatively untracked spaces of rural New England offer the most plausible setting for Bradstreet's account of wandering "silent alone, where none or saw, or heard, / In pathless paths." That Bradstreet enters the woods voluntarily, alone, and for no reason of practical necessity is striking in itself. By the nineteenth century many forms of literature, particularly the wilderness romance, would celebrate the solitary sojourning of male protagonists. But in the colonial era, literary examples of independent female explorers, or even of temporarily unattached daytrippers like Bradstreet, were exceedingly rare.

Though Bradstreet's orthodox theology controls the final direction of her reflections, visual cues do affect their sequence. Thus, her gaze flows reflexively from the massed splendor of fall foliage to one "stately oak," and proceeds upward from there to the "glistering Sun." As she shifts attention from oak to sun, she perceives a comparable inward progression toward heightened antiquity and glory:

> Then higher on the glistering Sun I gazed,
> Whose beams was shaded by the leavie tree;
> The more I looked, the more I grew amazed,
> And softly said, "What glory's like to thee?"
> Soul of this world, this universe's eye,
> No wonder some made thee a deity;
> Had I not better known, alas, the same had I. (205)

Some have construed Bradstreet's strongly emotive attraction to Phoebus as a temptation to embrace pagan or neo-Romantic sun-worship. In this view, the poet's drawing back from the sensuous attractions of nature religion is regrettably Puritanical. It shows her capitulation to a repressive ideology that triumphs over heartfelt experience. For Bradstreet, though, the aim of meditation is to unite head and heart. Neither indulging nor denying creaturely emotion, she tries through contemplation to set her feelings of rapture and amazement within the ordering frame of theology. As she sees it, the sun embodies indeed what she calls the "glory" of God—that is, a visible reflection of at least some dimension of God's invisible essence. Biblical usage agrees that divine glory can be apprehended through the senses, particularly through sight, while Bradstreet's conventionally masculinized imaging of Phoebus as the virile bridegroom of Psalm 19 suggests her erotic attraction to this sun-god who represents, in turn, the divine Son.

Nonetheless, the poet reminds herself that the sun is a created figure of God rather than God himself. So her homage is pointedly qualified: "Hail creature, full of sweetness, beauty, and delight." Even in strictly naturalistic terms, the sun must be deemed a necessary but not sufficient cause of life on earth. To worship the sun as if it were life itself would ignore the organically conjunctive process by which life is created. Bradstreet describes Creation as a divine process of reproduction. For the generation of "birds, insects, animals with vegative" to occur, solar heat must enter "the darksome womb of fruitful nature" (206).

Although much of the natural theology in "Contemplations" draws on conventional rhetoric associated with the argument from design, this process language implies a more intimate involvement between Creator and Creation than one customarily associates with a Puritan worldview. Such perceptions could be strengthened by meditating on the Christian doctrine of Incarnation, as confirmed by Bradstreet's colloquy in other poems with Christ as heavenly bridegroom and by many of Edward Taylor's Preparatory Meditations. Insofar as Bradstreet envisions biotic Creation as the fruit of God's intercourse with Mother Earth, she perceives God as different from the world, but not detached from it in strictly "monarchical" isolation.[13] In prose reflections addressed to her children she avows that in the face of doubts about God's existence and "the verity of the Scriptures," her faith had been sustained by "consideration" of the Lord's "wondrous works" as manifested seasonally within the "vast frame of the heaven and the earth." Her vision could even be described as "ecological" (from the Greek *oikos*, meaning household) in a peculiarly literal sense, since her prose statement goes on to expresses thankful amazement at God's "daily providing for this great household upon the earth, the preserving and directing of all to its proper end" (243).

As domestic manager of a large and politically prominent New England family, Bradstreet had firsthand knowledge of what it might mean to approach nature as a bustling household to which she belonged rather than a lifeless commodity or fearsome antagonist. "Contemplations" shows her wandering through a landscape that holds no terrors, an unpeopled place where she evidently feels at home. Still, she finds herself unable to share in the instinctual outpouring of divine praise voiced by other creatures, like the cricket and song-bird. She is a natural creature curiously alienated from nature. Though she aspires "To sing some song, my mazed Muse thought meet," she must struggle with words and face the "imbecility" of failing to magnify her "great Creator" justly and spontaneously. But why? Consistent with the natural flow of Bradstreet's meditation, her seemingly digressive rehearsal of biblical fables concerning Adam, Cain, and Abel recollects the fallen condition of humanity. Cain, the first city builder, is also the first creature to perpetrate fully deliberative violence against another. Hence Bradstreet perceives that other fall, Adam's primal fault, as infecting humankind more directly than the rest of Creation.

Made in God's image, the human animal qualifies as "by birth more noble than those creatures all, / Yet seems by nature and by custom cursed" (209).

Unlike "wat'ry folk that know not your felicity," humans are at once uniquely blessed and uniquely burdened with self-consciousness. And unlike the rest of nature's creatures, which are "insensible of time" but recover greenness in temperate climes when "spring returns, and they [are] more youthful made," mortal humans are excluded from earthly immortality. Unlike nature's eternally recurring spring, a human "grows old, lies down, remains where once he's laid." He is "No sooner born, but grief and care makes fall / That state obliterate he had at first" (209–210). But though nonhumans might evidence superior strength, beauty, or earthly endurance, humans are "made for endless immortality" on the transtemporal plane of eschatology. By virtue of the Resurrection, their ultimate destiny is enscribed on a "white stone" (from Revelation 2:17) located beyond geological history.

Thus, humans find themselves alienated in crucial ways from their creaturely kin in nature's household. Ordinarily, we are not so violently estranged from these distant relatives as Cain was from his brother Abel. Yet Bradstreet's meditations in this poem foster awareness of our existential divergence from, as well as our affiliation with, brute Creation. Accordingly, they combine two spiritual practices often distinguished, in contemplative tradition, as the negative and affirmative paths of interior ascent to God. By definition, meditation on the creatures draws largely on the *kataphatic*, or "positive way" tradition of Christian spirituality, which encourages engagement with words and images as a means of approaching union with the Creator. Bradstreet's attraction to literary art, to creaturely images, and to scriptural language all support this approach. Affirmative way spirituality is a fundamental element of her Christian humanism. By contrast, *apophatic* mysticism involves the systematic negation of all words, images, or concepts of the Divine. Insofar as God transcends all sense knowledge and human representations, the apophatic way leads toward pure contemplation—toward the soul's immediate, unverbalized apprehension of the Absolute. Though generally associated with pre-Reformation Catholic mystics, such as the author of the fourteenth-century *Cloud of Unknowing*, negative way mysticism also coincides with Puritan and Jewish impulses to set aside sacred icons.

In Bradstreet's "Contemplations," the speaker pursues a *via negativa* principle by repeatedly denying impressions of congruence between herself, as representative human soul, and the nonhuman creatures she interrogates. In one fundamental sense, insofar as she ponders her unlikeness to trees, birds, insects, and fish, she understands her spiritual state to be *not nature*. She is constantly noticing the limitations of natural analogies she has discovered. Yet insofar as she knows herself to be another "creature," like the sun, she accepts her membership in earth's "great household." In this *via affirmativa* mode, she recognizes a strand of spiritual and figurative continuity between humans and nonhuman objects of her meditation. More particularly, her bird and piscine meditations serve to highlight analogically the condition of humanity as an existential amphibian who inhabits both time and eternity, material nature as well as the immaterial spirit-world.

In common usage, the bird identified as "sweet-tongued Philomel" would correspond to the Old World nightingale. But in its literal derivation from the Greek and Latin *philomela*, meaning love of song, the name could reasonably apply to any songbird. Bradstreet was scarcely alone in failing to name precisely those American avians that, in Francis Higginson's words, looked like "strange fowls which we know not." John Josselyn, too, borrowed Old England's idiom in his seventeenth-century description of "*New-England* Nightingales painted with orient colors, white, blew, yellow, green and scarlet"; as late as 1791, the naturalist William Bartram was still referring to an American species as "the philomela or mock-bird."[14] Nor does Bradstreet's feminized depiction of Philomel square with a naturalist's recognition that the singer would typically be male.[15] Evidently, though, the bird she describes in stanzas 26–28 is a perching songbird, a migratory species that sings before dawn and may well belong to the thrush family, as does the nightingale. Which American bird, then, warbled so melodiously as to enrapture the poet "with wonder and delight"? It is impossible to say for sure. The wood thrush, with its haunting flutelike strains, may well have inspired Bradstreet's account of a singer that "chanted forth a most melodious strain / Which rapt me so with wonder and delight." Another kind of thrush (or member of the family *Turdidae*) could also satisfy Bradstreet's description, and Josselyn's testimony confirms the abundance of such songbirds in colonial New England.[16]

Whatever its species, this spirit-like fowl remains largely hidden from view. Its presumptive joy and freedom from care differ dramatically from the "sad thoughts" and "cruciating cares" of self-conscious humanity. In two crucial respects, however, the bird offers a positive natural analogy, or emblem, of our amphibious state as human creatures. The first dimension of the bird's double life is its ability to move in two atmospheric elements, earth and air. Bradstreet perceives human beings, likewise, as earthbound but aspiring to soar by divine grace toward the metaphoric heavens. Clearly the poet identifies her own urge to transcend mortal anxiety with the bird's ability to fly, declaring that she "wished me wings with her a while to take my flight." Moreover, Bradstreet's conventional analogy between winged creatures and the human soul is enlarged by her scriptural reference to Matthew 6: 26–33. Just as the ideal of unencumbered, steadfast human commitment to the Kingdom of God is imaged in the gospel by "fowls of the air" who "sow not, neither do they reap, nor gather into barns," so also Bradstreet admires the nonacquisitive, single-minded disposition represented in this "merry Bird" who "neither toils nor hoards up in thy barn."

Another dimension of the bird's double life is its migratory participation in two different environmental climates. Bradstreet recalls that after the "feathered crew" of Philomel "pass their youth in summer season," they leave northern winters behind by following "thee into a better region." Again, the connotation of "a better region" seems to be heavenly though its directional denotation is, of course, southerly. The Puritan principle of "weaned affections" stipulated that human beings, too, must cultivate enough detachment from the world to understand that they had no permanent habitation on earth.[17] Bradstreet believed that within the saints' cosmic calendar, she resided in New England only for a season.

Like Philomel, the fish Bradstreet describes in stanzas 24–25 remain insensible of time and of their own condition. To that extent, they present a *via negativa* comparison with the human mariner of stanzas 31–32, who also negotiates an aquatic medium but shows painful cognizance of his mortality. At another level, though, the fish also present one more positive analogy with amphibious humanity. These fish inhabit two different environments insofar as their spawning habits direct them "for each season" to alter their habitation, "Now salt, now fresh where you think best to glide." In Bradstreet's symbolic scheme, the river flow corresponds to temporal existence, whereas the saline ocean recalls that eternal reservoir of being "where all embrace and meet" (211).

To consider more fully this fluid element of the poem, it is helpful to recollect what we know materially about its probable setting. Settled after 1638, the inland plantation of North Andover lay about fifteen miles west of Ipswich, within two miles of the Merrimack River. Anne's husband, Simon, not only owned a twenty-acre houselot in the settlement but probably built a sawmill on nearby Cochichewick brook. The Shawsheen, a tributary of the Merrimack, and Lake Cochichewick could also be seen within a mile's walk of Bradstreet's home. Consistent with this geography, "Contemplations" describes a sizeable river, fed by numerous tributaries, that runs directly to the sea. When she addresses the river, Bradstreet mentions the "hundred brooks" that "in thy clear waves do meet." Her poem also mentions the "lakes and ponds" visited by spawning fish.

When Bradstreet's family moved to North Andover in the mid-1640s, the settlement had more of a frontier character than the poet had previously known in Ipswich. Wolves, bears, and other wildlife still roamed pathless territory near the village, which probably numbered fewer than five hundred residents by 1662. Still, Native Americans had cleared sections of the area for planting and seasonally burned forest underbrush, while observers such as Edward Johnson praised the fertility of Andover's meadow lands.[18] Thus, the parklike impression Bradstreet sometimes conveys of her environment in "Contemplations" corresponds to landscapes she would have found close to home. Her reflections on a "stately oak" near a "goodly river" teeming with fish are closely paralleled, in fact, by John Josselyn's observations in *Two Voyages*: "Eight miles beyond *Agowamin* runneth the delightful River *Merrimach* or *Monumach*, it is navigable for twenty miles, and well stored with fish, upon the banks grow stately Oaks, excellent Ship timber, not inferiour to our *English*."[19]

A tidal estuary near its mouth, the Merrimack (named by Pennacook Indians with the sense of "Strong Place" or "the place of swift water") runs with some force and little winding from North Andover to the sea (see fig. 2.1). Bradstreet likewise depicts her river as a "happy flood" that "to the longed-for ocean held its course"; she sees in it "nor crooks, nor rubs that there did lie /

FIGURE 2.1. Merrimack River near North Andover, Massachusetts. The probable setting of Anne Bradstreet's "Contemplations." (Photo by Ning Yu.)

Could hinder ought, but still augment its force" (210). Observers such as William Wood and William Hammond marveled over the abundance of fish—particularly sturgeon, salmon, and bass—in the Merrimack watercourse.[20] Thoreau, in his later account of touring this river, remarked that anadromous species, particularly salmon, had been plentiful here before the construction of dams and locks. Thus, we can identify the migratory fish in Bradstreet's poem as bass or salmon. Atlantic salmon would be the best bet, I think, because the poet refers to their offspring as "fry," one of whose applications the *Oxford English Dictionary* restricts quite specifically to salmon progeny in the second year of the spawning cycle.

By present-day standards, Bradstreet could have made her poem more effective by visualizing more concretely such material details of place and time. For all that, Bradstreet deserves Adrienne Rich's accolade as the first poet "to give an embodiment to American nature" (foreword to *Works*, p. xix). Though it reaches toward "divine translation" in another realm, "Contemplations" also expresses a divine sense of wonder about this world, and about some of the creatures who live beside us in the great household. As meditation, Bradstreet's work aspires to present not an argument from design but a psalm of praise centered on Creation. Beyond filing rational claims of God's existence, it stirs affections to discover God's presence, felt through senses enraptured by the

FIGURE 2.2. Great soft-shelled tortoise, drawn by William Bartram to illustrate his *Travels*. (Photo courtesy of Thomas J. Dodd Research Center, University of Connecticut, Storrs.)

beauty of Creation. Thoreau, who recorded his own meditations on the Merrimack in his first book, *A Week on the Concord and Merrimack Rivers*, lamented that books of natural history fail to "teach the divine view of nature." Published within the earliest phase of letters in British North America, "Contemplations" is a noteworthy effort to do precisely that.

Ethical Views of "Brute Creation" in Two Quakers: William Bartram and John Woolman

William Bartram's *Travels Through North & South Carolina, Georgia, East & West Florida* (1791) offers a startling contrast to Bradstreet's "Contemplations." Authored by a bona fide though largely self-educated naturalist from Philadelphia with scientific expertise in botany, this prose account examines at first hand that "better region" of southeastern, semitropical America that for Bradstreet was only a distant dream. Unlike Bradstreet, Bartram provides a wealth of concrete information about the creatures he observes during four years of exploration (see fig. 2.2).

He describes the region's flora and fauna in exhaustive detail. Anticipating

Whitman, he inserts lengthy catalogues to show the diversity of organisms in each habitat, tagging his list of names with scientific Latin. In addition to recording natural history, he was obliged to collect specimens and seeds for his trip's financial sponsor, Dr. John Fothergill of London. Yet Bartram's literary treatment of his experience in southern savannas, woods, and marshes is not simply an inert anatomy of biological specimens. Often disposed to write in a floridly Romantic style, Bartram enlivens his inventory with human interest stories of his interactions with colonists and with Creeks, Cherokees, and Seminoles. He relates adventures, verging on tall tales, of his close encounters with alligators, a "rapacious wolf," and other perils.

Above all, Bartram humanizes his scientific narrative by recording many subjective, emotional responses to the *biota* he observes. His repeatedly interrupts his factual descriptions with prose poems. Bartram's fondness for exclamatory rhetoric confirms his awestruck gratitude at receiving this world as "a glorious apartment of the boundless palace of the sovereign Creator . . . furnished with an infinite variety of animated scenes, inexpressibly beautiful and pleasing." Thus, from his own spiritual perspective influenced by Quaker values, Bartram nonetheless shared with Bradstreet a conviction that "meditating on the marvellous scenes of primitive nature" was at base a religious act allied to worship. As the writer James Dickey puts it, Bartram "moved in the midst of God's bewildering plenty" so that his "lists of plants and animals which modulate—or explode—into prayers, are from beginning to end praise" (xi).[21]

When Bartram describes the fundamental purpose of his travels, he presumes that his vocation to serve practical science is integrally bound to natural piety:

> Whilst I, continually impelled by a spirit of curiosity, in pursuit of
> new productions of nature, my chief happiness consisted in tracing
> and admiring the infinite power, majesty, and perfection of the great
> Almighty Creator, and in the contemplation, that through divine aid
> and permission, I might be instrumental in discovering, and intro-
> ducing into my native country, some original productions of nature,
> which might become useful to society. (82)

Bartram's effusive tributes to a numinous nature, which surface throughout the *Travels*, often reflect conventional sentiments about the exceptional beauty and perfection of God's works, or the "inexpressibly sublime" (160) character of outdoor scenes. Like his well-known father, the naturalist John Bartram, and others of his era, William shared typical deistic assumptions about the providential order and mechanical unity of Creation. Though he marvels at the splendid variety of organisms that he classifies according to the usual Linnean taxonomy, he never inquiries deeply into the origins of this diversity. Yet some distinctive features of William Bartram's theology of nature appear in the *Travels*. For example, he balances his acceptance of nature's utilitarian function with a rare insistence that nonhuman lives may also warrant respect as sacred in God's design apart from human designs. Though anthro-

pocentric in presuming the primacy of human needs, the outlook acknowledges human fellowship with other members of "brute creation," particularly
with other sentient animals.

So instead of emphasizing humanity's absolute sovereignty over nature by
virtue of our unique possession of a soul, Bartram perceives continuity and a
fair degree of ambiguity across linkages in the great chain of being. In his
vision of Creation, the most essential attribute of the Creator is not omnipo-
tence, or genius in ordering the world, but compassionate care for all creatures.
Far from accepting any doctrine of divine election or limited atonement within
the human race, Bartram envisions a universalism in which something of the
Creator's saving will that "peace and love may prevail in the earth" (103) extends
to nonhumans. Thus, a common soul, or life-principle, animates the whole of
creation.[22]

Bartram's skepticism about familiar dichotomies between Euro-Americans
and Amerindians, plants and animals, humans and animals indicates how his
biological perceptions support his theological belief in Creation as a unified
continuum. His inspection of the Venus flytrap (*Dionea muscipula*), for example, suggests to him a major ambiguity about plant/animal distinctions that
remains salient today.[23] "Can we," he asks, "after viewing this object, hesitate
a moment to confess, that vegetable beings are endued with some sensible
faculties or attributes, familiar to those that dignify animal nature; they are
organical, living, and self-moving bodies, for we see here, in this plant, motion
and volition" (15). He also shows skepticism toward racialist ideas of drastic
anthropological difference between Europeans and Native Americans.

By the same token, he perceives a substantial continuity between human
and nonhuman animals. While granting that humans stand at the apex of
creaturely development in rational consciousness, he questions traditional
views that our species is uniquely gifted with "soul" and reason in contrast to
beasts governed solely by instinct. "I am sensible," he writes,

> that the general opinion of philosophers has distinguished the
> moral system of the brute creature from that of mankind, by an epi-
> thet which implies a mere mechanical impulse, which leads and im-
> pels them to necessary actions, without any premeditated design or
> contrivance; this we term instinct, which faculty we suppose to be
> inferior to reason in man.

And yet, he insists, "the parental and filial affections seem to be as ardent,
their sensibility and attachment as active and faithful, as those observed in
human nature." If we so esteem the visible marvels of animal Creation, how
much more might we admire the unseen element, "that inexpressibly more
essential principle, which secretly operates within? that which animates the
inimitable machines, which gives them motion, impowers them to act, speak,
and perform, this must be divine and immortal?" (17).

Consistent with his Quaker background, Bartram finds the wellsprings of
his Creation spirituality more typically in personal experience, an inner sense
cultivated mostly outdoors in solitude, than in scriptural revelation. John Bar-

tram had been disowned by the Darby Meeting of the Society of Friends after denying Jesus' divinity,[24] and William's outlook in *Travels* differs unmistakably from the densely biblical imagination of Anne Bradstreet's orthodox Christianity. Yet William retained a Quaker perspective on the world. He practiced meditation and prayer each morning; even more emphatically than his father, he denounced inhumane treatment of animals.[25] His approach to naturalism embodies certain classic Quaker virtues: humility and patience in waiting upon the spirit, contemplative equanimity, and a nonviolent disposition equivalent to Asian *ahimsa*—that is, a refusal to inflict needless harm on any sentient creature.

Despite his essentially benevolent view of Creation, Bartram does not overlook the many troubling, threatening faces of untamed nature that his travels expose. His gripping tales of danger, especially the near-calamity he endures while canoeing in East Florida among a large brood of attacking alligators, discourage idealization of the South as a balmy paradise. He knows what it is to live in a predatory world that includes not only "subtle greedy" alligators and "rapacious" wolves but also vexing mosquitoes and gray caterpillars that ravage forests and fruit trees throughout the north. His famous account of "terrible conflict" (115, 145) among smoke-belching alligators could aptly illustrate Hobbesian claims that the true state of nature is indeed a state of war. All the same, Bartram periodically insists on declaring that animals such as the vulture, moccasin snake, and coach-whip snake are all "beautiful"—a judgment inspired, as in Coleridge's *Rime of the Ancient Mariner*, by a pre-Darwinian but effectively ecological recognition of their adaptive interaction with other organisms in a suitable habitat.[26] He also refuses to regard competitive struggle as the sole or dominant principle of natural processes. "Within the circle of my acquaintance," he admits, "I am known to be an advocate or vindicator of the benevolent and peaceable disposition of animal creation in general, not only toward mankind, whom they seem to venerate, but always towards one another, except where hunger or the rational and necessary provocations of the sensual appetite interfere" (222). Even rattlesnakes, he claims, can show generosity by passing up opportunities to strike vulnerable humans.

An ethical consequence of Bartram's perception is the unusual restraint he shows about destroying any form of life. Praying that the "universal Father" will look on the world with "pity and compassion," he asks in part 2 of his travel testimony that God will illuminate our understanding and warm our hearts "with a due sense of charity, that we may be enabled to do thy will, and perform our duty towards those submitted to our service and protection, and be merciful to them, even as we hope for mercy" (103). Though Bartram is a carnivore who sometimes hunts, kills, and fishes, he considers himself bound to practice mercy whenever possible to creatures requiring his "service and protection." Some people, he admits, consider him too partial toward Native Americans, whom he admires in a way his father certainly had not.[27] His humanitarian conscience is not fully or consistently developed, since he betrays insensitivity toward the condition of African slaves in Georgia, whom he imagines to be "contented and joyful" while they labor to prepare timber for market.

Denouncing slavery only later in life, he himself accepts slaves lent to him during his travels and had earlier owned slaves during an abortive attempt to become a planter in Florida.[28] Still, Bartram finds occasion to practice tender mercy toward the Seminole as well as toward deer, bear, and rattlesnakes. When he sees a large hawk bound up with a long coach-whip snake, he is moved to dismount his horse with the intent of liberating both from harm. Reproaching himself as "entirely insensible to gratitude or mercy" when, in earlier years, he might instinctually kill any snake he encountered, he later "promised myself that I would never again be accessary to the death of a rattle snake, which promise I have invariably kept to."[29]

Like other celebrated scientific naturalists, including Aldo Leopold in *A Sand County Almanac*, Bartram traces his promotion of environmental ethics to an emotionally charged episode of personal epiphany comparable to a conversion narrative. Bartram describes this defining moment toward the opening of his *Travels*. While ascending Florida's south Musquito river in a canoe, a hunter in his party spots and shoots a bear, which turns out to be a female with offspring. The surviving cub, discovering its mother has been killed, "approached the dead body, smelled, and pawed it, and appearing in agony, fell to weeping and looking upwards, then towards us, and cried out like a child." At this point Bartram, who reproaches himself for complicity in a kill he deems unwarranted, tries to avert the cub's destruction:

> The continual cries of this afflicted child, bereft of its parent, affected me very sensibly; I was moved with compassion, and charging myself as if accessary to what now appeared to be a cruel murder, endeavoured to prevail on the hunter to save its life, but to no effect! for by habit he had become insensible to compassion toward the brute creation: being now within a few yards of the harmless devoted victim, he fired, and laid it dead upon the body of the dam. (18)

Despite the failure of his intervention, Bartram experiences an inner motion toward divine compassion that later enables him to show mercy toward other members of brute Creation, including rattlesnakes. Within the *Travels*, this bear-killing incident sets the tone for Bartram's enlargement of Quaker spirituality toward a recognition that nonhumans, too, can qualify as "friends." Bartram sees this extension of a selectively qualified nonviolence arising not from rule-based obligation but from a "sense of charity" rooted in firsthand knowledge of the material world.

John Woolman, another prominent Quaker born almost twenty years before Bartram, sets forth remarkably similar ethical views in his *Journal* (first published 1774). Woolman scarcely fits usual images of the nature writer, since little of his work is devoted to landscape description or travel narrative. Best known for antislavery acts of conscience and other forms of social witness, Woolman devotes most of his spiritual narrative to showing how God's "motion of love" inspired his conversion toward a ministry of compassion and truth among human brethren. Yet the ethical theology he expounds in the *Journal* clearly includes the notion of human responsibility toward the nonhuman world. Woolman's chief illustration of human connection with the "brute creation," and a defining episode in his progress toward conversion of heart, concerns his mistreatment of animals. He recalls an incident from childhood when he saw a robin, obviously worried about her young, fluttering about her nest as he approached. On a perverse whim, he throws stones at her until one of them strikes her dead. His examination of conscience with respect to this deed, both originally and retrospectively, shows such penetrating earnestness that the relevant passage must be cited in full:

> At first I was pleased with the exploit, but after a few minutes was seized with horror, as having in a sportive way killed an innocent creature while she was careful for her young. I beheld her lying dead and thought those young ones for which she was so careful must now perish for want of their dam to nourish them; and after some painful considerations on the subject, I climbed up the tree, took all the young birds and killed them, supposing that better than to leave them to pine away and die miserably, and believed in this case that Scripture proverb was fulfilled, "The tender mercies of the wicked are cruel" [Prov. 12:10]. I then went on my errand, but for some hours could think of little else but the cruelties I had committed, and was much troubled.
>
> Thus He whose tender mercies are over all His works hath placed a principle in the human mind which incites to exercise goodness toward every living creature; and this being singly attended to, people become tender-hearted and sympathizing, but being frequently and totally rejected, the mind shuts itself up in a contrary disposition.[30]

Whereas acts of cruelty toward animals rarely appear in Puritan exhibits of depravity, the episode stands out in Woolman's recollections because he perceives that purely gratuitous malice toward the most helpless of God's creatures violates the deepest nature of humanity as well as of God. Though as a child he had been absorbed by remorse for his indiscretion, as an adult he dwells rather on the godly insight generated by his fall from grace. He now sees respect for "brute creation" as more than a supplementary ethical duty. It becomes instead a spiritual charism integral to his religious faith. Woolman comes closest to presenting a comprehensive credo in the first section of his *Journal*, when he declares the conviction he achieved as a young man

> that true religion consisted in an inward life, wherein the heart doth love and reverence God the Creator and learn to exercise true justice and goodness, not only toward all men but also toward the brute creatures; that as the mind was moved on an inward principle to love God as an invisible, incomprehensible being, on the same principle it was moved to love him in all his manifestations in the visible world; that as by his breath the flame of life was kindled in all

animal and sensitive creatures, to say we love God as unseen and at
the same time exercise cruelty toward the least creature moving by
his life, or by life derived from him was a contradiction in itself.[31]

Though expressed with rare eloquence, these sentiments that Woolman
first recorded around 1720 cannot be considered unique. Before the century's
close, Samuel Taylor Coleridge penned his own poetic argument for respecting
"brute creation" in *The Rime of the Ancient Mariner.* Although Coleridge approached this issue from the standpoint of cultural and theological traditions
well removed from Woolman's Middle Atlantic Quaker piety, he had read both
Woolman and Bartram with enthusiasm.[32] And within Woolman's own era and
nation, even the religious soil of Reformed Christianity—a less nature-friendly
tradition, on the whole, than Quakerism or Coleridge's Romanticism—offered
pockets of support for an environmental ethic. To consider this last claim more
closely, we might pause to assess the case of America's greatest colonial-era
theologian, Jonathan Edwards.

3

Intimations of an Environmental Ethic in the Writings of Jonathan Edwards

From Edwards to Aldo Leopold

Whether viewed as more essentially Neoplatonist or Calvinist, Jonathan Edwards was surely no naturalist by most familiar definitions of that term. The environmental determinism of late nineteenth-century literary naturalism, the picturesque naturalism of William Bartram's landscape commentary, the "Romantic naturalism" of Thoreau—none of these finds any exact counterpart in the work of a divine whose most ambitious writing is devoted to grandly bookish notions like the Freedom of the Will and Original Sin. The Edwards best known for invoking hellish terror in "Sinners in the Hands of an Angry God" seems even more remote from our image of the earth-centered conservationist. Yet the younger Edwards was evidently curious about insects, light, and other facts of nature. Reared amid placid rural scenes in East Windsor, Connecticut, he was shaped both there and later in Northampton, Massachusetts by the distinctive topography of the Connecticut River Valley (see fig. 3.1).
Despite his later preoccupation with mentalized abstractions, he did not "lose his grip upon the sheer facticity of nature."[1] Edwards shared the inquisitive mindset of Enlightenment naturalism in his well-known scrutiny of rainbows and spiders; he affirmed the epiphanic wonder of physical Creation in his "Personal Narrative"; and he anticipated Emerson in the insight that nature is a palpable symbol of Spirit.

This last point, broached decades ago in Perry Miller's classic essay "From Edwards to Emerson," has since received more considered analysis by students of Edwards's typology and religious imagination.[2] Innovative in his extensions of typology beyond the scrip-

FIGURE 3.1. Rural scene near East Windsor, Connecticut. The geographic setting of Jonathan Edwards's birth and childhood experience. (Photo by the author.)

tural text to the Book of Nature, Edwards nonetheless did not regard physical Creation as an autonomous equal of scriptural revelation. "The Book of Scripture," he insisted, "is the interpreter of the book of nature."[3] From one perspective, Edwards's theology of nature looks indeed like only a halfway house on the way toward Emerson's testimony to immediate revelations of the Universal Being felt amid the vital currents of open air. Still, Edwards's theology of Creation displays an original subtlety and force of its own. In fact, if we suspend our belief in strict chronology long enough to read Edwards in the light of the naturalist Aldo Leopold's 1948 plea for an "ecological conscience," we can find instructive parallels between the ethical philosophies of these two figures. Moreover, I think it possible to conclude from an assessment of Edwards's later writings that this religious philosopher, despite his image as America's last and most formidable Puritan, ends up looking no less "green" than Emerson in his ethical vision of how humanity relates to the larger cosmos.

Such I want to propose, at any rate, in an exposition whose first subtitle, "From Edwards to Aldo Leopold," must be qualified with all of Miller's disclaimers about indirect intellectual lineage. My focus is less on the obvious nature references in Edwards's early scientific musings, "Miscellanies," and "Images of Divine Things" than on the more theoretical implications of two late companion treatises written in Stockbridge: *Concerning the End for Which God Created the World* and *The Nature of True Virtue*. Highlighting what I take to be central impulses in these two works, I conclude among other things that while both the Edwardsean and early Emersonian writings present a symbolic rather than morally didactic view of the natural world, Edwards's view has at

least as much claim to be described as ethically comprehensive and nonanthropocentric. Emerson's Transcendental Idealism threatens to turn nature
finally into another, albeit richly ennobling, form of "Commodity" and human
creation. Edwards's theocentric Idealism, while admitting humanity's vocation
to render Creation aware of itself, sees physical nature as the refulgent emanation of divine glory. Though available for use by humankind, Creation is
thus for Edwards an aesthetic organism whose "end" is grasped solely by God.

As such, nature bears what later ethical philosophers would call inherent
worth, as opposed to purely instrumental value.[4] Neither the historical circumstance nor the personal temperament of Edwards encouraged him to pursue
the practical consequences of his protoecological vision. Nor, for that matter,
was Edwards inclined to explore the sociopolitical ramifications of other ethical
issues. As the historian George Marsden points out, "even though he pro-
claimed spiritual equality, the idea of social equality hardly occurred to him."[5]
Slavery presents the most flagrant contradiction between the nobility of Edwards's ethical pronouncements and the social degradation that his behavior
condoned. Usual though it may have been for an early eighteenth-century New
Englander of his social standing to own house slaves, Edwards's inability to
grasp the social import of his own far-reaching moral philosophy must strike
us as disappointing. By the same token, only the grander, more theoretical
shapes of Edwards's thought offer any suggestion of ideals that would, centuries later, gain explicit articulation as a "land ethic." To discern these shapes
more clearly, though, it is helpful to glance ahead to Aldo Leopold's classic
twentieth-century statement of environmental philosophy.

Sacred Grounds of Leopold's Land Ethic

First published in 1949, a year after Aldo Leopold's death, *A Sand County
Almanac* is revered by many as a "bible" of twentieth-century environmental
philosophy. As a prophet of conservation, Leopold underscored the integral
connection between "wild things" and the larger global community to which
humans belong. His conservationist orientation meant that in many cases he
assumed nature's instrumental or prudential value for humankind. He did
not, therefore, advocate the sort of biotic egalitarianism or rigorously ecocentric
viewpoint later championed by deep ecology spokespersons such as Dave For-
man. Leopold argued instead that the future welfare of humankind depended
on achieving a "shift of values" that would foster wiser, less profligate use of
the land that sustains our lives, as well as more critical assessment of technical
engineering applied in the name of "progress." At the same time, this conservationist's treatment of "The Land Ethic," in part 4, has also been canonized
as an incipient gospel of "preservationist" beliefs that the nonhuman world
has a life of its own, an inherent worth deserving respect and protection beyond
its utility in serving immediate human needs. Unlike Edwards, though, the
author of this secular gospel gained his professional training in forestry, not
theology. If anything, the foreword to *A Sand County Almanac* censures the

Hebrew Bible to the extent that it somewhat questionably attributes the baneful notion of earth as a "commodity belonging to us" rather than a "community to which we belong" to "our Abrahamic concept of land."[6] Where, then, are the lines of affinity between Leopold and Edwards?

One such affinity can be perceived in the personal, spiritually subjective character of Leopold's presentation. Encouraged by advisors and editors to present a form of nature writing that engaged readers beyond the factualism of objective science,[7] Leopold expressed the heartfelt sentiments of a distinctly defined personality who loved a certain plot of land in Wisconsin and could not live without knowing wild things. To foster authentic conservation it was not enough, he believed, to master all the subtleties of soil science, geology, and zoology. It was not enough to learn sound techniques of resource management. It was not even enough to replace the faulty conceptual view of land as mechanism with an organic model of ecological community, of land as a "fund of life" and "fountain of energy flowing through a circuit of soils, plants, and soils" (253). No, developing a right relation to land meant enlarging one's capacity to love. Stirring this impulse to love was, of course, crucial to Leopold's rhetorical purpose in the Almanac. For Edwards, too, neither religion nor godly ethics could be equated with cerebral knowledge. They were, at base, a matter of the heart and will.

In fact, through the pivotal section of the Almanac titled "Thinking Like a Mountain," Leopold links his testimony on behalf of the earth to his own personal confession of a change of heart. There he recalls his behavior as an impetuous young man who was lunching with others "on a high rimrock" in the West one day when he caught sight of half a dozen wolves. Immediately he joined in the fun of shooting them, on the simple assumption that wolves were nothing but nuisances who deprived hunters of their full take of deer. When he reached one old wolf at the point of death, however, he was struck by the sight of "a fierce green fire dying in her eyes" and "realized then, and have known ever since, that there was something new to me in those eyes—something known only to her and to the mountain" (138). He suggests that this troubling recognition allowed him, eventually, to achieve a leap of imaginative sympathy beyond shortsighted views of human-centered worth and utility. Appreciating as never before the role of predators within the larger ecology of plants and animals inhabiting the mountain, he had also learned to think and feel beyond the species boundary. Now he understood what it meant to "think like a mountain"—or, at least, to adopt a perspective broader than that represented in the culture's usual focus on nature as a purely humanized commodity. Without denying humanity's primal connection to the earth, Leopold gains new respect for the implacable otherness of wild things, as voiced by the "deep chesty bawl" (137) of wolves roaming the mountains at night. If mountains thus maintain "a secret opinion" about wolves, Leopold takes pains to inform his readers that "my own conviction on this score dates from the day I saw a wolf die" (138).

This key episode in Leopold's book, which appears in part 2 following the "almanac" section per se, amounts to what Edwards and earlier Puritans would immediately recognize as a conversion narrative. Surviving well beyond the Puritan era, it is a form in which one soul's passage from self-reproach and a "true sight of sin" to gracious self-renewal offers a public model of transformation for the benefit of others. To be sure, Leopold's admission of misconduct is not accompanied by an explicit, Puritan-style avowal of contrition for sin. Nonetheless, it draws on the rhetoric of traditional conversion narratives by demonstrating how an unsettling personal experience can lead not only to an amendment of life but also to a change of heart and mind that Edwards in another context calls a "new sense of things." The story is one that Leopold evidently hopes his readers can either match through their own experiences in the wild or enter vicariously through his narration. In any event, even Leopold's secularized account of conversion concludes with, and is introduced by, a statement of faith. This concluding statement affirms the fresh conviction of truths about oneself and the world that are, as Puritans would say, hidden from the carnal mind. Significantly misquoting Thoreau's famous declaration that "in Wildness is the preservation of the World," Leopold moves thereby one step closer to religious language in phrasing his own affirmation:

> too much safety seems to yield only danger in the long run. Perhaps this is behind Thoreau's dictum: In wildness is the salvation of the world. Perhaps this is the hidden meaning in the howl of the wolf, long known among mountains, but seldom perceived among men. (141)

Since for Leopold ethical conduct makes sense "only in relation to something we can see, feel, understand, love, or otherwise have faith in," some experience of awakened affection toward the nonhuman world must precede the evolution of a genuine land ethic. And Leopold believes that acceptance of such an ethic requires a long and gradual evolution in moral consciousness, on the part of individuals as well as whole cultures. Although "individual thinkers since the days of Ezekiel and Isaiah have asserted that the despoliation of land is not only inexpedient but wrong" (239), societies had been slow to develop these beliefs into a communally defined "ecological conscience." As Albert Schweitzer pointed out, notions of ethical responsibility had traditionally extended (in mainstream Western culture, anyway) no further than "the relations of man to man." Even when ethical claims had, after long stages of development, reached beyond kin, clan, tribe, or nation to the global community, that community of care usually did not include plants and animals. In Jewish and Christian teaching, loving both God and one's neighbor was an ethical imperative. Despite the famous parable in Saint Luke's gospel, it would not be easy to imagine extending the definition of "neighbor" beyond Samaritans to wolves. Schweitzer insisted, however, that someone can be "ethical only when life, as such, is sacred to him, that of plants and animals as that of his fellow men, and when he devotes himself helpfully to all life that is in need of help."[8] Leopold, in turn, may have been influenced by the "reverence for life" teachings of this slightly heterodox Alsatian Christian polymath, though his own ethical principles modified Schweitzer's solicitude for individual organisms and particles of matter by emphasizing instead the preservation of species and healthy ecosystems.[9]

Thus, Leopold argued that humans were responsible for protecting the life and health of biotic communities. He did not defend the right to life of every organism—a doubtfully tenable ethic in any case. Nor did he disavow hunting. Yet the flexible ideal of judgment at the core of Leopold's land ethic clearly assumes an intrinsic rather than a purely instrumental or utilitarian standard of worth. The land ethic is indeed ecocentric to the extent that human self-interest no longer figures as the sole or chiefly determinative criterion for judgment: "A thing is right when it tends to preserve the integrity, stability, and beauty of the biotic community. It is wrong when it tends otherwise" (262).

From the standpoint of environmental science and policy-making, the arresting word here is "beauty." A natural scientist might, in scientific terms, talk plausibly about the need to preserve the integrity or stability of existing systems. "Beauty," though, like "love," has no place in the vocabulary of physical science. Only in relation to Leopold's holistic ethical ideal of beauty and preordained harmony can such terms be considered meaningful. Or as Leopold remarks in the "Goose Music" section of the almanac:

> What value has wildlife from the standpoint of morals and religion?
> I heard of a boy once who was brought up an atheist. He changed
> his mind when he saw that there were a hundred-odd species of
> warblers, each bedecked like to the rainbow, and each performing
> yearly sundry thousands of miles of migration about which scien-
> tists wrote wisely but did not understand. No "fortuitous concourse
> of elements" working blindly through any number of millions of
> years could quite account for why warblers are so beautiful. . . .
> There are yet many boys to be born who, like Isaiah, "may see, and
> know, and consider, and understand together, that the hand of the
> Lord hath done this." (230–232)

Fully accepting Darwinian explanations for the origin of species, Leopold nonetheless gives credence to religious explanations for their beauty. As I hope to show, his aesthetic sense of the world, crucially linked to his land ethic and even to a residual belief in divine teleology, brings his vision surprisingly close to that of Edwards.

YES! in Thunder

To judge from Edwards's "Personal Narrative," this budding philosopher-theologian began early on to learn what it meant to enjoy divine beauty and glory reflected in the natural biosphere. Intimations of the divine presence seized him, he writes, as he walked alone "for contemplation" in his father's East Windsor pasture. As a child, he and his schoolmates "built a booth in a swamp, in a very retired spot, for a place of prayer." He also found and retreated to his own "secret places" in the Connecticut woods. Following his first youthful taste of true conversion, he entertained visions of "sweetly conversing with Christ" as one "wrapt and swallowed up in God" while "alone in the mountains, or some solitary wilderness, far from all mankind." He claims that often, in subsequent years, he conversed with God and sang "forth my contemplations" while walking alone in the woods, roaming the fields at Saybrook, or removing himself into "a solitary place, on the banks of Hudson's River."[10]

Granted, one must read the "Personal Narrative" cautiously since it was written some twenty years after the fact of conversion and may not present a reliable factual account of Edwards's earlier years. As an index of Edwards's adult attitudes, though, the "Narrative" reveals much by what it does *not* say by way of conventional responses to the nonhuman world. Edwards does not invoke natural elements to confirm God's existence and care for humankind, to support a traditionally intellectual argument from design. The writer's primary religious response to the physical world is not evidential—or, for that matter, morally didactic—but mystical and palpable. He registers not so much a knowledge of God, rationally deduced from his works, as a sensible grasp of God's body filling the grand garment of Creation. Led from his meditations on the creatures to sing forth his enchantment, Edwards testifies that he

> felt God at the first appearance of a thunder storm. And used to take
> the opportunity at such times, to fix myself to view the clouds, and
> see the lightnings play, and hear the majestic and awful voice of
> God's thunder: which oftentimes was exceedingly entertaining, lead-
> ing me to sweet contemplations of my great and glorious God.[11]

Colored by sentiments of the sublime, such effusions are not pantheistic—not quite the poetic raptures of Walt Whitman. But neither are they the sober proofs later offered by William Paley in his *Natural Theology* (1802).

It seems that the capacity of thunder and lightning to summon impressions of the numinous is not entirely spent even in our own age of skepticism. Or, at least, the human impulse to respond to such impressions remains vital in some Americans, as evidenced by a curiously Edwardsean spot of personal narrative that John Updike published not long ago in the *New Yorker*. Updike describes the experience of getting up and walking to the window during a sleepless night spent in a hotel room in Florence. There, overlooking the Duomo, "the fourth-largest church in Christendom," he finds unexpected assurance in witnessing a fierce storm:

> While I watched, the rain intensified, rattling on tile roofs near and
> far; it looked like rods of metal in the floodlight that illumined part
> of the Duomo's red-tiled dome. Lightning. Hectic Gusts. The rain
> was furious. I was not alone in the universe. The rippling rods of
> rain drove down . . . [but] the hulking old cathedral crouched like a
> stoic mute dragon, the thick tiles and gurgling gutters around me all

could withstand the soaking, the thunder, the shuddering flashes of light. I was filled with a glad sense of exterior activity. God was at work—at ease, even. . . . All this felt like a transaction, a rescue.[12]

But while God's voice might speak to Edwards and even Updike through thunder, God's essence remained shrouded in sacred mystery. Edwards's proclivity toward light imagery likewise follows biblical precedent in equating glory with God's *visible* radiance, as contrasted with God's inner, self-sufficient being. The more the heavens tell of God's glory, the more one can intuit untold depths of God's unrevealed majesty. So Edwards came to love thunder and lightning, heaven's most piercing image of divine sovereignty. The harmony Edward perceived from meditating on these earthly elements resembled less the tranquil, pleasantly uniform order connoted by "design" than the unity born of Heraclitean strife. Gazing into the clouds, the youthful Edwards saw and virtually tasted the conjunction of God's "awful sweetness," divine "majesty and meekness joined together." Paradoxically, his inward and immaterial "sense of divine things" found embodiment in a dramatically intense experience of sight, sound, and physical sensation.

For Edwards, such immediate insight into divine glory was not a stimulus toward belief but a fruit or consequence of grace. Only after genuine conversion, he indicates, had God's glory "seemed" to appear to him in "sun, moon and stars; in the clouds, and blue sky; in the grass, flowers, trees; in the water, and all nature." Then "the appearance of every thing was altered; there seemed to be, as it were, a calm, sweet cast, or appearance of divine glory, in almost everything."[13]

Though the emphasis on prior conversion experience derives from Edwards's Calvinism, non-Calvinist writers like St. John of the Cross have similarly testified that those brought to an advanced level of spiritual encounter with God may find the face of nature transfigured. Edwards also makes a telling concession when he speaks of nature's altered appearance. What we see in nature, he admits, is colored by our own cast of mind and soul as perceivers. To see the physical world most truly, he suggests, is to look not *at* it but *through* it toward the all-surpassing light of God.

The Divine Beauty of Creation

In the "Personal Narrative," as elsewhere in Edwards, the beauty of holiness complements the holiness of natural beauty. But Edwards regarded the first as necessarily antecedent in the growth of imaginative perception. He believed that only after discovering the inward sense of grace could a soul begin to understand its own part within the larger harmony of Creation. Paradoxically, this realization produced a vital passivity: the soul gained new access to power, but only as an instrument or conduit of divinity. Drawing imagery from domesticated nature, Edwards in the "Narrative" portrays his own version of organic unity between the Me and Not Me by comparing the soul to a small white flower basking in the vital glory of the sun in God's garden and rejoicing there "in a calm rapture."[14]

On a more telescopic plane, Edwards represents the unific beauty of God's cosmic garden in pieces such as "The Beauty of the World" (1725), "Images of Divine Things" (begun 1728), and the *Dissertation Concerning the End for which God Created the World* (1765; composed 1755). For Edwards, the loveliness discernible in nature is not merely pleasing but authentically revelatory. Because "the beauty of the world consists wholly of sweet mutual consents, either within itself, or with the Supreme Being," it reflects a cosmic harmony and continuity with the spirit world. For Edwards, scientific knowledge of how this natural beauty, "surpassing the art of man," is mediated to us physiologically through the senses need not diminish our wonder and joy at seeing:

> 'Tis very probable that that wonderful suitableness of green for the grass and plants, the blue of the sky, the white of the clouds, the colors of flowers, consists in a complicated proportion that these colors make one with another, either in the magnitude of the rays, the number of vibrations that are caused in the optic nerve, or some other way. . . . So there are innumerable other agreeablenesses of motions, figures, etc.: the gentle motions of trees, of lily, etc., as it is agreeable to other things that represent calmness, gentleness and benevolence, etc. The fields and woods seem to rejoice, and how joyful do the birds seem to be in it.[15]

Edwards's views on typology support the notion that Creation offers an authentic mode of divine revelation. It presents, to be sure, a lesser revelation than the Bible, and one whose fullest meaning requires scriptural elucidation. Nonetheless, "That the works of nature are intended and contrived of God to signify and indigitate spiritual things is particularly evident, concerning the rainbow, by God's own express revelation." Thus, "the visible world" is inscribed with its own "sacred language," or symbolic "hieroglyphics," to represent things invisible. "The works of God," Edwards maintains, "are but a kind of voice or language of God, to instruct intelligent beings in things pertaining to himself."[16]

As defined in traditional Reformed theology and spirituality, the biblical figures known as "types" had been perceived to operate on a strictly temporal plane. Old Testament persons, actions, or objects were commonly read as "shadows" or "types" anticipating later fulfillment in New Testament "antitypes" and, ultimately, in the person of Christ. Edwards looked to expand the definition of "types" to include the material signs evident in Creation. In so doing, he freed typology from temporality, from an exclusive bonding to sacred or ordinary human history. Yet he believed that scripture itself warranted such expansion: "That the things of the world are ordered [and] designed to shadow forth spiritual things, appears by the Apostle's arguing spiritual things from them." Natural types were potentially accessible even to the illiterate; and unlike the finite matrix of types in the Hebrew Bible, they were limitless in number and character. In his "Images of Divine Things," Edwards offers a typological exegesis of rivers, hills, mountains, spiders, and many other biotic or landscape features. Convinced that everything in material Creation bore anti-typal meaning, Edwards perceived "a great and remarkable analogy in God's works," a "wonderful resemblance in the effects which God produces, and consentaniety in his manner of working in one thing and another, throughout all nature." He considered this mutual "agreeableness and harmony" among the elements of Creation to be "very observable in the visible world."

Edwards's reading of natural types often amounted to brief moral allegory. In such cases, simple didacticism replaced visionary expression. "High mountains," for example, supply a predictable lesson that people cannot "attain to anything eminent or of peculiar excellence without difficulty." At other moments, though, Edwards's writing rises to a more poetic view, one that envisions the types as animating a universally comprehensive ecology:

> 79. The whole material universe is preserved by gravity, or attraction, or the mutual tendency of all bodies to each other. One part of the universe is hereby made beneficial to another. The beauty, harmony and order, regular progress, life and motion, and in short, all the well-being of the whole frame, depends on it. This is a type of love or charity in the spiritual world.[17]

Despite the dualistic aspects of Edwards's philosophy, this holistic vision prevails throughout "The Beauty of the World," "Images of Divine Things," and *The End for Which God Created the World*. In contrast to one traditional picture of a Creation only distantly joined to the Creator, these works largely confirm the world's dynamic participation in the beauty of divine being. Beauty conjoined to goodness is in fact so crucial to defining the perfection of God's identity that for Edwards it eclipses even "sovereignty," in the sense of a dis-associated divine power or brute force.[18] Edwards's doctrinal emphasis on the Trinity reinforces God's interactive relation to the world through the indwelling power of the spirit. In fact, the theologian Jürgen Moltmann suggests that Christian belief in the Holy Spirit, like the Jewish rabbinical and Kabbalistic doctrine of the Shekinah, reconciles Creator and Creation in a way that neither pantheism nor deism permits. It thereby bridges that chasm between God's transcendence and our finite world demanded by absolute monotheism.[19]

Still, even as Edwards displaces the notion of God's radical separation from God's world "dominion," he maintains a hierarchical model of Creation based on the traditional chain of being. Creatures of intellect stand above other creatures in the universal scale. Humanity is in some sense a conscious end for the rest of Creation. For Edwards, though, each link in the chain of being "had its own integrity," so that " 'the lower creatures' did not exist solely for man."[20] And Edwards is distinctive in stressing the upward line of connections along the chain. Edwards establishes in *The End for Which God Created the World* that the ultimate end of all works of Creation is not human commodity but divine glory, just as the end of God's being is nothing other than the irreducible fact of God's essence.

This pointedly antiutilitarian accent supports Edwards's contention that the fullness of glory God communicates to Creation and receives back from Creation are indeed one. Besides this resplendent vision of unity-in-reciprocity, all scaled distinctions within "the astonishing fabric of the universe" (419) must pale.[21] Edwards understands God, as undivided Trinity, to be the fountain of Creation's limitless flow. Transcendent in being yet consubstantial with the world in glory, God stands for Edwards at the center of an interlocking circle of analogies.

Thus, *The End for Which God Created the World* cannot accurately be described as human-centered at all. Not human salvation or happiness but rather divine glory must be deemed here God's "last end in the great work" of Creation (475).[22] Nonetheless, God takes pleasure in "communicating good to the creatures" (503). God rejoices, in fact, in seeking "the good of the creature" (533), in supplying that *summum bonum* or highest good in which "the moral part of the creation" (478) can most fully participate. Imaged principally as a ceaseless stream of divine Light, glory (or Hebrew *kavod*) represents God's self-communication as a transcendent reality made visible, at least by intimation, to the ocular sense: "The manifestation of glory, the emanation or effulgence of brightness, has relation to the eye" (513, 521).

In some later, more scripturally based sections of the treatise, Edwards rehearses conventional Reformed teachings about God's will to save humankind, or God's still more limited intent to rescue saints, through the course of a redemptive history culminating in Christ. In most of the work, however, he refers in sweeping generic terms to "the creature," not specifically or exclusively to human beings, in assessing God's relation to the world. Certainly humans occupy a privileged place in this scheme, since they most obviously represent the "intelligent part of the system" (470) and are uniquely qualified to know and to respond to the beauty of God's self-communication. Nonetheless, the material world does not exist solely to satisfy the will, pleasure, or self-defined happiness of human beings. Its purpose surpasses instrumental categories since for Edwards it is not mainly a resource but a human habitation and medium of revelation—as well as a "creature" in its own right. Without challenging the traditional subordination of nonhuman beings to human needs, Edwards affirms that even "lower" elements and creatures of the physical world belong to *oikos*, the ecology of our familiar habitation: "The inanimate, unintelligent part is made for the rational as much as a house is prepared for the inhabitant" (471). Nature, then, is not simply a storehouse of commodifiable goods but the very substance of our home as human beings. Insofar as Edwards understood its beauty as belonging preeminently to God, he would have consented most heartily to the final term of Leopold's dictum that "a thing is right when it tends to preserve the integrity, stability, and beauty of the biotic community."

From Aesthetics to Environmental Ethics:
The Nature of True Virtue Applied to Nature

If the *Dissertation Concerning the End for which God Created the World* rises to a unified, comprehensive vision of the cosmos in purely ontological terms, *The Nature of True Virtue* explores the ethical ramifications of this vision. There may be something like virtue even among thieves. Rule-based ethics likewise has a necessary function in the practical governance of societies. Yet true virtue, according to Edwards, yearns to embrace nothing less than the well-being of everything that is. It expands the sphere of ethical responsibility outward, beyond the first circle of neighbor and kin all the way to a "benevolence to Being in general."[23] And the crucial ambiguity about "being in general" lies in the phrase's concurrent reference to the whole created cosmos as well as to God as ultimate source and end of being.[24] True virtue finally has more to do with a disposition of heart than the commission of individually worthy deeds, more with a vision of symbiotic linkage among elements composing "the great whole" (541) of our moral universe than with reasoned choice or the satisfaction of legal duty.

Despite its underpinnings in philosophic idealism, Edwards's conception of true virtue is fundamentally derived from New Testament ethical teachings, particularly as set forth in that portion of Jesus' Sermon on the Mount that is commonly described as the evangelical counsels of perfection. Unlike the more clearly limited Deuteronomic principles, with their stipulated scheme of earthly punishments and rewards, the New Testament law of love can never be perfectly fulfilled by any human being. One is here enjoined to give to everyone who asks, to turn the other cheek, to banish from thought even the desire for illicit sex. Whereas it may be natural to "salute your brethren only" and to "love them which love you," Jesus' new law requires followers to "love your enemies, bless them that curse you, do good to them that hate you, and pray for them which despitefully use you and persecute you" (Matthew 5:44–47). There is no discernible limit to what this gospel love may require, no point at which persons may count themselves perfectly justified by virtue of their deeds. Edwards likewise takes pains to distinguish "true virtue" from the restricted, ultimately self-referential principles he attributes to natural morality. "There is no more virtue in a man's thus loving his friends merely from self-love," he insists, "than there is in self-love itself, the principle from whence it proceeds" (579). By the same token, "men love those who love them, and are angry with those who hate them, from the natural influence of self-love" (581). Only God, Edwards presumes, will ever manifest the full essence of true virtue.

In sum, Edwards's True Virtue is the perfected coalescence of imagination and love. What the Romantic era would enshrine as "Imagination" is first required if a person is to see things in what Edwards calls the most "comprehensive view," to perceive virtue in "its universal tendency." Such is the beauty wherein a being is loved "as related to every thing that it stands in connection with" (540, 541). Moved by their recognition of the aesthetic beauty and harmony that sustain Creation as a whole, humans can be drawn to exercise virtue. This consent of the will and affections presupposes an interior vision of things that unites the several spheres of physical, moral, and spiritual Creation resolved into a single community of love.

That this ethical extension bears some resemblance to Leopold's conservationist rhetoric should by now be apparent. Like Edwards, Leopold believed that developing an "ecological conscience" that reached beyond expediency would require an enlargement of love, faith, and vision. Given the force of humanity's self-serving instincts, this enlargement would not come easily or quickly. Although Leopold believed that humans bore obligations to land "over and above self-interest" (245), he knew that learning to recognize this claim of nature was not altogether natural. Leopold's pessimism on this score—a cast of mind not wholly different from Edwards's Calvinist sense of human depravity—was confirmed by the grave difficulty he faced having his book accepted for publication in the first place. Leopold knew he had to temper expressions of his own belief in the beauty and intrinsic value of wilderness areas with instrumental arguments outlining the human benefits of preserving roadless regions. He knew that fostering the spirit of cooperation that was needed to develop a broadly communitarian land ethic ran squarely against Darwinian suppositions about natural competition as well as against powerful economic motives for exploitation. Yet he also kept faith that it was possible, perhaps even inevitable within the course of natural or providential evolution, to awaken an ecological conscience in humankind.

To be sure, it would be implausibly anachronistic to expect Edwards's treatise to square too closely with later environmental statements. In *The Nature of True Virtue*, Edwards shows scant interest in the physical biosphere as such. Aside from a few passing references to flowers, the solar system, melody, and the like, this abstract work offers nothing by way of naturalistic description. Neither does it even begin to address the social and political issues raised by a land ethic. Still, the point here is not to imagine Jonathan Edwards as a hypothetical participant in the 1970 Earth Day, though one suspects he would have appreciated the revivalistic aspects of that event. Rather, his contribution in *The Nature of True Virtue* is to define on the level of visionary theory that which others would apply and interpret in concrete social terms. Just as it remained for Samuel Hopkins and the younger Jonathan to see what implications true virtue or disinterested benevolence should bear in the specific case of American slavery, so also a working environmental ethic had to be nurtured from various philosophic seeds, including those scattered through Edwards's treatise.

Another limitation of Edwards's natural philosophy involves the scaled hierarchy of being that he again portrays in *The Nature of True Virtue*. Although this work defines a comprehensive community of responsibility beyond that of human society, it is hardly a community of equals. Moreover, within the first chapter Edwards announces a crucial restriction on the scope of benevolence:

"when I speak of an intelligent being's having a heart united and benevolently disposed to Being in general, I mean *intelligent* Being in general. Not inanimate things, or beings that have no perception or will; which are not properly objects of benevolence" (542) It would seem, then, that we cannot exercise true virtue toward trees or spiders after all. Perhaps not even toward other mammals.[25]

Yet this qualification, too, is qualified by chapter 3, where Edwards defines a "secondary beauty" beneath the ontological category occupied by spiritual and moral creatures—that is, beneath humans and angels. The secondary beauty, in its attributes of proportion and harmony, does reflect "some image" of primary beauty. It constitutes a meditative language "found even in inanimate things," which participate thereby in the glory effused from "the fountain of all being and all beauty." "In how many instances," the author asks, has God "formed brutes in analogy to the nature of mankind; and plants in analogy to animals, with respect to the manner of their generation, nutrition, etc.?" (561, 551, 564) And this world of secondary beauty, because it resembles that of true spiritual beauty, offers moral benefit to human beings. "God has so constituted nature," writes Edwards,

> that the presenting of this inferior beauty, especially in those kinds
> of it which have the greatest resemblance of the primary beauty, as
> the harmony of sounds, and the beauties of nature, have a tendency
> to assist those whose hearts are under the influence of a truly virtu-
> ous temper, to dispose them to the exercises of divine love, and en-
> liven in them a sense of spiritual beauty. (565)

It follows, then, that true virtue must show some respect for the beauty and worth of all creatures, both for themselves and by virtue of their "connections in the universality of things." A virtuous agent will "seek the good of every *individual* being unless it be conceived as not consistent with the highest good of Being in general" (540, 545). In practice, Edwards's treatise persistently identifies the objects of benevolence in the most broadly generic terms—not as fellow humans but "fellow creatures" or "beings" (551–552). A person of "generally benevolent temper" (5) who possesses "a disposition to love Being in general" will set no self-regarding limits to love. It is enough to say simply that "a virtuous mind," enlarged by grace, "exercises true virtue in benevolence to created beings" (542, 559). Consistent with its etymology (from Latin *virtus*, or strength), "virtue" thus identifies not a discrete action but a strength of character with invariably universal application to all other beings.

Edwards does scale the ethical claim of all beings according to their presumed possession of existence, thereby ranking an archangel above a worm. He also perceives a definite hierarchy in the ability of creatures to function as moral agents. At least this last chain of distinctions between orders of morality in human and nonhuman Creation is also presumed, though, in nearly every other ethical system. To project human ethical standards uncritically onto the behavior of nonhuman organisms is to risk arriving at horrifying and distorting metaphysical conclusions about the nature of nature, as Annie Dillard observes in *A Pilgrim at Tinker Creek.*

Among earthly creatures, then, only humans are capable of practicing true virtue. Even they will do so imperfectly, or not at all unless they have first experienced the gift of regenerative grace. Edwards considers self-love the normal disposition of human beings apart from grace, and grace the crucial prerequisite to virtue. By present-day standards, herein lies the main obstacle of using Edwards to support an environmental ethic. If Edwards's Calvinism leads him to say—in contrast to fellow eighteenth-century moralists like Francis Hutcheson and Lord Shaftesbury—that benevolence and virtue are quite beyond the natural capabilities of man, can these qualities have ethical bearing on any human behavior, much less on behavior toward the brute order of beings? Or if, in present-day democracies, the shaping of green political policy must depend largely on the behavior of popularly elected representatives, how can the relatively few "saints" who possess true virtue hope to prevail?

In this respect Edwards's commitment to the doctrine of limited election poses a real difficulty, I think. By comparison, his assumptions about human depravity are not so problematic. If anything, Edwards's Calvinist shadings of skepticism about the nature of human nature may help to ground his vision in realism. Again, one need not share his doctrinal restriction of the "spiritual and divine sense" to regenerate souls to concur that true virtue rarely comes naturally. Contrary to Aristotle's assumptions in the *Nicomachean Ethics*—or, for that matter, to the educational programs found in many present-day schools—Edwards maintains that knowledge of the good may not always lead to virtuous action. In the realm of environmental ethics, one might agree that even well-intentioned souls can confuse private interest with the public good, and sentimental earnestness with the extension of imaginative sympathy.

As Edwards remarks pungently, in his denial that sentiments of instinctual pity constitute true virtue: "Some men would be moved with pity by seeing a brute-creature under extreme and long torments, who yet suffer no uneasiness in knowing that many thousands of them every day cease to live, and so have an end put to all their pleasure, at butchers' shambles in great cities" (606). This remark encapsulates those peculiar contradictions that still inform our responses to animal life. Edwards's observation is verified today by the immense slaughter of animals that supports the American fast-food industry, though many of those who consume such foods go to considerable lengths to protect the life and health of household pets.

Despite depravity, Edwards believed that grace does happen in the world. In fact, the Platonic side of him saw true virtue as all that truly is, and sin as insubstantial—to the point where he never quite acknowledged the metaphysical problem of evil that tormented Melville. Nor does his affecting, nonpolemical expression in this treatise lack "grace" in the more modern but related sense of beauty, charm, and free adornment. The leading and final instincts of *The Nature of True Virtue* are withal more gracious than they are censorious of self-love. Like Aldo Leopold, Edwards acknowledged the decidedly human angle of his vision and saw humankind as the chief moral executive in the world community of beings. This outlook, though theocentric in Edwards's case, cannot be described as ecocentric insofar as it does not affirm the egalitarian status of all beings or the final autonomy of "nature." Paradoxically, though, it might prove more salutary in sustaining the integrity of earthly life-forms than an approach that tries to respect nature as an absolute end in itself, apart from any other community of being. In contrast to Edwards's vision of humanity and nature as joint participants in the divine *gloria*, a physical world evacuated of spirit, randomly generated rather than created, can be regarded as all the more vulnerable to exploitation. *The Nature of True Virtue* thus rewards reading today as a document of more than historical interest. It is hard to find a plainer statement of what True Ecology might mean in comprehensively moral, spiritual, and biological terms than the theme Edwards sounds early on and develops with variations: "a things appears beautiful when viewed most perfectly, comprehensively and universally, with regard to all its tendencies, and its connections with everything it stands related to" (540).

4

"Revelation to US"

Green Shoots of Romantic Religion in Antebellum America

Surveying the Field

As the Erie Canal opened in 1825, painters of the Hudson River school were beginning to display impressions of the sacred sublime they had witnessed in American landscapes (see fig. 4.1). Religious feeling figures no less prominently in this period's writing, much of it reflecting an array of poetry, fiction, and nonfiction we are now disposed to view collectively as environmental literature. Such expression includes familiar poems by William Cullen Bryant, fictional romances by James Fenimore Cooper, and seminal essays by Ralph Waldo Emerson. Our attention in this chapter focuses on these three figures. To assess the greening of Romantic religion in nineteenth-century America one must, for example, take account of Emerson's famous statement of the case in *Nature*. I think it pertinent to interject here, too, a reading of Emerson's relatively obscure poem "The Adirondacs." But all antebellum writing on green themes, a domain explored with reference to major and minor authors in the following chapter as well, culminates in the work of Henry Thoreau.

There are several good reasons why Thoreau continues to stimulate discussion, even beyond English academies, as *the* presiding spirit of American environmental literature.[1] Not only the brilliance of his verbal artistry but also the reach of his philosophic imagination set him apart from the more prosaic, commonplace sort of naturalistic chronicler. For Thoreau, the accumulation of merely factual knowledge never offered sufficient ground for understanding the essential nature of nature. No literary figure of the antebellum era grasped more deeply than he what it might mean in religious terms

FIGURE 4.1. Thomas Cole, "The Clove," Catskills, New York. Oil on canvas; 25" × 33". New Britain Museum of American Art, Charles F. Smith Fund 1945.22. (Photo by E. Irving Blomstrann.) Cole, a prominent figure among the Hudson River painters, also published verbal testimony of his belief in the distinctively sublime character of American landscapes.

to extend revisionist notions of biblical hermeneutics toward formation of a new hermeneutics of nature. No one felt more intensely than he what Emerson's call to shift the locus of spiritual authority—away from the revelation preserved in scripture toward a "revelation to us" through nature—would mean in practical experience. And no one pursued more deliberately the spiritual implications of emergent "developmental" or evolutionary scientific discoveries.

At the same time, Thoreau sustains a naturalist's reputation for empirical honesty and attentiveness. His writings, whatever their standing as naturalistic science, present a sensibility steeped in the material reality of the nonhuman world. For most readers, his uncommonly vivid observations of life in the field offset the impulse toward abstraction associated with his Transcendental idealism. And particularly in essays like "A Succession of Forest Trees," Thoreau's writing is innovative by virtue of its explicit recognition of ecological systems and processes. Sometimes, too, his work raises questions of contemporary interest about how humanity's impact on the environment should affect public policy. Thus, in *Walden* he draws on biblical imagery to lament the way overzealous logging endangers not only individual trees but also the local avian habitat and his own artistic muse: "How can you expect the birds to sing when their groves are cut down?"[2] So it is only fitting that Thoreau be considered separately at some length in chapter 6.

Still, other nineteenth-century figures also warrant attention in this cultural narrative, and for reasons more compelling than their value in merely anticipating or elaborating Thoreau's sense of the material world as sacred space. Melville, for example, pursued the religious implications of nature's savagery more rigorously than Thoreau ever could. Though Thoreau's rhetoric abounds in "wildness," his writing tells us more about the untamed life of woodchucks and "wild apples" than about sharks, cannibalism, and the bloody strife that endures beneath the sea's sunny surface. We see little blood in *Walden*, whereas *Moby-Dick* offers ample exposure to the violent survival instincts of both humans and beasts. So Melville, emphatically religious yet nearly Manichean in sensibility, provides a more aggressive critique of pastoral Romanticism than Thoreau. Cooper, too, advances a style of naturalistic inquiry that probes the ethical and religious import of blood violence beyond the usual scope of sentimental romance. Whitman, meanwhile, was pressing the boundaries of environmental literature—and of Transcendental spirituality—beyond Concord's bucolic fields and woods to include urban and oceanic settings. Other figures discussed in this chapter and the next, ranging from Bryant to Margaret Fuller and Nathaniel Hawthorne, illustrate how religious responses to the nonhuman realm inevitably become absorbed in human concerns such as history and ethnography. But as early as 1815, Bryant's poetry registered the pivotal Romantic shift that enabled New England woodlots to inspire veneration as sacred groves.

From Reading Nature's Book to Worshiping in God's First Temple: Bryant and Cooper

Already in the Renaissance, the notion that God's sacred truths were inscribed in two books, that of the Bible and of Nature, had spread throughout European culture.[3] By the eighteenth century, this two-book metaphor gained further prominence, in America as well as Europe, in response to what Christian apologists perceived as growing threats of scientific materialism. In *The Analogy of Religion, Natural and Revealed, to the Constitution and Course of Nature* (1736), Joseph Butler linked his catalogue of instances from the physical world to theological commentary based on Scripture. William Paley's *Natural Theology* (1802) emphasized still more that observing nature's manifold "contrivances," even without benefit of scriptural teaching, proved "the existence of an intelligent Creator."

Commonly used as a college textbook, Paley's work began with the clichéd mechanical analogy of the world as well-regulated timepiece. It then amassed evidence from every known field of natural history to establish the sort of rational, optimistic, and teleological faith in design that won popular approval. Aside from one chapter devoted to "natural attributes of the deity," described in the vaguest of terms, Paley confined his attention to deducing God's existence.[4] *Natural Theology* has little to say about the character of God—or about salvation history, or religious experience. Some orthodox Christian thinkers, most notably Coleridge, tried to develop a sophisticated hermeneutic involving more substantial integration of natural theology with scriptural revelation. By the nineteenth century, though, pressure had mounted in some quarters to replace rather than to enhance the Bible with a "natural supernaturalism" that nonetheless fed more of humankind's spiritual hunger than had been dreamt of by the philosophers of deistic rationalism.[5] Thus, Romantic religion at once accepted and resisted the secularizing effects of science.

In North America, Emerson best exemplifies this definitive change in the character of natural theology. For Emerson and other Transcendental believers, the book of nature became the central text—with the Greek and Hebrew scriptures assuming at best an ancillary status shared, particularly in Thoreau's rhetoric, with sacred scriptures of other nations or with inspired writing penned by individuals. In the novel *Hobomok* (1824), Lydia Maria Child likewise suggests, through a sympathetically drawn character, that Creation rather than the Bible might be regarded as the most revealing text of divine revelation. For while the Bible is indeed " 'an inspired book,' " it presents such formidable obstacles to interpretation that it seems " 'the Almighty suffers it to be a flaming cherubim, turning every way, and guarding the tree of life from the touch of man.' " In Creation, though, "one may read to their fill" since "it is God's library—the first Bible he ever wrote."[6] Although the trope of the world as book is at least as old as Dante, it reaches its most vibrant fulfillment as an expression of Romantic religion after midcentury with Whitman's *Leaves of Grass* and the penultimate chapter of Thoreau's *Walden*.

In fact, the prevalence of forest-as-temple imagery in early nineteenth-century literature dramatizes the point that natural religion was now redefining not only the locus of revelation but also the locus of worship. William Cullen Bryant, for example, launches his blank-verse meditation in "A Forest Hymn" (1825) with the blunt assertion that "the groves were God's first temples." Drawing on a predictable comparison between forest canopy and cathedral vault, Bryant goes on to recommend that world-weary souls of his own day recover the benefits of worshiping in the woods:

> Ah, why
> Should we, in the world's riper years, neglect
> God's ancient sanctuaries, and adore
> Only among the crowd, and under roofs
> That our frail hands have raised?[7]

As a post-Puritan Romantic distant from the Calvinism he encountered in childhood, Bryant is likewise far from sharing the old New England theology's rejection of localized sacred space, its resolve to replace all physical temples with the secular meetinghouse. Bryant instead portrays an idealized forest retreat in which "sacred influences" prevail. Within this sanctified place, presumably an American version of the Old World's ancient groves, the poet also discovers a latter-day equivalent of the temples once constructed by Greco-

Roman, Hebrew, Celtic, and Roman Catholic worshipers. Yet even as he admires the solemn grandeur of medieval church architecture, which he finds comparably represented in the forest's dark silence, he betrays some Protestant distaste for the "fantastic carvings" and other emblems of "human pomp or pride" he associates with formal church edifices. For Bryant, an "aged wood" offers the more promising worship space not only because its features lack the impress of human vanity but also because its dynamic character reflects the ongoing creativity of a living God:

> The fresh, moist ground, are all instinct with thee.
> Here is continual worship;—Nature, here,
> In the tranquillity that thou dost love,
> Enjoys thy presence. Noiselessly, around,
> From perch to perch, the solitary bird
> Passes; and yon clear spring, that, midst its herbs,
> Wells softly forth and wandering steeps the roots
> Of half the mighty forest, tells no tale
> Of all the good it does. . . .
> . . . .
>
> That delicate forest flower,
> With scented breath and look so like a smile,
> Seems, as it issues from the shapeless mould,
> An emanation of the indwelling Life,
> A visible token of the upholding Love,
> That are the soul of this great universe. (80)

Influenced here by the mood of international Romanticism, Bryant does not strictly define the religious doctrine he brings to his forest worship. Picturesque Romanticism, the sublime, Wordsworthian natural piety, didactic moralism—all these notes and more can be heard in the syncretistic "hymn" of this nominal Unitarian.[8] The poem's final dictum, which recalls the well-known didactic close of the poem "To a Waterfowl" (1815), even sustains a tone of neoclassical rationalism:

> Be it ours to meditate,
> In these calm shades, thy milder majesty,
> And to the beautiful order of thy works
> Learn to conform the order of our lives. (27)

Overall, however, the faith reflected in "A Forest Hymn" amounts to a quasi-pantheistic form of Romantic religion. It is not quite pantheistic because Bryant's forest worship remains worship *in* the woods rather than *of* the woods. He see the woods as offering a "Fit shrine for humble worshiper to hold / Communion with his Maker," a setting fit to inspire wonder at the Creator's "boundless power / And inaccessible majesty" (79). The poem extols forest worship as supplementing, not replacing, traditional indoor observances. But in the sphere of religious revelation, it sees the book of nature presenting a more open canon than historical scripture. Traditionally, the biblical canon is regarded as definitively closed. The Bible is already complete by virtue of its concluding accounts of Jesus' death, resurrection, and the end of the world, beyond which there is no need or possibility of adding new texts inscribed in recent centuries. For Bryant, though, nature's text reveals more strikingly than Scripture the prospect of an unfixed canon and the marvel of God's continuous Creation subsequent to the original genesis:

> My heart is awed within me when I think
> Of the great miracle that still goes on,
> In silence, round me—the perpetual work
> Of thy creation, finished, yet renewed
> Forever. Written on thy works I read
> The lesson of thy own eternity. (80–81)

For Bryant, then, a major attraction of the groves is that here the solitary self confronts relatively unbounded forms both of revelation and of worship. Just as the woodland's revelation of God's "upholding Love" is temporally unlimited, so also the boundaries of the poet's devotions are physically unfixed and irregular. More than the village church, the forest remains open to perpetual worship and reveals God's continuous Creation. Yet for Bryant, the freedom of worship available in this "woody wilderness" can be practiced only by isolated individuals. Such sacred space is not settled space. Nor does any form of corporate worship have a place in the poet's forest temple.

Moreover, even if one perceives the nature of this New World temple to be vital rather than stationary, it must be rendered uniformly unthreatening to satisfy the poem's dominant ideal of a tranquil sanctuary. In his "Inscription for the Entrance to a Wood" (1815), Bryant muses on how humankind's original fault affected the nonhuman world. According to Saint Paul, the Fall had indeed corrupted nature, so that "the whole creation groaneth and travailleth in pain together until now" but would likewise participate in God's saving redemption (Romans 8:21–23). More optimistically, Bryant supposes that nature had been exempted from the most corrupting results of human sin: "The primal curse / Fell, it is true, upon the unsinning earth,/ But not in vengeance." So "these shades," he insists "Are still the abodes of gladness" (25). In "A Forest Hymn" he goes even further to imagine a wholly agreeable nature sanctuary. Admitting that evidence of God's sublime strength in the form of tempests, floods, and hurricanes might appear at any time, he nonetheless asks to be spared from encountering "these tremendous tokens" of divine power and "sterner aspects" of God's face to reflect instead, "in these calm shades," on the Creator's "milder majesty." The forest whose praises Bryant sings in "A Forest Hymn" becomes, in effect, a sanitized nature purged of fearful savagery. By the time Bryant was roaming the Berkshire hills of Massachusetts as a child, this terrain no longer presented the frontier terrors that first-generation English settlers found there. Bryant likewise wants to expunge, at least for the occasion of his poem, all threat of exposure to "the wrath / Of the mad unchained elements." His tranquil grove becomes a refuge not only from society but also from the more unsettling aspects of nature.

But just as Bryant's erasure of wildness remained temporary, self-consciously restricted in time and space, so also his religious philosophy remained unsteady. In the earlier "Thanatopsis" (1815), for example, confronting nature is the imagistic equivalent of entering not a temple but a tomb. Here the nature sanctuary looks more like a sepulcher. Although "Thanatopsis" begins with cheerful thoughts of "him who in the love of Nature holds / Communion with her visible forms," it moves quickly, as its title suggests, toward a meditation on death. Bryant envisions all living organisms coming to rest eventually in that "mighty sepulchre" of earth where every human being likewise goes, "surrend'ring up" its "individual being" and mixing "forever with the elements, / To be a brother to th'insensible rock / And to the slugglish clod, which the rude swain / Turns with his share, and treads upon." For one who ponders this sobering fact, and considers how "All that tread / The globe are but a handful to the tribes / That slumber in its bosom" (22), faith in the transcendent destiny of individual humans is hard to sustain. Accordingly, the poem in its fuller 1821 version concludes with a diffuse Stoic affirmation of "trust" rather than any statement of faith in God. Confidence in resurrectional immortality is conspicuously absent. Bryant instead exhorts his reader to accept death with such dignity that he or she can eventually,

> sustain'd and sooth'd
> By an unflattering trust, approach thy grave,
> Like one who wraps the drapery of his couch
> About him, and lies down to pleasant dreams. (23)

In "The Prairies" (1832), though, a broadly theistic—practically deistic—religious viewpoint surfaces again, this time as the easterner looks west to encounter the open fields of Illinois. Impressed by the freedom and "encircling vastness" of the scene, Bryant initially sees here a remnant of earth's prelapsarian sanctity:

> These are the Gardens of the Desert, these
> The unshorn fields, boundless and beautiful,
> And fresh as the young earth, ere man had sinned—
> the Prairies. (130)

Again, too, Bryant portrays the natural world as a divine temple, imaged here as an immensity extended to earth from the vault of heaven:

> Man hath no part in all this glorious work:
> The hand that built the firmament hath heaved
> And smoothed these verdant swells, and sown their slopes
> With herbage, planted them with island groves,
> And hedged them round with forest. Fitting floor

For this magnificent temple of the sky—
With flowers whose glory and whose multitude
Rival the constellations! The great heavens
Seem to stoop down upon the scene in love,—
A nearer vault, and of a tenderer blue,
Than that which bends above the eastern hills. (131)

Yet this unpopulated temple, unlike the one invoked in "A Forest Hymn," is not a space where actual worship occurs. Although Bryant finds the "great solitude" to be "quick with life" of diverse species and envisions an "advancing multitude" of settlers, he stands for now alone on the plains. Only by looking beyond this vacancy, and beyond the current vitality of insects, birds, and "gentle quadrapeds," can he imagine the prehistory of human races that once inhabited this land. He then finds the landscape haunted by ghostly powers. The poet reflects a popular but dubious racial ideology when he describes a people known as the "mound-builders," a presumably civilized and industrious society rendered extinct by "roaming hunter tribes, warlike and fierce" of the "red man," which have since moved farther west. For Bryant, then, the earth mounds of Illinois are at once sepulchers and ruined temples of an unrecoverable religion:

All is gone—
All—save the piles of earth that hold their bones—
The platforms where they worshipped unknown gods—(132)

Bryant supposes that the newest colonizers, filling these plains from the east, will bring their own religion to the scene. He fancies hearing already the "sweet and solemn hymn" of these "Sabbath worshipers." But one suspects he will not be joining their song, though he had himself authored hymns for Unitarian worship.[9] For such worship sounds saccharine compared with the potent mystique drawing his imagination toward those platforms dedicated to "unknown gods."

The most relevant biblical precedent for Bryant's phrasing can be found in Acts 17, where Paul's speech to the citizens of Athens centers rhetorically on an altar inscribed "to the unknown God." While using this occasion to preach the distinctive revelation of the Christian gospel, Paul acknowledges as well the universal human impulse to seek God, the transcendent "Lord of heaven and earth" who "dwelleth not in temples made with hands" (Acts 17: 24). Paul thus recognizes Greek worship of "an unknown God" to be religiously authentic albeit incomplete. For Bryant, the allusion helps associate the mound-builders with the highly renowned civilization of ancient Greece. More crucially, it offers him a way to affirm, from somewhere on the margins of Christian tradition, the valid religious aspirations of non-European cultures and civilizations. The poet's own religious stance at the close of "The Prairies" could be considered comparable, in fact, to the semiagnostic spiritual seeking that Paul attributes to the ancient Athenians. It seems that part of Bryant, awestruck by the West's undulating expanse of fields, wants to worship some perception of the numinous in this temple of wild nature, though the wildness will soon be retamed. Part of him wants to worship, at a vicarious distance, on the mound-builder's ancient platforms. And part of him, likewise enamored of civilization, endorses but will not join the Sabbath ceremonies of future settlers. In the end he is uncertain just where he stands. Bryant thus becomes a semipagan, semi-Christian observer who worships nowhere.

It remains debatable how far "The Prairies" defends a racist form of cultural imperialism in its favorable portrayal of mound-builders and European settlers by contrast with its savage depiction of Native Americans. "The Prairies" seems to shift uneasily between endorsement of America's Manifest Destiny and love of nature's "unchained" open fields. But the poem claims a place in the canon of American environmental literature—not only for its freshly evocative account of a land "For which the speech of England has no name," as a subsequent revision describes this setting, but also for its early recognition of the ways human history can be implicated in apparently pristine landscapes. It will take time, though, for the frustrated spiritual desires Bryant exposes in "The Prairies" to find freer expression in other writers as a consequence of their worshipful encounter with lands west of the Ohio River.

While Bryant touches on the ethnographic dimensions of nature writing in "The Prairies," James Fenimore Cooper broods continually on the interaction between "redskins" and "palefaces" throughout his five Leatherstocking novels. Here, too, one finds an author entranced by the sacred grandeur of the American frontier—and troubled by the need to locate a religious ethic suited to this untamed atmosphere. Within the five-novel series, environmental questions surface most prominently in *The Deerslayer* and *The Pioneers*. All of these questions converge in Cooper's portrayal of Natty Bumppo, that larger-than-life frontier hero who encapsulates the American saga by emerging from the eastern woods and dying on the western prairie. Leatherstocking, as he is sometimes called, embodies a natural piety strengthened by habits of forest solitude as well as by the decade he spent living with the Delawares. Thus, his temperament, habits, apparel, and bearing mark him as an honorary redskin. Yet he regards himself as purely paleface by blood, on account of which he sometimes betrays a distressing excess of racialistic pride. As allied to white settler culture, his career reflects a contradictory commitment to values of pioneering conquest as well as to a Christian ethic of nonviolent restraint. And like many later Americans, both fictive and real, this warrior scout ends up participating in the demise of the wilderness he loves. Pressing westward to escape the clearings of civilization, he becomes "the foremost in that band of pioneers who are opening the way for the march of the nation across the continent."[10]

Though composed last, *The Deerslayer* (1841) portrays Cooper's archetypal frontiersman in the prime of his youthful vigor. At later points in the saga, Natty Bumppo often presents himself as bumbling, comically loquacious, boastful, or downright cantankerous like Cooper, his earthly author. In his zeal to exterminate the Iroquois Mingos, or "bad Indians" who are villainized in *The Last of the Mohicans* (1826), this Hawkeye character even shows a distressing thirst for blood violence. But in *The Deerslayer*, Natty enters adulthood as an Adamic innocent. A figure "of gigantic mould" suggestive of the noble demisavage,[11] he emerges here as something akin to the *genius loci* or presiding spirit of the woods in New York's still-untamed Otsego region prior to the Revolution.

Nowhere, in fact, does Cooper evoke the solemn splendor of precolonized America so memorably as in the opening pages of *The Deerslayer*. The scene he describes already stands a century distant from him. By the time the author summoned from imagination, rather than from personal memory, the "vast expanse of woods" which in 1740 still stretched almost unbroken from the Atlantic to the Mississippi, this "virgin wilderness"(16) no longer embraced America's eastern seaboard. In fact, the land speculation of prosperous settlers like his father, William Cooper, had hastened the demise of the great woods. Yet as D. H. Lawrence and others have recognized, Cooper's main achievement as a historical romancer lay not in his fictive artistry but in his ability to represent the essential myth of America. And because America's mythopoeic sense of itself has much to do with the promise of returning continually to the time of origins, to the genesis moment of fresh beginnings in an unfallen Creation, it is fitting that Cooper should have worked backward to recover the most youthful Leatherstocking in the last book he composed in the series.

So when Cooper's hero affirms in *The Deerslayer* that "the whole 'arth is a temple of the Lord,' to such as have the right minds," the earth he imagines is sacred to the extent that it remains pristine—unsettled (by Europeans) and unfallen. In his simplest mood of moral innocence, Natty supposes that "all is contradiction in the settlements, while all is concord in the woods" (266). Accordingly, he avoids churches, worshiping almost exclusively in God's outdoor temple. In *The Pioneers*, he complains in fact that " 'I never know'd preaching come into a settlement, but it made game scearce' " (135–136). He loves the woods for "the impress that they everywhere bore of the divine hand of their creator," and "never did a day pass without his communing in spirit, and this too without the aid of forms and language, with the infinite source of all he saw, felt and beheld" (*Deerslayer*, 278). For a man of action, he is surprisingly disposed toward "conterplation" (455). And in his illiteracy, he looks first at features of the wilderness landscape rather than at biblical texts to study " 'the hand of God' " since " 'much l'arning may be got in this way, as well as out of books' " (248–249). Chingachgook and Wah-ta!-Wah likewise confirm their moral rectitude by showing themselves "sensible of the beauties" presented by the surrounding lake and forest (332).

In jarring contrast to the "holy calm of nature" (47) epitomized by the placid surface of Lake Glimmerglass, most of *The Deerslayer*'s specimens of human nature—especially white males other than Leatherstocking—seize our attention as sinful despoilers of the New Eden. Cooper frames a similar opposition in *The Last of the Mohicans*. In that fable, noisy strife of Europe's Seven Years' War invades the quiet sanctuary of Lake George, a body of surpassing loveliness attached in its French nomenclature to the Blessed Sacrament. In *The Deerslayer*, figures like Hurry Harry and Tom Hutter destroy the calm beauty of Cooper's original landscape portrait by their rapacious greed and a relish for violence unredeemed by Indian principles of rectitude. Such unholy men, like the clan of Ishmael Bush in *The Prairie*, reveal a deepseated depravity of human nature coupled with indifference toward spiritual uses of the non-human world. Moreover, they demonstrate no desire or capacity for regeneration.

Though originally innocent rather than depraved, Natty Bumppo *does* undergo a crisis of regenerative renewal when he first sheds human blood. Almost despite himself, he shoots and kills a Huron warrior who had treacherously sought to kill him. In the process he gains a new identity as frontier hero and a new name, "Hawkeye," in place of "Deerslayer." The episode, as recounted in the seventh chapter of *The Deerslayer*, amounts to a symbolic baptism, a rite of initiation combining elements of both pagan and Christian mythology.[12] Up to a point, it reflects conventional notions of chivalric heroism. Observing every rule of fair play, Hawkeye nonetheless triumphs in combat by virtue of his courage as well as his "quick and certain eye" (121). Throughout the Leather-stocking saga, he acts to defend and rescue helpless souls, often distressed maidens, who are plentiful by virtue of conventions inherited from the sentimental romance. But one dare not forget that Natty becomes and remains a killer. First he becomes a deer hunter, then a warrior-scout who is highly adept at killing people, and finally in old age (as presented in *The Prairie*) a mere trapper. To a striking degree, killing remains a primary occupation throughout his career.

What distinguishes his heroic identity from that of conventional chivalry, however, is his exceptional reverence for life in all its forms. Even when he kills, he often does so reluctantly. Hence the scene of his first human kill, despite its exposure of Natty's racial vanity and its implausibly prolix speechifying in the heat of battle, induces a poignant melancholy. After his kill, Natty feels pride but also "regret, with the freshness of our better feelings, mingled with his triumph" (122). The hero's success is qualified by his "fall" into adult consciousness, his piercing knowledge of mortality, guilt, and loss. Thus, Cooper develops here a kind of blood intimacy between slayer and slain. And the violent though stylized character of such scenes challenges the idyllic pastoralism that dominates the book's opening tableau of the frontier. Despite Natty's reverence for life, much of his connection to "nature" arises from his participation in violence and death. He achieves his baptismal renewal not through the usual Christian medium of water but by shedding "redskin" blood to acquire his new name.

By enacting his own version of America's cultural belief in "regeneration through violence," Natty participates ritually in a hunter myth that antedates and partly contradicts Christian teaching. Richard Slotkin argues that Cooper's main character in *The Deerslayer* identifies with Indian ways by "discarding the Christian name given him through baptism" in order to "make new names, new identities, for himself through his deeds as a hunter and warrior."[13] Yet the grace of renewal embodied in Leatherstocking's fable draws heavily on Christian as well as pagan mythology, particularly as supported by biblical par-

adigms in series novels composed after *The Last of the Mohicans*. Biblical stories, too, typically show characters adopting a new name when assuming a new
vocation or identity; and often, as in the case of Abraham, such tales are linked
to archaic blood rituals. Flannery O'Connor's fiction reminds us that New
Testament accounts of baptism are scarcely insulated from violence insofar as
they stress the believer's need to descend to the turbulent depths of primordial
chaos to embrace the christological mystery of death and resurrection.

Despite its artistic infelicities, then, Cooper's Leatherstocking series effectively dramatizes the mythopoeic reality that going "back to nature," if such an
atavistic project is feasible at all for those shaped by American settler culture,
would require accepting a way of life governed by hunting and violent death.
Deerslayer may relish those contemplative interludes when he gazes on the
beauty of his surroundings, but he achieves his fullest, most visceral involvement with the spirit of elemental nature when he kills and hunts. Showing
reverence for life even while taking life, he embodies what Cooper takes to be
Native American religious values. But particularly in later versions of his characterization, his ethical awareness is governed still more by the struggle to
integrate New Testament ideals of nonviolence, forgiveness, and restraint with
the brutal facts of life on the frontier.

In *The Deerslayer*, this ethical conflict reveals itself in much of the dialogue
as well as in practical questions raised by the story's action, such as how to
regard the taking of human scalps. Natty kills but refuses to scalp—in part
because he believes the practice glorifies personal heroism and violates the
dignity of human nature, in part because he perceives scalping to be a racial
marker against which he can measure pride in his own "whiteness." Yet neither
he nor the author condemns Indian scalpers, since presumably the distinctive
"gifts" of redskins justify behavior not ethically warranted for palefaces. " 'My
gifts are not scalper's gifts, but such as belong to my religion and colour,' "
Natty insists, and " 'I'll not unhumanize my natur' by falling into ways that
God intended for another race' " (85–86). Though all humans are God's children, and created " 'much the same in feelin's' " as well as essence, " 'A white
man's gifts are christianized, while a redskin's are more for the wilderness' "
(50). When Chingachcook longs to take Huron scalps, he loses nothing of his
moral stature or claim on our sympathy since this urge coincides with his
proper circumstance as a Delaware. Thus, Cooper gropes toward imagining a
theory of comparative culture that might include a divinely sanctioned principle of relativized or situational ethics.

That is not to say, however, that Cooper's ethical outlook in the Leatherstocking romances ever becomes *wholly* relativistic—or his religious outlook
wholly syncretistic. For while all gifts may be equally valid with respect to the
peoples they endow, some gifts look more equal than others in a picture dominated by Natty Bumppo's image. Christian principles enjoy a clear primacy in
this ethical hierarchy. Thus, Natty rejects Hurry Harry's ethic of retaliation,
" 'Do as you're done by,' " in favor of the Golden Rule, " 'Do as you *would* be
done by' " (89), and the more explicitly New Testament imperative to forgive
one's enemies. The very idiom of comparative "gifts," by which Cooper tries

to recognize difference within the supposition of fundamental unity, reflects Saint Paul's famous discourse in 1 Corinthians 12–13. And just as Paul identifies love as the highest spiritual gift, so also Natty demonstrates a willingness to sacrifice himself for others, as when he risks death to push the canoe containing Hist and Chingachgook beyond reach of their Huron pursuers.

To be sure, slow-witted Hetty Hutter is the only character in this book who adheres strictly to the pure eschatological ethic of Jesus represented in the Sermon on the Mount. Regarding nonviolence as an ideal often impracticable in real-life experience, Natty Bumppo affirms the right to kill humans in self-defense and is scarcely willing to turn the other cheek when affronted. Still, his code of restraint corresponds more closely to Christian principles than it does to the ethic of aggressive expediency practiced by frontiersmen like Tom Hutter, whose behavioral motto might best be represented as "doing unto others *before* they do unto you."[14]

In *The Deerslayer*, Cooper confirms his hero's "higher" ethic by emphasizing the forgiveness and solicitude he shows toward that first Huron warrior he has mortally wounded. Natty not only pardons his enemy but carries him to allay his thirst at the lake, shelters his head in his lap, holds his hand as he dies, and settles his corpse in an honorable posture. A plain-countenanced figure[15] whose "tongue was one that literally knew no guile" (96), Natty also insists on honoring an agreement with the Hurons by which he must return from "furlough" to face likely execution. He considers his pledge to be not mainly a human contract but a religious covenant, " 'a solemn bargain made atween me and God' " (405). Even the lovely, spirited Judith questions this " 'act of extraordinary self-destruction and recklessness' " (384).

So while Natty has little patience for sectarian controversy, he insists before the Hurons that " 'I am christian born' " (296)[16] and credits the Moravians with having shaped his early religious training. When Harry March derides the pietistic Moravian Brethren as too soft on killing, he accuses them of being " 'the next thing to quakers,' " that notably pacifistic community of faith to which Cooper's parents belonged before becoming Episcopalians. " 'If you'd believe all they tell you,' " scoffs March, " 'not even a 'rat would be skinned, out of marcy,' " and " 'who ever heard of marcy on a muskrat' " (89). Who indeed, in the United States by 1841 when *The Deerslayer* appeared?

Respect for nonhuman life becomes a prominent concern elsewhere in the Leatherstocking saga. In *The Deerslayer*, it emerges only in passing, as when Natty reminds Hurry Harry that " 'there's little manhood in killing a doe, and that, too, out of season' " (21). In broader terms, though, *The Deerslayer* conveys respect for the mystery of all life, extending beyond visible matter to invisible things. Pondering the great uncertainties of life after death, for example, Natty confides to Chingachgook his faith that " 'the great principle of christianity is to believe *without* seeing' " (455). Natty's baptism in blood seals his palpably sacramental encounter with life's unseen origins and ends. Unlike Bryant's poetry, then, *The Deerslayer* embodies a reverential yet unsanitized ideal of humankind's interaction with nature. In its portrayal of Natty, it also sustains a tension between the environmental expression of archaic and of Christian ethical values. Some question remains about the character of Cooper's personal faith, since he supported the Episcopal mission church his father had established in Cooperstown but became a communicant only weeks before his death.[17] Yet there is much in the Leatherstocking romances, and particularly in *The Deerslayer*, to support Donald Ringe's larger assessment of Cooper as "a *moraliste* whose work is the coherent expression of his fundamentally religious vision of life."[18]

Cooper illustrates the ethical imperative to respect all life, including non-human life, most obviously in *The Pioneers*, the first book in which Natty Bumppo appears. Natty's typical refusal to kill more game than he can eat stands in sharp contrast to the profligate attitudes that most settlers in New York's Otsego region display in this romance. Describing a period of rapid change in the cultural and physical environment, Cooper presents the upstate pioneers as impressively energetic in transforming the landscape from deep woods to farm settlements. As forests are cleared, a few ornamental poplars and willows replace pines; and so swiftly is the valley of the story's action in Templeton refashioned that "five years had wrought greater changes than a century would produce in countries, where time and labour have given permanency to the works of man" (46). Yet this civilizing initiative also brings destruction. Cooper frankly affirms that European settlers in the Middle States "dispossessed the original owners of the soil" (83). Moreover, in their zeal to conquer the wilderness, the pioneers show an appalling disregard for nonhuman life. They destroy life thoughtlessly and on a prodigious scale, beyond all prospect of human need. Cooper's romance includes several scenes of wanton slaughter, affecting not only large mammals but also birds, fish, and trees. Such overkill suggests a pathology, all too familiar in the way Americans have responded to the specter of superabundant resources, that cannot be justified even by the practical requirements of European settlement. It is likewise telling that Richard Jones, Templeton's county sheriff and a community leader, insists that town planning for thoroughfares should take no account of geographic features: " 'We must run our streets by the compass, coz, and disregard trees, hills, ponds, stumps, or, in fact, any thing but posterity' " (183).

Among the book's several depictions of needless carnage, none presents a more vivid impression than the account of the great pigeon slaughter in chapter 22. As birds migrate from the south, they soar over Templeton in such vast numbers that they darken the sky. It seems inconceivable that human attack could substantially affect an aggregation of animals larger than the eye can grasp. But infected by the enthusiasm of Richard Jones, who longs to "pepper" the birds with lead, the town quickly succumbs to a kind of festive mania that accepts no limits in assaulting the heavens. Townsfolk of all ages rush to join the kill with weapons ranging from ordinary firearms to arrows and even a miniature cannon. The result can hardly be described as sport. A first wave of birds having been attacked, "none pretended to collect the game, which lay scattered over the fields in such profusion, as to cover the very ground with the fluttering victims." After a second and even larger flock sustains a major assault that the perpetrators fancy to resemble glorious warfare, boys are sent to wring the necks of thousands of wounded birds brought to the ground. Natty stands apart from the scene, deploring a slaughter that he is helpless to prevent and warning darkly that " 'the Lord won't see the waste of his creaters for nothing, and right will be done to the pigeons' " (246). Although Cooper could not have known that the passenger pigeons he described would become extinct by the early twentieth century, he demonstrates throughout *The Pioneers* how human cupidity can not only destroy individual creatures but can also degrade whole species and habitats.

Natty often complains bitterly of changes that have ruined his former hunting grounds and " 'driven God's creaters from the wilderness, where his providence had put them for his own pleasure' " (356). Although he declares in *The Deerslayer* that " 'the whole 'arth is a temple of the Lord,' " he has to acknowledge in *The Pioneers* that for anyone who worships in wild nature, Otsego County by 1793 was already becoming a ruined temple. In fact, by the time Cooper publishes *The Pioneers* in 1823, he feels compelled to disclose in a preliminary footnote that depletion of the region's large mammal species— including bear, wolf, panther, and even deer—is virtually complete. Understanding the great woods to be God's temple, Natty nonetheless finds that all the acreage in his neighborhood is now legally owned and governed not by God but by a man whose name, ironically enough, is "Temple." From Natty's standpoint, Judge Marmaduke Temple represents the artificial imposition of a statutory order that confines the liberty of free-spirited individuals. Marmaduke encourages the ministry of Mr. Grant, an Episcopal clergyman who begins his worship service in Templeton's meeting house "with the sublime declaration of the Hebrew prophet—'The Lord is in his holy temple; let all the earth keep silence before him' " (125). Yet Natty regards the Judge as more nearly the destroyer than the preserver of God's sanctuary. Judge Temple's settlement, with its system of social regulation, threatens his more archaic relation to the environment as well as what little is left of Native American ways, as represented in the sadly degraded state of Indian John before his death. And Natty particularly blames Judge Temple for sponsoring change that endangers his livelihood: " 'Ah! the game is becoming hard to find, indeed, Judge, with your clearings and betterments' " (22).

Up to a point, though, the environmental attitudes of Natty and Judge Temple are surprisingly consonant. In matters of immediate practical policy, both insist that humans should restrain their killing instincts to take game only in proper seasons and circumstances, and as prompted by actual need. Thus, while Natty denounces the pigeon slaughter from the first, Judge Temple, too, comes to feel remorse for his role in assenting to the orgiastic massacre: " 'Thou sayest well, Leatherstocking . . . and I begin to think it time to put an end to this work of destruction' " (248). Raised as a Quaker, Marmaduke affirms the value of preserving nonhuman life whenever possible. And like Natty, he rejects emphatically the national myth of inexhaustible resources. The Judge believes that vegetative life, too, is worthy of respect. So he tells Monsieur Le Quoi, a foreign observer, that he is shocked by " 'the wastefulness of the settlers, with the noble trees of this country' " (108), as when they fell a great pine but leave all of it to rot except the minor portion they intend to use. He likewise refuses to consume sugar maples for household firewood, arguing that " 'really, it behooves the owner of woods so extensive as mine, to be cautious what example he sets his people, who are already felling the forests, as if no end could be found to their treasures, nor any limits to their extent.' " It is scarcely "wildness," he insists, " 'to condemn a practice, which devotes these jewels of the forest, these precious gifts of nature, these mines of comfort and wealth, to the common uses of a fireplace' " (105–106). And though he briefly participates, despite himself, in an indecently gigantic haul of bass from Otsego Lake led by Templeton's unrighteous sheriff, he again ends up assenting to Natty Bumppo's condemnation of the deed as " 'sinful and wasty' " (266).

Where Natty and Marmaduke fall into conflict, however, is in the nearly opposite theoretical bases for their environmental responses. In *The Pioneers*, unlettered Leatherstocking grounds his reactions to the nonhuman world in a piety that remains as much archaic as Christian—and, above all, in an individualistic ideal of natural law. His uncompromising defense of wilderness corresponds roughly to what would later be called a "preservationist" stance, except that he would ideally wish to preserve not just selected territories but virtually all of North America from encroachment by European-style "clearings." By contrast, Judge Temple's implicitly "conservationist" approach to environmental practice is rooted in a social philosophy that takes Europeanized civilization to be normative, that regards the nonhuman world as resource rather than divine presence, and that upholds the order of law as essential to regulating a well-ordered society.

In several respects, the narrative as a whole supports Leatherstocking's side of this conflict. Natty seems justified in his cynical view that Judge Temple can rarely see God's forest through the trees—that is, he fails to grasp the contradiction between his concern to preserve individual trees and the considerable pride he takes in having tamed and cleared large expanses of woodland. Moreover, the Judge's conservationist ethic has more to do with the perceived utility and commodity-value of natural resources than with any kind of interior, spiritual recognition of beauty. " 'It is not,' " he says frankly, " 'as ornaments that I value the noble trees of this country; it is for their usefulness' " (229). But Judge Temple most flagrantly exceeds the bounds of his partly self-granted authority when he insists that Natty be put in the stocks and jailed a full month for having killed a buck at a season technically forbidden by law.

Although Cooper himself was a litigious-minded landowner and his father a judge, he scarcely presents Judge Temple's legalistic response to this harmless old man in sympathetic terms. Temple can reasonably claim that respect for the rule of law is necessary for the governance of civilized communities. But he goes too far in attributing to humanly devised law not merely practical benefit in sustaining a culture's social contract but a sacred and absolute authority. " 'The sanctity of the laws must be respected,' " he argues, since "the laws alone remove us from the condition of the savages' " (382–383). In religious terms, Judge Temple affirms no definite form of Christian doctrine. One character describes the doctrinal content of his faith, such as it is, as " 'jist nothing at all'" (154). And even the Christian preaching of Mr. Grant, with whom Judge Temple is loosely connected, offers no direct support for an environmental ethic though it affirms very generally that " 'the fountain of divine love ... pervades creation'" (128). Inhabiting a culture where authentic experience of the sacred seems increasingly remote, Judge Temple is all the more tempted to idolize the law as the highest available object of faith.

Yet the Natty Bumppo portrayed in *The Pioneers* is not wholly attractive, either. Now in his seventies but still sporting his deerskin leggings and one gaping yellow tooth, he cuts a slightly ridiculous figure. In the uncompromising rigor of his solitary forest habits, he has become something of a self-righteous anachronism, since the era of the great woods has already ended in Oneida, never to return. Closely inspected, even his environmental attitudes cannot be deemed altogether preferable to those of Judge Temple. After all, when he cuts his knife through a buck's throat in Lake Otsego so as to call down Judge Temple's harsh punishment, he is impelled to kill not by any pressing need for food but by the sheer excitement of pursuing such a grand " 'pair of horns'" across the water (296). One might therefore conclude that this hunt violates his own stated principles as well as Judge Temple's law. Nor is he particularly sensitive about preserving human life when he expresses his feelings about Hiram Doolittle to Oliver Edwards: " 'If he harbours too much about the cabin, lad, I'll shoot the creater'" (290). Natty's free-spirited defiance of social convention is understandable enough when he demands to know " 'what has a man who lives in the wilderness to do with the ways of the law' " (311), but Leatherstocking forgets that Templeton is no longer wilderness territory.

He also forgets that in any densely settled community, the absence of established civil law would produce anarchy. Offended by the law's restrictions on his personal freedom, he is indignant about challenging the Judge to tell him " 'who ever heard of a law, that a man should'nt kill deer where he pleased!'" (25) Who, indeed, dares question an American's right to freedom of movement and action? Natty's anarchic individualism poses no threat to human or nonhuman life so long as individuals happen to share Natty's inner rectitude. But extending the lawless rule of the frontier into other social environments also enables persons of lesser conscience to prey freely upon others. Natty is distressed to realize that even in America, powerful people can often impose their will or practice malice without restraint, that " 'might often makes right here, as well as in the old country, from what I can see'" (22). He does not quite realize, however, the extent to which his own anarchic and antinomian philosophy would license the unfettered cruelty he deplores.

The limitations of Natty Bumppo's sensibility in the realm of environmental ethics emerge most clearly, I think, in the bass-fishing episode presented in chapters 23–24 of *The Pioneers*. As already noted, Sheriff Jones and others indulge themselves here by shamefully netting thousands of bass that they have no intention of consuming.[19] Judge Temple fails to prevent this killing spree, which occurs after all within proper season of the law he has procured. Arriving by canoe at the scene of the crime, Natty denounces the act in no uncertain terms as a sin of wasteful excess. The author doubtless concurs. Yet when the Judge notices that Natty was himself prepared to do some spear-fishing, he asks the righteous hunter to abandon that desire:

> "Approach, Leather-stocking, and load your canoe with bass. It would be a shame to assail the animals with the spear, when such multitudes of victims lie here, that will be lost as food for the want of mouths to consume them." (265)

Natty will have no part of the invitation. Declaring he will " 'eat of no man's wasty ways,' " he refuses to take anything from this sinful catch. He repeats his usual jeremiad against those who kill more animals than they eat. Rejecting the scores of edible fish that Marmaduke offers him, he insists instead on paddling off to kill a large fish of his own in suitably sporting fashion. In doing so, he preserves his own standard of absolute moral purity—but, if one may put it so, at the great fish's expense. The episode shows him enjoying more success in protecting his fixed ideal than in protecting the lake animals or ecology.

Within the full span of the novel, Judge Temple is probably less admirable, in personal moral terms, than Leatherstocking. Yet as environmental policy, the Judge's pragmatic counsel to use fish that are already dead makes more sense than Natty's pure-minded disdain. Thus, Cooper's romance questions the absolute character of Natty's preservationist idealism—as well as the temporizing, materialistic temper of the Judge's conservationist pragmatism. As an environmental text, the book's distinctive contribution is to expose both approaches to critical scrutiny, sustaining a major ideological ambiguity without denying the need for ethical engagement with the nonhuman world. *The Pioneers* is useful, too, in the way it dramatizes the point that those who represent a more settled, rule-based institutional order may end up protecting the earth's integrity more successfully than free-spirited lovers of a nature they wish to keep lawless.

Emerson's *Nature*

"Nature" is arguably the keyword of Emerson's early pronouncements as a post-Unitarian prophet of what came to be called "the newness" or the "Concord philosophy," an American version of Romantic religion that some New Englanders thought would supplant the revealed faith and institutions of historical Christianity. It supplies the title of his famous 1836 book commonly regarded as the charter statement of the Transcendentalist movement. It had already figured in his lecture on "The Uses of Natural History" (1833). It appears again in the title of an 1841 oration, "The Method of Nature," yet again in the essay "Nature" included in *Essays: Second Series* (1844), and repeatedly within many other prose works and poems. If one judges the 1836 publication by its capacity to inspire other naturalists, Emerson had indeed written the book on nature—not only for Thoreau but also for the likes of John Burroughs, John Muir, and Mary Austin. Yet despite the wealth of published commentary on Emerson, critics have rarely focused directly on his response to the biotic environment.[20] One can read book-length treatments of Emerson's relation to a host of other topics. Why doesn't nature make the list?

From the standpoint of present-day environmentalism, Emerson's obvious defect as a nature writer is the dearth of concrete particulars—of named organisms and objects—invoked in his writing. In contrast to Thoreau, whose hearty empiricism brings a world of sensory appeal to his work, Emerson typically dwells in metaphysical abstractions. His totalizing view of nature favors grand universals over the smell of Concord's ferns and swamps. Moreover, the idealistic philosophy set forth in *Nature* seems ultimately to reduce the nonhuman world from physical actuality to epiphenomenon. If the awakened human soul is all that matters, our physical environment becomes nothing more than the mind's projection. Emerson's song of the Orphic poet ends up not questioning but celebrating "the kingdom of man over nature." One might even suspect that the worldview represented in *Nature* is more radically anthropocentric than the Christian orthodoxy it sought to displace. Although the visible world remains a creation, it seems now to have been created not only *for* human beings—for their sole use and satisfaction, rather than for itself or to declare the glory of a transcendent God—but *by* humans, insofar as they realize their divinely creative powers of perception.[21] If the Oversoul then becomes just one more version of selfhood, we may find Emerson's theology of nature troubling insofar as it seems to endorse not pantheism so much as self-worshiping solipsism. Or, as the former Transcendentalist Isaac Hecker put it in his withering summation of Emerson, "Nature is his church, and he is his own god."[22]

It would be fairer, though, to acknowledge that for Emerson, the principle of enlightened self-reliance is quite unlike egotistical self-worship. In the notorious eyeball passage in *Nature*, the speaker discovers the world's transparency as well as his own, and thereby dissolves the cognitive distance between personal subjectivity and material objectivity. To declare that as transparent eyeball "I am nothing. I see all" (10) is, in fact, to affirm an ideal of self-emptying detachment or *kenosis* comparable to that recommended by Christian and other versions of mystical spirituality.[23] The instructed eye regards the physical world not as object but as religious icon: instead of gazing *at* the opaque surface of things, Emerson's "pupil" looks *through* Creation to apprehend that flow of animating energy otherwise known as Spirit. Emerson's public writings offer little concrete description of the physical world or recognition of nature's operations apart from human perception. But they amply confirm our connectedness to the creaturely order, the "occult relation" (10) between us and earth's other inhabitants. This sense of a limitless tissue of associations through diverse orders of Creation, which struck Emerson with peculiar force during his 1833 visit to the Jardin des Plantes in Paris, fed his early aspiration to become a scientific naturalist.[24] It also permeated his writing throughout his career.

After admitting Emerson's limitations as a nature writer, one can more readily perceive three major dimensions of his contribution to environmental theology: (1) an insistence on nature's ultimately nonutilitarian, sacred status as cosmos rather than as purely material commodity; (2) a reformulation of natural theology highlighting personal experience of God's presence rather than rational evidence of God's existence; and (3) a recognition of humanity's immense power to shape the world and its environment, ideally through the integrating influence of that higher faculty described by Kant and Coleridge as "Reason."

From Commodity to Cosmos

In *Nature*, Emerson briefly acknowledges the physical world's "final cause" as commodity before considering its value in satisfying "a nobler want of man . . . namely the love of Beauty." Both the ancient Greeks and Goethe confirmed Emerson's insistence on regarding the world as cosmos: "The ancient Greeks called the world Κόσμος, beauty." As cosmos, the visible sphere is not only picturesque but ordered, integrated within itself as well as with humanity's love of outward forms. For an eye attentive to the world's wholeness, beauty signifies moral rectitude and the divine order of spirit, since "Beauty is the mark God sets upon virtue" (12, 15). Well before "ecology" began to name a branch of biological science in 1866, Emerson's cosmos extended the principle of synergistic interaction beyond the visible world. Adapting Swedenborg's theory of correspondences, the author of *Nature* saw natural facts connected to the invisible domains of language and spirit. Laws governing the physical world and those operative in the moral dimension of our environment were presumably both rooted in "nature." Ralph Cudworth's seventeenth-century Neoplatonism offered Emerson further support for affirming, against the pressure of mechanism and materialism, an active divine presence in the world.[25]

Instead of recognizing nature's integrity as cosmos, those who see it in the lesser light of Understanding rather than Reason apply a dis-membering gaze that reduces land to a vulgar, lifeless form of commodity. Thus, the wood-cutter may not see the tree as a life-form but only as a "stick of timber" (9) in the forest landscape. Seeing the land as cosmos also demands appreciation of its spiritual and material status as common space. In *Nature*, Emerson's philosophic vocabulary sometimes obscures issues of material land ownership that the author knew to be topically relevant and contentious in Jacksonian America.

In 1836, the year *Nature* was published, an unsurpassed quantity of American land—twenty million acres—was transferred from public holdings to private property. Following completion of the Erie Canal in 1825, favorable credit and commodity prices spurred the development of western territories opened by the Louisiana Purchase. Soon railway transportation, combined eventually with lust for gold and military action, would press migration further. Yet most of the huge 1836 land sellout was transacted not by family settlers but by wildcat speculators.[26] Land acquired through an expansionist policy that often included the displacement of native peoples, a removal protested by Emerson in the case of Georgia's Cherokees, now supported the voracious cash-appetite of aggressive entrepreneurs. Senator Robert J. Walker of Mississippi, national chairman of the Congressional Committee on Public Lands, pointed out that within the single year of 1836 "an extent of territory as large as the combined states of New England had passed into the hands of speculators." Our territories, he complained, would soon be controlled by speculators rather than the elected national government:

> There is thus opened a golden stream from East to the West which, whilst it drains the East of millions of capital . . . condemns to a period of long sterility a vast portion of the beautiful valley of the West, containing soil inexhaustively fertile, but remaining in the hands of speculators barren and infertile.[27]

Family farms rather than large landholding interests still occupied much of New England's rural acreage. Yet the growing concentration of wealth in factory-dominated settlements represented an equivalent expansion of commercial culture. Already by the 1830s, new railways and the appearance of large linen mills in Lowell, Massachusetts, were changing the face of New England.[28] By 1841, the New England village, in its previously conceived pastoral autonomy, had begun to die when railways linked it to western cornfields and a national market economy.[29] And more ground than ever was devoted to serving only the immediate uses of "commodity." With more than 60 percent of the land cleared for agricultural fields and most of the remaining forest divided into small private woodlots, the countryside offered little space or suitable habitat for the survival of larger wildlife species. Even in Vermont, George Perkins Marsh began to notice as a child, before 1820, damaging effects of deforestation near his native Woodstock.[30]

Despite New England's small population by present-day standards, it had preserved surprisingly little publicly owned land by the early nineteenth century. In 1668, Concord set aside several thousand acres "for a free comon to the present householders of Concord, and such as shall hereafter be approved and allowed to be inhabitants."[31] But already by 1750, the town began to feel crowded because of population growth, its own rush of land speculation in frontier townships, and rising demand for agricultural space.[32] A town historian of Emerson's day lamented that while Concord had once reserved "several lots of land" for " 'the public good,' " most had been "disposed of without producing much permanent benefit."[33] In the vicinity of Concord, only about 10 percent of the countryside remained forested in the 1840s and 1850s.[34] Although Emerson was reluctant to accept Malthusian pessimism about the limits of land growth in relation to soaring population, he was at least cognizant by 1858 of English predictions about the dire consequences of seeing, as he put it, "the first comers take up the best lands; the next, the second best; and each succeeding wave of populations . . . driven to poorer, so that the land is ever yielding less returns to enlarging hosts of eaters."[35]

So one can glean, not far beneath the surface of Emerson's idealistic rhetoric in 1836, hints of tension over land distribution that ground the question of "nature" in the era's material and political culture. Within the town limits of Concord, fewer and fewer new arrivals could aspire to that version of self-possessed fulfillment epitomized at the close of *Nature* by ownership of "a hundred acres of ploughed land" (45). And yet, at a time when most of southern New England's territory had already been commodified into someone's real estate, while Irish immigrants and free blacks in Concord remained landless, Emerson assures his readers that "the universe is the property of every individual in it." Recognizing that the "charming landscape" he observes across twenty or thirty farmlots near Concord is defined legally under title of "warranty-deeds," he argues that none of the deed-holders "owns the landscape" since "there is a property in the horizon which no man has but he whose eye can integrate all the parts, that is, the poet" (15, 8). In this last reference, Emerson's idealistic confidence in the power of imagination seems to make private land ownership an irrelevance rather than a threat to the democratic distribution of goods or the preservation of viable ecosystems. In the 1846 poem "Hamatreya," though, his contempt for arrogant New England landowners who style themselves "landlords" is considerably more pointed. Although the poem does not picture damaging environmental results of human greed, it does belittles the vanity of "earth-proud" men who "added ridge to valley, brook to pond, / And sighed for all that bounded their domain." This complaint against the vanity of soil avarice is framed, moreover, in spiritual terms. Behind it lies familiar scriptural teachings—as recorded in the Book of Ecclesiastes as well as in the New Testament Beatitudes, when Jesus blesses the meek who shall inherit the earth. To refute the claims of human ambition, "Hamatreya" gives the earth its own voice, rising to exultant song:

> 'They called me theirs,
> Who so controlled me;
> Yet every one
> Wished to stay, and is gone,
> How am I theirs,
> If they cannot hold me,
> But I hold them.'[36]

These cultural considerations invite us to look again at the crucial opening chapter of *Nature* with an eye toward the transmutation of American soil from commonwealth to private commodity. That Emerson's sacred encounter with the landscape, rendering him glad to the brink of fear, takes place while "crossing a bare common" (10) is a detail worth pondering. It suggests, to begin with, Emerson's brief for the democratization of Transcendental experience. Discovering one's sacred connection to nature and the Oversoul does not require the luxury of a trip to some remote Alpine meadow or, as Emerson says in another context, "some desert cliff of mount Katahdin, some unvisited recess in Moosehead Lake."[37] It is available to anyone, virtually anywhere— even on the "common" place of a thoroughly domesticated village green. Emerson's first-person testimony of his epiphany on this occasion describes circumstances that, from the standpoint of Romantic exoticism, could scarcely be less promising. Although he approaches the moment in a state of receptive leisure, open toward whatever grace presents itself, he does stumble upon his "perfect exhilaration" while crossing the common "in snow puddles, at twilight, under a clouded sky, without having in my thoughts any occurrence of special good fortune" (10).

The common in question was probably situated in Concord. I think the available evidence favors Concord land over Boston Common, the other leading possibility. In November and December of 1834, just after Emerson had moved from Boston and Newton to board with his step-grandfather in ancestral Concord, he confirmed in his journal a personal affection for "the quiet fields of my fathers" and for Concord's small but venerable green, located within half a mile of the house and two-acre plot that he would purchase for his own residence the following year. "I do not cross the common," he wrote expressly of Concord green, "without a wild poetic delight notwithstanding the prose of my demeanor." The language here is strikingly similar to what he would write in *Nature*. "Thank God I live in the country," he added—though plainly Boston, too, preserved a common that had likewise become second nature to him.[38]

Traditionally, of course, New England's village common had been rendered wholly or mostly "bare" of trees to provide pasturage—and, especially, night protection—for livestock. Yet by the nineteenth century, this strictly utilitarian purpose was being supplanted by more loosely civic and recreational functions. Fronting the bustling commercial operations of the Wright Tavern and the Colonial Inn, Concord's green supplied an obvious focal point and gathering space for the community. The village green was scarcely "nature" as imaged according to a wilderness ideal of precolonial settlement. But it did mark a major intersection between Nature and Culture. Moreover, like the later institution of urban parks, it preserved a symbolic remnant of the national commonwealth. Corresponding to what we should today call "open space," the green belonged to each and all. It was a zone reserved from the production of cash crops. Situated physically at the center of a New England settlement composed of fragmented landholdings and increasingly dedicated to profit-yielding private enterprise, it also represented what was left of the community's belief in common spiritual values. It therefore recollected in microcosm the principle of cosmos rather than commodity—that is, collective ideals of wholeness, beauty, order, and play supposed to prevail in the "plantations of God" (10) equated with primeval forest.

The village common could be regarded, in fact, as the physical counterpart of values enshrined temporally in the New England Sabbath. And not coincidentally, the Congregational structure designated for Sabbath worship was typically located on or near the common. Even after leaving the ordained ministry, Emerson often commended the New England tradition of Sabbath-day observance but rejected its institutional expression in the historical forms of Christian worship. Thus, in "The Divinity School Address" he calls the Sabbath "the jubilee of the whole world."[39] The first chapter of *Nature* therefore embraces the irony of portraying a religious experience that is sited physically on the common yet apprehended spiritually in a decidedly individual if not private modality.

Emerson's sense of the fundamentally private, ineffable character of religious experience helps to explain the rarity not only of autobiographical illustrations but also of detailed nature writing in the public essays. The journals leave little doubt, though, that Emerson loved the outdoors and could describe with some particularity natural facts he encountered in the local landscape. When, for example, the author of *Nature* locates his second nature-based epiphany (likewise in chapter 1) not on the "bare common" but in a comparably open clearing of "bare ground" vaguely situated "in the woods," a journal entry suggests the actual site of his numinous self-discovery as "a transparent eyeball." For while the essay's crucial paragraph of narration ends with the general affirmation that in a tranquil wilderness landscape "man beholds somewhat as beautiful as his own nature" (10), the journal account attaches this same description to a well-known piece of local geography: "I went to Walden Pond this evening a little before sunset, and in the tranquil landscape I behold somewhat as beautiful as my own nature."[40] Similarly, while *Nature* presents only vague references to stars and other heavenly bodies, the journals convey in more graphic detail Emerson's fascination with astronomical spectacles.

Revelation to US: The Primacy of Experience

Whether or not Emerson is describing a response to specific features of the environment, he remains emphatic about the need to identify firsthand experience—what the Puritans called "experimental knowledge"—as the root of all natural theology. The opening paragraph of *Nature* asserts the necessity of a "religion by revelation to us," grounded in "insight," rather than the presumably closed and derivative "tradition" preserved by historic Christianity. And for Emerson, as elaborated in "The American Scholar," the antiquated faith to be supplanted goes beyond the doctrinal inheritance of Abrahamic religion to include America's traditional veneration of Europe. To believe in a "religion by revelation to us" requires a new national confidence in the U.S., a willingness to embrace "new lands, new men, new thoughts." Emerson presents his contemporary experience, outdoors in America, as the ground for rejecting every version of retrospective faith. He speaks not merely as a student of natural history who has examined the external evidence but as one who knows what it feels like to be "embosomed for a season in nature, whose floods of life stream around and through us" (7).

The prospect of "an original relation to the universe" is not merely to be deduced from methodical observation, then, in the mode of Paley's inquiry, but to be *enjoyed*. Unlike Paley, who interrogates God's design in nature objectively, with only brief eruptions of personal feeling, Emerson sets his argument within the subjective frame of a conversion narrative. This emphasis on experiential knowledge, which anticipates later neopragmatism, derives not only from Puritan tradition but also from Hume's skepticism about all forms of deductive knowledge and arguments from design.[41] Yet the concern of New Light preachers to discover intense feelings leading toward *metanoia*, or change of heart, remained central in Emerson's early view of experience. The affective responses of "delight," "exhilaration," and "fear" he discloses in the opening sequence of *Nature* support the progression toward his concluding eschatological vision of unity, grace, and perfected sight. Not the theoretical existence of God, as primordial creator, but the Spirit's palpable presence in the world animates this testimony. The "influx of the spirit" engenders the "redemption of the soul" and the re-creation of God's kingdom, "as when the summer comes from the south the snow-banks melt, and the face of the earth becomes green before it" (43, 45). Such confidence in the inward testimony of experience persists even for the later Emerson, whose chastened idealism leads him to admit that "Nature, as we know her, is no saint."[42] Even when he comes to modify his views about the character and teleology of the nonhuman world, he continues to rely primarily on experiential knowledge to define those views.

Reshaping Nature

From the standpoint of present-day green awareness, the Emerson of *Nature* lacks real appreciation of humankind's capacity to degrade the global environment. Initially, at least, he dismisses "art"—that is, the total impact of human activity on the planet's ecology—as no more significant, in metaphoric terms, than "a little chipping, baking, patching, and washing." George Perkins Marsh, in *Man and Nature* (1864), showed much better understanding of the "momentous" environmental effects of human intervention. Marsh described at length the perils of watershed loss, deforestation, and soil erosion. Unlike Marsh, Emerson failed to recognize that ecological systems might be damaged beyond repair and that human folly even threatened "extinction of the species."[43]

Emerson likewise failed to acknowledge the ways in which his sense of "nature," as contrasted rhetorically to the supposedly moribund values of "history" and "tradition," is itself historically mediated. Though we may aspire to see the world directly, as utterly "transparent," our view of it is inevitably colored by our cultural circumstance and personal disposition. Emerson in 1836 says he can bear any calamity that leaves him his eyesight, but he is already seeing the nonhuman world through multiple lenses—including the historical assumptions of international Romanticism, incipient industrialism, writings of Carlyle and Goethe, visual ideals of the picturesque, and philosophic notions of the sublime. The prospect of receiving a vital revelation of the sacred directly from nature, instead of straining from dead letters the history of someone else's divine experience, sounds attractive. But Jaroslav Pelikan is right, I think, to suggest that Emerson's opposition between "insight" and "tradition" amounts to a false dichotomy.[44] Even the "insight" enjoyed by a Romantic solitary in the woods must be seen as contextualized within human history, as mediated by cultural traditions and social attitudes.

Conversely, the sacred "tradition" affirmed by historic Christianity supposes that individual believers within a faith community can and must experience their own encounter with the living Spirit. Why should we "grope among the dry bones of the past," Emerson asks, instead of seeking "a religion by revelation to us" in the body of nature with its "floods of life"? But while this disparaging reference to "dry bones" applies principally to the Jewish-Christian tradition of scriptural revelation, the figure is itself a scriptural trope—drawn from Ezekiel's visionary account of a dispirited nation but fully assimilated into Emerson's active imagination. For that matter, the essay's concluding image of insight, epitomized by the blind man who enters God's dominion as he is "restored to perfect sight" (45) emerges unmistakably from biblical tradition.[45] Despite Emerson's antithetical portrayal of scriptural revelation (tradition) versus natural revelation (unmediated insight), modern hermeneutics suggests a need to interpret both texts—the Bible as well as nature—within the temporal contexts that produced them.

Yet even the anthropocentric outlook of *Nature* contains a certain ecological wisdom in the kind of human hegemony over nature that it extols. Though Emerson overlooks the negative perils of environmental degradation, he does recognize in a positive sense that the lordship our species exercises over the nonhuman world is at once inevitable and potentially limitless. He therefore exhorts his readers not to deny the scope of their control but to seek a more Transcendentally enlightened mastery of Creation. Boldly optimistic about the "plastic power of the human eye," he insists that under such influence "Nature is not fixed but fluid" and that a "correspondent revolution in things will attend the influx of the spirit." In this transfigured "kingdom of man over nature," the world appears in a new light" so that snakes, spiders, pests, and other "disagreeable appearances" (44, 45) vanish altogether. Emerson's point here, of course, is not to recommend physical extermination of these organisms but a transformation of one's outlook so that the beauty of common snakes, for example, like that of the water snakes in Coleridge's *Rime of the Ancient Mariner*, can be perceived in relation to an ecological vision of nature as cosmos.

For Emerson human consciousness, too, is fluid, perpetually evolving, and consequently able to endow the nonhuman world with ever-advancing forms of self-consciousness. This crucial nexus between human thought and the physical world is particularly well dramatized in a later poem, "The Adirondacs" (1858), describing Emerson's camping trip through the rugged north country of New York State. An underrated piece, "The Adirondacs" is worth reading on several counts. For one thing, it offers a candid, often humorous disclosure of the social class issues that arise when ten rustic guides, "stalwart churls in overalls," instruct Emerson and nine other "polished gentlemen" in the crafts of wilderness living. The genteel adventurers, a distinguished party that included the Harvard zoologist Louis Agassiz as well as the noted poet and literary critic James Russell Lowell, were enthusiastic but decidedly lacking in frontier learning (fig. 4.2). Unlike other Emerson writings, this blank-verse reflection also provides a clear factual narrative and a fair measure of concrete physical description. Thus, the poem begins on a note that attaches the myth-

FIGURE 4.2. W. H. Stillman, Philosophers' Camp in the Adirondacks (c. 1857). (Photo courtesy of Concord Free Library.)

ological aura of "sacred mountains" to specific place-names and sensory impressions of the rowing trip:

> We crossed Champlain to Keesville with our friends,
> Thence, in strong country carts, rode up the forks
> Of the Ausable stream, intent to reach the Adirondac lakes. At Martin's Beach
> We chose our boats; each man a boat and guide—
> Ten men, ten guides, our company all told.
>
> Next morn, we swept with oars the Saranac,
> With skies of benediction, to Round Lake,
> Where all the sacred mountains drew around us,
> Taháwus, Seaward, MacIntyre, Baldhead,
> And other Titans without muse or name.
> . . . .
> By the bright morn the gay flotilla slid
> Through files of flags that gleamed like bayonets,
> Through gold-moth-haunted beds of pickerel flower,
> Through scented banks of lilies white and gold,
> Where the deer feeds at night, the teal by day,
> On through the Upper Saranac, and up
> Père Raquette stream, to a small tortuous pass
> Winding through grassy shallows in and out,

Two creeping miles of rushes, pads and sponge,
To Follansbee Water and the Lake of Loons.[46]

Perhaps the most revealing feature of the poem, though, is its later description of how Emerson and his wilderness companions reacted to news that
the world's first transatlantic telegraph cable had been successfully laid across
the sea.[47] Though situated in a remote landscape, Emerson finds the civilized
world breaking suddenly into his awareness when one of his associates holds
"a printed journal waving high / Caught from a late-arriving traveller." The
technology of the printing press thereby confronts him, even in wild country
of the high peaks, with notice of still newer engineering in the form of a
marvelous wire now "landed on our coast, and pulsating / With ductile fire."
He and his companions are elated. They applaud the technical feat of linking
the hemispheres as a promise that "thought's new-found path / Shall supplement henceforth all trodden ways" and "Match God's equator with a zone of
art." Moreover, the poet feels a sympathetic urge to find the human triumph
represented by this geographic linkage shared sympathetically by the surrounding elements of nature: "Let them hear well! 'tis theirs as much as ours" (191–
192).

Given his historical circumstance, Emerson might be excused for his inability to qualify such noble expectations with proper skepticism about the long-
term human and environmental costs of technological progress. Thoreau came
closer than he to foreseeing that telegraph cables also opened a new conduit
for cheapened speech, leading eventually to that compulsive chatter facilitated
by on-line discussion groups and cell phones. Nor does Emerson's poem acknowledge that by 1869, much of the Adirondack's old-growth forest had already been assaulted by massive logging of hemlock, white pine, and red
spruce.[48] Yet Emerson was prescient indeed in recognizing that the oceanic
cable dramatized a crucial fact of modernity: no part of nature could henceforth
be considered wholly removed from human presence or influence. At its best
the undersea wire, a harbinger of today's cybernetically wired world, represented an extension of consciousness that was initiated by humans, yet reached
across the entire planet. Even the apparently eternal and remote Adirondack
lakes would now be changed, for good and ill, by this irrevocable tie to human
civilization. Long before they are denuded of fish by acid rain, they participate
in humanity's worldwide web so as to share the impact of that

> . . . spasm throbbing through the pedestals
> Of Alp and Andes, isle and continent,
> Urging astonished Chaos with a thrill
> To be a brain, or serve the brain of man. (192)

Nor does Emerson lament the need to return to urban life at the close of
"The Adirondacs." He does not suppose it either possible or desirable to live
in an autonomous state of nature that severs all ties to civilization. In his view,
"We flee from cities, but we bring / The best of cities with us." And when, "on
the verge / Of craggy Indian wilderness" (193), he unexpectedly hears strains

of Beethoven issuing from a piano played by someone in a log cabin, he welcomes the sound as an enhancement rather than an interruption of his wilderness experience. His Adirondack encampment does not, after all, represent any permanent change of life. It fulfills instead the usual Romantic aim of discovering a tonic, a restorative interlude, in some rustic locale. For Emerson, the trip qualifies as a "holiday" in two relevant senses. First, in simple modern terms, it is a vacation—a deliberately abnormal, leisure-class activity offering respite from more typical pursuits. But the poem's persistent invocation of religious language suggests that time spent in the region's sublime landscape also imparted "spiritual lessons" (189), thus satisfying the less worldly purpose traditionally assigned to "holy days." A sacred day is time set apart from profane existence that helps to define its ultimate character. True to both senses, then, Emerson declares that "The holidays were fruitful, but must end" (194).

"The Adirondacs" ends somewhere short of affirming that human science can uncover every secret of nature. The transatlantic cable reaches only part way toward explaining the world's inscrutable mystery, "As if one riddle of the Sphinx were guessed" (194). Yet the poem reasserts Emerson's confidence that human consciousness can achieve benign mastery, if not total knowledge, of the physical world. At the outset of *Nature*, he had imaged his representative self as a free spirit, a figure wholly immersed or, still more intimately, "embosomed" in nature's "floods of life." By the end, though, he is acknowledging the almost inescapable domesticity of the human condition, the need for all human beings to admit at least some measure of hegemonic separation from the wild. "Every spirit builds itself a house," he declares, "and beyond its house, a world, and beyond its world, a heaven" (44). The statement exudes Transcendental assurance but contains as well a concession to civilized custom. Even Thoreau, a freer spirit than Emerson, ended up building a solid frame house at Walden, destroying some pines in the process, though he admits he might have inhabited a cave or wigwam instead. Though Emerson did not literally construct his own dwelling, in 1835 he purchased and selected as his permanent home an imposing white structure once named "Coolidge Castle" after its original owner.[49] Whitman loafed on the grass, chanting in free verse his praise of "Nature without check with original energy," but never meant to reside permanently on the open meadow. Though "one of the roughs," he, too, normally wanted to sleep under a civilized roof. In fact, he had occasionally worked as a housebuilder in the early 1850s, before publishing his first edition of *Leaves of Grass*.[50] And by a telling coincidence in American letters, the same rented house in which Emerson began working on *Nature* later became Hawthorne's home in Concord. Here, in fact, Hawthorne mused on his own complex relation to nature and to history in ways that invite us to reconsider the prefatory essay to *Mosses from an Old Manse* as a form of environmental literature.

5

Variations on *Nature*

From the Old Manse to the White Whale

Hawthorne's Recovery of Eden

Nathaniel Hawthorne, another distinguished resident of Concord in
the early 1840s, rarely if ever claims a place in surveys of American
nature writers. This chapter begins, however, with a look at one of
Hawthorne's personal essays that offers a thoughtful assessment of
human interactions with the green world. The greenery in question
is not the pristine wilderness of "first nature" but a garden refuge
beside the Concord River displaying apple orchards and winter
squash. Hawthorne's essay thus describes a nature consistent with
that represented in women's nineteenth-century garden literature.
The environmental rhetoric of "The Old Manse" preface also has a
religious undertone. It reflects an incarnational theology of God's
Creation grounded in Hawthorne's gratitude for the grace made
manifest in vegetative life.

Written in an expansive mood of contentment, "The Old
Manse" preface first centers our attention on the venerable house
where Hawthorne wrote his second major collection of tales between 1842 and 1845. The manse holds the accumulated experience
of several clerical generations who inhabited it before him. Its garret
contains heaps of old books and newspapers. So in one sense the
house walls mark the outer boundary of Culture, as opposed to the
local forms of Nature with which it is "environed."[1] But as the essay
unfolds, in the meandering style of a personal meditation, the
house's integral connection to its surroundings becomes clearer. In
the author's creative mind, the house becomes more nearly a portal,
inviting free entry to nature's green space, than a wall against it.
The Old Manse serves, in fact, as Hawthorne's window on the green

FIGURE 5.1. The Old Manse, Concord, viewed from rear beside the Concord River.
(Photo by Ning Yu.)

world. Like Emerson before him, he can stand before any of his three study
windows to gaze upon the house orchard, the fields, and the Concord River
(see fig. 5.1). The scene before him, which includes a celebrated battleground
of the Revolution, is colored as well by his cognizance of weighty historical
events that transpired here. And yet, surprisingly for Hawthorne, the stimulus
afforded by his involvement in present-day outdoor life, especially its botanical
features, seems in this case more imaginatively fertile than his reflection on
America's historical past.

What version of nature does Hawthorne's sketch of Concord evoke? Parts
of the essay, in the Transcendental spirit of Thoreau and Emerson, remind us
that traces of a wilder, unfettered world survive even on the verge of this cultured village and its tranquil river. Because the listless river holds little use for
powering commerce, it offers boaters a rare opportunity to find solitude and
seclusion close to civilization. Hawthorne writes fondly of "wild days" (25) he
spent fishing with Ellery Channing on the Concord and Assabeth. As though
removed to genuine wilderness, he can relish from his boat the nonhuman
attractions of the "shy kingfisher," the pickerel "leaping from among the lily-
pads," or ducks that "skimmed along the glassy river, breaking its dark surface
with a bright streak." Amid the water's "rich scenery," Hawthorne also notices

turtles, cardinal flowers, hemlocks whose arms stretch across the stream, and "delicious" pond-lilies growing on the margin. When he and Channing kindle a primal fire for their noontime meal, spreading food "on a moss-grown log," he enjoys the sensation that "all seemed in unison with the river gliding by, and the foliage rustling over us." In this "sacred solitude," he breathes an invigorating air of freedom, presumably casting aside "all irksome forms and straight-laced habitudes" to "live like the Indians" that his romantic fancy represents as indigenous to the landscape. Celebrating a holy freedom "from all custom and conventionalism, and fettering influences of man on man," Hawthorne finds intimations of what Emerson would confirm to be wild nature's higher spiritual use as cosmos rather than commodity.

Yet the essay's prevailing sense of nature is clearly a version of pastoral, grounded in the settled agricultural landscape. Hawthorne frames our first impression of the Concord River in bucolic imagery. Conventional rhetoric of the picturesque likewise suffuses his testimony, as when he portrays the river, "in the light of a calm and golden sunset," as "lovely beyond expression" (7). Sometimes, too, the author turns natural facts into simple allegories, as when the white pond-lily offers him a lesson about moral ambiguity, or when he takes the river's tawny reflection to signify "that the earthliest human soul has an infinite spiritual capacity, and may contain the better world within its depths" (8).

For Hawthorne, though, the landscape's strongest emotional attraction lies closer to hand, in the manse's own garden and orchard. As the author describes the satisfaction he takes in harvesting the orchard's "wealth of fruits" and the garden's rich yield of vegetables, the Edenic flavor of life at the Manse is unmistakable. The orchard showers him with cherries and currants in the summer; and with pears, peaches, and an "immense burthen" of apples in the fall. First planted by Thoreau, the garden now demands little human effort to bring forth peas, a hill of beans, fat summer squash, "great yellow rotundities" of winter squash, and early Dutch cabbage "which swells to a monstrous circumference" (15). Here is Paradise indeed, where one has only to accept with gratitude the "infinite generosity and exhaustless bounty" of "our Mother Nature" (13). And just as the author looks with pleasure at the squash swelling in his garden during an extended "calm summer" of his "heart and mind" (34), so also he is happy to find his wife Sophia becoming pregnant and giving birth to Una, their first child, during this idyllic period of life together in Concord. "The Old Manse" presents us not with "the power of blackness," as Melville would have it, but rather with what we might term Hawthorne's "green phase" of artistic response to the world.

The theology that Hawthorne cultivates within this garden variety of nature Romanticism is not so apparent, however. I think it fair to say that Hawthorne, adapting familiar Christian vocabulary to express his own semiorthodox faith, understands the vegetative abundance that delights him to be a physical incarnation of divine grace. Delighted to gather fruit from trees he never planted, he rejects the nation's masculinized work ethic to announce: "I relish best the free gifts of Providence" (13). To be sure, the gardener invests a modicum of labor in his domestic plot—and to that extent, according to Hawthorne, qualifies as a cocreator with God of his own biotic environment. "Childless men," he observes, "if they would know something of the bliss of paternity, should plant a seed—be it squash, bean, Indian corn, or perhaps a mere flower, or worthless weed—should plant it with their own hands, and nurse it from infancy to maturity, altogether by their own care." He admits that he needed to revisit his own garden plot "a dozen times a day, and stand in deep contemplation over my vegetable progeny, with a love that nobody could share nor conceive of, who had never taken part in the process of creation" (14). This joyous activity of cocreation, he assures us, requires little labor. The pleasure of gardening, like the vegetables and fruits themselves, is something given rather than earned.

Accordingly, a seasonal mood of early autumn dominates this essay. Not the pressure of mortality that comes with late autumn, but the free flow of apples that Providence supplies in New England's harvest season. It is a moment of grace incarnate, best captured in Hawthorne's memory of a time when "in the stillest afternoon, if I listened, the thump of a great apple was audible, falling without a breath of wind, from the mere necessity of perfect ripeness" (13). This embrace of the Shakespearean wisdom that "ripeness is all" coincides with the author's disposition to accept rather than to conquer and subdue the earth.

For Hawthorne, such acceptance requires the inward maturity to rest one's spirit upon the material reality of the nonhuman world. "Grace" seems to name an abstraction, but the fruits and vegetables he receives as "free gifts" are decidedly palpable. Gazing at the winter squashes, he is delighted to recognize not only that he had had something to do with bearing "a new substance . . . into the world," but also that "they were real and tangible existences, which the mind could seize hold of and rejoice in" (15). This insistence on the "real presence" of the physical world, which Hawthorne saw challenged by several forms of philosophic idealism and apocalyptic fantasy, surfaces repeatedly in writings collected for *Mosses from an Old Manse*.[2]

In emphatically secular terms, Wallace Stevens later declared: "The greatest poverty is not to live / In a physical world."[3] The Hawthorne of the Old Manse period would, I think, endorse this sentiment but within a comparatively religious context that acknowledges nature's "blessed superfluity of love," the world's creation by a "beneficent God" and "the promise of a blissful Eternity" (27). Though not christocentric, the view of Creation presented in "The Old Manse" might thus be characterized as incarnational.

Hawthorne's remarks about the many clergymen who once inhabited the manse also shed light on the implicit theology of nature that informs this essay. Recalling that the Manse had never been "prophaned by a lay occupant" (4) before he arrived, he pokes gentle fun at these clerics, who are largely associated with the lifeless prints of Puritan ministers that once darkened the walls of his study. Because nothing of the religious writings they had collected in the attic "retained any sap," the author "tossed aside all the sacred part, and felt myself none the less a Christian for eschewing it." He notes facetiously that such books "seldom really touch upon their ostensible subject" and that most holdings of theological libraries might be safely ignored "so long as an unlettered soul can attain to saving grace" (19, 20).

Hawthorne grants that at least the last of the Manse's clerical residents *did* create a legacy of sacred worth—but not through the usual channels of ordained ministry. This minister, now deceased, had "penned nearly three thousand discourses" in addition to countless oral homilies. Hawthorne imagines him conceiving sermons while absorbing a "variety of natural utterances," including "solemn peals of the wind, among the lofty tops of the trees!" (4) Yet his gift to future generations had nothing to do with what he wrote, read, or preached, but with the orchard trees that he planted beside the Manse. Though already advanced in years when he set out the orchard, for the sake of later generations if not himself, he surprised his neighbors by living to harvest apples from mature trees. His progenitive act of faith extended life, unlike those grim prints of dead Puritan ministers and volumes of religious writings that retained no sap. The minister's participation in botanical Creation is ultimately comparable to the author's artistic cultivation of a "few tales and essays, which had blossomed out like flowers" (34) at the Manse—and perhaps also, by implication, to Hawthorne's fathering of children. Above all, the minister's work in the orchard represents an enduring act of love:

> He loved each tree, doubtless, as if it had been his own child. An orchard has a relation to mankind, and readily connects itself with matters of the heart. The trees possess a domestic character; they have lost the wild nature of their forest-kindred, and have grown humanized by receiving the care of man, as well as by contributing to his wants. (12)

Thus, Hawthorne's essay supports Christian beliefs insofar as it presents the clergyman's orchard work as an expression of *agape* and regards nature's gifts as incarnations of divine grace. At the same time, Hawthorne presses imaginatively to displace the moribund, formal religion of dead clerics with what he takes to be a more vital and "natural" form of *religio*—that is, a connective or ligature to the divine origins of life, as embodied by the minister's planting. Hawthorne's description of the orchard and garden underscores, too, the sense that what we call nature is often indivisible from civilized human life. Even the domesticated nature that constitutes his primary environment in Concord retains plenty of sap, beauty, and capacity for spiritual sustenance. At the Manse, he is heartened to see culture wedded to horticulture. Biologically equivalent forms of uncultivated moss grow on the log where Hawthorne once dined in a wild stretch of the Assabeth River *and* on the Manse's external walls during most of his stay there. By the same token, nature blends into history at every turn of the panoramic view that he contemplates from his study windows.

Secret Gardens: Women's Plot, Women's Work

More than most other male authors of the period, Hawthorne has frequently been associated with a culturally feminized sensibility. Accordingly, his contentment with the placid outdoor activity of gardening, as revealed in "The Old Manse," calls to mind the ample body of women's garden literature that lesser-known figures like Celia Thaxter and Anna Warner produced during the nineteenth century.[4] Sometimes linked to landscape painting, the plots described in these popular garden books often served ornamental functions. As such, they supported middle-class and ruling-class social beliefs about the need to cultivate beauty on the domestic premises. At the same time, gardening offered the genteel woman a rare opportunity to interact with the outdoor physical world—not simply by observing it but by taking "a direct hand in creating her environment."[5] Victorian women in the eastern states were, of course, discouraged from standing behind the plow, from roaming forests in pursuit of wildlife, or from joining dangerous expeditions on the high seas. Yet they were encouraged to study botany along with ornithology, and gardening supplied a useful opportunity to apply this botanical knowledge. The domestic garden also gave women an outdoor space of their own for reflection and creative expression.

Besides contributing to general beautification of the home grounds, gardening offered other practical benefits. Catharine Beecher, assisted by her sister Harriet Beecher Stowe, described these benefits in *The American Woman's Home* (1869), which devoted three full chapters to horticultural education, including advice about how to propagate plants. Beecher and Stowe reminded readers that gardening provided healthful exercise for women, as well as good moral training and recreation for their children. Plants such as ferns, swamp-grasses, and ivy could enhance the home indoors, while the wise use of spade labor outdoors could supply flowers "to ornament the table and house" in addition to plenty of edible fruits and vegetables. Home gardening reaffirmed the dignity of human labor, particularly for leisure-class women. It supported artisanal culture in an industrial age. By cultivating fruits and vegetables within the household, women could also contribute to a self-reliant economy yielding direct material benefit.[6]

Writing of this period indicates that women looked to their home gardens to satisfy spiritual needs as well. Medieval monastic tradition prized the enclosed garden as a kind of sacred ground upon which religious brothers or sisters could combine active labor with contemplative reflection. In his sixth-century *Rule for Monasteries*, Saint Benedict included manual labor, typically centered on spade agriculture, in the daily discipline prescribed for brethren living in community. Benedictine practice in subsequent centuries, recollecting the ancient motto *Ora et labora*, continued to stress the link between prayer and work. Celia Thaxter showed a comparable recognition that one seeking refuge from worldly anxieties and space for inward meditation would do well to work the soil outdoors. Certainly, too, Thaxter's troubled marriage and unruly children encouraged her to seek a place of repose beyond the turmoil of family life. Dedicating herself to the care of a small plot on Appledore Island off the New Hampshire coast, this "Island Miranda" (as Hawthorne had called her in her younger years) lavishes such attention on her plants that she comes to regard them as friends and comforters. Unlike Beecher and Stowe, she shows no interest in edible flora but concerns herself entirely with flowers suited to "feast the souls that hunger for beauty" and to " 'delight the spirit.' " " 'God Almightie first planted a Garden,' " she cites Lord Bacon as recalling, " 'And indeed it is the purest of Humane Pleasures, it is the Greatest Refreshment to the Spirits of Man.' "[7]

In *An Island Garden* (1894), Thaxter elaborates her belief that horticulture can be a practical expression of love, divine praise, and worship. Her own religious beliefs, never very close to orthodox Christianity, involved flirtations during various phases of life with Unitarianism, Darwinian agnosticism, Buddhism, Hinduism, spiritualism, and theosophy. Toward the end of her life she attended Unitarian services at Portsmouth but never joined any church.[8] Nonetheless, she sustained a lifelong commitment to rituals of planting, weeding, and harvesting. Beyond offering detailed advice about gardening techniques, she confides to readers: "Dearly I love to sit in the sun upon the doorstep with a blossom and meditate upon its details" (119). By the same token, she believes the beauty of the wild rose

> cannot be learned in a single glance, nor indeed, in many glances: it must be carefully considered and lovingly meditated upon before it yields all the marvel of its delicate glory to your intelligence. "Consider the Lilies," said the Master. Truly, there is no more prayerful business than this "consideration" of all the flowers that grow. (93)

Thaxter approaches even the simple task of planting seeds as a religious act:

> I always do it with a joy that is largely mixed with awe. I watch my garden beans after they are sown, and think how one of God's exquisite miracles is going on beneath the dark earth out of sight. . . . Yes, the sowing of a seed seems a very simple matter but I always feel as if it were a sacred thing among the mysteries of God. (25, 27)

Striving to capture in words the surpassing loveliness of the California poppy, Thaxter remarks on how "the petals spring from a simple pale-green disk, which must needs be edged with sea-shell pink for the glory of God" (77). For her, the craft of flower arranging also has religious import, as when she writes of creating an "altar of flowers" upon a table she calls "The Shrine" (96).

Nineteenth-century women who are today better known than Thaxter—figures such as Margaret Fuller, Harriet Beecher Stowe, Susan Cooper, and Edith Wharton—likewise wrote of the spiritual sustenance available in gardens. For Margaret Fuller, recollecting the enchantment she felt as a child while gazing on flowers in her mother's garden became crucial to the project of defining her soul's identity as an adult woman. In her "Autobiographical Romance," she describes the small plot in Cambridge, Massachusetts, as "the happiest haunt" of her childhood. She recalls that the flower and fruit-tree garden of her "mother's delight" was "carefully kept"—but through her mother's labor rather than her own. For Fuller, then, this patch of green, from which a gate "embowered in the clematis creeper" opened into the surrounding fields, becomes the site not of blessed labor but of pure contemplation. The garden offers a feminized dream of refuge from the world's utilitarian expectations and from her father's zealous, often dominating ambitions on her behalf. Its brilliant flora emblematizes for Fuller a Transcendental realm of beauty and love located beyond the pain of her subsequent depression and self-doubt. This vegetative life touches the maternal and creative spirits stirring in her soul, while the spirit of her actual mother, whose presence Fuller's writing almost never describes or visualizes directly, hovers over the scene like an unseen deity:

> Of late I have thankfully felt what I owe to that garden, where the
> best hours of my lonely childhood were spent. Within the house every-
> thing was socially utilitarian; my books told of a proud world, but in
> another temper were the teachings of the little garden. There my
> thoughts could lie callow in the nest, and only be fed and kept
> warm, not called to fly or sing before the time. I loved to gaze on
> the roses, the violets, the lilies, the pinks; my mother's hand had
> planted them, and they bloomed for me. I culled the most beautiful.
> I looked at them on every side. I kissed them, I pressed them to my
> bosom with passionate emotions, such as I have never dared express
> to any human being. An ambition swelled my heart to be as beauti-
> ful, as perfect as they.[9]

Fuller perceived her mother's garden as a bounded domestic space that, paradoxically, lifted her spirit beyond domestic boundaries. An integral feature of her deeply religious but unorthodox sensibility,[10] this Edenic sanctuary affirmed the prospect of safe nurture for the secret, creative recesses of her soul; and it reinforced her developing feminist conviction that "all the secret powers are 'mothers.' "[11]

Fuller believed she was never far removed from the mystical spirit-world, a domain she typically experienced in natural settings removed from society. It is telling, for example, that in her journal account of a spiritual awakening that occurred when she was twenty-one, she finds herself able to pray only after she walks out of a church service in Groton, Massachusetts, to wander for hours through the surrounding fields. Bathed in November sun beside a woodland pool, she gains fresh appreciation of the soul's capacity to "sow new and immortal plants in the garden of God." On that Thanksgiving Day, 1831, she believes she received mystical confirmation that she "had only to live in the idea of the ALL"; and before the earth grew dark around her, "I was for that hour taken up into God."[12]

In her travel account of *Summer on the Lakes* (1844), Fuller looked beyond

New England landscapes to venture as far west as the Wisconsin Territory. She is struck by the wild splendor of midwestern lakes; she is intrigued to observe the daily routine of Pottawattamies and other native peoples. She regards Native Americans as possessing "profound sympathy" with wild animals and as distinctively allied with "the majesty of nature in this American continent." But she thinks they are already living in a degraded state, soon to become extinct or insignificant as white settlers transform the West. For Fuller, in fact, visiting the frontier stirs no momentous interior change. Neither her effort to recover the Romantic sublime at Niagara Falls nor her pleasure at observing pastoral scenes in Illinois provokes an episode of religious awakening comparable to what she had experienced earlier in fields of Massachusetts. She was usually more attracted to New England's familiar gardens, fields, and woodland than to wilder territory. Fuller recognized, after all, that life on the frontier could be especially brutalizing for women, and that "wherever man is a mere hunter, woman is a mere slave."[13]

That is not to say, however, that Fuller's writing always presents a tamely benign, picturesque view of nature. Particularly in poems and lesser-known prose works written through 1844, during a period of personal crisis for Fuller, wilder images of elemental nature emerge. In a mystical essay titled "Leila," Fuller describes a goddess figure who becomes for her an evocative representation of woman's capacity for fecundity and self-renewal. At once a transcendent goddess and an unsettling presence within the writer's psyche, Leila bears a name that "stands for night," for the darkness that brings forth stars, "as sorrow truths." In Fuller's feminist revision of theology, divine powers that Emerson had already attributed to the poet-Transcendentalist are associated now with the darker female presence of Leila. Thus, Leila's eye reflects the human soul, or subliminal self, as well as the limitless soul of nature—particularly as seen in the elemental ocean, night, star, wind, moon, and fire. In relevant verse pieces as well as in prose, Fuller dramatizes Leila's access to chthonic powers through images of the snake, which are emblematic in turn of the archetypal fertility goddess: Leila, she insists, is "one of those rare beings who seem a key to all nature." When the narrator gazes in her dream-vision "steadily and in the singleness of prayer" on a lake framed by "solemn oaks and pines," Leila appears there, rising and walking as the very spirit of "the vasty deep." As such, Leila reflects Fuller's view not only of godly womanhood but also of the darkness of divinity and the permanently elusive, untamable soul of nature.[14]

Erotically charged essays such as "Yuca Filamentosa" and "The Magnolia of Lake Pontchartrain" further demonstrate Fuller's cognizance of a wild side even in floral displays and garden settings. Extending a key line from Emerson's peroration in *Nature*, Fuller confirms that " 'The Spirit builds his house, in the least flowers.' " But the revelation of this spiritual fact, when she perceives it in yucca plants she had cultivated "for several years" in her own garden, is arrestingly strange. On a night of full moon, the plants "burst into flower together"—abruptly, unpredictably, and uncontrollably. Their blossoms "rose to meet the moonlight" after the plant's "palmetto-shaped leaves . . . had, as it were, burst asunder to give way to the flower-stalk, leaving their edges rough with the filaments from which the plant derives its name."[15] By the same token, Leila's apotheosis beside watery depths reminds us that an untamed environment confronted Fuller even close to home, on the populated eastern seacoast. Eventually, in fact, the fierce power of the Atlantic would claim her own life after the ship in which she was returning from Italy foundered off Fire Island, New York, in 1850.

God's Grassy Handkerchief: Walt Whitman's World

Oceanic settings also loomed large in Whitman's imaginative response to the nonhuman world, particularly as dramatized in the third (1860) edition of *Leaves of Grass*. Best known as a gregarious urban personality, this major American poet "of Manhattan the son" is often overlooked in broader assessments of American nature writing. Yet his writing presents a distinctive contribution to environmental poetics. One can scarcely fail to notice Whitman's omnivorously tactile response to the physical world, his lovingly detailed recognition of animals, plants, and all forms of matter ranging from microparticles to stars and planets. Erotically conjoined with the totality of his environment, he blurs customary boundaries between human and nonhuman orders of being in at least two crucial ways. First, his characteristic technique of identification with others extends to a sympathy with nonhuman life, particularly birds and mammals, that often surpasses literary conventions of personification. Second, his celebration of urban landscapes, in poems like "Song of Myself" and "Crossing Brooklyn Ferry," blurs the geophysical distinction between natural facts and human artifacts, including structures of commerce. Just as he envisions a dilation of himself as private person into a universalized, Transcendental "kosmos" called Walt Whitman, so also he presents an expanded and culturally variegated model of "nature."

Thus, the close of "Crossing Brooklyn Ferry" (1856) shows the splendor of "mast-hemm'd Manhattan"—with its profusion of flags, vessels, dock structures, curious passengers, and foundry chimneys—merging with the scene's natural wonders of "river and sunset and scallop-edg'd waves of flood-tide." The poet regards all these things among "the glories strung like beads on my smallest sights and hearings." Such Transcendental vision discerns beauty even in the grubby articles of freight commerce. Meditating on the enduring presence of physical objects enables the poet to project his spirit beyond the otherwise oppressive frontier of mortality. Luminescent within the poem's sundown atmosphere, these outward and visible signs become a sacramental means of realizing one's invisible ties to others—including the vast crowd of humanity that crosses, will cross, or might only imagine crossing the East River to Manhattan—as well as to ultimate reality. Thus, Whitman's sacramental vision transfigures material objects into "gods," "dumb beautiful ministers" that "furnish your parts toward eternity" and the soul.[16]

The religious intensity of Whitman's ecopoetic worldview, which suffuses

Leaves of Grass from 1855 through all subsequent editions, can scarcely be ignored, though its theology is notoriously hard to define. What one can deduce of the poet's beliefs indicates a peculiar blend of Transcendental philosophy, Quaker mannerisms, shamanistic occasions of ecstatic mysticism, rearticulations of Old Testament prophecy, and adaptations of ethical precepts from the New Testament Beatitudes.[17] Whitman seems, in fact, to have regarded his 1860 *Leaves* as "the New Bible" that was needed to address spiritual aspirations of a democratic people in the United States.[18] His non-Christian spirituality sustained but modified the New Testament apprehension of God as love, while his prophetic style implicitly challenged the Bible's claims to unique scriptural authority:

> This is what you shall do: Love the earth and sun and animals, despise riches, give alms to everyone that asks, stand up for the stupid and crazy, devote your income and labor to others, hate tyrants, argue not concerning God . . . [and] read these leaves in the open air every season of every year of your life. (Preface to 1855 *Leaves*, 716–717)

Because Whitman enjoyed contradicting himself, his representation of God shows considerable volatility throughout his poetic corpus. Most often, his radically democratized version of Transcendental faith led him to scorn the idea of a personal, uniquely divine and superior godhead, as figured in traditional images of God the Father. Accepting Jesus as brother, he celebrated instead the universal divinity of humanity. At times, though, Whitman's exaltation of the "me myself" as representative soul overflowed into simple self-worship, fostering creation of a Whitmanian ego cultus to which others paid homage. One might argue that Whitman came closer than Emerson to making himself his own god and his own church. At any rate, Whitman certainly intends to be provocative when he insists "Divine am I inside and out" and commends the "scent of these arm-pits" as an "aroma finer than prayer" ("Song of Myself," 53).

Frequently, too, Whitman extends this fascination with his own body to embrace what he takes to be the grand incarnation of God's body throughout the material world.[19] Sometimes he even personalizes this incarnate deity as a familiar presence, distinct from himself, who "comes a loving bedfellow and sleeps at my side all night and close / on the peep of the day, / And leaves for me baskets covered with white towels bulging the house with their plenty."[20] Whitman likewise perceives this godly lover, his unseen *camerado*, to be the indwelling spirit of Creation whose whiff and feel are everywhere at hand in the burgeoning grass:

> Or I guess it is the handkerchief of the Lord,
> A scented gift and remembrancer designedly dropped,
> Bearing the owner's name someway in the corners, that we may
>   see and remark, and say *Whose?* (33)

Whitman's classic account of God's body filling the world appears in section 5 of "Song of Myself." Here the poet articulates a mystical vision of Creation that arises strangely and spontaneously from his meditation on a blade of grass while loafing in the open air "on a transparent summer morning in June" (1855 wording). The transparent atmosphere recalls not only Emerson's penetrating gaze as a "transparent eyeball" in *Nature* but also that essay's persistent emphasis on looking beneath physical surfaces into the life of things. To see nature as transparent rather than as opaque is, in Emersonian terms, to realize the organic connection between the ME and NOT ME. Earlier, in section 3 of "Song of Myself," Whitman has announced a comparably lucid gift of insight by declaring: "Clear and sweet is my soul, and clear and sweet is all that is not my soul." Whitman's ecstatic testimony in section 5 can be read, in fact, as a considered revision of Emerson's illuminative experiences on a "bare common" and on "bare ground" in chapter 1 of *Nature*.[21]

Like Emerson, who urges readers to enjoy "an original relation to the universe," Whitman promises his disciples: "you shall possess the origin of all poems" by recovering your felt relation to "Nature without check with original energy" (30, 29). Emerson does not engineer his Transcendental discovery of Spirit in nature. Such occasions of grace occur when he has no anticipation of "special good fortune." Similarly, Whitman loafs without effort or ambition on the open grass, seeming to expect nothing. But as ancient masters of contemplation attest, one can at least prepare oneself for the influx of divine energy by giving over exertions, waiting in a state of receptive leisure that invites access to hidden depths both of nature and of psyche. As Whitman waits, his fascination with the hum of his own "valvèd voice" draws him toward the instinctive vibrations of what Emerson called the "aboriginal Self." And like Emerson, whose epiphanic experience brings a sacred gladness tinged with fear, Whitman's joy is a piercing gift, mixed with something of physical violence as he feels a tongue plunged to his "barestript heart." In this enigmatic episode, Whitman realizes at once several orders of conjunction—between body and soul, personal ego and transcendental self, humanity and nature.

But though Whitman celebrates here the equivalent of Emerson's wedding between ME and NOT ME, he makes some notable changes in the ceremony. The most prominent difference, of course, lies in the erotic and bodily accents of Whitman's account, his arresting literalization of marital metaphors. Playing on the supremely sacred language of Exodus 3:14, Whitman declares his body, his other "I AM," to be no less god-bearing than the soul. In section 5, their union as equals gives birth to the Transcendental Self celebrated in the poem's opening lines. By contrast, Whitman had to notice how thoroughly the language of Emerson's primary epiphany in *Nature* reduces that experience to a cerebral event—an uplifting of the head away and apart from the body. Instead of Whitman's orgasmic, interpenetrative union with the body, involving a plunge downward from tongue to heart, Emerson records his bodily evaporation—to become a head "uplifted into infinite space," then an eyeball, and finally "nothing." While Emerson enjoys transparent commerce with "currents of the Universal Being" circulating through "the blithe air,"[22] Whitman thrills to an immediate touch of nature's chthonic, procreative rhythms surging from below. And unlike Emerson, the poet of "Song of Myself" perceives his merger with the NOT ME not primarily through ocular sight but through tactile sense impressions:

> I mind how once we lay such a transparent summer morning,
> How you settled your head athwart my hips and gently turn'd over
>   upon me,
> And parted the shirt from my bosom-bone, and plunged your
>   tongue to my barestript heart,
> And reach'd till you felt my beard, and reach'd till you held my
>   feet.

Thus inspired by a mystical encounter with God's body, known first through recognition of his own body, Whitman uses a chant cadence redolent of church confessions to declare his creedal faith:

> Swiftly arose and spread around me the peace and joy and
>   knowledge that pass all the art and argument of the earth;
> And I know that the hand of God is the promise of my own,
> And I know that the spirit of God is the brother of my own,
> And that all the men ever born are also my brothers, and the
>   women my sisters and lovers,
> And that a kelson of the creation is love,
> And limitless are leaves stiff or drooping in the fields,
> And brown ants in the little wells beneath them,
> And mossy scabs of the worm fence, heaped stones, elder, mullein
>   and pokeweed. (33)

At the heart of this ecospiritual litany is Whitman's pronouncement that "a kelson of the creation is love." Rhetorically, at least, the emphasis again swerves away from Emersonian precedent. After all, in Emerson's postillu-minative credo, "the name of the nearest friend sounds then foreign and ac-cidental." "To be brothers, to be acquaintances,—master or servant, is then a trifle and a disturbance" for him who has become "the lover of uncontained and immortal beauty."[23] Emerson calls himself a lover. But in this crucial sec-tion of *Nature*, his Platonic idealism leads him to declare more affection for abstract "beauty" than for brotherly or sisterly humanity, to say nothing of pokeweed. Whitman, though, wants to claim palpable kinship with every nat-uralized embodiment of the world-soul, including human nature. He begins, in effect, with the leaves, the starting point of his meditative journey and the punning nexus between the common grass in nature's book and the physical body of his own book. But his vision reaches from the astronomical heights, where later in the poem his mental travel speeds him "through heaven and the stars," down to the lowliest order of concrete particulars—elder, mullein, and pokeweed. The episode in section 5 expands to embrace animal, vegetable, and mineral categories of Creation. Like Dante in the concluding canto of the

Divine Comedy, Whitman finds the "limitless leaves" in the book of Creation bound together by love.

In Whitman's case, of course, the love forming Creation's keel must be considered fully secular insofar as it arises not from a Creator who is worshiped as wholly Other but from a God whose hand is the "elderhand" of his own (1855 wording), whose "rough deific sketches" are imaged in himself and everyone he meets.[24] Still, the poet's vision of love as a kind of living tissue stretched across every species and mineral feature of global ecology also qualifies as *religio.* Though Whitman applauded "materialism," "positive science," and "exact demonstration," his binary instincts never allowed him to embrace secular materialism alone. And though he was apt to speak familiarly rather than deferentially of God, he acknowledged: "I hear and behold God in every object, yet understand God not in the least" (51, 86).

To appreciate the peculiar temper of Whitman's Creation spirituality, we might focus on the homely forms of nonhuman life named toward the close of that expansive credo in section 5 of "Song of Myself." The sequence studiously avoids showcasing conventionally attractive landscape features. There is nothing picturesque about "heap'd stones," or about "brown ants" as the passage's sole representative of animal life. The vegetation pictured here includes "mossy scabs," bryophytes that cling parasitically to wood reshaped by humans into an artifact bearing the unglamorous name of "worm fence." Plants with more immediate human appeal—such as lilac or sweet flag (*calamus*), which figure prominently in later Whitman poems—are not brought to light here.

In fact, Whitman's grand vision of a cosmos unified by love—roughly equivalent, in biological terms, to synergistic interaction among life-forms—reaches an almost comic culmination with the naming of elder, mullein, and pokeweed. Usually found in waste places on the margins of civilization, all three plants have been disdained as weeds. Pokeweed (*Phytolacca americana*), for example, is an invasive flowering plant with toxic potential. As introduced species, neither elder (a common hedgerow tree or shrub) nor mullein (an ungainly-looking plant, often cursed by gardeners, that typically appears on disturbed land) qualify as "pure" specimens of American nature. Yet Whitman may have known that traditional herbalism has identified medicinal or other practical uses for each of these plants. The sequence with which he ends section 5 clearly demonstrates, in any case, his conviction that Transcendental awakening to the ecological integrity of Creation must extend even to organisms customarily dismissed as unattractive. If the poet's own sweaty armpits belong to God's body, so do nature's unsightly extremities in the shape of mullein or pokeweed.

As Whitman moves into his comparatively "tragic" phase with poems newly featured in the 1860 *Leaves of Grass,* this supremely optimistic reading of natural revelation undergoes a crucial change. Without disowning his Transcendental faith, the poet admits more deeply now the spiritual challenges posed by death, by life's implacable boundaries, by his own terror of self-dissolution. Without abandoning the joy of feeling the physical world, epitomized in the way he had invited ocean waves to "dash me with amorous wet" (49), he turns his gaze more and more by 1860 toward seaview meditations, dwelling particularly now on "The World Below the Brine." The greatest of these sea poems, "Out of the Cradle Endlessly Rocking," dramatizes Whitman's chief crisis of creativity, his central fable of personal loss and recovery. From an ecocritical standpoint, the poem is striking in the way it fuses private memory of boyhood sensations on Paumanok's shore with universally imagined recollection of life's primeval origins in the sea. The poet also fuses his own psychic pain, his crisis of midlife humanity, with a sympathetic re-creation of animal emotion, as enacted in the tale of mated mockingbirds from Alabama who are separated by death. If the torment of frustrated love leads Whitman to ponder the more fundamental alienation posed by death, the poem shows him looking particularly toward the ocean, nature's "endlessly rocking" cradle of life, for a "clew" to our origin and ultimate destiny. In interrogating the waves, Whitman seeks "the word final, superior to all" (252).

This survival of a teleological longing, once focused primarily on the biblical "word," has shifted definitively now to a hermeneutic of natural revelation. As the poem appeared in the 1860 and 1867 editions of *Leaves*, it was actually titled "A Word Out of the Sea." For Whitman, at least, the triumph of "natural supernaturalism" over scriptural piety seems complete. Christianity's venerable Book of Revelation simply dissolves here into the Oceanic Psalm, whose still small voice conveys "the word stronger and more delicious than any" (247). Yet when the poet finally hears the sea whispering to him "the low and delicious word death," the revelation defies rational exegesis. This "hissing melodious" sound is certainly repeatable, and richly evocative—but not quite translatable into discursive or doctrinal language. Its existential import cannot, therefore, be spoken or preached. This "word of the sweetest song and all songs" (252, 253) can only be sung, blended harmonically with the art of Whitman's rediscovered chants.

In "As I Ebb'd with the Ocean of Life," another poem first collected in the 1860 *Leaves*, Whitman shows even less confidence in his ability to interpret nature's revelatory signs. Though he paces the shore of Paumanok with his "electric self" looking for "types" that might illuminate "the real Me," he finds only a trail of debris: "Chaff, straw, splinters of wood, weeds, and the sea-gluten, / Scum, scales from shining rocks, leaves of salt-lettuce left by the tide." And if spiritual signifiers no longer appear in nature, how does one suppress the fear that "I too but signify at the utmost a little wash'd-up drift"? (253, 254)

This poem, Whitman's nearest approach to Melvillean skepticism about the purposefully benign character of nature, is dominated by the specter of modern meaninglessness. The shore environment is defined by unsightly, disordered fragments of driftwood and debris. Whitman dares to doubt that in his previous effusions he has even "once had the least idea who or what I am"; he images himself now as a drowned corpse, bubbly white "ooze exuding at last" from his lips. He finds no psychic consolation in the sea, pictured as a "fierce old mother" (254, 256, 255). Nor can he accept the spiritually fatherless state of humanity in our post-Cartesian world,[25] since he expresses a desperate urge to find meaning and solace by clinging eternally to Paumanok, figured here as a kind of surrogate Father God.

Such desire seems futile, though, within the mood of this poem. Resisting the ebb tide of his Transcendental faith, Whitman assures himself that "the flow will return." Yet he can state this promise only parenthetically. Dreading self-dissolution in a swirl of random currents, he ends his nightmare vision as mere detritus, his body spread "in drifts" among "Tufts of straw, sands, fragments" (256). Still, nihilistic doubt could never hold Whitman's attention for long. It would remain for more skeptical "deep divers," such as Dickinson and Melville, to pursue the implications of living in an apparently spiritless world without benefit of divine parenthood. I have not tried in this study to pursue Dickinson's multilayered scrutiny of the matter. Tracing the lifelong development of Melville's beliefs about God and the physical world through his sizeable corpus of writing is a project no less daunting. But some reflections on Melville's greatest novel may serve to highlight the character of one naysayer's artful response to the prospect of natural theology and teleology set forth in Emerson's *Nature*. Such remarks, combined with a look at Thoreau's contrary response, may also be a fitting endpoint to the story of how antebellum writers address green themes touching Romantic religion.

"Heartless Voids and Immensities": The Inscrutable Nature of *Moby-Dick*

In the second chapter of *Nature*, Emerson begins his discourse on "Commodity" by rhapsodizing about "the steady and prodigal provision that has been made" for our "support and delight" as we float through the heavens on a "green ball" splendidly ornamented with "this ocean of air above, this ocean of water beneath, this firmament of earth between."[26] It is hard to imagine a sharper critique of this idyllic naturalism than the one Melville supplies in *Moby-Dick*. Ishmael's narration brings to light, from below the Pacific surface, lurid counterimages of predatory strife. Perched aloft on the masthead, Ishmael lapses briefly into a Transcendental reverie in which he takes "the mystic ocean at his feet for the visible image of that deep, blue, bottomless soul, pervading mankind and nature."[27] Increasingly, though, his spirit is seized by a proto-Darwinian recognition of nature's underlying savagery and vulturism. Whereas Jesus invited his hearers to consider the lilies of the field, Melville dwells instead on the fierce underside of oceanic life:

> Consider the subtleness of the sea; how its most dreaded creatures glide under water, unapparent for the most part, and treacherously hidden beneath the loveliest tints of azure. Consider also the devilish brilliance and beauty of many of its most remorseless tribes, as the dainty embellished shape of many species of sharks. Consider, once more, the universal cannibalism of the sea; all whose creatures

prey upon each other, carrying on eternal war since the world began. (225)

Circling above this dark realm of sharks and killer whales, a pack of land-based human animals indulges not only in gory pursuit of other large mammals but also, the book suggests, in various forms of cannibalism. Ishmael insists that we are all savages, all killers. Like other Euro-Americans addressed in his narrative, he shrinks at first before the otherness of a Queequeg but comes to wonder rhetorically who among us "is not a cannibal" (242).[28] Inevitably, then, this fable about the pursuit of "a Job's whale" poses grand questions about the nature of evil, the nature of whatever deity may have formed "this visible world" and "the invisible spheres" (158, 169), and the nature of nature. In assessing evil, the book confronts not only immorality, epitomized by the reckless egomania of Captain Ahab and the sinister shadow of Fedallah, but also the problem of metaphysical evil. How, in other words, could a just, benevolent, and omnipotent God permit evil and affliction to prosper in the world? If God is good, why are so many things so dreadfully wrong with humankind and the rest of God's Creation? Or, as Queequeg sums up the matter with characteristic pungency, " 'de God wat made shark must be one damn injun' " (243).

Since the seventeenth century, Jewish and Christian tradition has assigned the term *theodicy* to discourse that aspires in some manner to reconcile the existence of evil with God's goodness and justice. The Book of Job is often cited as the classic biblical expression of this subgenre. Melville, though, had no intention of justifying the ways of God to human beings. *Moby-Dick* cannot be mistaken for an orthodox theodicy if one regards its author's skepticism or its mostly impious response to the problem of metaphysical evil.

Yet generations of readers have perceived the religious passion driving its inquiry, the ultimate reach if not grasp of the quest for meaning occasioned by Ahab's quest for the Great White Whale. No major American writer has been more painfully haunted by the problem of God than Melville. None has struggled more incessantly with his or her religious heritage. Melville scorned the Calvinism to which he was exposed in childhood through the Dutch Reformed Church—but could never quite banish it from his mind and soul.[29] Beyond his antimissionary and anti-Christian polemics, he feared that God might be either hopelessly unlovable or dead indeed. Not only dead but decimated and dispersed throughout the cosmos. Still, he retained to the end an insatiable hunger for the numinous. How else to explain the sacramental intensity of his famous disclosure to Hawthorne: "I feel that the Godhead is broken up like the bread at the Supper and that we are the pieces"? Even if God were dead and fragmented, or eternally hiding out, God's ghost refused to go away. "Take God out of the dictionary," he confided again to Hawthorne "and you would have Him in the street."[30] Melville's mind had more than enough skeptical sophistication to realize that a divine presence—or whatever fragments of God survived the onset of Victorian modernity—could never be physically located in a "Holy Land." Nonetheless, as Alfred Kazin points out, his heart finally impelled him, somewhat pathetically, to seek *something* in those traditionally sacred sites of Judaism and Christianity, situated in what had become the sordid emptiness of Turkish Palestine. "What he could never get over," Kazin suggests, "was the unlimited power of divinity on a cosmic scale which he had torrentially poured into *Moby-Dick*."[31]

Thus, from its deliberately mythologized "Extracts" sequence to its apocalyptic conclusion, *Moby-Dick* unfolds as a version of sacred text.[32] One source of the religious aura surrounding Melville's fish story is its pervasive biblicism, anchored especially in the Old Testament books of Job, Jonah, and Ecclesiastes but manifest also in its elevated rhetorical style. Other impressions of the sacred are generated by Melville's characterizations. The author shades his portrayals of Ahab, Fedallah, and the white whale with hints of the numinous that enlarge upon the already larger-than-life characterization endemic to symbolic romance. Above all, the book's status as religious literature derives from its "deep diving" interrogation of the visible world to discern what unseen powers, if any, might lurk beneath the "pasteboard mask" of appearances. Principally through Ishmael, Melville in *Moby-Dick* also pursues the question of ethical consequences, of how our knowledge or ignorance of ultimate realities ought to affect our bearing toward ourselves and others.

Ahab feels certain that his quest to destroy Moby Dick carries monumental and even cosmic significance. If he begins the hunt as simple revenge against the animal that destroyed his leg, his campaign soon acquires broader and deeper justification. Looking beyond his private physical injury, Ahab sees himself sympathetically engaged with the larger spiritual plight of all humankind. For him, the fiery quest offers an active, practical means of responding to the world's "intangible malignity." Ahab sees himself, in fact, as a Prometheus, acting heroically to exact "supernatural revenge" on behalf of the entire human race (156, 158). Killing the whale would consummate his rebellion against the indifference of a cosmos—or of whatever divine or demonic power *might* govern reality—that permits affliction to be visited on innocent humankind.

Thus, Ahab embodies the incipient modernity of an existential character later identified by Albert Camus as the metaphysical rebel. According to Camus, such a figure "contests the ends of man and of creation," "rejects his mortality," and "attacks a shattered world in order to demand unity from it." Recalling Starbuck's complaint that rage for vengeance against a "dumb brute" seems not only irrational but "blasphemous," one is struck all the more by the relevance of Camus's generalization to Ahab's precise circumstance:

> At the same time that he rejects his mortality, the rebel refuses to recognize the power that compels him to live in this condition. The metaphysical rebel is therefore not definitely an atheist, as one might think him, but he is inevitably a blasphemer. Quite simply, he blasphemes primarily in the name of order, denouncing God as the father of death and as the supreme outrage.[33](24)

Ahab sees the whale not as an actual animal but as a transcendental signifier for all that provokes him to blasphemy. He insists on turning Moby Dick into "the monomaniac incarnation of all those malicious agencies which some deep men feel eating in them." He wills to control not only the whale's lifespan but also its figurative meaning, so he ends up affixing his own symbology to its body along with his harpoon:

> all the subtle demonisms of life and thought; all evil, to crazy Ahab, were visibly personified and made practically assailable in Moby Dick. He piled upon the whale's white hump the sum of all the general rage and hate felt by his whole race from Adam down. (156)

To what degree might the author have shared Ahab's impious sentiments? Though one should not overstate the old case for an authorial "quarrel with God,"[34] it is safe to say that Melville's unsettled agnosticism, combined with his general distaste for Christian orthodoxy and disdain for evangelical mission efforts, engendered sympathy for metaphysical rebellion. Ahab, too, draws at least some personal sympathy, insofar as we are assured that " 'stricken, blasted, if he be,' " he nonetheless " 'has his humanities' " (79). If a sperm whale's head sees enough undersea horrors to " 'make an infidel of Abraham' " (249), Ahab has reason indeed to rage against the specter of unredeemed evil and suffering.

Still, critical reaction for several decades has emphasized that Melville's philosophic viewpoint, if it can be located at all within this book's multilayered ironies and competing voices, should be more closely associated with Ishmael than with Ahab. Even if Ahab is warranted in his diagnosis of the world's ills, one must be appalled by his prescription, an insanely personalized vengeance that achieves nothing but instead causes yet more pain and death for members of his crew. Thus rejecting Ahab's "woe that is madness," Ishmael has stared at the fires of affliction long enough to recognize the "wisdom that is woe" (328). Without trying to solve Ahab's metaphysical queries, he reaches a Stoic accommodation with pain and fear by heeding the earthy advice of Ecclesiastes to accept one's lot, to savor life's ordinary satisfactions. While Ahab pursues the "ungraspable phantom of life," Ishmael learns to grasp the tangible satisfactions offered by visible things—"the wife, the heart, the bed, the table, the saddle, the fireside, the country." He succeeds thereby in lowering his "conceit of attainable felicity" (20, 323). As the chapters "The Monkey Rope" and "A Squeeze of the Hand" confirm, Ishmael also finds solace from brooding on woe by holding fast to those common bonds of humanity that connect him to others even, or especially, in moments of shared peril.

By contrast, Ahab's imperial egotism isolates him increasingly from other selves. He longs to make even the physical world conform to his will. Two features of his manic pursuit of Moby Dick bear particularly on the ecocritical import of this book. One is the flagrantly arbitrary quality of Ahab's reading—or misreading—of natural facts associated with the whale. Another is the anthropocentric excess of his response.

That Ahab "piled upon the white whale's hump" (156) blame for everything that has ever gone wrong dramatizes the capricious, perversely willful tenor of his misreading. Dismissing any pretense of organic symbology, he simply *chooses* to interpret Moby Dick as a supernatural signifier. To make the whale his scapegoat, he must not only kill it but must first impose his meaning on it. What, if anything, the whale signifies beyond itself within Melville's text, or within the larger text of Creation, remains inscrutable. But Ahab refuses to accept this indeterminacy. He will claim authorship of Creation by simply decreeing what the whale means regardless of other evidence. His stirring speech in "The Quarter-deck" contains the admission that a purely subjective hermeneutic, rather than anything inherent in nature's text, shapes his reading of the whale:

> How can the prisoner reach outside except by thrusting through the wall? To me, the white whale is that wall, shoved near to me. Sometimes I think there's naught beyond. But 'tis enough. He tasks me; he heaps me; I see in him outrageous strength, with an inscrutable malice sinewing it. That inscrutable thing is chiefly what I hate; and be the white whale agent, or the white whale principal, I will wreak that hate upon him. (140)

A second troubling feature of Ahab's outlook is its anthropocentric excess. One already expects agents of the nineteenth-century marine industry to value whales chiefly as commodities, as items esteemed for their usefulness in serving an array of human needs. One likewise expects every literary work, including Melville's, to betray at least some measure of anthropocentric concern since writing is invariably produced by and for human beings. But when Ahab looks at Moby Dick, exclusively human and private interests become so magnified in his fevered fancy that the living animal becomes nothing but a "wall," a fixed screen on which he projects his totalizing ideology.

Though Ahab remains oblivious to every manifestation of whale suffering, Ishmael and some others can see beyond the joy of the kill. As Lawrence Buell observes, Ishmael describes the *Pequod*'s first kill in graphically gory terms, without shades of triumph. When the ship encounters a great herd of sperm whales in "The Grand Armada" chapter, Ishmael is evidently touched by the "peaceful concernments" of cow and newborn calves who sport lovingly beside their boat's gunwales while a solitary whale bearing an "agonizing" wound, flailing lethally among his fellows with a loose cutting-spade, presents an "appalling spectacle" (303–304).[35]

Recognizing that whales possess a life of their own apart from human commerce, the author, too, displays his fascination with them through the book's full ballast of cetological commentary. That is not to say that Melville can be enlisted under the banner of present-day campaigns to save whales. Nor was he in a position to acknowledge that sperm whales faced a serious risk of extinction.[36]

Still, the book takes zoological details seriously. Its account of Moby Dick's behavior suggests that whales might exercise mental powers well above the level of "blindest instinct" assumed by Starbuck. Its surmise concerning the bifurcated sense impressions produced by "the peculiar position of the whale's eyes" in its head (262) even shows some effort to see things, literally, from the animal's point of view. Particularly in "The Whiteness of the Whale" chapter, Melville suggests, in fact, that most of what humans have to say about the nonhuman world amounts to a colossal projection.

But what if a more responsible reader than Ahab tried to decipher nature, to assess its spiritual import beyond idiosyncratic forms of human projection? Would Melville credit such a hermeneutical project as feasible at all? Perhaps not. Whereas Emerson could still ask "to what end is nature," Melville doubts whether nature has any larger purpose or design. Just as *Pierre* destroys vestigial credence in America's pastoral myths, so also *Moby-Dick* casts doubt on all essentialist doctrines of nature's meaning. Neither Christian Providentialism nor Transcendentalist confidence in the unity and design of Creation finds support in Melville's narrative. Far from declaring "the glory of God" (Psalm 19), the great squid presents itself as a "chance-like apparition of life" (226), a mass that appears to be faceless, formless, and blind. God does not visibly govern the *Pequod*'s fate; and the sea neither knows nor cares what happens to the ship when it is finally sucked into the "yawning gulf" of a watery vortex. Nature shows total indifference to the human catastrophe once "all collapsed, and the great shroud of the sea rolled on as it rolled five thousand years ago" (427).

Thus far, Melville's view of things bears some resemblance to the gritty pessimism and skepticism toward religious absolutes reflected in later versions of literary "naturalism."[37] If the nonhuman world has no inherent meaning, one's response to it might be a purely subjective relativism. This relativistic hermeneutic is often illustrated with reference to "The Doubloon" chapter, in which characters express radically divergent interpretations of a gold coin riveted to the ship's mast. Alternatively, pondering the "dumb blankness" of a godless universe could lead one to nihilism. Such is the frightening prospect Ishmael envisions in "The Whiteness of the Whale" chapter. What if we admitted that the colors, the impressions of beauty that we attribute to the visible world are "but subtile deceits, not actually inherent in substances, but only laid on from without; so that all deified Nature absolutely paints like the harlot, whose allurements cover nothing but the charnel-house within"? Pascal recorded his fright at perceiving the emptiness of outer space. Two centuries later, Melville voices the terror of feeling that our total planetary environment is devoid of spiritual meaning or divine presence. If Ishmael's orphaned state figures our plight as post-Cartesian human beings,[38] as souls presumably bereft of a Divine Father's loving kindness, then the world's whiteness betokens the possibility of a hopelessness worse than death at the very heart of material being:

> Is it that by its definiteness it shadows forth the heartless voids and immensities of the universe, and thus stabs us from behind with the thought of annihilation, when beholding the white depths of the milky way? Or is it, that as in essence whiteness is not so much a color as the visible absence of color, and at the same time the concrete of all colors; is it for these reasons that there is such a dumb

blankness, full of meaning, in a wide landscape of snows—a color-
less, all-color of atheism, from which we shrink? (165)

Yet the book's critical skepticism is so penetrating that we are likewise
urged to doubt the final validity of nihilism and relativism. At a little lower
layer of reflection, Melville exposes even doubt to skeptical scrutiny. As Hawthorne astutely observed, Melville could "neither believe nor be comfortable in
his unbelief; and he is too honest and courageous not to try to do one or the
other."[39] Characters like Ahab are *probably* wrong to believe they can discover
some absolute truth that is "the key to it all"(20)—but for Melville, not even
this point can be established with absolute certainty. If any character in *Moby-
Dick* does encounter ultimate reality, it is Pip, the black cabin boy from Connecticut who almost drowns during a chase when he jumps from a whaleboat
into the ocean's "heartless immensity." During the trauma of what might be
called a near-death experience, Pip receives something like a mystical vision
of Creation in the very process of divine formation. Such, at least, is the suggestion conveyed by Melville's poetic report of how the lonely castaway had
been

> carried down alive to wondrous depths, where strange shapes of the
> unwarped primal world glided to and fro before his passive eyes;
> and the miser-merman, Wisdom, revealed his hoarded heaps; and
> among the joyous, heartless, ever-juvenile eternities, Pip saw the
> multitudinous, god-omnipresent, coral insects, that out of the firma-
> ment of waters heaved the colossal orbs. He saw God's foot upon
> the treadle of the loom, and spoke it; and therefore his shipmates
> called him mad. So man's insanity is heaven's sense. (321–322)

But Melville insists that even if someone managed, on unpredictable occasions of unearthly insight, to glimpse "God's foot upon the treadle of the
loom," that person could never assimilate the vision into normal human life
in the world. Pip is dismissed as mad. His discovery, whether or not it is
religiously authentic, remains incommunicable. It remains useless, too, because "heaven's sense" is so far removed from the worldly facts of everyday
life. Melville next novel, *Pierre*, elaborates this point by setting the absolute
standard of "Chronometricals" apart from the worldly measure of "Horologi-
cals." For all practical purposes, therefore, the "end of nature," if nature has a
telos, must be deemed inscrutable, like the undecipherable marks on Queequeg's coffin. Ironically, both well-tempered Ishmael and hot-tempered Ahab
agree that the whale's meaning is naturally inscrutable. But Ishmael accepts
this limitation, whereas Ahab says he hates it, resolving to control both the
animal and its import.

What conclusions, then, might be drawn about the dominant response to
natural theology presented by *Moby-Dick*? Through rather than despite its skepticism, the work's prime contribution to religious thought is what I take to be
a critical pursuit consistent with the via negativa tradition of Jewish and Chris-

tian spirituality. Thus, beyond all his teasing ambiguities, Melville offers some fairly clear indications of who God is *not*, where God is *not* to be found, and what the nonhuman world is *not*. For if God exists, God remains unknowable within the usual conditions of human life. Scattered hints of the divine might be gleaned from Pip's epiphany, or from the engagement with affliction embodied by "the Man of Sorrows" who was "the truest of all men" (328). For the most part, though, God is a felt absence rather than a presence in *Moby-Dick*. The Word remains silent, the Weaver of fate invisible.

So we may reliably conclude that Captain Ahab is not God, though Peleg calls him a " 'grand, ungodly, god-like man' " (78), and though his arrogance leads him to claim divine sovereignty over nonhuman creation as well as his crew. Moby Dick, too, is assuredly not God—or, for that matter, the Devil, which for Voltaire amounted to the same thing. Though Ahab knows better, he willfully attributes supernatural powers to Moby Dick for the sake of expressing his quarrel with the gods. Superstitious crew members imagine the whale to be ubiquitous and immortal. Both parties are wrong. This whale is not God, and Melville portrays its behavior as perfectly explicable in secular terms. And insofar as Moby Dick stands in this story for the whole Creation, it follows that the nonhuman world is not divine. Nature may or may not appear "good," in the light of human moral judgments, but it is not God. Nor is it demonic.

This Melvillean postulate has far-reaching implications. It assaults the foundations of all nature religion, including traditional animism as well as Transcendental idealism. In itself, though, it poses no direct conflict with the teachings of revealed religion preserved in Abrahamic faiths. These traditions typically understand Creation to be good, perhaps even a vessel of pneumenal energy and godliness, but not a personal presence identical with the Creator. C. S. Lewis argued that transcendent monotheism can actually heighten appreciation not only of nature's commonplace earthiness but also of its potential for spiritual signification. "It is surely," he wrote, "because the natural objects are no longer taken to be themselves Divine that they can now be magnificent symbols of Divinity." So "by emptying Nature of divinity—or, let us say, of divinities—you may fill her with Deity, for she is now the bearer of messages," whereas "there is a sense in which Nature worship silences her."[40]

Melville's naturalism does run squarely against the religious orthodoxy of his day, however, in its skepticism toward usual views of divine Providence. Sustaining Calvinist tradition, Father Mapple delivers a fearful warning that God's will immediately directs every event, every detail of life in nature and human affairs. The behavior of Jonah's whale, the tempest that surrounds Jonah's ship when he tries to escape, and even the "shrieking, slanting storm" that accompanies Mapple's preaching—for Father Mapple, all of these apparently natural phenomena directly manifest God's Providence. There is no room for chance, secondary causality, or genuine tragedy in this worldview, which interprets all actions as signs of God's scheme for human reward-and-punishment. God himself might remain hidden, inscrutable in essence,[41] but his intentions were usually plain. Father Mapple means to leave no ambiguity in the minds of his hard-salted listeners that " 'wilful disobedience of the command of God' " (49) produces direct, visible consequences in this world.

Of course Melville disagreed. Although Ahab's demise *might* be construed as just punishment for his hubris, little else in Melville's tale supports a Providential reading and much belies it. That Ishmael survives from the *Pequod*, for example, while Queequeg and all the rest perish scarcely demonstrates the narrator's singular virtue. It is just a quirky, amoral turn of events that illustrates life's unpredictability rather than divine justice. Particularly through Melville's elaborated zoological comments, *Moby-Dick* portrays whales and other sea animals not merely as agents of some higher will, whether human or divine, but as creatures with lives of their own that may strike us as implacably alien. This wild alterity often looks terrifying when it takes the form of a shark or great squid.

Moby Dick's victory over Ahab dramatizes the free, uncontrollable dynamism of nonhuman creation despite aggressive human efforts to control the sea. To be sure, humanity's hegemony over nature, including oceanic nature, has expanded enormously since Melville's era of perilous whaling voyages in wooden ships. Yet, even today, the nonhuman world retains a certain freedom insofar as countless of its organisms still act in ways beyond our immediate knowledge or control. This secular principle of an inherent freedom in nature also bears theological implications. For as Milton demonstrates throughout *Paradise Lost*, God endowed human beings with a radical freedom that ensures the persistence of moral evil.[42] Similarly, God may allow a free dynamism to operate through nonhuman creation as well, thereby opening space for that wild amorality we perceive as metaphysical evil. Such, at least, is the logic embraced by some contemporary theological movements—including versions of process theology and what has recently been called "open theism."[43] As I will discuss later, this affirmation of Creation's radical freedom, involving rejection of a strictly interventionist Providence, is likewise a major premise of Annie Dillard's spirituality in *Pilgrim at Tinker Creek*. Admittedly, Melville's agnostic outlook cannot be brought into precise focus with these theistic perspectives since the wild liberty of the sea world in *Moby-Dick* is linked to the felt absence of God, for Melville a possibly permanent void.

But insofar as the author of *Moby-Dick* entertained the possibility that scriptural theism offered a true expression of the "wisdom that is woe," he found the most compelling text for that possibility in the Book of Job. Long recognized as a crucial point of reference for *Moby-Dick*, Job's interactive dialogues clearly influenced Melville's fictive struggle to confront evil and affliction. Furthermore, the Book of Job offered Melville rare biblical precedent for a nonanthropocentric theology of nature.[44] The divine voice that speaks from the whirlwind in chapters 37–41 presses Job to envision the splendidly unfettered bearing of creatures such as the lion, wild goat, raven, ostrich, and eagle. Job cannot hope to domesticate or to understand fully those grand presences named, in language familiar to Melville through the Authorized Version, as Behemoth and Leviathan. What is more, even the Creator does not choose to exercise direct mechanical control over such free-spirited beasts. "Who hath sent out the wild ass free?" God demands of Job, and "Wilt thou hunt the prey for the lion?" (Job 39:5, 38:39). The whirlwind voice, which Job heeds in silence but Ahab hears too late if at all, fairly drips with sarcasm toward humanity's Faustian dream of total resource management: "canst thou draw out leviathan with an hook? or his tongue with a cord which thou lettest down?" (Job 41:1).

We know that Melville was ill disposed to emulate Job's final act of abject repentance before an awful, omnipotent deity. Yet the philosophy of nature embodied in *Moby-Dick* does coincide with Job's vision of a divinely unknowable and unfettered Creation beyond the scope of human mastery. Ahab sees the whale as nothing but an inert wall on which to project his rage. Job, however, is forced to look beyond himself, beyond the furthest horizon of human pain, toward a cosmically expansive view of life. Viewed within this grand tableau of all Creation, human suffering is not explained or erased—but it does look smaller than it had. It comes indeed as a revelation to Job that untold numbers of sentient nonhuman beings who know or care nothing of him are sustained each day in lives of their own while connected to the world's One Life. The Job-author's vision of a genuinely free, sometimes terrifying dynamic at the heart of the material world stands in sharp contrast to all fixed categories of fate, chance, and foreknowledge. Wherever "the truth of it all" lay for Melville, it did not lie with the conventional pieties dispensed by Job's false counselors. Even Job's whirlwind God, who also insists on correcting Job, confirms these men to be liars. Despite differences in their advice, all of them cling to the Deuteronomic creed, with its confidence in a moral order governed by God's law of reward and retribution.

Faith in such certainties, and in manifest interventions of a benevolent Providence, had ebbed so far by Melville's time that one no longer expects to hear a God-voice emerge from the tempests in *Moby Dick*. We hear Ishmael's voice, but all the rest is silence by the story's close. And though Ishmael survives, he ends up bereft not only of soulmates and kin but even of a definite land address to call home. Orphaned in the "heartless voids" of an unstable world, he claims no positive knowledge of where, or even if, the divine parent's presence survives. The work gives heartfelt testimony, though, to the spiritual uses of critical skepticism. For Melville, such skepticism combined Kantian techniques of doubt, as dialogically set forth in the two Critiques,[45] with rigorous scrutiny of creaturely nature—a project consonant with the mystic's negative way in both Western and Eastern traditions.

6

"Rare and Delectable Places"

Thoreau's Imagination of Sacred Space at Walden

Spirits of Concord

Few classic works of American literature are so intensely identified
with a particular geographic site as Thoreau's *Walden*. Today the setting of this experiment in solitary living near the village of Concord,
Massachusetts, remains a tourist mecca—and qualifies, for many, as
a literary shrine. In fact, an energetic woman who resided in my
corner of Connecticut helped for some years to lead a group called
Walden Forever Wild, Inc., in its efforts to designate the pond area a
Massachusetts State Sanctuary on the grounds that "its spiritual
sanctity should be preserved beyond demands for local use."[1] Textual
evidence suggests that Thoreau, too, regarded the pond precincts as
sacred space but in a more complicated—and, I think, more deeply
Transcendental—way. His most celebrated book underscores the belief that this place he had known from childhood, this remnant of a
wilder New England so close to civilization, was not just an attractive place to live cheaply and freely. As the focal point of Thoreau's
Romantic naturalism, it was also the locus of his worship and spiritual discovery. In other published writings Thoreau offers descriptive commentary on diverse sites he had visited, including Cape
Cod, the Maine Woods, the Concord and Merrimack rivers, and Wa-
chusett Mountain. But in the singular case of that book, originally
subtitled "life in the woods," Thoreau reflects at length on a place he
had not only visited but inhabited.

Much has been written, of course, about the crucial matter of
Thoreau's response to the nonhuman world. That Thoreau sustained a lifelong belief in the spiritual significations of nature, despite the heightened attention he showed after 1850 toward scientific

details of his material environment, has generally been acknowledged.[2] But
what did it actually mean for Thoreau to regard Walden Pond and the surrounding woodlands as sacred space? For that matter, just how might one
define Thoreau's sense of the sacred, as conjoined with his fundamentally
religious apprehension of nature? And how, finally, did Thoreau's syncretistic,
largely non-Christian theology of nature nonetheless incorporate selected
themes of biblical Christianity? Such are the main questions I want to address
here.

Consistent with the richly allusive character of *Walden*, Thoreau sounds
several dimensions of the sacred in his portrayal of the pond and its environs.
While the Transcendental belief at issue here is largely "pagan" in orientation,
a faith commonly described as pantheistic and as substantially influenced by
Asian philosophy and religion, Thoreau also drew heavily on scriptural and
other elements of Christian tradition to map the distinctive spiritual geography
represented in Walden. There is, for example, clear biblical precedent—especially throughout the Exodus narratives—for the paradoxical tension Thoreau
sustains between devotion to his own "Holy Land" of Concord and his self-
description as a "saunterer" journeying perpetually through the world without
attachment to home or property.[3] He is at once well rooted to place, or (as he
puts it in "The Bean-Field" chapter) "attached . . . to the earth," and the unencumbered sojourner. He has, in short, "travelled a good deal in Concord."[4]
Despite Thoreau's rejection of organized religion and his unceasing jibes
against Christian churches and clerics, his allusions to biblical texts actually
became more pervasive in *Walden* than they had been previously in the *Week*.[5]
And despite disdainful remarks about God's "personality,"[6] Thoreau's version
of nature mysticism incorporates elements of traditional Christian belief in a
personal Creator and in the world as divine Creation.

Did Thoreau, then, believe in a personal God? Because of his fondness for
Transcendental inconsistency and distaste for articulated doctrine, the question
admits of no simple answer. On the one hand, his writing commonly personalizes the deity through its pronoun references and its figurative portrayals of
God as Creator, as the "original proprietor" of Walden Pond—and as congenial
artisan, speaker, or musician. The journal confirms that in his maturity, Thoreau was more often willing than Emerson was at a comparable phase to address God as a presence beyond himself, as a someone he could imagine to
be both the object and the source of love. Not surprisingly, this affective dimension of Thoreau's tentative theism appears more prominently in journal
entries recorded soon after the gruesome death of his brother John in 1842,
when the pain of Henry's loneliness was most acute. On the other hand, it is
hard to know just how seriously or literally to take Thoreau's playful images
of divinity—or for that matter, his related personifications of the Pond and
other features of nature. Moreover, other references in the journal and elsewhere seem to support the more typically Emersonian conception of a thoroughly internalized or impersonal deity. Though the coloration of Thoreau's
beliefs changed over time, he remained emphatic in his rejection of Jesus'
unique divinity and of the Hebraic image of a stern and jealous "Jehovah." In

a journal entry recorded in April or May of 1850, he expressed his preference for the "purer more independent and impersonal knowledge of God"[7] he saw represented in the contemplative writings of Vedic Hinduism; yet Hindu tradition is itself elusive and elastic with regard to concepts of divine personality or polytheism.

Above all, Thoreau insisted that "God," if authentically divine and transcendent, must transcend all human images and description. This apophatic awareness of God as truly ineffable Being appears in many sacred texts of Hinduism and Buddhism (including the Upanishads and Zen works not known to Thoreau by the time he wrote *Walden*) as well as in Christian writings such as the *Mystical Theology* by Pseudo-Dionysius the Areopagite, a sixth-century Syrian monk, and the fourteenth-century *Cloud of Unknowing*. For Thoreau, however, the personal God that Christian churches of his day purported to worship was nothing more than a frightfully enlarged human person, a grossly anthropomorphic projection. "All the gods that are worshipped have been men," he declared in his journal for 1849, "but of the true God of whom none have conceived—all men combined would hardly furnish the germ" (*PJ* 3: 7). If he could not describe such a Being, he nonetheless regarded naturalistic experience as his chief means of pursuing "the true God." *Walden* marks a critical stage in his lifelong quest to embrace a sacred reality whose essence he could not hope to explain.

Perhaps the first thing to notice, rhetorically, in approaching *Walden* is the regularity with which Thoreau uses the word "sacred"—to evoke not a distinct supernatural order, but a transcendent dimension of this physical world antithetical to the "profane."[8] For Thoreau, the "profane" is associated not just with overt degradation but also with commonplace dullness or inertia, with failure to realize the divine fullness of Transcendental imagination. Often, too, he links the profane quite physically to human alterations or deformations of the landscape. He remarks, for example, on how the "the woodcutters, and the railroad, and I myself have profaned Walden" (*W* 197).

In Mircea Eliade's classic formulation, sacred space is a place set apart as "exceptional," a spot regarded as auspicious for experiencing some opening toward the transcendent. For Eliade, the sacred place "constitutes a break in the homogeneity of space, so that archaic peoples readily perceive it to stand symbolically as the Center of the World and nearest abode to heaven."[9] And insofar as the sacred corresponds most broadly to an experience of the numinous—that is, to an encounter with something "wholly other," beyond the usual bounds of human culture, the nonhuman world of nature is evidently allied to the numinous. Confronting nature's "wildness" has at least a potential religious value, then, insofar as it helps us, in Thoreau's words, "to witness our own limits transgressed, and some life pasturing freely where we never wander." Despite his occasional labor as a surveyor setting boundaries, Thoreau is most intrigued by the human hunger for boundlessness, our desire "that all things be mysterious and unexplorable, that land and sea be infinitely wild, unsurveyed and unfathomed by us because unfathomable" (*W* 317–318).

Eliade's description of how "primitive peoples" ritualize space is, I think, strikingly applicable to Thoreau's project of reaching beyond the desacralizing tendencies of post-Enlightenment civilization to recover a spiritually archaic or "original relation to the universe."[10] It is particularly relevant to the second chapter of *Walden*, which is replete with place references, both geographic and figurative. When Thoreau presents his central statement on "Where I Lived and What I Lived For," even the chapter title ties his broader search for existential purpose to a particular locale. Just as Thoreau's reasons for living at Walden go well beyond his initial plan to finish writing *A Week on the Concord and Merrimack Rivers* there, so also his cognizance of the place itself—or, as we might say colloquially, of "where he's at"—expands beyond the mapspace to further planes of perception. In this key second chapter we are urged to believe that meditating on *where* the author lived will also clarify just *what* makes life worth living. After first describing the physical coordinates of his address—by a small pond, low in the woods, about "a mile and a half south of the village of Concord" (*W* 86), Thoreau looks toward loftier horizons of space and time to see himself seated indeed at the divine center of things. What he calls "one of the best things which I did," his morning practice of bathing daily in the pond, becomes a "religious exercise" (88) not only of interior self-renewal but also of ritualized connection to his outdoor environment. Like the communal purification rites of traditional peoples, yet in terms consistent with Christian understanding, such activity becomes for Thoreau a true "sacrament"—that is, an " 'outward and visible sign of an inward and spiritual grace' " (69).[11] If *where Henry lives*, legally speaking, is only a parcel of Waldo's real estate,[12] he has nonetheless claimed it by power of imagination—and by squatter's rights of occupation—as the property of his own spirit.

One way Thoreau imaginatively establishes Walden's status as a sacred place is through his application of temple imagery to the pond, to the pine groves and forest topography, and especially to the author's self-constructed house. "Verily," he writes in his journal for 1845, "a good house is a temple—A clean house—pure and undefiled, as the saying is. I have seen such made of white pine" (*PJ* 2:156). For Thoreau, of course, the temple's aura of localized sanctity derived from Greco-Roman and Asian religious systems as well as from Hebrew scriptures and Christian tradition. Yet Walden, envisioned with vital particularity in all seasons, is clearly Thoreau's place of worship—his church, in the physical sense of a finite space. Punning on the place-name of this "Walled-in" refuge from competitive society (183), the author envisions the shores of his pond—elsewhere litanized as "God's drop" (194)—to be set apart from the profane world. Walden is "a gem of the first water" (179), a reservoir of original cosmogonal purity said to be bottomless.[13] Here indeed "the morning wind forever blows, the poem of creation is uninterrupted" (85). Though we are "wont to imagine rare and delectable places" of divine presence in the far reaches of outer space, Thoreau discovers that his "house actually had its site in such a withdrawn, but forever new and unprofaned, part of the universe." If "in eternity there is indeed something true and sublime," Thoreau confirms that "all these times and places and occasions" of transcendence "are now and here" since "God himself culminates in the present moment and will never be more divine in the lapse of all the ages" (88, 97).

Thus, Thoreau's contemplative engagement with Walden, supported by the physical involvement of his daily immersion ritual, amounts to a centering exercise. For Thoreau, the pond defines "where I lived" not only geographically but also on that spiritual, existential plane at a right angle to the *axis mundi*. Walden qualifies all the more as a sacred center because the author can imagine the unpeopled space around him to be "as much Asia or Africa as New England" (130).

But just how welcome, in the face of our current environmental predicament, should we find Thoreau's emphasis on the sacred potential of wildness? Should we really believe that in "Wildness is the preservation [or, in Aldo Leopold's telling misquotation, the "salvation"] of the World?"[14] How helpful to our circumstance is Thoreau's insistence on preserving "rare and delectable places" at some remove from urban society? Not very, according to some recent commentators. In fact, the impulse to valorize wilderness terrain as uniquely godly by contrast with the presumably fallen, corrupted state of all settled landscapes has been called unfortunate and even pernicious. Some, including the distinguished environmental historian William Cronon, have blamed Thoreau for contributing to this enduring myth of the Romantic sublime. According to such critics, present-day wilderness advocates inspired by Thoreau typically fail to recognize that wilderness is always a cultural construct and that the ideal of recovering a pristine, sanctified face of nature is always illusory. Nature is, by its very nature, ever-changing. So to make a fetish of protecting roadless territories from human influence will only distract us, say some, from the real environmental challenge, which is learning how to make our home wisely in this physical world. Thus, Cronon includes in his published edition of symposium pieces on the theme of "reinventing nature" an essay of his own significantly titled "The Trouble with Wilderness; or Getting Back to the Wrong Nature."[15]

Now it is certainly true, as I've already noted, that Thoreau sacralizes features of his physical landscape, often drawing on temple imagery in the process. For him the leaves of the wild andromeda were, according to one journal entry, "stained windows in the cathedral of my world" (*PJ* 4:471). It is likewise evident that some of the author's descriptions of untamed nature, including his well-known account of ascending Mount Katahdin in *The Maine Woods*, reflect an awestruck fascination with wilderness—responses linked to notions of the sublime that had become commonplace by the eighteenth century.[16]

Yet in several key respects, Thoreau's spirituality of place transcends those naive versions of Romantic wilderness worship with which it is often equated. Instead of fetishizing the Concord woods as exotic or monumentally sublime, Thoreau cherishes them as his home ground. The authorial consciousness of *Walden* shows an elaborate self-awareness of how imagination, in the spirit of Wordsworth, half-creates what it perceives about a place's hierophanic power. Particularly in his concluding chapters, Thoreau presents Walden's landscape—despite his fondly detailed delineation of it—as more exemplary than unique. This place, in other words, becomes for him at once exceptional and commonplace—and as Transcendental commonplace, opens toward anyone's spiritual epiphany much as the village common does in chapter 1 of Emerson's *Nature*. By centering attention now on two epiphanic moments in *Walden*, we might begin to grasp how this work imaginatively recreates the author's spiritual relation to his environment.

Active and Contemplative Religion

The first telling episode is Thoreau's account of morning meditation toward the beginning of the chapter "Sounds." Having first declared his love for a "broad margin" to his life, the author relates how he had sometimes confined himself quite narrowly within the frame of his doorway for an entire summer morning. There he simply sat in the sun, "rapt in a revery, amidst the pines and hickories and sumachs, in undisturbed solitude and stillness, while the birds sang around or flitted noiseless through the house." Thus oblivious to the passage of time, he says he "realized what the Orientals mean by contemplation and the forsaking of works" (111–112).[17] The sacred character of such repose is confirmed by journal entries in which he aspires to be "as still as God is," or praises that animal contentment which he supposes "comes of resting quietly in God's palm" (*PJ* 1:349, 371).

Particularly noteworthy for my purposes is the way Thoreau sets his account of meditative engagement with nature squarely inside a domestic portal. The open doorway, like the window at which the observer-listener sits later on in "Sounds," corresponds to Eliade's image of the mythical threshold. It marks a boundary not only between two physical spaces but also between "two modes of being, the profane and the religious."[18] For Thoreau, though, the doorway becomes a fluid, not fixed, frontier between indoor and outdoor environments, just as the chapter as a whole recollects a mélange of sounds produced by civilized commerce and nonhuman creatures. While birds pass freely *into* his house, the author's soul passes outside its wood frame to encounter the uncut pines, hickories, and sumacs. As Sherman Paul and others have stressed over the years,[19] Thoreau's primary interaction with nature's wildness at Walden occurs not amid geophysical wilderness but in more settled territory. For Thoreau, as for Aldo Leopold, "wildness" is not synonymous with "wilderness." *Walden* conspicuously lacks the emphasis on exoticism, on images of scenic grandeur, associated with most wilderness travel literature. And it is certainly concerned with how to make a home in nature, starting at the most graphically literal plane of construction.

Thoreau, unlike some present-day deep ecologists, does not condemn every human alteration of the landscape as a deformation. This point is evident from his willingness to cultivate the earth in chapter 7, "The Bean-Field." Beyond the practical value of raising crops such as beans and corn, his spade labor in a "half-cultivated field" (*W* 158) near his house connects him more solidly to the soil—and to the original dust of his own nature. It also reinforces his spiritual kinship with Native Americans who once worked the same plot, likewise raising beans and corn. While censuring typical farming practices of his day, Thoreau insists that agriculture qualified in ancient tradition as "a sacred art," and that something of the sacred calling of "husbandry" might still be recovered through morally reflective engagement with the soil.

Granted, Thoreau's own garden version of farming never became a full-time occupation or sole means of support. His hoeing and weeding in the dirt nonetheless offer a much earthier picture of encounter with sacred nature than does the tourist's awestruck gaze at some titanic cataract. Thus, the author's much-discussed pastoralism bears religious as well as sociocultural significance. Though American pastoral often supports an unreflective and regressive ideology of nostalgia,[20] the version of agrarianism cultivated most assiduously in "The Bean-Field" is self-consciously religious insofar as it offers a ritual discipline, a practical means of working out one's salvation. Growing beans not only helped Thoreau heal his culturally inherited alienation from the earth but also mediated his limited connection with human society through the market economy. Unlike the subsistence farmer, this planter bartered his beans for rice.

That Thoreau typically calls his habitation a house, not a cabin or shack,[21] underscores his willingness to enrich his life in the woods with what he takes to be the best things of civilization—including books and writing instruments. Toward more intrusive activities of the industrial world, such as the noisy rush of the Fitchburg Railroad or the winter work of ice cutters on the pond, he betrays attitudes ranging from scornful satire to cheerful acceptance. Even commerce, though, can sometimes find a place in Thoreau's sacral vision of nature. After telegraph wires reach Concord in 1851, Thoreau testifies in his journal to the delight and "revelation" he experiences in hearing celestial music of the "telegraphy harp" (*PJ* 4:89–91, 5:436). In *Walden*, he muses with satisfaction that when New England merchants sell pond ice to India, the "pure Walden water," which he likes to consider "as sacred as the Ganges," might mingle in fact "with the sacred water of the Ganges" (*W* 192, 298).

Sandbank Visions of Numinous Evolution

Nowhere is this comprehensive quality of Thoreau's vision more apparent than in the justly renowned railroad-cut passage found in the book's penultimate chapter, "Spring." This stunning etymological rhapsody starts from the simple act of observing the flow of sand and clay on the bankside of the rail cut, at the pond's western edge, during spring thaw. Warmed by sunlight, the icy sand flows down "like lava" (see fig. 6.1). The cosmogonic story continues as sand-streams form themselves into leaves and vines. Then, swept by a copious stream of linguistic correspondences emanating from the word "lobe," these vegetative leaves turn into fatty leaves suggestive of animal parts and, finally, of the human body. For, after all, "what is man but a mass of thawing clay?" (307).

FIGURE 6.1. Sand foliage from deep cut on railroad, Concord, Massachusetts, March 17, 1900. (Photo by Herbert W. Gleason. Courtesy of Concord Free Library.)

What Thoreau envisions in this common earthbank, which is clearly an artifact of rail commerce rather than a fact of wilderness nature, is nothing less than Lucretius's nature of all things. With benefit of imagination, one gazes here into the mystery of life itself. Before Thoreau's eyes, the world evolves almost instantly from chaos to cosmos, from primordial energy to the leaves of his own book-in-progress. The full course of Creation appears, in a progression from lava sand through vegetable leaf to human consciousness, as imaged in the great tree of language.[22] Exposed through the centering omphalos of the deep cut are both Culture and Nature, art and animality.

Within this dynamically evolutionary tableau of Creation, Thoreau none-theless finds room for a divine maker with personal attributes. Rather than pantheism, such a theology has been aptly termed panentheism, because it regards the whole universe as a divine milieu while recognizing the presence of a Transcendent God who in some manner exceeds the bounds of this created universe.[23] Earlier, Thoreau had playfully described his pleasure at receiving winter visits from that "old settler and original proprietor, who is reported to have dug Walden Pond, and stoned it, and fringed it with pine woods; who tells me stories of old time and of new eternity" (137). This congenial deity had, the author teases, used a "divining rod" (182) to site the excavation for Walden's well. Through another pun, Thoreau had likened a legal bequest to the deter-minations of a personal Creator who "rounded this water with his hand, deep-ened and clarified it in his thought, and in his will bequeathed it to Concord" (93). Now he is moved to describe a God who combines the scientist's *sapientia*, in this case involving zeal for experimental knowledge, with the artist's love of cosmos, or beauty:

What makes this sand foliage remarkable is its springing into exis-tence thus suddenly. When I see on the one side the inert bank,— for the sun acts on one side first,—and on the other this luxuriant foliage, the creation of an hour, I am affected as if in a peculiar sense I stood in the laboratory of the Artist who made the world and me,—had come to where he was still at work, sporting on this bank, and with excess of energy strewing his fresh designs about. I feel as if I were nearer to the vitals of the globe, for this sandy overflow is something such a foliaceous mass as the vitals of the animal body. You find thus in the very sands an anticipation of the vegetable leaf. No wonder that the earth expresses itself outwardly in leaves, it so labors with the idea inwardly. The atoms have already learned this law, and are pregnant by it. The overhanging leaf sees here its proto-type. *Internally*, whether in the globe or animal body, it is a moist thick *lobe*, a word especially applicable to the liver and lungs and the leaves of fat. . . . Thus it seemed that this one hillside illustrated the principle of all the operations of Nature. The Maker of this earth but patented a leaf. What Champollion will decipher this hieroglyphic for us, that we may turn over a new leaf at last? This phenomenon is more exhilarating to me than the luxuriance and fertility of vine-yards. True, it is somewhat excrementitious in its character, and there is no end to the heaps of liver lights and bowels, as if the globe were turned wrong side outward; but this suggests at least that Nature has some bowels, and there again is mother of human-ity. (306–308)

In the cutaway moment, Thoreau comes to a place where the Creator is "still at work." While he ends up recapitulating the entire course of temporal cosmology, he testifies above all to the essential dynamism of *bios*, the encapsulated drama of a continuous creation. And within this drama he, too, plays a discernible role. Thoreau's representation of numinous nature advances, therefore, from more conventionally static images of sacred space to this dynamic icon of sacred mystery. To perceive the wonder of inhabiting a continuously regenerative and divine creation is, above all, to appreciate the wildness of life as *bios*. For "it is in vain," Thoreau tells his journal in 1856, "to dream of a wildness distant from ourselves. There is none such. It is the bog in our brain and bowels, the primitive vigor of Nature in us, that inspires that dream."[24] The elemental bios revealed in the railroad cut, which runs from the excremental depth of bowels to the mental heights of humankind's cranial "lobe," encompasses more than botany and zoology to embrace those interlayered zones of reality that the philosopher Ken Wilber discusses under the headings of physiosphere, biosphere, and noosphere.[25] Geography, then, is consequential but never sacred unto itself. The railroad deep cut, though discovered near Walden, could run as well through the Bronx or anywhere else.

The sand foliage passage seems to me remarkable not for its exposé of the author's personal psychology—or pathology, as some analysts would suggest—but for its bold intellectual synthesis, its bid to reenvision nature's numinosity in the new light of evolutionary theory. Some years before encountering Darwin, Thoreau had already begun to reflect seriously on competing views of evolutionary change (or, in the contemporary idiom, of "development") debated in scientific works such as Robert Chambers's *Vestiges of the Natural History of Creation* (1844), Asa Gray's *Manual of the Botany of the Northern United States* (1848), and Louis Agassiz's *Principles of Zoology* (1851, coauthored with Augustus Gould).[26] Like most of the new biology, and likewise consonant with the new geography of Alexander Humboldt and new geology of Charles Lyell, Thoreau's naturalism had by midcentury recognized the vast expanse of time required for changes in landforms and species. In an earlier but revised journal version of the sand foliage passage, while pondering that grand "interval" between earth's preorganic state and the appearance of "luxuriant vegetation," Thoreau refers incredulously to Bishop Usher's quaint chronology in which God "is reputed to have built this world 6000 years ago" (*PJ* 2:577). Yet Lyell could observe by 1830 that even geologists needed to revise drastically their estimation of time after discovering they had misread physical signs of change once believed to take "thousands of years where the language of nature signified millions."[27] In the same era, higher criticism was highlighting the historical, time-conditioned circumstances of biblical revelation. Just as scientists were discovering the vast temporal scale of natural history and the prevalence of process rather than permanence in environmental analysis, theologians were advancing an evolutionary hermeneutic that found the Bible's eternal truths incarnated in ever-changing circumstances and fallible personages.[28]

Though gathered into a single moment, then, the evolutionary vision Thoreau perceives in the sandbank is expansive across immense intervals of time. It is also teleological and spiritual rather than purely materialistic. Like Robert Chambers, Thoreau had largely disavowed traditional versions of natural theology that featured an argument from design, the special creation of diverse species, and belief that God frequently intervened in physical processes. In fact, the anonymous author of *Vestiges of the Natural History of Creation* was widely suspected of teaching pernicious atheism. Privately, Chambers apparently did wrestle with religious skepticism.[29] His book nonetheless affirmed that God was "ever present in all things." Although the First Cause did not create by "some sort of immediate or special exertion," the organic universe reflected an unfolding of divine will in accord with primal law, including "advances of the principle of development" through "the whole train of animated beings." For Chambers, the observable facts of life "clearly shew how all the various organic forms of our world are bound up in one—how a fundamental unity pervades and embraces them all" in a system conceived from one "law or decree of the Almighty," though "it did not all come forth at one time." So the creative flux of development is ongoing, just as the processes by which bodies come to be formed in space are "still and at present in progress."[30] Chambers's account of a continuous creation, of an evolution inspired from within matter rather than manipulated successively and supernaturally from without, anticipates Thoreau's own portrayal of sacred cosmology toward the close of *Walden*.

A century later, the scientist-theologian Pierre Teilhard de Chardin would find ways of reconnecting such an evolutionary theology of radical immanence to overtly Christian spirituality. But Thoreau, and subsequently Whitman, were the first Americans to turn a theology of natural "development" into poetry. As Boudreau suggests,

> perhaps the emergent Darwinian view of nature demanded a muse that had its expression in Thoreau, for *Walden* attains its climactic vision over a thawing bankside in a way to anticipate the tangled bank in the concluding teleological and—dare it be said?—transcendent vision in *The Origin of Species*, published five years after *Walden*.[31]

Yet the microcosmic revelation of the deep cut only reveals itself by virtue of a human interpreter. If "this one hillside illustrated the principle of all the operations of Nature" so that "the Maker of this earth but patented a leaf," such disclosure requires a discerning reader of the hillside—and, by extension, of Thoreau's text. Thus, the sand foliage passage must in some sense be read through the book's chapters on "Reading" and "Sounds." There Thoreau insists that serious reading involves a reflective discipline capable of leading us to gaze upon divinity and, as he subsequently affirms, to look "always at what is to be seen." Since "much is published, but little printed," one must learn to read nature by decoding its visible and aural signs—just as one must know the "particular written languages" of books to discern their meaning (W 99, 111). To read birds, for example, requires familiarity with the articulated sounds of each species. Learning to look with understanding at what is already "before you" in the text, field, or sandbank is essentially, then, a problem of hermeneutics. For Thoreau, the material facts of nature are usually significant, but their transcendental import is never self-evident. Sustained reflection is needed to discern those "essential facts of life" lurking in Walden's woods. So while Thoreau's linguistic, psychological, and other concerns have been usefully discussed in connection with the sand foliage passage, I think its most innovative contribution to the environmental imagination is hermeneutical.

In this light, the episode dramatizes a highly developed recognition that humans always and inevitably interpret the facts of nature. Thoreau's ideal is to read—and thereby to live—deliberately, so that the interpretive act becomes fully self-conscious. In so interpreting nature, the integrative imagination reunites the divided realms of human and nonhuman life. When the poet "takes a fact out of nature into spirit," he becomes conscious of that grander, cosmic consciousness in which nature speaks "along with him" (PJ 69).

Of course, the idea of "reading" the book of nature in a manner comparable to that of scriptural revelation had already been entertained by many in America. In a previous century, Edwards had found "the Book of Scripture" to be "the interpreter of the book of Nature." In Thoreau's own day, Emerson had not only responded to new biblical approaches associated with the "higher criticism" of Herder and Eichhorn but had gone so far as to envision nature and the "aboriginal self" replacing Scripture as the primary locus of "revelation."[32] Yet Emerson's theory of correspondences implied a smoothly incremental progression from nature to language to spirit. And as originally formulated, Emerson's Transcendentalism discounted the world's physicality in favor of an Idealism that regarded nature as a function of human perception, an "apocalypse of the mind."[33]

While accepting much of Emerson's formulation, Thoreau ordinarily displayed more acute awareness of the split between material nature and the dynamics of human interpretation. Insofar as the physical world presents "inhuman" and "unfathomable" sites in which to "witness our own limits transgressed" (PJ 339; W 318), nature retains a transcendent otherness, a resistance to assimilation by the self.[34] "I love nature," he insisted in 1853, "partly *because* she is not man, but a retreat from him" (PJ 5:422). Accordingly, Thoreau was more insistent than Emerson about humanity's need to decipher nature's hieroglyphics. In the "Spring" chapter of *Walden*, he himself becomes the Champollion graced to transliterate the meanings inscribed in leaf and hillside.[35] And in etymological terms, to approach the nonhuman world as *hiero-glyph* (from Greek *hieros*, or sacred, and *glyph*, carving or script) was already to affirm its religious signification as sacred script. But deciphering this script required an imaginative fusion of subjective and objective sources of revelation. While thus developing his own views concerning a hermeneutics of nature, particularly around 1848 when he was shaping early drafts of the sand bank passage, Thoreau found notable inspiration in his reading of Coleridge.[36]

Since Emerson was more involved than Thoreau in ecclesiastical controversies of the day, one should not expect Thoreau to react directly to questions about the authority of biblical interpretation raised by higher criticism. Yet clearly he did respond to Coleridge, and not only by way of accepting the famous Reason versus Understanding distinction from *Aids to Reflection*. Coleridge's views on biblical hermeneutics are relevant, therefore, to appreciating Thoreau's project of developing a hermeneutics of nature even though Thoreau modified the Christian suppositions apparent in works such as *Confessions of an Inquiring Spirit* and *Hints Towards a More Comprehensive Theory of Life*.

A Coleridgean principle of scriptural exegesis directly applicable to nature is the need to interpret each particular element of the text "by the Spirit of the whole." The letters or words written in the "plain sense" of Scripture cannot, therefore, be simply equated with God's revelatory Word. To avoid naïve "bibliolatry," one must look beyond historical literalism to discern the animating "Spirit of the Whole." Thus, a kind of ecological vision of the Bible's variegated life-forms is needed to read the text rightly. And for Coleridge, it is through the subjective exercise of determining what "finds me" in the text that one verifies the Bible's objective authority as vehicle of the Holy Spirit: "Revealed Religion (and I know of no *religion* not revealed) is in its highest contemplation the Unity (the identity or coinherence) of *Subjective* and *Objective*."[37]

For Thoreau, naturalistic science would replace the church and biblical historicism as the objective component in this equation. Hence "the religion I love is very laic" (*PJ* 1:289). Rather than the company of visible saints, the visible facts of Creation became his chief source of revelation and spiritual authority beyond the human soul. His individualistic temper led him to reject Christianity's social frame of worship, its tradition of collective textual exegesis and communal spirituality.[38] Yet his exegesis of biospheric signs maintained a teleological and decidedly religious cast. The sandbank passage fulfills extravagant claims made earlier in *Walden* that "God himself," at play within the full breadth of natural history, "culminates in the present moment" and that "it is the chief end of man here to 'glorify God and enjoy him forever' " (*W* 97, 91).[39] But only a contemplative disciple of true science can see beyond prosaic materialism to find the earth revealed as "living poetry" (309). Elsewhere, Thoreau expresses the simple ambition of devoting "his life to the discovery of the divinity in Nature." His vocation as Transcendental scribe is to report "the glory of the universe"(*PJ* 4:390). The Hebrew prophet Habakkuk testifies that he stood waiting on the tower of Jerusalem for a final vision of the Lord's glory. Thoreau likewise commits himself to watching metaphorically "a whole year on the city's walls," but actually amid earth's "rich & fertile mystery," for "some trace of the ineffable." Such revelation, he insists, is more joyous than that reported by the Hebrew prophets. Yet his "profession" is comparable to theirs insofar as commits himself "to be always on the alert to find God in nature—to know his lurking places" (*PJ* 4:53–55, 315).

Thoreau pursued this spirit quest with an acute awareness of the subjective, imaginative grounds of his response to nature. At the same time, he was determined to respect the objective materiality of the nonhuman world, tirelessly presenting concrete facts to demonstrate how the *bios* of Walden sustained what Coleridge would call "a life of its own."[40] Thus, the lofty account of personal contemplation that opens "Sounds" is followed presently by an earthy catalogue of seasonally differentiated plants—including groundnut, goldenrod, pitch pine, and sand-cherry (*cerasus pumila*)—growing beside his house. The book's bestiary features not only conventionally inspiring cases such as the wild-sounding loon and the hawk sporting freely in "fields of air" but also insects such as the ant and mosquito. In "Where I Lived, and What I Lived for," Thoreau even claims that he relished hearing "the faint hum of a mosquito" passing through his living quarters at dawn. That a mosquito buzz could stir recollection of "the heroic ages" and suggest "something cosmical" about "the everlasting vigor and fertility of the world" sounds at first preposterous. More incredibly still, an earlier journal draft of the passage equates this trumpeting of a solitary mosquito directly with "θειον"—that is, with divinity (PJ 2:235). My students want to know: What's with this guy, anyway, that he brushes aside the obvious annoyance of insect bites so as to find God in a mosquito? Can this be for real?

Part of Thoreau's idea here, surely, is to extend the Romantic definition of nature beyond picturesque landscapes and appealing fauna to embrace that wealth of commonplace facts and organisms contained within the earthly "cosmos." So the mosquito becomes a homely synecdoche for Emerson's array of "natural facts," as well as a token of that biotic vigor that Annie Dillard would later describe more darkly as "fecundity." In addition, Thoreau wants to press the logic of Transcendental correspondences, though not so antagonistically as Melville or Dillard, to see whether meditative scrutiny of "particular natural facts" might confirm Emerson's supposition that "Nature is the symbol of spirit." If God is immanent throughout the cosmos of this planet's ecological systems, then why not indeed within the bios of every species, including small and reviled insects? What better test case for a nonanthropocentric view of ecology than to try imagining the mosquito from something like God's point of view?

Or, by way of returning to the sandbank episode, how better to demolish overidealized human constructions of nature than to imagine "excrements of all kinds?" Animal waste is, of course, a universal fact of material life on earth. It not only plays an essential role in ecological processes of growth and decay but supplies a graphic reminder of Creation's objective ontology. It is implacably *there*, whether or not humans wish to think about it. But according to Julian of Norwich, the fourteenth-century English mystic, we can experience even the act of elimination as a sign of God's homely love and care for Creation. Excremental imagery likewise pervades writings influenced by the biblical and Reformed religious tradition of Puritan New England. Though commonly related there to the fallen condition of the world and humankind, it can also bear more positive allegorical association with God's bowels as the seat of divine mercy. Edward Taylor, for example, portrays in one memorable poem a saving kinesis in which "Gods Tender Bowells run / Out streams of Grace."[41] Similarly, the "excrementitious" character of Thoreau's sandbank vision reflects the divinely deep origin of regenerative processes in the bowels of a living earth, for "Nature has some bowels, and there again is mother of humanity." Just as Whitman cheers himself by remembering that his corpse will eventually make "good manure," so also Thoreau exults in imagining that insofar as we are dungishly linked to earth, its great bowel movements "will heave our exuviae from their graves" (*W* 309). Most impressively from the standpoint of religion, such images of physical elimination help define a view of natural evolution that is at once material *and* spiritual. Surely, then, there is nothing ethereal—and "nothing inorganic" (*W* 308)—about the spirituality of creation Thoreau witnesses in the sandbank. To regard the world as sacramental is to believe that spirit reveals itself through rather than despite materiality.

Thoreau's sense of place in *Walden* embraces a comparable paradox. "Where he lived" is a real location as well as a state of mind and soul. His book depicts a physical site, objectively situated a mile and a half from Concord, as well as an idyllic refuge, which he constructs subjectively and imaginatively. Part of the work's genius lies in its self-conscious preservation of this polarity, the interplay between nature's resistant autonomy (allied to what Coleridge called Life's "tendency to individuation") and humanity's rage for unifying order.[42] The hermeneutical breakthrough Thoreau achieved in *Walden* was to demonstrate how nature could be read and reinterpreted imaginatively as a sacred text in the new light of developmental science combined with recent forms of critical exegesis applied to biblical texts. But to rediscover divine revelation in and through the Creation, one had to study nature correctly—not merely by accumulating scientific data but by learning to perceive "her true meaning" so that "the fact will one day flower out into a truth."[43]

Particularly in the book's final chapter, Thoreau likewise reminds his audience that the experience of discovering God's presence in nature cannot be geographically restricted to Walden—or, for that matter, to any other single location. Despite his thorough involvement with local landscapes, Thoreau ends by urging readers to look beyond New England boundaries because "Thank Heaven, here is not all the world." Finding our place in the scheme of things first requires, apparently, recognizing our own ignorance of the globe, discovering that "we know not where we are" (*W* 320, 322). A wild nature preserve might disclose the numinous not by any potency of the place itself but, once again, by enabling us to "witness our own limits transgressed."

So if part of Thoreau's sensibility coincides with more ritualized traditions of Christianity, according to which the sacred can be physically connected to sanctified space, Thoreau's ancestral link to more iconoclastic traditions of Protestantism suggests a countervailing tendency. This Protestant impulse would resist any attempt to confine movements of the spirit within a given location. It insists that the power of the sacred does not reside materially in the place or thing itself but rather, as Emerson observed, in the interactive harmony between nature and the human imagination. Thus, it promotes an attitude more phenomenological than the archaic essentialism presumed by Eliade's theory. It might even regard the fixation of present-day tourists on Walden Pond, to the exclusion of less crowded and degraded landscapes, as a species of idolatry. Accordingly, Thoreau in his "Higher Laws" chapter follows something of a Pauline argument by displacing his temple imagery away from structures or places in the outer landscape to the human body. "Every man," he asserts, "is the builder of a temple, called his body, to the god he worships, after a style purely his own, nor can he get off by hammering marble instead" (*W* 221).

Few writers have recorded so richly sensual an immersion in the particularities of place as Thoreau does in *Walden*. Nonetheless, the book consistently urges readers to apprehend the geography of the sacred in terms that transcend the literalism of physically defined mapspace. If Thoreau saw his Walden house planted figuratively at the world's center, he also understood himself to be living on the margins of society. If the deep cut lays bare the very center of Nature's splendor as *bios*, it lies also at the physical periphery of Walden's estate. That Thoreau should see the world not so much in Blake's grain of sand but on the sideslope of Fitchburg Railroad's sandbank, a byproduct of mechanized industry, may reflect a suitable adaptation to the largely decentered mythological perspective of Western culture by 1854. One suspects the author would, in any case, heartily endorse the reluctance of another New England writer and nature lover, the contemporary poet Mary Oliver, to follow his footsteps to the actual scene of Walden Pond. As Oliver writes in her poem "Going to Walden," some regard her as "half a fool" for refusing the chance to make her own daytrip to Concord. "But," she concludes,

> . . . in a book I read and cherish,
> Going to Walden is not so easy a thing
> As a green visit. It is the slow and difficult
> Trick of living, and finding it where you are.[44]

Thoreau himself, by the time he published *Walden*, no longer located his life in the house by the pond. But by then he had made another dwelling place, a text that would offer readers, too, a site from which they could learn to read nature as hiero-glyph, or holy writ, and to witness their own limits transgressed.

7

Post-Darwinian Visions of Divine Creation

Beyond Deicidal Darwinism

After 1855, belief in a sacral world was shaken by several developments impinging on citizens of the Republic. To be sure, the publication of Charles Darwin's book *The Origin of Species* in 1859 did not immediately destroy either the religious faith or the nature Romanticism cherished by large numbers of Americans. For a time, many considered it possible to assimilate Darwinism into preexisting conceptions of natural history, natural theology, and providential design. After all, theories about the mutation or "development" of biological species had been entertained for at least half a century before *Origin*, most conspicuously in Robert Chambers's *Vestiges of the Natural History of Creation* (1844). The full import of evolutionary thought, as initially mediated through Herbert Spencer and often implicated with Social Darwinism, took decades to permeate American culture.[1] As the Tennessee Scopes Trial of 1925 confirmed, this process took still longer in sectors of popular culture concentrated regionally in the South and West.

Even among naturalists in the National Academy of Sciences, nineteenth-century views about the extent of divine intervention in the modification of species differed considerably. The Harvard botanist Asa Gray, for example, became an outspoken defender of Darwin's transmutation hypothesis after having scorned Chambers's explanations of how new species emerged. Yet even Gray questioned Darwin's focus on natural selection as the chief means of adaptive change and, contrary to Darwin, wanted to charge some otherwise elusive variations in organic etiology to divine Providence.[2] By the same token, America's intellectual leaders in other spheres included not only atheistic materialists but also Idealists and theistic evolutionists of many stripes. Despite Darwin, they held a wide spectrum of views about the extent to which God might occasionally work miracles of "special creation."[3] Thus, particularly after 1875, mainstream Protestant church leaders largely abandoned previous efforts to deny that organic evolution could be accommodated to truths preserved in biblical revelation. Committed theists became more and more inclined to argue that evolution was simply God's preferred method of creation.[4]

Eventually, though, the age's fascination with several forms of scientific materialism gave yet freer rein to the skepticism previously unleashed by "higher criticism" of the Bible and other challenges to historically revealed Christianity. Moreover, the colossal carnage of the Civil War called into question nearly every antebellum version of civic, natural, and revealed religion. Horrid battles were fought amid scenes of surpassing natural beauty, such as Virginia's Shenandoah Valley and Tennessee's Lookout Mountain. Although John Muir managed to escape military service, he was impressed by the signs of devastation he witnessed during his long walk through the South in 1867. As Melville wrote in *Battle-Pieces* (1866), with something of an I-told-you-so-earlier-do-you-get-it-now satisfaction, "Nature's dark side is heeded now." Emily Dickinson, later in the century, represented the era's crisis of faith by lamenting in verse that God's right "Hand is amputated now / And God cannot be found." She must have known then that amputation of limbs had been the treatment of choice for countless blue and gray soldiers maimed in the conflict that raged some twenty years earlier. Surely this hateful bloodletting, inflicted by Americans upon their fellows on an unprecedented scale, contributed to what Dickinson called "the abdication of Belief."[5] Nor did the nation's postwar atmosphere—with its worship of entrepreneurial greed, its corporate and civic corruption, its expansionist pride, its vulgar materialism as sanctioned by the "Gilded Age"—offer much to renew belief in things of the spirit. The triumph of large-scale industrial capitalism, together with the official closing of the frontier around 1890, further assured America's fall from the Jeffersonian ideal of free-spirited individuals planted in free soil.

Much of the literature produced between the Civil War and World War I reflects a markedly pessimistic reading of the Darwinian fable of survival through fierce competition.[6] Other readings were possible. The philosopher Herbert Spencer's optimistic reconstruction of Darwinism defended not only laissez-faire economic policies but also expectations of evolutionary progress vaguely allied to an apotheosis of force he termed "the Unknowable." Yet writers identified with literary "naturalism" accented the grimly impersonal, morally indifferent identity of nature in a godless world. Personal freedom now seemed illusory, as implacable forces, chance, and instinct shaped the lives of characters fictionally portrayed by Stephen Crane, Frank Norris, and Theodore Dreiser. In Dreiser's *Sister Carrie* (1900), for example, ethical pursuits or spiritual aspirations have no bearing on the career of the title character. As Carrie Meeber adapts from the rural setting of her childhood to the new nature of dynamic Chicago, she finds herself driven by elemental urges to secure the food, sex, and social position she craves.

What spirits, then, might be left to inhabit nature after evolutionary materialism seemed to have replaced "creationism" with hard science? How, too, could anything of nature Romanticism survive the ever-accelerating consumption of wild acreage in the post–Civil War period as a result of burgeoning cities, population surges from the new immigration, and the western land rush?

Despite literary naturalism's denial of God's real presence in the material world, Romantic naturalism did survive in some quarters. Traces of Romantic religion survive, for instance, in Mark Twain's hauntingly lyrical evocations of the Mississippi River, a current saturated with the primal spirits of American nature as venerated and recollected from his boyhood. In the form of paeans to grand, unknowable forces beyond human will, they persist even in spots of narrative exposition scattered throughout the fictions of Theodore Dreiser and Jack London. America's ineluctable optimism simply could not allow total or permanent acceptance of pessimistic materialism. Where postwar expressions of spiritual naturalism do emerge, however, they typically differ from their antebellum counterparts. Resurgent forms of Romantic religion had to be adapted to the new frenetic era of progressivism, robber barons, and Teddy Roosevelt's cult of the "strenuous life."

The most obvious change in focus presented by this later, neo-Romantic literature is its geographic shift from East to West Coast sites of numinous encounter. If the gods once so accessible to imagination in the forests of Massachusetts and New York State had died or retreated, other spirits arose to access the numinous for Mary Austin in the desert Southwest and for John Muir in California's Yosemite Valley. Beyond the traditional nature temples planted in northeastern woodlands, other ecological systems and landscapes came to be acknowledged as sacred space. Such territory included Mary Austin's Mojave Desert and, eventually, Willa Cather's Nebraska prairie and Ed Abbey's arid Moab territory in Utah.

With respect to ethnic communities, too, the base of religious involvement in nature moved beyond traditions previously fixed within Anglo-Saxon culture. Thus, Willa Cather's fiction reveals her fascination with the pioneer struggles of Scandinavian and eastern European immigrants. Mary Austin describes appreciatively the customs and rituals of several non-Anglo peoples, including Shoshone Indians and the semipagan, Catholic Hispanics who inhabit settlements comparable to El Pueblo de Las Uvas (the Town of the Grape Vines). And at a time when great Indian cultures of the Dakotas and other western regions were threatened with dissolution, many in white settler culture were captivated by images of the Indian as Romantic Other. This inclination, already encouraged by the artist George Catlin's pictorial renderings of Great Plains tribes during the antebellum period, continued into the twentieth century. Members of the dominant and increasingly mechanized culture combined their sponsorship of ethnographic research and the publication of indigenous testimonies with bids to recover what they sometimes perceived to be the atavistic wisdom of Native American nature religion. In 1902, for example, when Gertrude Bonnin (Zitkala-Sa, or Red Bird) published a personal essay on "Why I Am a Pagan" for the *Atlantic,* the outlet presumed a mostly non-Indian audience for her argument on behalf of a counter-Christian religion. By 1932, curiosity about this ethnically and attractively "strange" spirituality was addressed by the publication of *Black Elk Speaks: Being the Life Story of a Holy Man of the Oglala Sioux.* The book's publication date falls roughly midway between 1890, when Black Elk had witnessed the massacre of Sioux Indians at Wounded Knee, South Dakota, and 1973, when a second conflict took place on the same site. Significantly, though, this well-known testimony of an Oglala Sioux, otherwise known as Hehaka Sapa or Ekhaka Sapa, was presented to readers through the mediating influence of the poet John G. Neihardt.

Another trait of the ecospirituality voiced during this extended period is an ethical commitment disdainful of the amorality that had commonly been identified with evolutionary determinism or Social Darwinism. For John Muir, preserving the integrity of wild places and wild things became an ethical passion. Comparable forms of ethical urgency inform the natural history writings of later figures such as Aldo Leopold (as already discussed in chapter 3), Rachel Carson, and Loren Eiseley. Leaders of the nascent environmental movement agreed that instead of capitulating to doctrines of economic, historical, or physical necessity, Americans must assume direct responsibility for preventing the despoliation of the earth.

Insofar as the theory of organic evolution contributed positively to the reshaping of religious faith in America, its chief long-term influence was to foster what John H. Roberts has called "more immanentist conceptions of God's relationship to the world."[7] Divine immanence, the doctrine of God's palpably incarnational involvement in Creation, had always been at least theoretically part of Jewish and Christian teaching. Yet even for orthodox believers, old dividing lines now blurred more than ever—not only between Creator and Creation but also between spirit and matter, human and animal. Evolutionary science also encouraged religious thinkers, whether inspired by Judeo-Christian or Asian traditions, to reconceive the world's formation as a continuous creation rather than a one-time performance by a deity who subsequently withdrew from earth's stage into heavenly solitude.

In the closed system envisioned by scientific determinists toward the close of the nineteenth century, all natural and social processes were regarded as theoretically knowable and predictable. Though complex, the universe and all its systems were essentially finite. They operated in accord with fixed laws, all of which scientific inquiry could eventually discover without recourse to supernatural hypotheses. Thus, in *Le Roman Expérimental* (1880) the French novelist and critical commentator Émile Zola contrasted scientific determinism, which offered humans the hope of eventually knowing and regulating the forces governing nature, with fatalism, which required belief in the teleological intervention of irrational and unknowable powers. As an experimental novelist, Zola believed he followed sound scientific principles by studying in his work "the natural man, governed by physical and chemical laws, and modified by the influences of his surroundings." Though Zola rejected conventional notions of free will, he retained a Baconian confidence that as humans gained knowledge of what caused organisms to behave as they did, they gained power to control the outcome of life's experiment. "We are not fatalists," Zola insisted, "we are determinists, which is not at all the same thing."[8]

This worldview had changed by the twentieth-century era of Werner Heisenberg and Alfred Einstein, when physics began to overshadow biology as *the* paradigmatic science of the world for Western culture at large. For the modern cultural imagination, Heisenberg's Uncertainty Principle (announced in 1927) and Einstein's General Theory of Relativity suggested a more indeterminate model of nature than either actual or vulgar Darwinism had previously outlined. Quantum physics made matter, energy—and perhaps "spirit" as well— seem mysteriously coextensive. Recently, the sense of nature's unpredictability has been further enlarged by popular accounts of chaos theory and self-organizing processes. The limits of strictly empirical investigation become more apparent even as computerized technology becomes more sophisticated. Astronomical science, too, now favors an "open" rather than "closed" model of cosmological development toward the future.

In fact, outside the fundamentalist enclave of creationism, present-day theological reflection on the possibility of divine presence and purpose in the world focuses more on the future of things than on past origins.[9] Once a literal reading of the Genesis cosmology had lost all currency for writers and serious theologians, it no longer seemed plausible to narrow the search for God's creative presence to those first milliseconds of momentous change following the Big Bang. If the universe is now considered to be some thirteen billion years old, surely "Creation" must be accounted longer than the blinking of an eye. Moreover, if Christian faith is defined as "the substance of things hoped for, the evidence of things not seen" (Heb. 11:1), the primary locus of religious hope and belief about Creation must shift toward the future. By the same token, even secular expressions of what Lawrence Buell calls "environmental apocalypticism"[10] continue the religious tradition of the American jeremiad, warning that sinful violations of the earth may be revealed in future cataclysm. For more than a century, the environmental nonfiction with broadest popular appeal has centered attention not on life's origins but on an imagined endtime. Rachel Carson's *Silent Spring* (1962) and Jonathan Schell's book *The Fate of the Earth* (1982) are cases in point.

In several respects, then, post-Darwinian scientific developments have encouraged the modern resurgence of ecospiritual attitudes and beliefs. As Annie Dillard observes in *A Pilgrim at Tinker Creek*, modern physics enables scientists to become "once again mystics."[11] Some latter-day consequences of this perception for religious-minded nature writers will be pursued in the book's final chapters. But at this stage it is worth wondering how, within a late nineteenth-century climate of deterministic skepticism, John Muir managed to evolve a neo-Romantic nature philosophy steeped in religious mysticism. How is it, too, that the author of *Silent Spring*, writing half a century or so after Muir, showed herself to be not only an accomplished rhetorician and scientist but also a poetic mystic entranced by invisible as well as visible aspects of nature? The resurgence of mystical spirituality in figures like Muir can be viewed as a reaction against turn-of-the-century mechanistic determinism—or as an anticipation of later scientific trends more hospitable to sacred mystery. In any case, much of the environmental literature considered in this chapter reflects forms of spirituality that are only tenuously or ambiguously linked to traditional theism.

Godliness Writ Large in John Muir's Sierra

At the outset of "The Story of My Boyhood and Youth," John Muir sounds the central theme of his life: he is perpetually a lover "of wild places and wild creatures." In Muir's recollection, this "natural inherited" attraction to untamed nature stands painfully at odds with the severe regimen of labor and punishment that his father first imposed in Scotland.[12] After the family moved to Wisconsin, John continued to chafe against the influence of Daniel Muir, an authoritarian figure who became an itinerant preacher for the evangelical Christian sect known as Campbellism.[13] Having been confined too long by his repressive father, who forced him to commit to memory most of the Bible, John Muir understandably welcomed the chance to breathe freer air—first by studying science at the University of Wisconsin, then by taking a long excursion through the South, and at last, in 1869, by entering the high temples of his heart's desire in Yosemite Valley. In Muir's mind, the path that eventually led him to become America's foremost apostle of wilderness also opened an escape route from his father's narrow brand of Christian discipleship.

Still, when John Muir began walking south from Indianapolis in 1867 at the age of twenty-nine, he did not know quite where he meant to end his journey. Having contracted malaria by the time he reached the Gulf Coast of Florida, he eventually found his way to San Francisco and from there to the rugged terrain of California that would thereafter possess his soul. Many other expeditions preceded and followed his "thousand-mile walk to the gulf." But Muir's marriage to Louie Strentzel in 1880 concluded an unusually restless period of wandering that has been called his "ten-year pilgrimage to the wild."[14]

In the course of this grand passage, Muir walked away from the God of his cultural inheritance. Feeling "joyful and free" as he began his unencumbered sojourn, he also wanted to shed the burdensome piety of bourgeois Christianity. By the time he reached Cedar Keys, Florida, his journal entries betray total disillusionment with the presumption that a "civilized, law-abiding gentleman" could be worshiped as Creator of the vast cosmos. Such a deity, narrowly fixated on the welfare of human beings, was "purely a manufactured article" no better than an idol.[15] All the same, he felt powerfully drawn to pursue a godliness beyond his own ken. Though he confessed, before embarking on his great walk, "I wish I knew where I was going," he felt "doomed to be 'carried

FIGURE 7.1. John Muir at Yosemite. (Photo from the Library of Congress.)

of the spirit into the wilderness.' "[16] It was satisfying enough to think how far he had removed himself from the stifling piety of Daniel Muir.

Nonetheless, John Muir's sense of the world remained passionately religious. If anything, Muir became more intensely absorbed by godliness once he moved outside the bounds of Campbellite control. His writing is everywhere permeated by a conviction that humans could personally encounter transhuman spirits of the material world, that the whole of nature—not just humanity—displays a divine image, and that godliness was inscribed most clearly on faces of nature least marked by human colonization. "God's glory is over all His works, written upon every field and sky," he declared in 1870 after spending his first winter in Yosemite Valley. Yet he insisted that "here it is in larger letters—magnificent capitals" (see fig. 7.1).[17]

Accordingly, Muir's expression abounds in references to "Godful wilderness," or "the Godful woods." The water-ouzel's haunting song as well as "the utterances of torrents and storms" were "only varied expressions of God's eternal love." "In our best times," he insisted, "everything turns into religion, all the world seems a church and the mountains altars."[18] The interior glow of such beliefs is what fired Muir's outward activism, including his cofounding of the Sierra Club in 1892 and his political crusade to preserve inviolate large tracts of uninhabited land.

Defining the theological character of Muir's adult faith more closely poses difficulties, however. When assessments of Muir take any account of his religion, they represent him variously as a pantheist, a Transcendentalist, a mystic, an ecocentric evolutionist, an idiosyncratic Protestant Christian, or a post-Christian Romantic.[19] Each of these labels carries some validity for a figure struggling to define his innate spirituality within the unsettled intellectual climate of post-Darwinian America. Because Muir saw himself primarily as a lover and defender of wild places, rather than as a literary artist or as any kind of systematic philosopher or theologian, one cannot expect to locate a definitive statement of his beliefs. But despite the eclectic character of Muir's earth-centered religion, his faith preserved some essential traits of biblical Christianity. His heterodox yet robust piety drew constantly on biblical paradigms of grace, conversion of heart, evangelical poverty, and a loving Creator.

Muir was drawn away from conventional Christianity not only by his father's whip but also by growing discontent with what he perceived to be the human-centered and book-centered character of revealed religion. Though he was willing to advocate the preservation of roadless areas for practical reasons of human welfare, he was more committed to an ecocentric vision that affirmed the intrinsic value of all Creation. This principle placed him at odds with his culture's commonly taught religious views concerning the biblically sanctioned, hegemonic right of human beings to exploit every aspect of nature. Compared with the ecstatic faith that Muir professed in Yosemite and later in Alaska, the faith of most Christian churches struck him as too narrowly anthropocentric, the God they worshiped too anthropomorphic, and their indoor worship too bland to rival the numinous impressions he received in Sierra's "Range of Light." No revelation could surpass the "magnificent capitals" written at Yosemite.

Yet even these upper-case letters of glory needed interpretation to reveal their full meaning. Persistently invoking script metaphors, Muir insisted that scientific training enhanced rather than impeded one's ability to read the poetry inherent in earth shapes "whose many books and chapters form the geological Vedes of our glorious State." Having so thoroughly "learned the alphabet of ice and mountain structure,"[20] he believes he can appreciate all the better how "Yosemite comes to us an endless revelation" even as it remains "mysterious," in some measure "unreadable, immeasurable." Its scripted revelation must be deciphered with care because the multilayered nature of Sierra geology involves features that, "like palimpsests," are "written line upon line and crossed again and again."[21] In fact, Muir confessed in an 1866 letter that he could "take more intense delight from reading the power and *goodness* of God from 'the things which are made' than from the Bible," though he maintained that the two sources of revelation "harmonize beautifully."[22]

Thus, Muir never explicitly disavowed Christianity, even when he distanced himself from conventional faith to embrace a more earth-centered godliness. The era's liberal forms of Christianity encouraged, after all, the kind of eclectic spirituality that Muir sought to develop.[23] So Muir's faith incorporated the religiously liberalizing influences available to him through his friendship with Jeanne Carr, the wife of one of his university professors, through exposure to Transcendentalism from several sources, including a meeting with Emerson himself in Muir's cabin near Yosemite Falls, and through reading figures such as the geographer Alexander von Humboldt and the zoologist Louis Agassiz, whose work suggested to him a holistic view of the world's geophysical unity. All of these influences supported Muir's inclination to envision a more immanent, dynamic, benign deity than his childhood Christian training had allowed.

At the same time, Muir's naturalistic piety retained a greater sense of God's personal presence and care than antebellum Transcendentalists had typically acknowledged.[24] Muir accepted the transmutative premise of evolutionary theory, believing that Darwinism confirmed our human kinship with other creatures and fostered a proper humility about our place in the cosmos.[25] Yet he was reluctant to describe nature's primary *modus operandi* in terms of "Darwin's mean ungodly word 'struggle.' "[26] Moreover, he affirmed that the divinity suffusing Creation was, in fact, an intelligence rather than a randomly directed or heartless force.[27] With the Bible impressed on his verbal consciousness in childhood, he fastened in adulthood on theological keywords of natural piety that he had held in memory from the scriptural Word.

Most plainly within the scriptural canon, Saint John's Gospel expounds on two theological motifs favored by Muir: God as Love, and God as Light. He found a God who is love—neither indifferent nor punitive—manifested in the marvel of creatures vitally connected to one another in ecological harmony. "How wholly infused with God," he once exclaimed, "is this one big word of love that we call the world!"[28] And he found sensory corroboration of the "God who is Light"[29] by apprehending the splendor that irradiated the Sierran high peaks.

The "divinely beautiful" luminosity of these heights (315) sets the tone of his account in *The Mountains of California.* Pressing toward the summit of Mount Ritter, he perceived the rosy evening alpenglow to be "one of the most impressive of all the terrestrial manifestations of God." He concluded that even "the darkest scriptures of the mountains are illumined with bright passages of love that never fail to make themselves felt when one is alone" (350). After a power beyond himself carried his defeated body to "blessed light" at the pinnacle of Mount Ritter, "the sunlight in which I was laving seemed all in all" (355).[30] Muir's experience also follows the biblical precedent of Saint Paul, insofar as he underwent an illuminative conversion and change of life after he was nearly blinded by an accident suffered while working with factory machinery in 1867.[31] He became all the more convinced, as he later testified in *The Mountains of California,* that wild places were uniquely capable of "leading one far out of himself, yet feeding and building up his individuality" (350).

Thus, the version of Christian spirituality most closely allied to Muir's religion was at once mystical and Protestant. The mystical strain appears in Muir's accounts of envisioning the ineffable, his testimony to experiencing the unseen divine unity of the cosmos. It is telling in this regard that Jeanne Carr should have compared him to Saint Francis of Assisi, Christianity's foremost example of the ecological mystic and lover of Creation. Muir also reflected a zeal for righteous reform springing from his Protestant heritage.[32] Accordingly, he devoted his life to saving and changing the world—but in a more immediate physical sense than his forebears had presumed. Only that prophetic charism classically given to the reformer could embolden an ordinary citizen to preach to the president of the United States, as Muir did to Theodore Roosevelt, about his moral fault in hunting wild animals for pleasure.

Temperamentally, Muir was also sympathetic to the traditional Protestant emphasis on human depravity. All that he observed about humanity's defacing of Creation, culminating in his failure to prevent the damming of Hetch Hetchy Valley in Yosemite, confirmed his suspicion that greed and vanity were deeply rooted in human nature. Thus, although the Sierra offered a prosperous environment for the giant sequoia, its future was seriously endangered because "unfortunately, *man* is in the woods" so that "waste and destruction are making rapid headway" (*Mountains of California*, 436). Yet Muir departed from religious orthodoxy in his conviction that wild nature remained peculiarly exempt from the universal corruption linked to the Fall. He exulted in the pure divine beauty displayed by Douglas squirrels, woodchucks, white lilies, and water-ouzels but scorned domestic sheep as "in great part misbegotten, without good right to be, semi-manufactured, made less by God than man" (*My First Summer*, 208). "Strange that mankind alone is dirty" (186), he observed, while commenting on clothing customs but implying deeper skepticism about our moral condition. Whereas moles, seals, or fishes lead tidy lives, "man seems to be the only animal whose food soils him, making necessary much washing and shield-like bibs and napkins" (198). In a fit of annoyance, he had even claimed that "more than aught else mankind requires burning" if one were to cleanse the planet of its genuinely "deplorable evils."[33]

My First Summer in the Sierra is a logical text to examine for indications of how Muir transposed Christian and Romantic paradigms into his own idiom of earth-centered spirituality. Blending traditions of travel literature and personal narrative, the book as reworked from journals late in the author's career does not describe what Muir then perceived to be humanity's menacing incursions into his favorite place. Unlike many of Muir's later writings, *My First Summer* includes no explicit statement of preservationist ideology or call for government action to create parks and forest reserves. Yet by recalling the experiential origins of Muir's full-blown commitment to wilderness preservation, the work as published in 1911 took readers back to what Muir regarded as the spiritual heart of the political movement he had initiated. In offering the story of his own "conversion" in Yosemite, Muir clearly hoped to stir in others a recognition that landscapes like those witnessed in the Valley display "divine hieroglyphics" (164) in grand relief. Such ground, which "seemed holy, where one might see God" (180), must therefore be saved from destructive profanation.

By his thirty-first year, when he first met the exhilarating freedom of Yosemite, Muir had already been devoutly enamored with wild things. So the "conversion" in question involves no abrupt turn from previous ways but rather an elevation and consummation of his commitment:

How glorious a conversion, so complete and wholesome it is, scarce memory enough of old bondage days left as a standpoint to view it from! In this newness of life we seem to have been so always. (161)

To convey the spiritual impact of his encounter with the mountains, Muir often invokes the expressive idiom of biblical Christianity. Do such allusions to conversion, baptism, and pilgrimage indicate a faithful revision of Christianity, or a rejection of Christian doctrine wherein the old vocabulary is reduced to analogy? The liminal quality of Muir's ecospirituality makes it hard to say for sure. Probably Muir, too, felt some uncertainty on this score. Yet his commitment to pursue incarnate godliness at all costs follows the spirit of Jesus' call to abandon all other attachments and possessions for the sake of the gospel. When Muir testifies, after "gazing awe-stricken" at the glory of Horseshoe Bend in Merced Valley, that he "might have left everything for it" (160) and later wants to carry only scraps of bread for his sustenance, he knew that Jesus' disciples, too, had embraced the ascetic rigors of traveling light. And when, after reaching the eleven-thousand-foot summit of Mount Hoffman he hears nature inviting him again to "Come higher" (240), the whisper urging him toward more sublime elevations must have echoed another divine voice fixed in literary remembrance: "Friend, go up higher" (Luke 14:10). We are apt to forget that Muir situates his most celebrated ecological aphorism within a religious vision of interconnectedness shaped by God:

> No Sierra landscape that I have seen holds anything truly dead or dull . . . everything is perfectly clean and pure and full of divine lessons. This quick, inevitable interest attaching to everything seems marvelous until the hand of God becomes visible; then it seems reasonable that what interests Him may well interest us. *When we try to pick out anything by itself, we find it hitched to everything else in the universe.* (245, emphasis added)

Among the most evocative, biblically inflected images of sanctified space that Muir develops throughout *My First Summer* is that of the temple edifice. As noted in previous chapters, the trope of the forest as spiritual temple had already become something of a cliché by the Jacksonian era. The title of Muir's 1876 essay "God's First Temples: How Shall We Preserve Our Forests" scarcely sounds original to anyone acquainted with Bryant's "Forest Hymn." Nor could Muir, in his account of Yosemite, resist pursuing the imagery of church architecture when the Valley presented him with a grand structure that was actually named "Cathedral Peak." "No wonder the hills and groves were God's first temples," he wrote, "and the more they are cut down and hewn" into confined worship sites, "the farther off and dimmer seems the Lord himself." Unlike these structures, Cathedral Peak stood to the east of his camp in "living rock" as "one of Nature's cathedrals," soaring roughly "two thousand feet high" and "nobly adorned with spires and pinnacles, thrilling under floods of sunshine as if alive like a grove-temple" (237–238).

In *My First Summer*, however, Muir found novel ways of playing out the conventional temple and tabernacle imagery, thereby raising some noteworthy considerations for green theology. For one thing, he reconceived this traditionally static figure in more dynamic, expansively geophysical terms. Saint John's Gospel records Jesus' declaration "In my father's house, there are many mansions." In Muir's vision, the many living mansions of God's dwelling extend from the human body to the entire cosmos. Just as the body's "flesh-and-bone tabernacle seems transparent as glass" to the Valley's surpassing beauty and godliness (161), so also particular sites such as Cathedral Peak reflect the larger "grandeur of the Yosemite temple" (228) as a whole. And just as some attending church worship remain indifferent to the services performed there, so also Muir laments that some visitors to Yosemite failed to recognize the numinous, even though "the sublime rocks were trembling with the tones of the mighty chanting congregation of waters gathered from all the mountains round about, making music that might draw angels out of heaven." Such souls reacted as though "their eyes were bandaged and their ears stopped,"[34] while "God himself is preaching his sublimest water and stone sermons" (263).

With the benefit of his studies in geology and evolutionary biology, Muir also understood that the apparently inert, unchanging features of nature's tabernacles were in constant flux. Despite the seeming solidity of Sierra's great peaks, even they participate in that play of continuous creation affecting every particle of nature: "From form to form, beauty to beauty, ever changing, never resting, all are speeding on with love's enthusiasm, singing with the stars the eternal song of creation." And despite the "enormous waste" one might perceive in nature's fertility and evolutionary processes, Muir saw instead a perfectly divine dynamism that confirmed his faith. Nature, he believed, "is eternally flowing from use to use, beauty to yet higher beauty; and we soon cease to lament waste and death, and rather rejoice and exult in the imperishable, unspendable wealth of the universe" (226, 296).

In *The Mountains of California* and other writings, Muir also modified the impression of static invulnerability that is usually attached to temples-of-nature imagery. Aside from Henry Thoreau and George Perkins Marsh, antebellum writers had not underscored humanity's capacity to desecrate America's sacred groves with permanent, large-scale effect. By contrast, Muir came to believe that thoughtless humans could indeed destroy or horribly deface God's finest works. He saw Yosemite's sanctuary threatened by dams, irresponsible logging, and overgrazing. He was appalled to see the shores of glacial lakes ruined by sheep, trampling across the meadows like "a horde of hoofed locusts." As he puts the case succinctly, with biblically charged indignation, in *The Mountains of California*, "the money-changers were in the temple" (387). The evangelical passion with which Muir later campaigned to "save" redwoods and other singular American creatures and places is already evident, though, in *My First Summer*. Disturbed by the apparent deafness of his shepherd associate, Billy, to "all stone sermons," Muir admits that he "pressed Yosemite upon him like a missionary offering the gospel, but he would have none of it" (238).

For Muir, Yosemite becomes a privileged site not only of worship but also of holy habitation. Herein lies another uncommon feature of Muir's temple imagery. In literary tradition, the forest cathedral—or, for that matter, the humanly constructed temple—had usually been portrayed as a space of occasional refreshment for the soul. By the same token, modern environmental rhetoric usually construes "wilderness" as a domain that humans are permitted to visit without remaining or residing.[35] Yet Muir developed such strong attachment to unsettled land that he considered it, paradoxically, his true home. Yosemite was at once God's favored temple, a domain in which "God himself seems to be always doing his best," and Muir's preferred dwelling place. "I should like to live here always," Muir confesses, because he finds the place "so calm and withdrawn while open to the universe in full communion with everything good." Devoted as he is to Sierra's forests, meadows, and streams, he solemnly declares: "I should like to dwell with them forever." With just "bread and water," he would be content to remain here, observing "storms and calms,—a new heaven and a new earth every day." Here he could delight in attending "an endless Godful play"; here he could know what it meant to see "Creation just beginning, the morning stars 'still singing together and all the sons of God shouting for joy' " (187, 273, 278).

Muir's ecstatic expression in this passage brings together biblical phrasing from several disparate sources—including Genesis, Job, and the Book of Revelation. From the standpoint of temple imagery, however, Muir echoes most crucially the familiar conclusion of Psalm 23: "I will dwell in the house of the Lord forever." Intoning his own form of prayer, "I should like to dwell with them forever," he voices his desire to enjoy holy habitation in a place not customarily inhabited by humans—or not, at least, by Europeans. He wants to abide in a place he neither owns nor governs.

Muir likewise draws on biblical rhetoric to drive home his conviction that final lordship of the Sierra belongs only to the divine Lord, not to any human individual or group. He apparently sensed that an older Hebraic piety, reminding us of our small physical and spiritual stature within the endless expanse of nature, held greater promise than Transcendental self-deification for restraining willful plunder of the earth. In posthumously published remarks from his journal, he refutes "erroneous views" of God and Creation, including the "presumption" that the world "was made for man." "Why ought man to value himself as more than an infinitely small unit of the one great unit of creation?" he asks. "And what creature of all that the Lord has taken the pains to make is not essential to the grand completeness of that unit?" Challenging the view that other creatures are simply our underlings, he describes them instead as "earthborn companions & fellow mortals."[36] Thus rejecting conventional beliefs in total human "dominion" over the earth as justified from Genesis 1:28, he nonetheless presents a "Godful" vision of ecological unity consistent with the biblical sentiment of Psalm 24: "The earth is the Lord's, and the fulness thereof; the world, and they that dwell therein."

Frequently, then, Muir's writing sustains credence in a transcendent, monotheistic Creator—and even in a form of providential Romanticism one might have thought implausible after Darwin. Most of his nature writing shows little engagement with specifically Trinitarian Christianity, but it also shows a reluctance to embrace Thoreau's humanistic confidence that "he who has visited the confines of his real estate, looking out on all sides into space—will find a new inducement to *be* the Lord of creation."[37]

Muir never presumed to call himself Lord of Creation, or the master of all he surveyed. At several critical junctures, Muir's pantheistic feelings give way to more outer-directed, theistic statements of reverence, as in the culminating words of *My First Summer*:

> Here ends my forever memorable first High Sierra excursion. I have
> crossed the Range of Light, surely the brightest and best of all the
> Lord has built; and rejoicing in its glory, I gladly, gratefully, hope-
> fully pray I may see it again. (309)

One must admit that Muir's extreme privileging of wild Nature over all forms of human Culture can be vexing to anyone interested in extending the benefit of environmental understanding to populated regions of America. If Yosemite is a holy place "where one might see God," does it follow that San Francisco is a Godforsaken place where one might see only cars and corruption? If so, should the clamor from residents of Saint Francis's city for a clean water supply be ignored? And if natural as well as anthropological science assures us that there is no such thing as a pure American nature, untainted by human contact, how can we take seriously Muir's belief that pristine places deserve special protection, if not veneration, as sacred ground?

In confronting such concerns, I think we need first to acknowledge Muir's limitations as a figure of single-minded passion. Like other prophetic personalities, he felt drawn toward hyperbolic rhetoric to dramatize the case for preservationist policies that were not always popular and were never profitable. The excess evident in his language and attitudes accords with the topographical extremes of his favorite landscapes. Unlike Barry Lopez in our own day and Thoreau in the earlier nineteenth century, Muir lacked a sophisticated awareness that Romantic "wilderness" is constructed from the interplay between material substance and our own cultural imagination. Though a brilliantly charismatic leader, he was a less subtle and original thinker than Thoreau. Nor was he fully conscious of the ways his own writing mythologized the western wilderness, or fully attentive to the possibilities for environmental reform in settled communities.

In pragmatic terms, however, I think Robert L. Dorman is right to defend Muir's rhetoric of numinous nature because it succeeded, against formidable opposition, in winning public acceptance of national parks and wilderness preservation systems that become all the more valuable as population pressures mount.[38] Nor should Muir's sacralization of monumental scenes be dismissed as hopelessly naive. Human apprehensions of sacred space are, after all, always determined in some measure by cultural consensus rather than by wholly intrinsic or "natural" attributes. So far as physical science can determine, there is nothing materially unique about the Ganges River, the Black Hills, Chartres

Cathedral, or any other site that has become the focal point of contemplative worship.

Thus, when Muir describes "the sculpture of the landscape" (160) in *My First Summer*, we notice that his impressions of sacred wonder flow largely from his powerful *aesthetic* response to the land's shapes and lighting. Yet it would be a mistake to regard this aesthetic dimension as unreal or wholly arbitrary. As centuries of sacred art and music confirm, religious experience is often conditioned by sensations of "the beauty of holiness." The beauty Muir perceived in Yosemite's spectacular scenery, like that discernible in a Rembrandt canvas or at Chartres, amounts to more than a projective fantasy. Many others have shared his admiration. Granted, we "half create"[39] from our inward sense what we outwardly perceive in nature. Granted, Muir's response to the high peaks was culturally conditioned, and his western wilderness something less than pristine. By proportionate comparison with many other settings, though, even the heavily touristed grounds of Yosemite qualify as wilderness. As Gary Snyder points out, large reserves are "the locus of big rich ecosystems" and thus afford "a living place for beings who can survive in no other sort of habitat." Moreover, academic bids to deconstruct preservationist ideals on the simplistic premise that all wilderness is a "cultural construct" have the dubious real-world consequence of bolstering "global developers," "corporate clear-cutters," and "those who would trash the Endangered Species Act."[40] Beyond the demonstrable protection that roadless expanses afford to species and biotic systems, such territory offers spiritual as well as many practical benefits to humans.

Muir's bid for government support to preserve the aesthetic and ecological integrity of less settled landscapes represented a turning point in environmental history. It never purported to be a comprehensive program of environmental reform. That enterprise would also require the efforts of more urban-minded reformers, and more worldly conservationists, than Muir could ever become. Yet, as Lawrence Buell illustrates in *Writing for an Endangered World*, Jane Addams's campaign to open up green spaces in working-class Chicago should ultimately be recognized as complementing—not contradicting—John Muir's style of advocacy.[41] Contemporary understanding of bioregionalism also tends to confirm Muir's skepticism about the viability of large-scale water diversion projects in the arid West. One need not disdain cities to recognize that populations cannot ultimately be supported beyond the limits of local watersheds to sustain them. Otherwise the environment's larger capacity to sustain diversity of life, for humans and nonhumans alike, becomes compromised beyond repair.

Earthspirits of Other Peoples in Mary Austin and Black Elk

Muir accepted the common view that disruptions imposed by Euro-American "progress," not Indian styles of living on the land, now endangered the wild nature of America. After his first trip to Alaska in 1879, he also developed new respect for aboriginal people whose communities and customs he came to know during his exploration of Glacier Bay. For the most part, though, Muir showed surprisingly little sympathy for Indian cultures surviving in California or elsewhere in the lower states. He was apt to regard such societies as hopelessly degraded, to feel repelled by aboriginal traditions of hunting as a means of sustenance, and to fix most of his attention on the healing power of unsullied nature for members of the dominant, largely Anglo-Saxon culture.[42]

Mary Austin's best-known work, *The Land of Little Rain* (1903), reflects a different ethnography—and a different face of California. For Austin, the search to encounter preindustrial "otherness" in the Mojave country south of Yosemite required attentiveness to spirits of the land that had already been encountered there by other humans. Her mystical response to this environment conjoined close observation of the desert's nonhuman nature with meditation on its peoples. She pondered not only their struggles to survive, alongside other organisms in a severe environment, but also the spiritualities that endure within this varied population. Numbered among the desert's human inhabitants are Ute, Paiute, Mojave, Shoshone, Hispanic Mexicans, and a tough, mostly Anglo-descended breed of miners and prospectors whose collective life centers in the frontier town she calls "Jimville." Austin shared with Muir, whose work she knew and whom she later met personally in Carmel, California, belief in the redemptive mystery accessible in "the spirits of the wild." Yet she did not share Muir's "pietistic" view of these earth spirits as "angels, who bore him on their wings through perilous places." Her own "Naturist" spirituality fed not only on the physically "uncorrupted corners" of desert land but also on the Paiute's culturally mediated encounter with "ultimate, immaterial reality."[43]

Born in the Midwest town of Carlinville, Illinois, Austin was twenty-two when she moved to the far West to live on a homestead in California's Tejon district. The readership first served by *A Land of Little Rain* remained concentrated, however, in the Northeast. Initiated as an article in the *Atlantic Monthly* and likewise first printed in Boston as a book, Austin's work is mainly addressed to easterners who inhabit "an environment of asphalt pavements."[44] The appetite of easterners for news of the wild West emboldens Austin to suggest that such readers, far removed from her desert land of lost borders, may suffer an aridity of heart and spirit worse than the Mojave's physical desiccation. "You of the house habit can hardly understand the sense of the hills," she chides, since "no doubt the labor of being comfortable gives you an exaggerated opinion of yourself, an exaggerated pain to be set aside." So she ends up exhorting jaded city-dwellers, "you who are obsessed with your own importance in the scheme of things, and have got nothing you did not sweat for," to "come away," at least in imagination, to "the brown valleys and full-bosomed hills," to the "kindliness, earthiness, ease" (200, 281) of places like the pueblo of Las Uvas.

Austin likewise had her own motives for seeking refuge here from the pain of an alienated American life on the cusp of the twentieth century. Having already suffered two nervous breakdowns in college,[45] she began writing *The*

Land of Little Rain in the face of a troubled marriage, financial worries, struggles to define a vocation open to her as a woman, and the strain of dealing with a mentally impaired daughter. Amid these dispiriting facts of modern life, the desert's elemental beauty gave solace to her soul. So did her embrace of a syncretistic religion linked to love of the earth, to Native American practices of nonpetitionary prayer, and to mystical impressions that first seized her psyche in childhood. By the age of six, she had experienced a powerful but ineffable presence and energy—which she later called "God"—in an orchard near her home.[46] This recollection of how "God happened to Mary under the walnut tree" carried lifelong significance, as Austin tried to blend theoretical views gleaned from her reading of Darwin, Spencer, Engels, and William James with her own contemplative sense of the world.[47]

Having cast aside the Methodist Church, to which she belonged for a time in her youth, Austin mostly disavowed the notion of a personal God and in her book *Christ in Italy* (1911) declared herself to be "not a Christian." In *Earth Horizon*, she concluded that "the dark cloud of the Hebrew Tribal God" had been permanently dissolved. Yet she could never embrace the materialistic faith of atheistic determinism. "I wish I could come to the conclusion that there is no Maker," she averred in 1923, and that "I am just a by-product of evolution," but "I can't believe that."[48]

During her later travels in Italy, where she made a retreat at Florence's Convent of the Blue Nuns in 1908, she came to recognize that early Christian teachings concerning the mystical way were surprisingly consonant with spiritual disciplines she had long admired among peoples of the American Southwest. During a 1922 trip to England, she also met Evelyn Underhill, a leading authority on the mystical traditions of Western Christianity; and it is telling that she draws on phrasing derived from Brother Lawrence, a seventeenth-century French Carmelite, when she refers more than once in her autobiography to "The Practice of the Presence of God."[49] Though some considered the author of *Christ in Italy* and *The Man Jesus* (1925) to be scandalously unorthodox, Austin confessed to a correspondent in 1919 that "a woman whose love life had been as unhappy as mine, who had no religion, would have gone mad or bad or committed suicide." In the same letter she goes on to verify that through her faith, supported by "indispensable High States" of experience, she had found compensation for painful privations in her personal life:

> Once you accept God as a reality in life, a near, friendly reality, more powerful than your father, wiser than your friends, more understanding than your brother, more competent to produce exalted states than a lover it seems inevitable that you turn to him in the failure of any of the lesser relations.[50]

In *The Land of Little Rain*, Austin leaves the failure of her own social relations unstated. From the start, however, she displays a heartfelt involvement in the land she describes. In addition to surveying the desert's topography and life-forms, the author includes character sketches and local anecdotes of the sort readers expected to find in period travel narratives. Her book gives colorful account of the region's "chrome and vermilion painted" hills (4), of creosote shrubs spreading green into Death Valley, of the blue wash of lupine, and of the white splendor arising from columbine sprouting in the uplands. It demonstrates that this reputedly lifeless land supports a crowd of animals, including buzzards, coyote, red foxes, lizards, insects, deer, hawks, and rabbits. Still, Austin will not market this work as a tourist guide for those seeking new sites for "a month's vacation." Insisting that she is "in no mind" to direct others "to delectable places toward which you will hold yourself less tenderly than I," she underscores her intention to "keep faith" with this place—"the loneliest land that ever came out of God's hands" (x, ix, 16)—and to devote herself to its contours like a true lover. Underlying the travel narrative of *The Land of Little Rain* is this white woman's testimony to a passage of self-discovery resembling a Native American's vision quest. Austin exudes an assurance that in "my country" of lost borders (viii), she has found an enveloping presence that, in phrasing borrowed from the theologian Paul Tillich, might be called the ultimate ground of her being.

Arid landscapes supply peculiar wellsprings of life for the spirit. Precedent for Austin's exposition of this major theme appears in several cultural traditions. It figured in traditional practices of Native American peoples, as is reflected in the author's account of Winnenap' a Shoshone-Paiute medicine man; it also marked the Eurasian legacy of biblical Judaism and Christianity, as well as the teachings of those ascetic Desert Fathers and Mothers who withdrew to lonely places in Egypt during the fourth and fifth centuries C.E. Later in the twentieth century, Ed Abbey fixed his search for "a hard and brutal mysticism" on the same sort of forbidding landscape at Arches National Monument in Utah when he wrote *Desert Solitaire* (1968).[51] The desert's elemental conditions of survival seem to reduce life to lowest terms, for humans as well as for all other organisms. "Somehow the rawness of the land favors the sense of personal relation to the supernatural," writes Austin, since "there is not much intervention of crops, cities, clothes, and manners between you and the organizing forces to cut off communication" (120). Just as the Book of Deuteronomy shows Moses presenting the Law to fellow Hebrews in the desert with the radical injunction that this day "I have set before you life and death" (Deut. 30:19), Austin reminds her reader that no matter how far you venture into such "lonely land, you cannot go so far that life and death are not before you" (13).

According to Austin, even the everyday dynamic of weather change seems more suggestive of the numinous when played across skies of a rugged landscape. Remarking on this point, she evidently likes to recall that the etymological origin of "spirit" is wind:

> The first effect of cloud study is a sense of presence and intention in
> storm processes. Weather does not happen. It is the visible manifes-
> tation of the Spirit moving itself in the void. It gathers itself together
> under the heavens; rains, snows, yearns mightily in the wind, smiles;

and the Weather Bureau, situated advantageously for that very business, taps the record on his instruments and going out on the street denies his God, not having gathered the sense of what he has seen. Hardly anybody takes account of the fact that John Muir, who knows more of mountain storms than any other, is a devout man. (246–247)

For Austin the harshness with which the desert forces human beings to consider the root terms of their existence is balanced, though, by intangible gifts. The desert's contemplative atmosphere, again described with the benefit of biblical coloring, stirs spiritual humility and gratitude for powers beyond human control:

For all the toll the desert takes of a man it gives compensations, deep breaths, deep sleep, and the communion of the stars. It comes upon one with new force in the pauses of the night that the Chaldeans were a desert-bred people. It is hard to escape the sense of mastery as the stars move in the wide clear heavens to risings and settings unobscured. They look large and near and palpitant; as if they moved on some stately service not needful to declare. Wheeling to their stations in the sky, they make the poor world-fret of no account. Of no account you who lie out there watching, nor the lean coyote that stands off in the scrub from you and howls and howls. (21)

Unlike buzzards, who perform a crucial scavenging function, civilized humans who fail to appreciate their supporting role within "the economy of nature" end up as blunderers who leave "disfigurement" on "the forest floor" (60). Yet most of the desert-dwelling humans whom Austin portrays in a favorable light reflect the same tenacious hold upon the earth, the same struggle to survive, as other biotic creatures in "the land of little rain." Thus, the apparently nomadic, sturdily independent prospector she calls "the pocket hunter" had actually found deep roots in this land, which "tolerated him as it might a gopher or a badger." Undisturbed by foul weather because he has become so "saturated with the elements," this man had migrated for a time to London in the aftermath of one of his lucky gold strikes. He was compelled, however, by what Austin presents as a kind of naturalistic determinism to return to California's barren country. "No man," she concludes, "can be stronger than his destiny" (68, 70, 80).

Her memorable sketch of Seyavi, the Paiute basket maker, likewise dramatizes a form of transcendence that is fully attached to the earth. After suffering early widowhood, this woman manages for years to sustain herself and her son through the practical artistry of basket weaving. As a literary artist with feminist inclinations, Austin is drawn to celebrate Seyavi's dignity, spiritual self-possession, and courage in accepting her eventual blindness. Clearly, too, the author admires Seyavi's standing as a naturist cocreator with the gods. Her art involves fashioning material drawn directly from nature: "The weaver and the warp lived next to the earth and were saturated with the same elements" (169). In fact, Austin idealizes this woman as an ethnic heroine comparable to Deborah, the Israelite prophet and sage honored in the Book of Judges: "In her best days Seyavi was most like Deborah, deep bosomed, broad in the hips, quick in counsel, slow of speech, esteemed of her people" (175).

Austin's romanticized view of ethnic otherness likewise colors the book's concluding account of Las Uvas. To be sure, the Mexican-Americans in this utopian pueblo are portrayed as implausibly merry, lively, and colorful. Yet by praising so extravagantly a settlement in which "every house is a piece of earth" (180), Austin plainly intends to convey her social criticism of the dominant culture. Whereas in her view bourgeois Protestants "go to church to be edified" and thus reflect an effete indoor spirituality, the people of Las Uvas "go for pure worship and to entreat their God" (280). Through their eclectic mix of Roman Catholicism with semipagan folk piety, the racially mixed residents of this town of the Grape Vines ensure their connection with the material world. Their gardening, festivities, and sacraments are all of a piece. Austin has no illusions about joining such a community herself. Yet she idealizes it by way of underscoring the absence of genuinely corporate, earth-linked bodies of faith in twentieth-century Anglo culture.

Some three decades after Austin's work appeared, in *Black Elk Speaks*, a Sioux holy man offers another ideal image of sacred community—this one situated all the more distantly, and elegiacally, in the past. At the tender age of nine, Black Elk had first received his great vision, "seeing in a sacred manner the shapes of all things in the spirit."[52] His interviewer, John G. Neihardt, recognized him as an authentic prophet who could recall a unified, sacred sense of the world that Wasichu (white) influences had obscured in the age of automation. Above all, his historical and personal narrative dramatizes "the story of all life that is holy and is good to tell, and of us two-leggeds sharing in it with the four-leggeds and the wings of the air and all green things; for these are children of one mother and their father is one Spirit" (1). Having met the spirit Powers of the Six Grandfathers at the center of the earth, Black Elk sustains his reverential conviction of kinship with buffalo and elk, with spotted eagles and split-swallows.

Such belief endures even when he feels compelled to kill animals; it persists, too, amid his recollection of momentous events such as the death of his relative Crazy Horse, or the rise and fall of the Ghost Dance movement. According to Black Elk, the Lakotan vision of organic unity is best represented when he and the fourth Grandfather plant a red stick, understood to signify a vibrantly blooming tree of life, into " 'the center of the nation's circle' " (28). Together with the sacred pipe, with its four appended ribbons representing the quartered geophysical order in which humans strive to situate themselves, the great hoop remains Black Elk's chief symbol of sanctified communion. The hoop binds the nation's two-legged members together with its nonhuman members in an unbroken circuit. It lies directly on the Dakotan earth, trails to the four quarters intersecting at its flowered core. Thus signifying "the living center of a nation," this mandala-like conjunction of a "flowering stick" with the hoop's "endless" circle of power (28, 34, 35) epitomizes the religious ecology that John Neihardt sought to preserve.

Black Elk's holistic vision was linked, however, to a model of tribal cohesion that no longer existed at the time of his testimony in the early 1930s. He concludes his account by declaring through John Neihardt that after the "butchering" of his people by U.S. soldiers at Wounded Knee, South Dakota, in 1890, "the nation's hoop" had been "broken and scattered" (270). His ecological vision depends as well on a palpable sense of communion with the bestial order that could not survive decimation of the great buffalo herds that once roamed the Plains. Black Elk records that by the fall of 1883, the Wasichus had destroyed the last herds. "When we hunted bison, we killed only what we needed," he recalls, whereas the whites slaughtered so recklessly that they sometimes took whole animals solely for their tongues. Around this time, too, the people had to abandon their traditional tepees to face confinement on the reservation in "square gray houses" (213–214).

So by 1930, when John Neihardt first met Black Elk at Pine Ridge Reservation, the glory days of the Lakota people were a distant memory. This *wichasha wakon* (holy man) had long since given up his own exercise of healing rituals and some other practices associated with his native religion.[53] Yet Neihardt found Black Elk's vision and symbology immensely compelling. To his mind, this thoroughly earthbound piety offered religious sustenance not only to Lakotans intent on preserving a sacred legacy,[54] but also to spiritually starved Wasichus who constituted his primary reading audience. When the two men met at Pine Ridge, they recognized each other as kindred spirits across the racial-cultural divide. "I think he knew the kind of person I was when I came to see him," Neihardt later recalled. "I am referring to the mystical strain in me and all my work," he added. This lyric and epic poet, already long absorbed in Sioux ethnography when he met Black Elk, went so far as to claim: "My attitude toward what he said to me is one of religious obligation."[55]

Yet Black Elk and Neihardt did part company in some of their theological allegiances. One of the two chief contributors to *Black Elk Speaks*, now recognized to be a religious classic of the twentieth century, was a publicly committed Roman Catholic who had served for decades as a catechist and Christian missionary. The other maintained a lifelong contempt for Christianity. Ironically, it was Neihardt, not the old Native sage, who scorned biblical religion. Sharing the skeptical view of Christianity displayed by both his parents, Neihardt greatly admired Native American beliefs and practices as well as the Hindu scriptures. His father, Nicholas Neihardt, had openly embraced unbelief, revering Charles Darwin along with two other champions of agnosticism, T. H. Huxley and Robert Ingersoll.[56] Thus, Neihardt epitomized those heirs of cultural Christianity who were looking for "alternative" spiritualities suited to the era of T. S. Eliot's poem *The Wasteland* and high modernism. To these vision seekers, the wichasha wakon's old religion held something of a new age allure. Aptly, *Black Elk Speaks* first drew popular acclaim, well after its early critical endorsement, in the countercultural mood of the 1960s. By then, Carl Jung and various anthropologists had recognized the mythological and symbolic richness of this book's narrative.[57]

Neihardt welcomed the visionary statements of Black Elk as contributing to the formulation of a post-Christian spirituality that explicitly honored the earth and might be selectively appropriated by whites. For Black Elk, however, Christianity remained viable. Moreover, most evidence suggests that he saw gospel faith as compatible with the ancient faith of his people—even if *Black Elk Speaks*, the rhetoric of which was heavily influenced by Neihardt, gives little hint of how he personally integrated these two belief-systems. Other evidence confirms, however, that he regarded the Great Spirit, often invoked as "Wakon Tanka" in later testimony recorded by Joseph Epes Brown,[58] as congruent with the God of Western monotheism. He also seems to have appreciated the parallels between Lakotan rituals involving physical objects like the sacred pipe and Catholic sacramental practices—perhaps even between seven major Lakotan rituals and the seven sacraments.[59] Whether Nicholas Black Elk, as he was called after his baptism in 1904, ever felt a tension between his ancestral religion and the faith he learned from Jesuits remains a controversial question. He did not, at any rate, expose such a tension in *Black Elk Speaks* or in any other undisputed record preserved for critical scrutiny. Understandably, though, Neihardt sensed that inviting his subject to speak of his Christian faith in *Black Elk Speaks* would detract from the book's force and coherence as an account of the old ways. Doubtless, too, Neihardt preferred to maintain a slightly Romantic image of the authentic Indian—that is, of one whose outlook seemed uncontaminated by modernity or the acceptance of Western influences.[60]

Black Elk's rhetorical opposition between the circle and the square is an aspect of sacred geometry that is particularly germane to the cultural milieu of Neihardt's twentieth-century readers. Lamenting that the Wasichus "put us in these square boxes," Black Elk observes that "everything the Power of the World does is done in a circle" (196, 194). The patterns governing nature, like that represented in the sacred hoop, are primarily circular rather than rectolinear: "The sky is round, and I have heard that the earth is round like a ball, and so are all the stars." Like tepees, the course of the seasons is circular, as is "the life of a man" running "from childhood to childhood" and indeed "everything where power moves" (194, 195). Given the interviewer's investment in this narrative, I suspect Neihardt recognized that the circularity theme also held topical meaning in the realm of social criticism. By the 1930s, many of the rounded, often uneven contours of America's landscapes were being pressed into linear forms under strict human control. Straight lines defined the layout of plowed fields in the Midwest, the squared lines of most townships west of Pennsylvania as mandated by the Land Ordinance of 1785, and the street grid of Manhattan. Despite the Depression, the expansion of industrial commerce during the century's first half saw the manufacture of countless linear commodities: rail lines, factory assembly lines, box cars, warehouses, and freshly paved roads. When the book first appeared in 1932, the Empire State Building, a singular display of environmental mastery raising lines into the sky, had just been completed the year before.

Even if one judged technology to be generally advantageous to human welfare, might civilized culture now threaten to supplant rather than to enhance the vital powers of nature? And as the American nation consolidated its vast powers of commerce and mechanized warfare, what might it be losing by way of commerce with the powers of earth—with the sacred community represented in the hoop of life? Such were the questions Neihardt knew that Black Elk's testimony, particularly as concentrated in chapter 17, must raise for non-Indian as much as for Indian readers. Nor were Sioux holy men like Black Elk and Lame Deer[61] the only Americans to have expounded on this theme. That "there can be no power in a square" (194) is also a persistent principle, albeit a recessive one, in Euro-American culture. Many non-Indian traditions have likewise revered the circle as an emblem of divine unity, perfection, and eternity. In nineteenth-century America, Emily Dickinson had written "My Business is Circumference" and that "Success in Circuit lies." Ralph Waldo Emerson not only elaborated a Transcendental-Romantic account of sacred circularity in his essay "Circles," but also had his poet Uriel declare succinctly that " 'Line in nature is not found; / Unit and universe are round.' "[62]

Thus, beyond its specific anthropological contribution, *Black Elk Speaks* also speaks directly to the modernist concerns of what Neihardt called "the white world." Neihardt admitted that the work's "beginning and ending are mine; they are what he would have said if he had been able to."[63] So when the book's presumed author concludes by mourning that "there is no center any longer, and the sacred tree is dead" (270), we should not be surprised to note how closely this sentiment resembles T. S. Eliot's expression of modernist disillusionment in *The Wasteland* or, for that matter, W. B. Yeats's classic proclamation in "The Second Coming" (1921) that "Things fall apart; the centre cannot hold."[64]

Rachel Carson's Reverence for Hidden Pools of Life

As the century wore on, however, Americans gained new faith that science pointed the way toward accomplishing total and benign technical mastery of the environment. This faith grew particularly strong during the years following World War II. Confidence ran high that harnessing the power of nuclear reactors would now provide a cheap, limitless energy source. Under the glow of General Electric's assurance that "Progress is our Most Important Product," corporate America offered 1950s consumers a dizzying array of new products: labor-saving home appliances, faster and larger cars, miracle chemicals for home and garden, and electronic marvels including televisions and high-fidelity phonographs. Advertising rhetoric of this period illustrates the popular apotheosis of "scientism," a supreme trust that technical knowledge conferred miraculous, nearly infinite power to recreate the world for the sake of human happiness and wholeness.[65] Nobody challenged this uncritical faith more effectively than Rachel Carson.

Employed for several years by the U.S. Bureau of Fisheries, Carson was a dedicated scientist with training in zoology and marine biology. As such, she could scarcely be considered a foe of scientific inquiry. She presumed that thoughtful human intervention in natural processes was often appropriate and necessary. Despite the charges of extremism leveled at her by opponents, she did not even censure all uses of chemical pesticides. Still, recognizing the destructive powers released in the atomic era, she deplored the notion that humankind should claim to act as godly "overlord of all creation," or enjoy free license to remake the world. "Mankind has gone very far into an artificial world of his own creation," she lamented, and has "sought to insulate himself, with steel and concrete, from the realities of earth and water." She admitted the need for humans to exercise control over the global environment, so long as this power was tempered by humility and self-imposed limits. For certainly, she thought, those "old ideas" that nature itself set bounds on the excesses of human exploitation and mismanagement had been exploded by 1958:

> It was pleasant to believe, for example, that much of Nature was forever beyond the tempering reach of man—he might level the forests and dam the streams, but the clouds and the rain and the wind were God's. . . .
>
> It was comforting to suppose that the stream of life would flow on through time in whatever course that God had appointed for it—without interference by one of the drops of the stream—man. And to suppose that, however the physical environment might mold Life, that Life could never assume the power to change drastically—or even destroy—the physical world. . . .
>
> I still feel there is a case to be made for my old belief that as man approaches the "new heaven and the new earth"—or the space-age universe, if you will, he must do so with humility rather than arrogance. . . . And along with humility I think there is still a place for wonder.[66]

For Carson, organic evolutionary theory had likewise hastened the demise of old ideas—about the permanence of nature, as well about humankind's special creation apart from the dynamic of biological processes. By the time she completed her formal zoological training in the 1930s, Darwinian ideas as modified by newer genetic findings had been well assimilated into scientific culture. Rachel Carson assumed their validity and seminal importance in everything she wrote about the natural world. Still, she disdained the amoral determinism with which Darwinism, and especially Social Darwinism, had long been identified. Throughout her life, she also insisted in diverse ways on the reality of the spirit. Against the strictly materialistic appraisals of nature and human nature presumed by many empirical scientists, she continued to argue the "affinity of the human spirit for the earth" and claimed that "natural beauty has a necessary place in the spiritual development of any individual or any society." Linda Lear's gripping biography of Carson outlines a career that itself rehearses much of the Darwinian fable.[67] It demonstrates that a surprising proportion of this writer-scientist's life involved a hard-fought struggle to survive, financially and psychologically as well as physically. All the same, the contemplative undercurrent of Carson's prose style shows a deeply personal love of beauty and mystery that runs against evolutionary images of lurid strife.

Thus, two impulses contrary to objective empiricism run prominently throughout Carson's naturalistic writing: its ethical passion, and its affirmation of a spirituality inherent in all creatures. The first impulse clearly animates *Silent Spring*; the second, tied to poetic praise of the world's inexhaustible wonder and mystery, is particularly evident in the sea commentaries. It also suffuses Carson's popular essay, "Help Your Child to Wonder," a version of which appeared posthumously under the title of *A Sense of Wonder* (1965). There the scientist as mentor testifies from experience that "those who contemplate the beauty of earth," recovering the child's "inborn sense of wonder," "find reserves of strength that will endure as long as life lasts." She believes "there is something infinitely healing in the repeated refrains of nature." And she witnesses personally to the value of "preserving and strengthening this sense of awe and wonder, this recognition of something beyond the boundaries of human existence."[68] Challenged by a reader of *The Sea Around Us* (1951) to explain why she had omitted God from her account of how life forms developed in and beyond the sea, she professed belief in a fairly standard accommodation of religious faith with Darwinism:

> It is true that I accept the theory of evolution as the most logical one
> that has ever been put forward to explain the development of living
> creatures on this earth. As far as I am concerned, however, there is
> absolutely no conflict between a belief in evolution and a belief in
> God as the creator. Believing as I do in evolution, I merely believe
> that it is the method by which God created and is still creating life
> on earth. And it is a method so marvelously conceived that to study
> it in detail is to increase—and certainly never to diminish—one's
> reverence and awe for the Creator and the process.[69]

However, Carson's spirituality never found much sustenance in formal religious allegiances. Early on she had formed some connections, by childhood experience and ancestral loyalty, to the Presbyterian Church. She gained further exposure to Christian influences while a student at Pennsylvania College for Women. During this period in the 1920s she took required Bible courses and attended Episcopal worship services. Her mature correspondence shows a fondness for blessings and occasional phrases inspired by theistic traditions. But she cultivated no adult relation to an established community of faith. Her funeral instructions, subsequently ignored, called for a simple memorial service to be performed by a Unitarian clergyman whom she found congenial. And though she embraced with the utmost seriousness the reverential ideals of Albert Schweitzer, to whom she dedicated *Silent Spring*, she was more disposed to profess reverence for "life" than for life's Creator. She felt little attraction toward worship that posited a deity set apart from the planet she loved.[70]

In her secular but earnestly spiritual orientation, as in so much else, Carson resembled her beloved friend Dorothy Freeman, who once confided to Rachel a fear that she had "denied formal religion too much." For her part, Rachel confessed to Dorothy that "part of my trouble is finding anything definite I can really feel is true" religiously. Perhaps they had to "talk more" about what they "do believe," beyond affirming the existence of some "great and mysterious force that we don't, and perhaps never can understand."[71]

Yet Carson's version of faith did coincide meaningfully with orthodox religion insofar as this scientist felt the world to be sustained by unseen realities no less than by visible marvels. For her, the sacred harmony of Creation, equivalent to what the Nicene Creed describes as the interfusion of "all things visible and invisible," remained a key article of faith. Her imagination was particularly drawn toward the less visible, relatively hidden features of nature that are rarely noticed by the multitude. In *The Sense of Wonder*, for example, she tells us she has been haunted by the voice of a black mole cricket, a sound "so ethereal, so delicate, so otherworldly, that he should remain invisible." In *The Sea Around Us*, she reflects at length on the many "hidden lands" stretched across the ocean floor. Like Melville, she wonders what must occur at dark depths, beneath our normal sight, in the colossal strife between sperm whale and giant squid. Impressed by the force of great ocean currents, she remarks on "the sense of a powerful presence felt but not seen, its nearness made manifest but never revealed." [72]

Above all, Carson was enchanted by the concealed beauty of tidal pools set in ocean caves. In the sea books, particularly in *The Edge of the Sea*, she marvels at the persistence of unseen life against all odds: "half hidden, it descends into fissures and crevices, or hides under boulders, or lurks in the wet gloom of sea caves. Invisibly, where the casual observer would say there is no life, it lies deep in the sand, in burrows and tubes and passageways." [73]

That an unseen web of connections unites the earth's multitudinous and seemingly disparate life forms is a fundamental premise of "ecology," a nineteenth-century term that Carson and Aldo Leopold helped to charge with new moral force for the modern era.[74] As a writer, Carson wanted to show readers the hidden life of nature, to bring to light the ecological threads binding together species in a given environment and to render visible the invisible worlds of cellular biology and genetics.

The truth of things unseen is also a common theme that links the polemical urgency of *Silent Spring* with the more contemplative, calmly appreciative mood of Carson's three oceanic books: *Under the Sea Wind*, *The Sea Around Us*, and *The Edge of the Sea* (see fig. 7.2). Despite obvious differences in tone, both forms of writing draw attention to the nexus between visible and invisible dimensions of the nonhuman world. The sea books highlight the rich profusion of life usually hidden from us because it is literally below the surface—

FIGURE 7.2. Rocky seacoast in Maine, a setting to which Rachel
Carson was perennially drawn. (Photo by David Beaucage.)

dwelling underwater, or flourishing at night, or abiding secretly in water caves.
Silent Spring likewise dramatizes the significance of nature's unseen activities
and interconnections—in this case, though, by way of highlighting the insid-
iously invisible effects of DDT and other synthetic pesticides.

Arguing that natural processes are not so self-cleansing as had previously
been imagined, Carson changed public awareness concerning the very notion
of environmental pollution. She pointed out how residual DDT was carried
cumulatively, but at first imperceptibly, along the food chain. Such contamination lay concealed in soil, waterways, and living tissue. No longer could the
spoliation of nature be simply equated with the sight of trash heaps, clear-cut
landscapes, filthy water, and smoky air. People now had to grant that the gravest
threats to them and to other living things might well be invisible. This deadly

array of forces included not only chemical pesticides but also nuclear radiation—and, eventually, PCBs in the Hudson River and excess CO_2 as well.[75] By 1961, when Carson offered a new preface to *The Sea Around Us*, marine disposal of radioactive waste made her question an earlier confidence that humankind "cannot control or change the ocean." We have yet to identify all of the subtler environmental conditions leading to human cancers. Nor was Carson unaware of the irony that she was herself dying of breast cancer even as she wrote of the "ever-widening wave of death" that human arrogance had created.[76]

In the "Fable for Tomorrow" that opens *Silent Spring*, Carson sets visible appearances—imaging a town "where all life seemed to live in harmony with its surroundings"—drastically at odds with the invisible reality of chemical ruin. One might even suspect that such baneful unseen powers were demonically inspired, as though in Carson's words "some evil spell had settled on the community." Not witchcraft, but a perversely self-destructive "chain of evil" created by humans was responsible.[77] Yet for all its apocalyptic elements of warning and denunciation, *Silent Spring* reflects an underlying faith. Like the classic American jeremiad sermon, which offered its hearers hope for change, Carson's book maintains hope in the future and in the receptivity of her readers. As such, the naturalistic attitudes of *Silent Spring* build on those presented in the marine books.

In *The Edge of the Sea*, Carson portrays a biotic community whose distinctive character is peculiarly suited to stir holy amazement. The liminal zone of the sea edge presents an ever-shifting, "elusive and indefinable boundary" between land and water, constancy and change. Though this restless space of harsh tidal extremes seems hostile to life, "yet it is a world that keeps alive the sense of continuing creation and of the relentless drive of life." "Each time I enter it," Carson adds, "I gain some new awareness of its beauty and its deeper meanings, sensing that intricate fabric of life by which one creature is linked with another, and each with its surroundings."[78]

The author expresses special delight at finding an ephemeral beauty hidden in the tidal pool of a sea cave at low tide. This place, a "pool hidden within a cave that one can visit only rarely and briefly," offers a singular "revelation of exquisite beauty." Kneeling on a carpet of sea moss, she peers into the darkened recess. Her patience is rewarded by glimpses of the pool's elusive *biota*—including sponges, sea squirts, apricot-colored coral, and delicate pink "pendent flowers of the hydroid Tubularia."[79]

Another personal epiphany that looms large in this prose poem takes place when Carson comes upon a small ghost crab while wandering at night with her flashlight on the Georgia shore. The crab lies alone in a sand pit, "as though watching the sea and waiting." Feeling enveloped in primeval blackness, "the darkness of an older world, before Man," she is struck by an extraordinary sense of this animal's otherness and embodiment of that "delicate, destructible, yet incredibly vital force that somehow holds its place amid the harsh realities of the inorganic world." Though she had already observed ghost crabs elsewhere, she insists that, on this occasion, "suddenly I was filled with the odd sensation that for the first time I knew the creature in its own world—that I understood, as never before, the essence of its being." She felt that time had been suspended, and that "the world to which I belonged did not exist and I might have been an onlooker from outer space."[80]

The most lyrical passages in *The Edge of the Sea* express a mystical sense of the world that, while not explicitly theistic, is far from narrowly positivistic. In a letter to Dorothy Freeman, Carson applauded Einstein's statement that " 'The most beautiful and most profound emotion we can experience is the sensation of the mystical,' " and that recognizing the impenetrable " 'is at the center of true religiousness.' "[81] She believed that not only nature but human love and sublime works of music all testified to life's impenetrable mystery and beauty. And like Whitman, she looked most intently toward birds and the sea for nature's finest hints of that ineffable "something that takes us out of ourselves, that makes us aware of other life."[82] Within the opening chapter of *The Edge of the Sea*, Carson suggests that "underlying the beauty of the spectacle" presented by the sea's evolutionary history, "there is meaning and significance." What this cosmic or existential meaning might be she declines to specify but concludes simply: "It is the elusiveness of that meaning that haunts us, that sends us again and again into the natural world where the key to the riddle is hidden." In the book's concluding epilogue, which Carson asked to have read at her funeral, she again invokes an intuitive, interrogative spirituality of nature bearing intimations of an upper-case Presence:

> Contemplating the teeming life of the shores, we have an uneasy sense of the communication of some universal truth that lies just beyond our grasp. What is the message signaled by the hordes of diatoms, flashing their microscopic lights in the night sea? What truth is expressed by the legions of the barnacles, whitening the rocks with their habitations, each small creature within finding the necessities of its existence in the sweep of the surf? And what is the meaning of so tiny a being as the transparent wisp of protoplasm that is a sea lace, existing for some reason inscrutable to us—a reason that demands its presence by the trillion amid the rocks and weeds of the shore? The meaning haunts and ever eludes us, and in its very pursuit we approach the ultimate mystery of Life itself. [83]

Carson also departed from scientific materialism and disinterested positivism by arguing that the earth's poisoned atmosphere confronted humankind with an ethical imperative to set matters right. It is obvious enough that moral passion, duly regulated by logic and evidence, propels the rhetoric of *Silent Spring*. Thus, the author insists that the enormous damage to animal life caused by indiscriminate spraying against Japanese beetles in eastern Illinois raises "a question that is not only scientific but moral." Instead of cooperating with natural processes by means of thoughtful intervention, Western technological civilization had resolved to "wage relentless war on life." It thereby endangered not only its own welfare and the health of the planet but also its very "right to be called civilized."[84]

For Carson, moreover, the ethical demands flowing from "reverence for life" were so powerful and unpredictable that she sometimes felt moved to defend creatures and habitats in ways that seemed more absurd than practical. Once, for example, she noticed that a firefly near her cottage in Maine, confused by a phosphorescent glow on the night beach, was foundering in sandy water. Carson quickly waded in, rescued the solitary insect, and carried it to safety. Another time she managed, after several tries, to work a beached octopus back to open sea with a broom. In *The Edge of the Sea*, she describes returning a large starfish to water at the same tidal level from which she had previously taken it so the animal would feel "at home."[85]

Such peculiar yet hopeful gestures anticipate the central action of an essay by Loren Eiseley titled "The Star Thrower." In that work an enigmatic, numinously shaded figure rescues starfish he finds stranded on the beach by hurling them back, one by one, into the sea. In practical or objectively scientific terms, his deed is clearly futile. Most of the animals will perish anyway, or be seized for profit by mercantile-minded collectors. In a world of endless death, what does it matter if a few individuals survive? Yet Eiseley's speaker ends up emulating the star thrower's action because of the ethical stance it represents. This speaker begins in a state of pitiless desolation, having absorbed too thoroughly the Darwinian view of life as stark warfare, "as a purely selfish struggle, in which nothing is modified for the good of another species without being directly advantageous to its associated form." The essay traces the speaker's spiritual recovery as he moves from detached scientific objectivity verging on cynicism, through a desire for engagement with lives beyond one's own, to an embodiment of love. Eiseley's narrator finally understands star throwing to be "the expression of love projected beyond the species boundary by a creature born of Darwinian struggle."[86]

Carson did not live long enough to read this powerful essay, first published in 1969.[87] Plainly, though, she had already joined forces with Eiseley's compassionate rescuer, in spirit as well as in deed. Moreover, she was fascinated by starfish—and, for that matter, by eels and many other marine creatures. It is fitting that Eiseley, himself a noted paleontologist and anthropologist, had conspicuously defended Carson's testimony in *Silent Spring* when that work first appeared. Carson likewise admired what she had read of Eiseley's writing, including *The Immense Journey* and *Firmament of Time*.[88] Like her, Eiseley was an accomplished writer-scientist who accepted the physical explanations of evolutionary theory but questioned the amoral assumptions of scientific determinism.

Another naturalist whose work Carson admired was none other than John Muir. Though Muir's imagination rested chiefly on the high peaks while Carson's ran to the sea, both figures initiated major environmental campaigns against determined opposition. Both aroused the ire of large corporate interests and of government agencies including the Department of Agriculture.[89] In fact, Carson reported to Dorothy Freeman that she had been reading Muir during the last months of her life. And during the last autumn before her death in April 1964, she made her first trip west to California. After delivering a speech in San Francisco, she welcomed the chance to view some of the region's natural splendors, at the invitation of David Brower, the executive director of the Sierra Club. By then, however, her health had deteriorated drastically.[90] On October 19, 1963, Rachel Carson paid final homage to one who had led the way to her own form of prophetic witness. That Saturday she toured Muir Woods in a wheelchair.

8

Imagined Worlds

The Lure of Numinous Exoticism

Swamp Spirits of African America

Every landscape is exotic, from the perspective of those who stand apart from it. Even places we assume to be familiar remain, on some plane of perception, implacably strange. So the appeal of exoticism is not always escapist. Barry Lopez points out that not only Arctic space but any physical landscape exceeds our grasp, shows itself "baffling in its ability to transcend whatever we would make of it."[1] And that which surpasses our understanding and control draws us inevitably toward religious experience.

Yet this sense of strangeness, of forbidding or alluring resistance to human hegemony, arises most palpably from encounter with places regarded as uncivilized, unmapped. Long before Frederick Turner articulated his "frontier thesis" in the 1890s, Americans had associated dreams of freedom and inner renewal with unsettled territories. In *Nature*, for example, Emerson linked his Transcendental call for the emergence of "new men" bearing "new thoughts" with the opening of "new lands" to Euro-Americans. By 1912, with borders of the lower forty-eight states firmly established, settler culture had to image its exoticism elsewhere. John Muir had already been drawn to visit and describe Alaska. Later prose writers of note, including Barry Lopez and John McPhee, were also inspired by Arctic settings. Other American writers looked to liminal territories beyond America—Ernest Hemingway for example, looked to Africa, and Peter Matthiessen looked to remote sites throughout the developing world.

Even within official U.S. borders, though, exotic or heterotopic spaces can sometimes be found in close proximity to centers of civilization. From the start of slave deportations through the aftermath of eman-cipation, African Americans have been peculiarly disposed to seek refuge in such countercivilized spaces. Granted, the experience of laboring in southern fields has rarely led slaves and their descendants to embrace forms of nature Romanticism favored by white literary culture. As demonstrated by the 1920s Harlem Renaissance, African Americans have usually found northern cities more appealing than recollections of rural poverty in the old South. They have had ample reason to scorn the pastoral conventions extolled in proslavery plan-tation novels. Must one therefore discount the idea of African-American nature writing as a contradiction in terms?

Evidently not, to judge from the land-rooted dramas of human endurance featured in works by writers such as Jean Toomer, Zora Neale Hurston, Alice Walker, and Toni Morrison. But such "nature writing" typically challenges the mainstream culture's impulse to segregate animal Nature from human Cul-ture.[2] Southern swamplands set geographically on the margins of white settle-ment likewise became centers of black resistance during the slave and Recon-struction eras.

Desperate to survive, fugitive slaves were understandably drawn toward these otherwise repellent grounds where damp footing, snakes, and tangles of vegetation discouraged pursuit. Some blacks even managed to establish social communities there. They cleared plots for farming and constructed dwellings. Members of these "maroon societies" might also plot political uprisings or conduct their own forms of worship. They constituted something of an alter-native nation, even as they developed trade links to poor whites and to blacks on surrounding plantations. Yet these "wild solitudes," as Harriet Beecher Stowe described maroon territory in her novel *Dred*,[3] remained inaccessibly exotic to southern slaveholding interests. As the anthropologist Victor Turner points out, a culture's religious experience is sometimes best imaged not along the axis of a common center but within the more liminal space of a sacred periphery.[4] The presence of maroon societies within yet beyond United States boundaries recalls the religious tenor of African-American ties to green sanc-tuaries on the margin of known settlements.

Nat Turner, for example, who escaped an overseer by retreating to the woods for thirty days in 1825 before returning to lead an 1831 slave rebellion in Southampton County, Virginia, testified to having nurtured his resolve by communing with the Holy Spirit. According to *The Confessions of Nat Turner* (1831), this ill-fated but literate insurgent believed he had been called in child-hood to become a prophet. Eventually his visionary, intensely devout disposi-tion seized not only on select passages of scriptural revelation but also on the signs he found inscribed in nature.

Though Turner's fellow slaves thought he must have run off "to some other part of the country" when he first escaped the plantation, he had been brooding alone in the nearby forest. Even after returning from the woods to work in the fields, he often withdrew himself from others to ponder the revelation conveyed through "lights in the sky" and other natural elements. The Holy Ghost had, after all, urged him: " 'Behold me as I stand in the heavens.' " Consistent with his meditation on the saving passion of Christ, he had "discovered drops of blood on the corn, as though it were dew from heaven." During wanderings at the plantation's edge, he also believed he had "found on the leaves in the woods hieroglyphic characters and numbers, with the forms of men in different attitudes, portrayed in blood." He believed, in fact, that "the leaves on the trees bore the impression of the figures I had seen in the heavens." Inwardly authorized to interpret the revelation presented by hieroglyphic leaves in conjunction with celestial signs, and scriptural prophecies, Nat Turner felt more and more convinced that God had ordained him to destroy his enemies "with their own weapons."[5] For him, the forest leaves carried bloody rather than bucolic meaning. And it seems fitting that Turner should have fed such transgressive ambitions by wandering from settled space to the uncultivated edge of his plantation, the place where he thought God spoke most clearly to God's children.

Frederick Douglass, too, reports in his autobiographical writings that he sought at least temporary refuge from the lash of the overseer Covey by running to the wooded periphery of Covey's plantation. He writes that in this "solemn silence," where he was effectively hidden "from all human eyes; shut in with nature and nature's God," he would have prayed for deliverance had his religious faith not been eroded by exposure to corrupt Christianity. In the forest at night Douglass also receives a consoling visit from Sandy, a fellow slave and "religious man" who retains belief in "the so called magical powers" of conjure revered in Africa. Accordingly, Sandy urges Douglass to accept the protection he attributes to herbal roots gathered in the woods.[6]

Henry Bibb, the author of a slave narrative published in 1849, often looked toward the woods because he began learning "the art of running away to perfection" as a child in Shelby County, Kentucky. Eventually Bibb settled permanently in Canada, where he participated in antislavery enterprises as well as the Methodist church. But during his earlier life as perennial fugitive, he often mourned his condition "while sauntering through the forest, to escape cruel punishment." Once, while trying to escape a brutal owner in Louisiana, Bibb faced a decidedly hostile "wilderness" environment. Ironically, Bibb fled the plantation after Francis Whitfield, an ostensibly pious Baptist deacon, became incensed that Bibb had presumed to attend a prayer meeting without his permission. Bibb, with his wife and child, then wandered for over a week through briers and cane-breaks in Louisiana's Red River swamps. His party had to contend with snakes, alligators, and "a gang of savage wolves" before they were hunted down by Deacon Whitfield's bloodhounds.[7]

Historically, though, southern swamps have been surprisingly hospitable to fugitive slaves and African-American revolutionaries. No such specimen of marginal terrain is better known than the Great Dismal Swamp of southeastern Virginia and northeastern North Carolina.[8] The almost supernaturally "magnificent" figure of Dred, whom Harriet Beecher Stowe portrays as the son of real-life insurrectionist Denmark Vesey, grows directly out of this fierce environment (see fig. 8.1). In Stowe's evocative account, the "wild desolation" of these "vast tracts where the forest seems growing out of the water" nurtures

FIGURE 8.1. Scene in the Dismal Swamp, Virginia, 1906. (Photo from the Library of Congress.)

Dred's iconoclastic piety and independent spirit. The Dismal Swamp's foliated luxuriance embraces the maroon community while defying slave-catchers. This apparently "impenetrable" domain becomes home ground for Dred, since "So completely had he come into sympathy and communion with nature, and with those forms of it which more particularly surrounded him in the swamps, that he moved about among them with as much ease as a lady treads her Turkey carpet."[9] The dread powers of God seem indeed to stand behind this character.

Stowe's impressions of the Dismal Swamp were doubtless influenced by what she had read about "The Virginia Maroons" in *The Colored Patriots of the American Revolution* (1855), by the African-American historian William C. Nell. Drawing in turn on a previously published account, Nell remarks on the "curious anomaly" presented by this "city of refuge, in the midst of society." The Swamp's lawless expanse shelters "a large colony of negroes, who originally obtained their freedom by the grace of God and their own determined energy, instead of their owners, or by the help of the Colonization Society."[10]

The former slave William Wells Brown, in his pioneering novel *Clotel* (1853), also pictures this environment of maroon culture. "The Dismal Swamps," writes Brown, "cover many thousands of acres of wild land, and a dense forest, with wild animals and insects, such as are unknown in any other part of Virginia." Brown describes a fierce runaway named Picquilo, whose "bold, turbulent spirit" has been roused to militant violence during the two years he has made the Swamp his home. Abducted from his native land at the age of fifteen, Picquilo deliberately maintains what he can of African practices, manners, and beliefs.[11]

In fact, the religious life of maroon communities often blended elements of traditional African belief with charismatic Christianity. Even slaves who were bound to plantations removed at night to secluded outdoor sanctuaries called "hush harbors" to practice their "invisible" religion, a folk piety involving distinctive patterns of scriptural exegesis. The owner Peter Randolph testified that plantation slaves "assemble in the swamps" to conduct their own forms of worship, sometimes risking severe punishment "for Jesus' sake." But runaways in geographic isolation developed more fevered, subversive understandings of biblical faith. For example, the religious motives that inspired Denmark Vesey's uprising included Methodism and folk spirituality as well as conjure.[12]

The spiritual legacy of the swamps survived in African-American memory into and beyond the Reconstruction era. (It survives even today in Lowcountry of the Carolina Sea Islands among Gullah communities of former West African slaves.) This point is aptly illustrated in the earliest novel written by the social critic and activist W. E. B. Du Bois. All but forgotten today, *The Quest of the Silver Fleece* (1911) opens in the swamps of Tooms County, Alabama, sometime in the postbellum era. Chain gangs, Jim Crow, and the economic hegemony of Southern plantation owners have kept most rural blacks in a condition of de facto slavery. Nonetheless, Du Bois shows how the spiritual wellsprings of African-American identity continue to flow from swampland inhabited by Zora, an exotic and vivacious young woman who personifies the place. Even when this "outcast child of the swamp" encounters literate culture by venturing into a school founded at the edge of her wild "paradise" and by falling in love with upward-aspiring Bles Alwyn, her soul remains bonded to the wetland's "black earth."[13]

Zora is eventually converted to a racially enlightened revision of social Christianity under the spell of a soulful black preacher in Washington, D.C. Transfixed by imagery of the Lamb of God, she finds herself inspired to work for "the salvation of the world." For a time, she believes she has "found the Way" (295–296) beyond her wandering in Christian terms.[14] Zora has, in fact, "been brought up almost without religion" in the formal sense, "save some few mystic remnants of a half-forgotten heathen cult" linked to her disreputable mother. From the first, however, she derives visionary power from those uncleared places "where the Dreams lives" (372, 78). Although Bles Alwyn assures her that after experiencing the benefits of education and cultural assimilation she "won't want to live in the swamp," she finds a sacred dynamism—a mystery "always moving" (50, 245)—residing there. "We blacks is got the *spirit*," (46) she insists; and she sees no ground more fecund for cultivating this spirit than the dark places of her own origin.

But for Zora and Bles, the swamp is more than a place to entertain otherworldly dreams. When they plant some rare cotton seeds there on a hidden island, the space also shelters their hopes for worldly prosperity and liberation. The island promises to become at once a spiritual and a commercial sanctuary from the economic tyranny that surrounds them. Discovering the first shoots of a small but extraordinarily fine crop of cotton, Zora welcomes the appearance of something miraculous:

> In the field of the Silver Fleece all her possibilities were beginning to find expression. These new-born green things hidden far down in the swamp, begotten in want and mystery, were to her a living wonderful fairy tale come true. . . . They were her dream-children, and she tended them jealously; they were her Hope, and she worshipped them. (125)

Even when white landowners rob Zora of her marvelous yield, she persists in believing that "this beautiful baled fibre was hers; it typified happiness; it was an holy thing which profane hands had stolen" (215).

Ultimately, though, the novel embodies its author's ambivalent attitude toward the Alabama swamps. On the one hand, the place is evidently a field of dreams for Zora—and, by extension, for African Americans—because it offers natural refuge from domination by white landowning society. However far African Americans may advance their social standing in the modern world, "the souls of black folk," to borrow the title of Du Bois's most celebrated work, still reside largely in southern swamps. On the other hand, *The Quest of the Silver Fleece* also portrays the terrain of Zora's birth as a backwater of disease, ignorance, and superstition. Even Zora recognizes that " 'the heart of the swamp' " is " 'where dreams *and devils* lives' " (52; emphasis added). Though there is "something holy" (98) about Zora's original state of untamed innocence, there is also for Du Bois something repellent about a nostalgic primitivism that would discourage black folk from pursuing education and radical social change.

Accordingly, the conclusion of *The Quest of the Silver Fleece* shows Zora and Bles Alwyn returning to Alabama from northern sojourns, finally reunited as lovers after each has learned much in the wider world. But they are now more concerned to improve the swamp than they are to recover affiliation with its primal spirits. Zora proposes "a bold regeneration of the land" (400) in which dispossessed people purchase and clear an ample piece of Tooms County swamp for farming. Decades before anyone doubted the environmental wisdom of clearing and cultivating wetlands, Du Bois plainly applauds Alwyn's socialist plan to preserve one hundred acres of this terrain as common land. A model farm created on the plot, beside the old school and newly formed industrial projects, will be worked cooperatively. Only a few twenty-acre portions will be sold for individual production. The novel corroborates such aspirations by showing that when formerly oppressed tenant farmers contribute voluntarily to working the first twenty acres of cleared land, they succeed in producing a "magnificent crop" (408) of cotton.

This "Silver Fleece" signifies hope that, even in the rural South, African Americans might foster the emergence of a new economic order offering them fuller autonomy. But the changes Du Bois extols come at a price. What physical setting could now fulfill what he had elsewhere called "the deep religious feeling of the real Negro heart, the stirring, unguided might of powerful human souls who have lost the guiding star of the past and are seeking in the great night a new religious ideal"?[15] The novel 's final chapter begins in springtime, with Zora musing while she sits in "the transformed swamp—now a swamp in name only" (426). To be sure, Du Bois wants us to understand that much of the surrounding terrain remains unimproved. Apparently, too, he wants to believe that when Zora looks deeper into the darkness, she can still perceive the residual wilds as "living, vibrant, tremulous." On this comparatively sanctified ground, where "there pulsed a glory in the air," Zora proposes marriage to Bles. The novel's closing words are a biblically inflected appeal for justice with transcendent resonance: *"Let my people go, O Infinite One, lest the world shudder at* THE END" (433–434).

Yet the swamp's peculiarly dynamic and diverse biosphere, too, fast approaches its end—and with it, the regenerative spirituality that Du Bois attributes to that setting. Sometime after the locale's hallowed spaces have been quite commodified into cotton, later generations must also learn that large-scale swamp clearing breeds environmental ills that Du Bois could scarcely have anticipated. Marginal lands might, through engineered "improvement," bear the burden of social reform for marginal citizens that ruling-class interests otherwise conspire to thwart.[16] So, at least, it was reasonable for Du Bois to think in the short run. The subtler, long-term costs of such reform have yet to be tallied—in America at large, as well as in the microcosm of Du Bois's novel. Born and raised in western Massachusetts, Du Bois was finally of two minds about the wisdom of continuing to link the spiritual identity of African Americans with traditionally wild tracts of southern soil. Nor is such tension between a people's attachment to indigenous places and its urge for progressive mobility unique to African-American culture.

Discerning the Invisible Landscape in Barry Lopez's
Arctic Dreams

Far removed from semitropical swamps, the stark terrain surveyed by Barry Lopez in *Arctic Dreams* presents a disparate image of the extreme or forbidding landscape. In fact, this northern expanse of tundra and ice more nearly resembles desert space. It is imposingly "spare, balanced, extended, and quiet" (xxiii). For most of us, the Arctic and Antarctic represent quintessentially severe endpoints of all earthly exoticism. Inherently hostile to human habitation, the North American Arctic strikes us as an alien land, the proper locus not of our lives and labor but of dreams. After years of travel and observation in the region, Barry Lopez knows a good deal about its peculiar character. *Arctic Dreams* displays extensive knowledge of the natural, anthropological, and exploratory history of a bioregion that lacks clearly defined boundaries. Yet the author never establishes permanent residence here. Unlike the native peoples he describes, he remains an outside observer. He himself remains exotic, as it were, as he confronts this comparatively "unknown landscape" (13).

Cached within the visible scene and its creatures, what Lopez perceives is a residual strangeness, an unfamiliar and untouchable essence.[17] Moreover, he suggests that such strangeness, colored by imagination, affects the perception even of native inhabitants:

> A Lakota woman named Elaine Jahner once wrote that what lies at the heart of the religion of hunting peoples is the notion that a spiritual landscape exists within the physical landscape. To put it another way, occasionally one sees something fleeting in the land, a moment when line, color, and movement intensify and something sacred is revealed, leading one to believe that there is another realm of reality corresponding to the physical one but different.
>
> In the face of a rational, scientific approach to the land, which is more widely sanctioned, esoteric insights and speculations are frequently overshadowed, and what is lost is profound. The land is like poetry: it is inexplicably coherent, it is transcendent in its meaning, and it has the power to elevate a consideration of human life. (274)

Arctic Dreams testifies to the way in which gaining scientific and personal familiarity with a place heightens respect not only for that environment but for all other faces of the planet. Even for readers who discover the region at second hand, knowledge fosters the sort of ethical attentiveness that helps turn vacant Arctic "space" into a "place."[18] But Lopez's book testifies still more to the way in which the place defies rational and sensory comprehension. It is, above all, a spirit of reverence for things unseen that the author admires in the man he once met in a village of Alaska's central Brooks Range called Anaktuvuk Pass. The man disclosed that when entering a new place, he simply waits and watches appreciatively with trust that through his self-silencing, "respectful manner," the "land would open to him" (257). Lopez finds the same spirit of reverence leading nineteenth-century American landscape painters to "conceive of the land as intrinsically powerful: beguiling and frightening, endlessly arresting and incomprehensibly rich, unknowable and wild." In the light of imagination, they saw and declared it to be " 'the face of God' " (257).

For his part, Lopez embodies the spirit of reverence[19] when he finds himself bowing before birds whose nests he sees exposed on the tundra during his evening walks. The action, described at the outset of *Arctic Dreams*, begins when the author pays homage to a single horned lark. At first instinctual, the gesture becomes habitual. Adopted at last as self-conscious ritual, it appears in retrospect to be the book's defining expression of environmental reverence: "I would bow slightly with my hands in my pockets, toward the birds and the evidence of life in their nests—because of their fecundity, unexpected in this remote region, and because of the serene arctic light that came down over the land like breath, like breathing" (xx). The book closes with Lopez offering a grand bow toward the icy waters of the Bering Strait. "I bowed," he explains, "to what knows no deliberating legislature or parliament, no religion, no competing theories of economics, an expression of allegiance with the mystery of life" (414).

To bow in this manner is to enact an outward, physical sign laden with inward, spiritual meaning. A reverential gesture in many cultural traditions, lowering the upper body thus qualifies as sacramental worship. For Lopez, it comes to bear a religious import not defined solely or principally by the Catholic Christianity in which he was raised. Within the larger course of *Arctic Dreams*, bowing from the waist expresses at once the author's involvement in Arctic nature—and, by extension, in all Creation—*as well as* his necessary standing apart from it.

Discovering ourselves to be paradoxically engaged with, yet estranged from, the sacred mystery of nonhumanity lies at the very heart of Lopez's environmental ethic. For unless we learn to respect the distinctive "otherness" of polar bears, musk oxen, narwhals, and snow geese, we will treat them as mere projections of our will and desires. Unless humans develop regard for the autonomy of such animals, and deeper "tolerance for the unmanipulated and unpossessed landscape" (313), fragile ecosystems of the North cannot survive the colonizing ambitions of Western industrial culture. It is important to notice what, in the polar bear's way of walking, is *not* our way at all. We bow to admit the dignity of its singularity. The narwhal's sense of the world, based mainly on acoustics and tactile cognizance of pressure rather than on sight, is nothing like ours. But this via negativa insight must be ethically conjoined with positive training in prayerful awareness. For unless we also bow affirmatively, to *celebrate* our invisible kinship with the horned lark, we cannot feel our full participation in the community of Creation.

In remarks recorded elsewhere, Lopez points out that his now-characteristic bow reflects "a technique of awareness." He goes on to clarify the via affirmativa aspect of spirituality embodied in the posture:

> We often address the physical dimensions of landscape, but they are inseparable from the spiritual dimensions of landscape. It is in dismissing the spiritual dimensions that we are able to behave like barbarians. If the land is incorporated into the same moral universe that you occupy, then your bow is an acknowledgment of your participation in that universe and a recognition that all you bow to is included in your moral universe. If you behave as though there were no spiritual dimension to the place, then you can treat the place like an object.[20]

Like Coleridge before him, Lopez understands the Imagination to be that unifying faculty of mind by which humans know themselves to be "incorporated into the same moral universe" as the horned lark, snow owl, or (in the case of Coleridge's Ancient Mariner) Pacific albatross. A bodily sign aptly displays this "incorporated" vision. We are indeed bound corporeally and atomically, as well as spiritually, to the rest of the material world. Just as Lopez admires without romanticizing the "archaic affinity for the land" (266) that connects Eskimos to their environment, so also his literary treatment blends depiction of these human lives with portraits of the Arctic's nonhuman inhabitants. The book also illustrates how debased forms of imagination reflect delusions of wealth and grandeur. Corrupt imagination stirs dreams of environmental exploitation, since "desire causes imagination to misconstrue what it finds" (256). But an imagination that is grounded in restraint, humility, and reverence draws inevitably on that truer, more integrative desire known as love:

> There is a word from the time of the cathedrals: agape, an expression of intense spiritual affinity with the mystery that is "to be sharing life with other life." Agape is love, and it can mean "the love of another for the sake of God." More broadly and essentially it is a humble, impassioned embrace of something outside the self, in the name of that which we refer to as *God*, but which also includes the self and *is* God. We are clearly indebted as a species to the play of our intelligence; we trust our future to it; but we do not know whether intelligence is reason or whether intelligence is this desire to embrace and be embraced in the pattern that both theologians and physicists call God. Whether intelligence, in other words, is love. (250)

This affirmative, illuminative spirituality is highlighted in three pivotal chapters: "Ice and Light," "The Country of the Mind," and "The Intent of Monks." The more speculative sequence follows directly upon several chapters offering materially dense reports of discrete zoological and geographic phenomena. Chapter 5, for example, conveys the sense of abundant life one derives from seeing huge numbers of migratory snow geese. "Each bird," writes Lopez, "while it is part of the flock seems part of something larger than itself." Finding their ancient paths of transit "a calming reminder of a more fundamental order," he suggests that "it is easy to feel transcendent when camped among them" (154–155). But in chapter 6, "Ice and Light," Lopez narrows his outward focus toward the elemental, seemingly inert image of sunlit icebergs. These gleaming blocks—"utterly still, unorthodox, and wondrous"—invite the soul toward a peculiarly intense contemplation. Simply staring at them for hours from a cargo ship during his first encounter, Lopez admits gazing with such desire that "it was as though I had been waiting quietly for a very long time, as if for an audience with the Dalai Lama" (208, 205–206).

This chapter also dwells on the presence of light, the literal and elemental foundation of all spiritual illumination. From starkly immediate impressions of light in Arctic space and reports on witnessing the aurora borealis, the narrative moves to reflect on our ageless longing for transcendence, peace, and blessing. The photons constituting light are, after all, both particle and wave, both material and immaterial. No wonder Christian tradition affirms that "God is light" (248). Lopez pursues the meditative, metaphysical implications of "our passion for light" with analogical reference to two expressions of human art: medieval cathedrals and nineteenth-century "luminist" paintings.

For Lopez, late medieval church architecture demonstrated that "not only was God light, but the *relationship* between God and man was light." "The cathedrals," he adds, "by the very way they snared the sun's energy, were an expression of God and of the human connection with God as well" (248). The author casts doubt on usual assumptions that the evolution of Western culture from the medieval "age of mystics" to our own era of technical mastery, an age "of singular adepts, of performers," represents pure progress. Ecological wisdom demands that we recover a contemplative, rather than solely manipulative, relation to Creation. Lopez also looks back with appreciation to productions by nineteenth-century American painters such as Fitz Hugh Lane and Frederic Edwin Church. Through canvases suffused with light that was "a living, integral part of the scene," they tried "to locate an actual spiritual presence in the North American landscape." The authority of their work lies "with the land"; their artistry evokes a landscape that "is numinous, imposing, real" (227, 245).

At the same time, Lopez understands that dimensions of the via negativa can be discerned even within the luminosity of paintings, cathedrals, and Arctic landscapes. A negating feature of those "silent and contemplative" (245) luminist paintings is the effacement of personal egotism demonstrated by their creators. The artist's absence highlights the presence of light and the observed landscape. By the same token, agape, verbal appreciation of which Lopez associates with "the time of the cathedrals," implies a self-abnegating disposition of love. Love that enables one to "embrace something outside the self," to "share life with other life," requires a proportionate negation of self. In New Testament terms, the Christian ideal of *agape* is inevitably wedded to kenosis— that self-emptying denial of all higher prerogatives epitomized by Christ through his incarnation and death.[21] It could also be regarded as the spiritual essence of "exoticism"—that is, in literal terms, a standing *outside* one's typically possessive self, or a sometimes painful discovery of what one is *not*. Saint John of the Cross once observed that mysticism best describes a secret hidden not from others but from "the very one who receives it."[22]

Physical landscapes likewise contain a wealth of imaginative life that is *not* seen, even when they offer observers a moment of epiphany:

> Whatever evaluation we finally make of a stretch of land, however, no matter how profound or accurate, we will find it inadequate. The land retains an identity of its own, still deeper and more subtle than we can know. Our obligation toward it then becomes simple: to approach with an uncalculating mind, with an attitude of regard. To try to sense the range and variety of its expression—its weather and colors and animals. To intend from the beginning to preserve some of the mystery within it as a kind of wisdom to be experienced, not questioned. And to be alert for its openings, for that moment when something sacred reveals itself within the mundane, and you know the land knows you are there. (228)

Lopez later elaborates the point that genuine "mystery," as contrasted with life's "puzzles," involves inexhaustible plenitude. To appreciate the "fundamentally mysterious" (257) character of earth is to welcome all that natural science reveals about its identity—and all that social science reveals about our interactive perceptions of it. But such knowledge ultimately enhances rather than diminishes mystery. Coming to know that even physical landscapes we thought we knew well are "not entirely fathomable," we can more readily discover "the simple appreciation of a world not our own to define" (151). Kallistos Ware, a Greek Orthodox bishop and theologian, explains that

> in the proper religious sense of the term, 'mystery' signifies not only hiddenness but disclosure. . . . So, in the Christian context, we do not mean by a 'mystery' merely that which is baffling and mysterious, an enigma or insoluble problem. A mystery is, on the contrary, something that is *revealed* for understanding, but which we never understand *exhaustively* because it leads into the depth or the darkness of God.[23]

As approached along the apophatic or negative way, therefore, religious mystery stirs awareness of a deeper presence surrounded by absence. And for Lopez, Arctic scenes confront the observer with impressions of absence at every turn. Temperate zone feelings about nature's beauty and solace, commonly supported by greenwood imagery, are negated here. The author reminds us that "regimes of light and time in the Arctic are so different" as to challenge our fundamental assumptions about space and temporality—and, indeed "the complacency of our thoughts about land in general" (12). Forbidding features of this environment sometimes provoke Lopez to voice sentiments shaped by traditional notions of the sublime. He writes, for example, that the "icebergs were so beautiful they made you afraid" (251). For the most part, though, his account represents the Arctic's attitude toward *us* as blankly indifferent. Interrupting his geophysical survey with tales of death, disappointment, and peril faced by explorers, Lopez portrays the North as an ideal place to be stripped of sentimental illusions about nature or oneself. In a setting where life is inevitably reduced to lowest terms, humans can nonetheless find solace through the Buddhist meditative principle that "we are saved in the end by the things that ignore us."[24] Although *Artic Dreams* copiously illustrates the idea that these bleak lands hold beauties of their own, it sees the place as a whole—apart from the projections of human desire—as preserving a kind of holy indifference. Elsewhere Lopez has characterized Antarctica, too, as a land "informed by indifference." "If you returned" to such a place you had once visited, he says wryly, "it would be to pay your respects, for not being welcomed."[25]

Lopez knows well that the spiritual geography of such landscapes has been previously mapped in several religious traditions, including that preserved from ancient Christianity through writings of the Desert Fathers and Desert Mothers. Inwardly, therefore, the environment of *Arctic Dreams* is connected to remote arid spots in the Middle East. Lopez studied at a Jesuit high school and took his undergraduate degree at Notre Dame. At one point he considered entering a monastery. He has since distanced himself from the Church and from some elements of his religious training. Selectively critical of his university education, he has complained that while attending Notre Dame, "that profound mystery I sensed in wild animals (which reading Descartes had done nothing to dissuade)—was regarded as peculiar territory by other nascent writers at the university."[26] But he continues to respect the traditions and practices of contemplative prayer, which single-minded souls have long pursued especially though not exclusively in isolated places. Appreciating the traditional regard in Benedictine monasticism for work as a form of prayer, Lopez extends the principle to his own work when he observes that "there must be moments in your life when you are saying your prayers better, and that's what writing is for me." Thus his writing, though rarely theological in its overt expression, is often contemplative in its orientation. His conviction that a divine energy surrounds human interactions with the land developed not only from years of outdoor experience in diverse settings but also from early training and later reflection:

> I grew up in a Roman Catholic tradition, and was deeply affected by it—especially the Desert Fathers, the Jesuits, and the monastic tradition—not the things one normally hears about Catholicism. An image I have from childhood is of a group of men and women praying somewhere in the desert. The reason chronically myopic and selfish people have not destroyed us with nuclear weapons is that, in a rarefied and metaphorical way, there have been these enclaves of monastics praying. What keeps these things from exploding, perhaps, is that each of us in his own way is saying his prayers.[27]

Applying verbal rather than visual artistry, Lopez seeks in *Arctic Dreams* to create the spiritual equivalent of a luminist painting—to convey impressions of "an actual spiritual presence in the North American landscape," but in a different region and through another medium. In fact, *Arctic Dreams* encompasses multiple subgenres of writing. It is at once a travel narrative, personal narrative, and prose poem. It combines discursive treatment of geography, ethnography, and zoology, with adventure tales drawn from the history of polar exploration. It is also a study in environmental hermeneutics, one person's reading of the interplay between land and what humans construct or project upon it.

Yet beyond all this, *Arctic Dreams*, like Matthiessen's book *The Snow Leopard*, records the fruits of interior exploration. As a rhetorically shaped meditation, Lopez's book resembles prayer because it looks to connect the deep psyches of both author and reader to something larger than themselves, something dreadfully yet alluringly alien. It testifies as well to our society's need to redevelop a contemplative, rather than a thoughtlessly manipulative, relation to the nonhuman world. But though Lopez deplores the injuries imposed on Arctic lands and peoples by resource-hungry nations, his book is more celebratory than apocalyptic. He can still say, after walking the iced northern sea edge of Canada's Baffin Island, "I feel blessed" (124). *Arctic Dreams* stands within an established tradition of American nature writing that contributes to what Lopez has called "a literature of hope."[28]

Seeking the Unseen Snow Leopard

Not merely the environment but the central organism as well in Peter Matthiessen's book *The Snow Leopard* (1978) emerges as "exotic"—that is, as inspiring Western travelers to envision a symbolic order beyond normal bounds of human perception. In fact, the author of this evocative nonfiction never catches a glimpse of its title character. The snow leopard becomes an elusive, unseen presence one can revere all the more because it defies casual inspection. Its hidden life is revealed only indirectly, through signs and reports. But it is solely within its native Himalayan setting that the species maintains this nearly numinous reputation. In captivity, deprived of dignity, it strikes observers as a sadly diminished creature.[29] Just as Lopez portrays musk oxen and polar bears as perfectly adjusted to the realms they inhabit, so also the snow leopard deserves to live where it belongs. So do human beings—presuming they can ever find a real homeplace amid modern mobile civilization.

Thus, the exoticism of *The Snow Leopard* is no idle diversion or end in itself but a route by which humans wander beyond familiar habitats to pursue their proper place in the world before returning home. For some, this pursuit may involve travel to distant lands, as it has for both Lopez and Matthiessen. Both writers embrace this itinerant vocation as a way of gaining global perspective and of supporting their engagement with social justice issues.[30] Matthiessen's spiritual journey, too, has led him on paths removed from the chief thoroughfares of U.S. religious culture. Like Lopez, for example, with whom he is personally acquainted, he has developed a well-informed esteem for the beliefs of Native Americans and other traditional peoples.[31] And like Gary Snyder, the poet Margaret Gibson, and other environmentally minded writers of our day, he has committed himself to meditative disciplines and habits of mind more derived from Buddhist traditions of Asia than from the Abrahamic religious heritage of Europe and the Middle East.

Having begun serious study and practice of Zen Buddhism in 1970, Matthiessen subsequently visited ancient shrines in Japan and became particularly enamored of writings by Dogen Zenji, a thirteenth-century Soto Zen master. In *Nine-Headed Dragon River*, he describes his attraction to that form of "not-knowing" that enables us to accept our true "Buddha-nature" and "to be at one with our element." Interior healing is thus seen as welded seamlessly to environmental philosophy. Matthiessen recommends the sitting Zen practice known as *zazen* as a way of discovering the liberating emptiness of resting "in the present" and thereby of returning "to natural harmony with all creation." Recalling as it does "that natural religion of our early childhood, when heaven and a splendorous earth were one," Zen practice is open to all. The author of *Nine-Headed Dragon River* also credits the nineteenth-century Transcendentalists Emerson and Thoreau with spreading Zen teachings to the New World. He writes that Thoreau, "inspired by 'my Buddha,' wished 'to go soon and live away by the pond, where I shall hear only the wind whispering among the reeds.' " Since 1981, when Matthiessen was ordained a Zen priest, he has continued to attend *sesshins* at a Soto Zen community.[32]

So after *The Snow Leopard* appeared in 1978, Matthiessen continued to publish books of nonfiction while extending his study and practice of Zen Buddhism. He understands Zen as "a way of seeing the world that is closely tied in with the way American Indian people see the world."[33] By contrast, the conservative Protestant missionaries who invade the Amazonian jungle in Matthiessen's novel *At Play in the Fields of the Lord* (1965) are portrayed as ignorant, controlling, and condescending toward traditional peoples. They seem motivated less by Christian love than by imperialist arrogance. In the deadly ambition of their enterprise, they lack all sense of the wilderness as a divine gift, an opportunity for joyous play in the field of God's Creation.

At first one might perceive some contradiction between Peter Matthiessen's Buddhist resolve to savor life in the present moment, as expressed in books such as *The Snow Leopard* or *Nine-Headed Dragon River*, and his preoccupation with the historical past throughout his Watson trilogy—a monumental work of novelistic fiction completed in 1999. In a 1989 interview, for example, Matthiessen confirmed that "we waste our lives regretting the past, anticipating the future," whereas "all Zen teaches is to pay attention to the present moment" so as to perceive "this humble subject" as "full of power and resonance."[34] But the Buddhist principle of "mindfulness" actually connects these two sides of Matthiessen's imaginative sensibility. In 1948 a disciple of Gurdjieff first impressed upon Matthiessen the importance of cultivating disciplined mindfulness, of "paying attention to the present moment."[35] Since then, books such as *The Miracle of Mindfulness: A Manual on Meditation* (1975), by Thich Nhat Hanh, have given this element of the Eight-Fold Path even broader exposure in the West. In any case, the spiritual discipline of mindfulness involves qualities of concentration and attentiveness to detail that shape Matthiessen's discipline as a writer in fictional as well as nonfictional modes. Attention to the world's textured abundance likewise shapes the mood of all his nature writing.

During a lifetime of peregrination, Matthiessen has endeavored to bring genuine mindfulness to his study of each locale that figures in his writing. Though some of his work qualifies as travel writing, it is not conventional tourist literature. Typically focusing full attention on the relevant spot of earth, he develops a historically and scientifically grounded sense of place through research conducted both in the field and in books. Since 1960, when he settled permanently on a six-acre tract in Sagaponack, Long Island, he has also found a kind of geographic anchor for his wandering disposition by maintaining his home in this community once dominated by potato farming.

In addition to mindfulness, a preoccupation with wildness could be identified as another keynote of Matthiessen's writing across a broad span of decades and subgenres. Plainly, much of the writing is concerned with representations of wildlife and with often exotic wilderness landscapes in Asia, Africa, or North and South America. Early in his career, his study *Wildlife in America*

(1959) surveyed the full story of untamed animals on this continent, beginning with the era of European contact, and assessed the long-term impact of humanity's presence on the scene. A landmark statement of modern environmentalism published three years before *Silent Spring, Wildlife in America* gave cogent illustration to the point that something invaluable was being lost when thoughtless intervention threatened animal habitats and species diversity. Attentiveness to the natural history of endangered wildlife and habitats in Africa likewise suffuses the author's several volumes of nonfiction about that continent. His writing often images once-undisturbed ecosystems that are fast disappearing or under threat.

Yet Matthiessen's imaginative sense of the wild extends beyond the physical wilderness of roadless areas. In both fiction and nonfiction, he shows himself drawn repeatedly toward the uncharted place that he calls, in the spirit of Thoreau, "the wildness of the world." Having presumably lost this sense of primal vitality in early childhood, Matthiessen writes of endeavoring to recover it through much of the rest of his life. In an early interview, he described his fiction as "realistic only in the most superficial sense; someone has called it *surreal,* in the sense of intensely or *wildly* real, and I think this is correct."[36]

Accordingly, his writing shows a perennial fascination not only with wild places and animals but with untamed or archaic human beings as well—and with deviations from the normative values, beliefs, and practices of middle-class Americans. Thus, the E. J. Watson of Matthiessen's trilogy is himself a violent, passionate figure whose story is mostly played out in the lawless territory of Florida's Everglades in the late 1800s. The urge to defend or to recover association with archaic peoples likewise remains prominent throughout the corpus of Matthiessen's work. Although he is not so atavistic as to suppose that his own Western culture ever could or should return to a premodern state of nature, much of his writing underscores the point that any initiative, including scientific exploration, by which industrialized peoples encounter primitive peoples must be intrusive if not destructive. It also probes the question of how technological societies can gain environmental understanding that effectively incorporates the spiritual wisdom of traditional peoples.

Matthiessen's most celebrated book of nonfiction, *The Snow Leopard,* seems at first a straightforward journal of an arduous 1973 expedition across remote Himalayan regions of Nepal to the Tibetan Plateau. Enfolded within this factual chronicle of adventure, though, is a richly evocative version of the archetypal quest narrative. The journey-quest proceeds on at least three planes. On the first and most obvious level, the trip's purpose is to seek further knowledge of the Himalayan bharal, or blue sheep. This scientific aim had initially motivated Matthiessen's zoologist friend George Schaller to propose the trip. Schaller invited the author to join him because of their shared zoological interest, but Matthiessen would find other reasons, too, for joining the expedition. Thus, the author observes that "where bharal were numerous, there was bound to appear that rarest and most beautiful of the great cats, the snow leopard" and that "the hope of glimpsing this near-mythic beast in the snow mountains was reason enough for the entire journey" (3).

The tantalizing mention of a "near-mythic beast" suggests at the outset motives for journeying that are less rationally determined than those encompassed by naturalistic science. On a second plane, this best-selling work unfolds the story of a spiritual and religious quest. Already committed to Buddhist meditative practice, Matthiessen welcomed the chance to journey "step by step across the greatest range on earth to somewhere called the Crystal Mountain" as "a true pilgrimage, a journey of the heart." Here, after all, in the Land of Dolpo, lay the Crystal Monastery, where one might find the lama of Shey, "the most revered of all the *rinpoches*, the 'precious ones,' in Dolpo." Dolpo was "said to be the last enclave of pure Tibetan culture left on earth" (3–4). Tibetan culture, in turn, represents for many Westerners a depth of spiritual possibility and interiority that seems elusive in today's commercial world. As the book proceeds, Matthiessen often interposes explanatory accounts of Buddhist belief and practice with physical descriptions of the journey. Such explanations offer a cultural-historical context for understanding particular versions of Zen, Mahayana, and Tibetan Buddhism. Yet Matthiessen also invokes a variety of Western writers—including Thomas Traherne, William Blake, Rainer Maria Rilke, Hermann Hesse, and Henry David Thoreau—to suggest the universality of the spirit-quest.

A third dimension of the book's journeying toward discovery is intensely interpersonal and emotional insofar as it focuses on the author's absent family. In the prologue, Matthiessen mentions that his second wife, Deborah Love, had died of cancer in the winter before his departure. This apparently casual reference takes on considerable meaning as the author returns repeatedly in memory to Deborah and the time of Deborah's death even as he progresses physically on his trek to Shey. In other ways, too, the book shows recursive stylistic traits that play against its linear progress through time and space, a progress signified outwardly by the inclusion of maps and dates.

The author's search to comprehend his relation to Deborah reaches an emotional climax in the entry for October 11, where a poignant account of her final days marks a turning point in the author's own sense of life and mortality. Particularly insofar as Deborah had shared Matthiessen's engagement with Zen, this interpersonal strand of the book's narrative is closely interwoven with its portrayal of the spiritual quest. Matthiessen constantly juxtaposes reminders of the existential solitude demanded in spiritual journeying with vignettes about the self-discoveries he has made, paradoxically, through encounters with other human beings—with Deborah, above all, but also with figures like Tukten, his Sherpa porter, and with his redoubtable, enigmatic, and sometimes exasperating companion, George Schaller.

Substantially rewritten from initial journal entries, the finished book sounds a religious note from the first with its epigraph from Rilke extolling the courage to confront strangeness, visionary experience, and the divine "spirit world." In subsequent expositions on the historical character of Zen, and of Buddhism more generally, the work offers a useful summary of belief-systems unfamiliar to most Western readers. But what lends force to such bookish discourse are Matthiessen's frequent insertions of personal testimony.

This personal narrative of spiritual journeying begins with a vague rest-lessness. It is as though "one were being watched" but cannot say who or what is watching. Matthiessen confides that he had still felt inwardly confused in his first books, having then pursued a kind of religious understanding by ex-perimenting with hallucinogenic drugs during the late 1950s and early 1960s. He even admits he doesn't quite know why he has taken this long trip on the Tibetan Plateau: "To say I was making a pilgrimage seemed fatuous and vague, though in some sense that was true as well." He had earlier described his "wandering from one path to another with no real recognition that I was em-barked upon a search, and scarcely a clue as to what I might be after." He knew only "that at the bottom of each breath there was a hollow place that needed to be filled." All the same, he comes increasingly to feel "that there is a source for this deep restlessness; and the path that leads there is not a path to a strange place, but the path home" (44, 125, 43).

Beyond the book's exotic landscapes, the undiscovered country that mat-ters most at the level of spiritual quest is a space or path in the psyche that Matthiessen associates with the classic Chinese way of Tao. Such mysteries are likewise evoked by Buddhist traditions of "a hidden kingdom—Shambala, the Center—in an unknown part of Inner Asia" (55). As *The Snow Leopard* pro-ceeds, Matthiessen reflects deepening awareness that his goal is not simply to reach the physical destination of Shey in Inner Dolpo. In fact, his trip could be considered something of an outward failure. He never manages to see the snow leopard—and when, after endless delays and difficulties, he reaches the fabled Crystal Monastery, he cannot view its interior. It is actually vacant. Be-fore the snows, its lama and monks had already retreated across the mountains to Saldang. His journey therefore involves not only movement toward a geo-graphic target but also a painful education in mindfulness and understanding along the way.

To be sure, the remote physical locale plays a critical role in this path of discovery pursued by what Michael Heim calls "the new mystical naturalist."[37] Though the environment is often forbidding in a way that reduces life to lowest terms, there is indeed "a blessedness to this landscape" with its occasional rest walls and tea houses. And as the author testifies, the silence and sublime grandeur of the high places readily encourage his practice of meditation. He also cultivates an attentiveness to more ordinary features of the Asian setting: "In the glory of sunrise, spiderwebs glitter and greenfinches in October gold bound from pine to shining pine. Pony bells and joyous whistling; young chil-dren and animals jump as if come to life" (16, 73). Who could fail to be dis-tracted from petty egotism by the thrill of encountering animals like the red panda, Asiatic black bear, wolf, and bharal ram? Still, the book shows wariness toward the lure of popular exoticism, toward the cultural mythology of escape to James Hilton's distant utopia of Shangri-La.

Accordingly, *The Snow Leopard* seeks in many ways to dispel images of the heroic adventurer who confronts spectacular perils while traversing exotic ter-ritory. As Lawrence Buell observes in *The Environmental Imagination*, the typ-ical hero of the wilderness quest-romance in classic American literature is a solitary male protagonist in the mold of Cooper's Natty Bumppo and Faulkner's Ike McCaslin.[38] By contrast, the narrator of *The Snow Leopard* portrays himself largely as an antihero. Prone to error and fits of petty anger, he rarely behaves nobly. There is little glamorous adventure in what he tells us of his leaking tent, bad shoes, and soggy sleeping bag. He even tells tales on himself, as when he confesses that envy may have stirred him to quarrel with George Schaller. He accuses himself of having behaved badly toward his now-deceased wife, of neglecting his motherless children, and of foolishly refusing the better judgment of Tukten. Native peoples, too, are portrayed as decidedly fallible, in contrast to the Western stereotype of saintly Tibetans. Matthiessen often complains about the stubborn, unruly, slothful, and deceitful conduct of the porters. By the end, though, he conveys a profoundly unsentimental appreciation of the humanity embodied in figures like Tukten.

In this regard, the book's periodic comments about interpersonal relations enrich its narrative of inward quest and refute the American wilderness myth of solitary heroism. Matthiessen's sporadic musings on a dead wife and absent children may seem at first only to distract him from involvement in the current expedition, but they play a crucial role in helping him cultivate the sort of mindful discipline that embraces the whole of life. Thus, the apparently intrusive remembrances of Deborah Love offer vital sustenance for his inward journey toward universal acceptance and love.

The central recollection of Deborah Love surfaces abruptly in the entry for October 11. Here Matthiessen relates a moving episode in which Deborah responded appreciatively to his gift of an elegant ceramic bowl even while she lay drugged and in pain during the final stages of her illness. The Himalayan peaks stirred memories of another mountain trip, when he had visited the French Alps with Deborah the year before her death. In the midst of his stormy relationship to this woman "lovely in person and in spirit" (76), he secretly purchased the antique bowl she had admired with him in Geneva. He had intended to surprise her with it on her birthday. When they quarreled, he set it aside indefinitely. He did not present his gift until she lay on her deathbed, when he feared she could no longer know or care what was happening. Yet her surprising recognition of the bowl—and, by implication, of his love—now looms large in memory as a moment of grace. It becomes a critical landmark in the author's journey toward acceptance of his own pain, remorse, and mortality.

For Matthiessen, reflection on the death of Deborah Love also figures conspicuously in his growth toward that paradoxical spirituality in which the self can be at once sympathetically engaged with others and inwardly detached. At the summit of his trip, on Crystal Mountain, the contentment he enjoys in solitude is not an escape from the world but rather a transcendent acceptance of death, affliction, and the satisfaction available in life's "common miracles" (232). That paradoxical capacity, as T. S. Eliot once described it, of caring yet not caring likewise describes an ideal to which the author aspires in his complex relationships to other figures—including George Schaller, Tukten, and his absent eight-year-old son.

Thus, in the painful process of seeking oneness with the whole Creation, the author finds Deborah Love becoming at once a presence and a palpable absence in his consciousness. The snow leopard, too, takes on growing significance in this book as both presence and absence. Its living presence is confirmed by November 9, when the author finds its print and scat along the Black River Canyon beyond Tsakang. Persuaded that the unseen animal is watching them, Matthiessen and Schaller develop a strong sense of its proximity. "It is wonderful," writes Matthiessen, "how the presence of this creature draws the whole landscape to a point" (247). While traveling apart from Matthiessen, Schaller finally manages to sight a snow leopard.

Yet Matthiessen never does. Because this creature is "wary and elusive to a magical degree," its absence from his gaze assumes an ever-deepening spiritual meaning. He would like to see a snow leopard but ultimately accepts his deprivation with serenity: "In the not-seeing, I am content" (152, 242). Perhaps he is not yet inwardly prepared for such vision. Perhaps, too, the leopard's presence-in-absence corresponds to that pregnant emptiness of the universe recognized by the spiritual sages—the emptiness into which Lao-tzu and Bodhidharma both passed.

Or perhaps the snow leopard should remain unseen because it serves as presiding spirit of an elusive, mysterious wilderness threatened by imminent destruction. Along his way through Nepal and across the Tibetan Plateau, Matthiessen sees many signs of environmental degradation, including land erosion, deforestation, and diminishing wildlife. He thus confronts an Asian equivalent of the sad tale he had told earlier in *Wildlife in America*. As long as the snow leopard remains unseen, one can celebrate its survival as an unconquered remnant of primitive nature in a world dominated by the meddlesome technocracy of "new barbarians" (62) from the West. Anticipating the gesture that Barry Lopez would enact in *Arctic Dreams* and other writings, the author of *The Snow Leopard* finds himself bowing involuntarily before the still beauty of nature revealed in the Dhaulagiri snowfields.

Beyond his obvious failure to see the leopard, Matthiessen must confront other forms of diminishment toward the close of his narrative. Inevitably, the thrill of discovery wanes during the return phase of his two-month trip, as he descends from the high point of his contentment with the beauty of Shey and Crystal Mountain. He feels a strange sense of regret following his safe return. Finally, on the day appointed for his last rendezvous with Tukten at a nearby shrine, Tukten fails to appear.

Even this last note of absence is consistent, though, with the book's broader theme of accepting the world as it is. Though physically absent at the close of the narrative, Tukten had already affected the author's soul through his example of unencumbered simplicity and inner freedom. In fact, "this leopard-eyed saint" (303) ends up becoming Matthiessen's teacher and spiritual guide in a way that partly supersedes George Schaller's guidance while recalling the elusive freedom of the snow leopard. In an interview, the author later confirmed that he regarded Tukten as his teacher and, indeed, as a kind of snow leopard.[39] What is more, Tukten's openhearted acceptance of life matches the affirmative outlook Matthiessen had encountered when he eventually met the disabled Lama of Shey. "Of course I am happy here," the lama insists when asked how he has borne eight years of silent isolation and infirmity. "It's wonderful! Especially when I have no choice!" (246).

Renewed capacity to accept the world as it truly is, beyond the passing distortions of social injustice, can be counted the greatest gift the narrator carries home to America. The exotic journey outward and upward leads toward deeper knowledge—for the reader, too, as mental traveler—of how to live in gracious harmony with one's home environment. Learning to say "Of course I am happy here" is a lifetime endeavor. *The Snow Leopard* does presume that an unseen presence and unity subsists at the heart of the phenomenal universe. It presumes further that the goal of spiritual search is to discover one's identity with this "Jewel in the Heart of the Lotus," to share in the cosmic rhythm evoked by the great "Om" mantra (104). But the hidden jewel also rests broadly across the visible landscape, adorning America no less than Asia. Those cosmic rhythms voiced in chant also govern the life cycles operative in actual, smelly, inexpressibly varied ecosystems. And the snow leopard, unlike mythical beasts, exists for real. Even those privileged to glimpse this animal are challenged by Matthiessen's book to respect the richly unseen, unknown life of nonhumans who act independently of our ambitions.

God, Satan, and Uncle Sam in the Everglades

Such respect has not always been apparent during the ever-quickening march of material civilization in America, particularly since the onset of industrialism. In his epic Watson trilogy, Matthiessen presents an environmentally colored critique of unbridled capitalism. The trilogy begins with *Killing Mr. Watson* (1990), continues through *Lost Man's River* (1997), and ends with *Bone by Bone* (1999). These historically inspired novels dramatize not only the deformations of place that fierce development has produced in the Florida Everglades but also the debased religious mythology that has often viewed conquest of indigenous lands and peoples as the sacred, civilizing mission of Euro-Americans. Matthiessen sums up his contempt for this perverted providential ideology when a character of his describes his trilogy's central character, Jack Watson, as looking " 'like God' " and " 'like Satan' " and " 'like Uncle Sam, all three at once.' "[40] Though Uncle Sam's material ambitions can be construed as godly progress, they can also be experienced as demonic and rapacious by those who stand in the way.

Read most profitably as a single unified work, Matthiessen's three novels deal exhaustively with the historical figure of Edgar J. Watson (aka "Jack"), a commanding personality who becomes a prosperous sugar cane planter and entrepreneur after he makes his home at Chatham Bend in the swamp country of Florida's Everglades in the 1890s. Though capable of adopting a gentlemanly and neighborly bearing, "Jack" Watson also has a violent temper and the reputation of a cold-blooded killer. Word of his misdeeds follows him from his previous lives in the Oklahoma Territory and north Florida to south Florida, where more tales of murder and illegitimate children grow so plentifully around "Bloody Watson" that he assumes larger-than-life stature in the frontier settlements of the Ten Thousand Islands region. Though not responsible for all the killings charged to him, this apparently likeable neighbor is indeed a serial murderer.

The trilogy, which examines Watson from every conceivable angle for over thirteen hundred pages, focuses particularly on the last dramatic episodes of his life. An apocalyptic mood develops as Watson's end follows the ravaging effects of the Great Hurricane of 1910, the return of Halley's Comet, and a triple murder that is attributed to him though it was committed by his foreman, Leslie Cox. Ironically, it is this crime that leads to Watson's showdown with a self-appointed "posse" of neighbors, who shoot him with thirty-three bullets when he returns to Chokoloskee on October 24, 1910. *Killing Mister Watson* (1990) tells the story through a polyphonic array of ten voices that, along with documentary statements from a fictive historian, reveal disparate judgments of the central character. In *Lost Man's River* (1997), the narration also draws on multiple witnesses but operates from a single, albeit unstable, center of consciousness in the person of Watson's son Lucius, while *Bone by Bone* (1999) revisits the story one last time from Watson's own point of view.

The work as a whole captivates by revivifying forgotten facts of regional history while capturing that sense of place peculiar to the wilds of southwest Florida at the turn of the century. Moreover, Watson becomes the focal point here for an even larger, distinctively American cultural drama. A peculiar folk hero who embodies the wild energy of America's frontier, this desperado nonetheless defies usual views of the outlaw in his attentiveness to documented land claims as well as in his zeal for Florida's economic and industrial development. More than one of Watson's murders is impelled by a desire to silence those he fears will harm his reputation as aspiring business leader or thwart his schemes to expand the production of high-grade sugar syrup.

Particularly in the last two novels, Matthiessen shows how Watson's lawless ambition is symbolically linked to the unfettered voraciousness of leading capitalists and to the nation's expansionist designs as epitomized by the Spanish-American War. Despite his killing and carousing, Watson is a hard worker with "big plans"[41] who stands for "progress." As one of his old neighbors testifies, Ed Watson " 'never let nobody stand in the way of progress' " (*LMR* 373). Watson believes in paying his bills, in exploiting hired labor to grow and process his sugar cane efficiently, and in realizing optimal profit through whatever means he deems necessary. For the sake of promoting his own economic empire, he would like to see southwest Florida developed by draining the Everglades for new acreage and building new railways.

No wonder Watson is eventually honored by agribusinessmen as a progenitor of Big Sugar—and as one who helped pave the way for Florida's great plenty of highways, causeways, malls, and retirement complexes. No wonder, then, he bears the composite image of God, Satan, and Uncle Sam. Yet by way of religion, he believes in nothing beyond nihilistic materialism.[42] Revering no god except himself, Watson has no comprehension of his ability to desecrate and destroy. Though gifted with certain virtues, he lacks all virtue of reverence for other persons and creatures.

It is germane to the dream of white mastery implicit in this cultural fable that Watson should have planted his sugar farm on top of an Indian mound left by displaced Calusas, and that two field hands he later kills for the sake of "eliminating agitators who caused serious trouble" should have been black. Watson concedes there may be some truth in the claim of Mr. Sam Clemens, an author admired by his second wife, that "our nation's bold new spirit of industrialism and imperialism was based on nothing more nor less than racism and greed" (B 349, 184).

Still, Watson "always spoke as a stern supporter of the capitalist system" since he "meant to become a capitalist" himself and knew that "rough methods were sometimes necessary in the name of progress" (B 179, 195). Watson invokes the precedent of those "great capitalists building America" who "let nobody and nothing stand in the way of progress, especially their own" (B 193). "I have taken life," he confesses, and "for that, I will always be sorry." Yet he claims: "Generally, I have not done it for financial reasons," and asks: "How many of these 'robber barons' who are making America's great fortunes can say the same?" (317). When Henry Flagler developed his Model Land Company at Palm Beach and completed his railway project in east Florida, he ignored the hundreds who labored and often died "in that humid heat to make his fortune." So to Watson it seemed "unjust—in fact, it enraged me—that a small cane planter on a remote frontier should be slandered for a few deaths among his workers when the powerful men building great empires were permitted to write off human life as simple overhead" (340–341). As a champion of progress, Watson wants to think he has more in common with two distinguished Florida visitors, Henry Ford and Thomas Edison, than he does with any celebrity killer. But Watson is scarcely the first or only self-deceived American to believe that ethical scruples must be set aside to realize some grand ambition. The author deftly leads readers to sympathize with Watson, despite his evil reputation, by exposing his troubled upbringing and the great pain he has endured.

In the end, Watson exemplifies both the self-confident individualism *and* the violence endemic to American culture. His relation to the natural environment is similarly paradoxical. On the one hand, he readily adapts to living in what the critic John Cooley calls that "singular bioregion" of the Everglades.[43] Protected by wild mangroves, he thrives in the lawless isolation of the subtropical frontier. As Lucius observes, he has more instinctive talent for working with "crops and farm animals" (LMR 52) than anybody else in the islands. On the other hand, Ed Watson's zeal for "progress" and disregard for life incite him to destroy the very wilderness he loves. When he first reaches the islands, he confides: "Seeing so much wild, virgin coast awaiting man's domination, I felt better and better" (B 148–149). He cannot perceive the beauty of wild creatures as clearly as his son Lucius or his son Rob, who later bemoans "'the desecration of Creation'" (LMR 509) displayed in the wanton slaughter of alligators. Hungry to shoot up "the best rookeries in spring" (KMW 48), he fails to grasp, as does the later-generation townsperson Bill Smallwood, that the loss of plume birds and eventual disappearance of large cats and bears are hastening the time when there " 'ain't goin to be one bright-eyed bit of life left in south Florida' " (*LMR* 371). Never having glimpsed a sacred face of nature or of human nature, Watson cannot abhor the desecration of either.

One must therefore recognize more than one sort of wildness. Watson's version of untamed energy more often destroys than preserves the endangered remnants of aboriginal life. Matthiessen has elsewhere defined wild people and places as those "that still have their own integrity."[44] In *Lost Man's River*, even the creation of Everglades National Park raises troubling questions about what is truly wild when park management tries to erase every sign of previous human settlement from this wilderness enclave.

The Watson epic, which reflects the dense empiricism of real-life investigation, also bridges the usual gulf between fact and fiction. Clear boundaries no longer exist by which the historical facts of Watson's case can be set apart from the Watson myths and from Matthiessen's fictions. The work's exoticism effectively transports us to another place and era, enabling us to enter the mindset of a decidedly aberrant central character. Highlighting the indeterminacy of boundaries between here and there, present and past, familiar and unfamiliar impressions of the American landscape, this anatomy of an outlaw expresses a mode of exotic imagination quite different from that represented in *The Snow Leopard*.

The Snow Leopard will probably remain Peter Matthiessen's best-known achievement. Yet his grand trilogy also deserves recognition for its searching analysis of the interplay between Nature and Culture in America. It should also stimulate readers to reassess what "nature writing" is all about. The term is still commonly equated with nonfictional prose and, above all, with writing from which human beings have mostly been evacuated. While challenging such assumptions in his colossal Watson novel, Matthiessen has continued to reap artistic benefit from his multidisciplinary knowledge of zoology, religion, history, and literature. Doubtless, too, he will continue to live up to his Zen name, Muryo, which as one commentator points out, is amazingly apt in its sense of one "without boundaries."[45] Such exoticism reveals itself not in fantasies of escape, but in unbounded zeal to explore the wonders of this earth.

9

Reclaiming the Sacred Commons

The Gifted Land of Wendell Berry

Exotic nature writing need not display disdain or indifference toward life on the writer's home ground. But it invariably expresses the reactions of an itinerant observer. Another significant strain of American environmental writing presents the settled resident's account of a particular locale. Familiar instances would be Henry Thoreau's *Walden*, or Edwin Way Teale's book *A Naturalist Buys an Old Farm* (1974). Instead of recounting his solitary trip into some majestic wilderness, Teale tells of settling with his wife in a quiet corner of northeastern Connecticut. There, toward the close of his career as naturalist writer, he devotes himself to sauntering with "Nellie" through the ordinary but companionable fields and woods of a former farm.

In present-day America, the voluminous prose writings of Wendell Berry epitomize this homewatching brand of environmental literature. Like other works considered in this chapter, Berry's nonfiction also denies the Romantic solitary's view of nature as a functionally private arena of self-transcendence. That human community should be viewed as an integral member of nature's ecological "household" is a persistent theme of Berry's writing and also figures conspicuously in Gary Snyder's vision of bioregionalism. In fact, all the writers discussed in these final chapters perceive a need to deepen our culture's sense of environmental reverence. And they generally understand this virtue of reverence to embrace a spiritual component, as well as a concern for social justice across the common landscape of North America. It is sometimes assumed that serious literature of the postmodern era must deny all transmaterial presence, purpose, or moral imperative. Yet the spiritual renaissance unfolding in present-day environmental literature is striking, richly variegated in its thought and expression.

This vein of spirituality runs through the nature writing of many modern and contemporary figures. Such figures include not only Barry Lopez and Peter Matthiessen, as I have shown, but also prose writers as disparate as Alison Hawthorne Deming, Barbara Kingsolver, Norman Maclean, N. Scott Momaday, Kathleeen Norris, Chet Raymo, Leslie Silko, Gary Snyder, and Terry Tempest Williams. Poets of note include A. R. Ammons, Denise Levertov, Marilyn Nelson, Mary Oliver, Theodore Roethke, Pattiann Rogers, and Gary Snyder. These writers, whether or not they personally accept or practice any tradition of organized religious worship, affirm the validity of interactions with the nonhuman world that disclose realities beyond ourselves, and beyond the play of our linguistic signifiers.

From the long list of writers whose works invite ecospiritual commentary, I have chosen here to examine prose pieces by four: Wendell Berry, Annie Dillard, John Cheever, and Marilynne Robinson. All four scrutinize the relation between Nature and Culture in self-consciously critical ways, declining to glorify pristine wilderness landscapes. All of them likewise press readers to inquire how, in postindustrial America, human settlements can become genuine communities coexisting in sustainable harmony with natural ecosystems. According to Gary Snyder, "the commons" upheld in traditional societies was an undivided land "embracing both the wild and the semi-wild." Since it embodied "the contract a people make with their local natural system," the commons had to be overseen by a cohesive community grounded in some definite place.

This shared sense of a homeplace is, of course, elusive in present-day society—though, as Snyder observes, "recollecting that we once lived in places" remains "part of our contemporary self-discovery" and "grounds what it means to be human."[1] A few modern Americans have consciously tried to renew this recollection in their own lives.

By turning away from the urbane academic world of New York to farm and write at the scene of his ancestral origins, Wendell Berry rediscovered communal roots that reached backward in time as well as deep into the remembered earth of Henry County, Kentucky. Berry's decision to settle with his family at Lane's Land Farm in Port Royal, Kentucky, in 1965 linked him to five generations of his family who had previously worked the land in this same locale. Over the years, Berry also taught at the University of Kentucky and elsewhere. But farming has remained central to his prophetic office as social critic and literary environmentalist.[2]

Accordingly, Berry's stance has often been linked to American traditions of virtuous agrarianism and pastoral innocence. Here and there, the writing does reflect a Jeffersonian strain of antiurban individualism. This impression is strengthened all the more by Berry's often-stated preference for farming with draft animals instead of motorized machines. To many contemporary U.S. readers, family farming already sounds like a quaintly anachronistic or "marginal" occupation. Such urbanized readers may not share Berry's passion for agricultural reform, though they must feel the economic effects of agribusiness. They may also doubt the virtue of a southern pastoralism that has, in the course of Berry's own family history, profited from slavery and tobacco planting.[3] Yet they have often admired the disarming candor of Berry's essays, the rare integrity of this writer's commitment to place in a society obsessed with mobility. No contemporary figure embodies more visibly, in both personal and literary terms, a Thoreauvian dedication to "living deliberately" amid the complexities of global economics. Again and again, Berry's essays remind us that "nature" is a place of human labor and livelihood, not merely of recreation and observation. And particularly in later volumes such as *Home Economics* (1987) or *Sex, Economy, Freedom and Community* (1992), Berry's meditations on the practice of moral economy and preservation of community clearly extend to settings beyond the rural south. For Berry, then, discovering how to sustain the planet's environmental health and to make oneself "responsibly at home both in this world" and in one's "native and chosen place" cannot be construed as a purely private challenge, but as a shared problem of household management.[4]

The religious grounding of this vision is easy to overlook. Berry has, after all, denounced institutional Christianity for failing to preach or to practice environmental healing. Though raised within the community of Kentucky's New Castle Baptist Church, he complains that "the organized church" typically "makes peace with a destructive economy and divorces itself from economic issues because it is economically compelled to do so." Too closely allied with worldly powers of militarism and exploitative industry, modern Christianity "connives directly in the murder of Creation."[5] Berry's Sabbath poems, reflecting decades of worshipful wandering through fields and woods near his home, pointedly displace his regular participation in Sunday church services.

Nonetheless, Berry has identified himself with those "who are devoted both to biblical tradition and to the defense of the earth." In recent years he has become increasingly willing to consider himself a Christian writer despite his unchurched status. He has argued repeatedly that the Bible, read deeply and sympathetically, gives powerful support to appreciating the world's sanctity as divine Creation, as "the continuous, constant participation of all creatures in the being of God." Discovering the Bible's untamed, outdoor identity helps us realize that God is not a supreme executive but "the wildest being in existence," that "the presence of His spirit in us is our wildness, our oneness with the wilderness of Creation." Far from siding with "anti-Christian environmentalists" who dismiss the value of scriptural testimony, Berry insists on weighing its moral claims seriously albeit critically.

While admiring other religious traditions, most notably Buddhism, Berry doubts that environmental reformers born into Christianity best advance their cause by rejecting their naturally inherited religion. "A better possibility," he writes "is that this, our native religion, should survive and renew itself so that it may become as largely instructive as we need it to be." "On such a survival and renewal of the Christian religion," he concludes, "may depend the survival of the Creation that is its subject."[6]

The Bible's reputation as paradigm of the Word accounts for at least part of Berry's attraction to this tradition. For a writer steeped in biblical language, and mindful that words hold prophetic power, scriptural texts inevitably merge with personal creativity. Berry's nonfiction testifies to the necessity of "standing by words." It also confronts readers with biblically framed arguments for metanoia, for an immediate change of heart in their responses to the earth and to other humans. As Berry writes in the essay "Christianity and the Survival of Creation," "probably the most urgent question now faced by people who would adhere to the Bible is this: What sort of economy would be responsible to the holiness of life? What, for Christians, would be the economy, the practices and the restraints, of 'right livelihood?' "[7]

A religious sense of the world lies at the heart of Berry's ecological conviction that land must be treated as a divine gift and sacrament. To approach the earth as sacrament is to embrace its materiality while reverencing its worth beyond the horizon of visible use. It is to regard land as a provisional endowment rather than a permanent possession, as a natural and social commonwealth rather than a private estate. In "The Gift of Good Land," Berry offers his clearest exposition of these themes. This essay develops its generalized argument by drawing heavily on biblical texts, chiefly from the Old Testament. Elsewhere, though, Berry reminds us that genuine love "is never abstract," so as to care only for the planet at large, but must address itself to particular people, places, and neighborhoods. That such love enfolds "singular sparrows of the street, the lilies of the field, 'the least of these my brethren,' "[8] also follows from Christian teaching about the localized Incarnation of Christ. So I think the best place to begin reflecting on this sacramental sense of land is with Berry's detailed account of his own return to farming in Kentucky, as narrated in "The Making of a Marginal Farm" (1980) and *The Long-Legged House* (1965). The tale that emerges from "The Making of a Marginal Farm" is at once personal and socially prophetic.

From the outset of "The Making," Berry refashions usual expectations of pastoral idealism. Though to him the land at Lanes Landing looked familiar, since it had been hallowed in his memory and in family tradition, it showed little promise of fertility when he returned to Kentucky in 1964. And Berry found little room there for farming, starting as he did by purchasing a mere twelve-acre plot with rundown house and barn. Even when he expanded his holdings to seventy-five acres, he discovered much of the land had been badly abused by a developer's bulldozers. It abounded in weeds, hilly thickets, and gashed soil. "What we had bought," he observes ruefully, "was less a farm than a reclamation project."[9] It was less pastoral refuge than wasteland. The ruined farm thus epitomizes a mechanized, slash-and-burn policy of land use that has also spread abandoned stripmalls, stripmines, and factory lots across postindustrial America. Nor does Berry himself claim to be pastoralism's perfect embodiment of the happy farmer. He admits to having made mistakes, such as trying to excavate a pond on a wooded hillside. He knows, too, that while pursuing his farm experiment on damaged land, he could derive his chief livelihood from other sources.

Nonetheless, Berry sees in this small project of land reclamation a much larger promise of healing and restoration. Such hope of healing extends beyond the practice of enlightened farming techniques toward renewal of the author's spiritual estate—and toward redefining humanity's economic relation to the planet. Although the farm's eroded river bank "stands literally at the cutting edge of our nation's consumptive economy" (340), the farmer's cocreative labor with nature saves enough earth to restore hope of fecundity. Berry begins the work with a few simple measures conducted on a modest scale. He repairs the old house, plants a garden, and buys a team of horses to work the steep ground. He learns how to use otherwise wasted wood for fuel, and how to recycle animal wastes:

> Because we did not want to pollute our land and water with sewage, and in the process waste nutrients that should be returned to the soil, we built a composting privy. And so we began to attempt a life that, in addition to whatever else it was, would be responsibly agri-cultural. We used no chemical fertilizers. Except for a little rotenone, we used no insecticides. As our land and our food became healthier, so did we. (332)

For Berry, sharing in this transformation whereby wounded land becomes fruitful ground for habitation is palpably sacramental. Perceiving restored fer-tility to be the outward and visible sign of inward and invisible grace, he literally works out his salvation—in the root sense of finding *salvus*, healing—on a marginal site that becomes spiritually central:

> As we have continued to live on and from our place, we have slowly begun its restoration and healing. Most of the scars have now been mended and grassed over, most of the washes stopped, most of the buildings made sound; many loads of rocks have been hauled out of the fields and used to pave entrances or fill hollows; we have done perhaps half of the necessary fencing. A great deal of work is still left to do, and some of it—the rebuilding of fertility in the depleted hillsides—will take longer than we will live. But in doing these things we have begun a restoration and a healing in ourselves. (334)

As the collective pronoun suggests, Berry's ongoing sacrament of engage-ment with land also bears a social dimension. Tanya remains an essential working and domestic partner in this project of reinhabiting the land. And among the seven discrete sacraments traditionally named in Catholic Christi-anity, marriage best defines Berry's enduring relation to the world. So refer-ences to marriage, both actual and metaphorical, abound throughout Berry's writing. Henry County becomes his "country of marriage"[10] in several senses. The writer weds not only Tanya but also a place he is committed to cherishing through physical "husbandry." Unlike Thomas Merton, who lived not far from Lanes Landing in the Trappist community of Gethsemane, Berry never took an official monastic vow of stability.[11] Yet in "The Making of a Marginal Farm," he testifies to initiating "a profound change" when he returned to Kentucky. Disavowing worldly paths of freewheeling ambition, he now sees himself committed to living "according to a kind of destiny rooted in my origins and in my life" (330).

To remain married for decades to the same spouse, to reside in the same community inhabited by generations of one's ancestors, to farm the land organically with animal labor—all of this would once have described an ordinary American life. But in the context of contemporary society, these self-limiting conditions of Berry's life have come to seem prophetically anomalous. Without expecting others to imitate such a life directly, Berry does call for a cultural shift toward more integral involvement with the places we inhabit. Even in densely settled landscapes, humans can choose to be "stickers," pursuing lives "adapted to available technology" and "to a known place" instead of "boomers" who lack caring connection with any environment.[12]

For Berry, envisioning the land as sacramental also means acknowledging its naturally social and ecological character as commonwealth. It means looking beyond private deeds and individual farm management toward the environmental health of "creaturely orders and communities that are whole." It means grounding our lives on solid earth, and in some kind of faith that reaches beyond ourselves. For Berry, then, faith is necessary—and inherently ecological and communal, since it expresses "our life's instinctive leap toward its origin, the motion by which we acknowledge the order and harmony to which we belong." He argues that as creatures of faith, "if we don't direct our faith toward God or into some authentic 'way' of the soul, then we direct it" inevitably toward lesser ends such as "progress or science or weaponry." If we are not faithful in some manner, we are inclined to embrace superstition, particularly in modern shapes of reductive materialism.[13] Caring for Creation "rests upon genuine religion" since "care allows creatures to escape our explanations into their actual presence and their essential mystery." It implies recognition that nonhumans "are not ours" though they share much of our living space.[14]

Berry's most explicitly religious argument on behalf of a sacramental, community-occupied environment appears in the essay "The Gift of Good Land" (1979). Identified at the outset as "a Biblical argument for ecological and agricultural responsibility,"[15] the essay focuses not on the old problem of human dominion over all Edenic nature, as raised by Genesis 1–2, but on the localized narrative concerning the gift of the Promised Land elaborated in books such as Deuteronomy, Leviticus, and Numbers. Berry grants that the story of settling Israel is morally problematic, too, because of the violent means by which Hebrew tribes wrested much of their territory from Canaanite inhabitants. Nonetheless, he finds the biblical account of this occupation paradigmatic because of the crucial limitations and reminders attached to it. The Promised Land was "a divine gift to a *fallen* people" rather than something earned or merited by human virtue. To act otherwise would be to confuse fallible humans with gods—or with the one true Creator. Nor could any member of Israel lay claim to the revered soil as a permanent possession. Berry points out that "it is 'given,' but only for a time, and only for so long as it is properly used." This contingent ownership, tenancy, or principle of usufruct must invariably acknowledge that " 'the earth is the Lord's' " (269, 270–271, 275).

Understandably drawn toward scriptures exposing Israel's intensely earthy affection for agricultural plots, Berry highlights rituals that supported the land's status as sacrament rather than as humanly ruled property. One such observance is the land Sabbath, whereby Israel's fields had to be left fallow at regular intervals. Other stipulations enforced compassionate treatment of animals. Though such provisions served practical ends, they also ritualized religiously "the limits of human control" (271).

Like countless other writers and theologians, Berry links biblical calls for human restraint to an environmental model of "stewardship." Yet his argument in "The Gift of Good Land" reaches beyond the rationalistic moral view of stewardship as prudential resource management. Its sacramental vision incorporates New Testament perspectives on neighborly charity. It also extends the notion of material community beyond space into time, and beyond human households to the household of all Creation. "One lives in the neighborhood," Berry insists, "not just of those who now live 'next door' " (272) but also of those who lived before, as well of those who will in future receive the land's inheritance.

For Berry, neighborly care extends beyond the space of immediate human proximity to become an ecological virtue. He sees this virtue founded, in turn, on the theological virtue of charity. Berry thus recommends an expressively dynamic, relational model of environmental stewardship. This fresh view of stewardship draws theologically on biblical ideas of *caritas*, as famously embodied in Saint Luke's Parable of the Good Samaritan:

> What we are talking about is an elaborate understanding of charity. It is so elaborate because of the perception, implicit here, explicit in the New Testament, that charity by its nature cannot be selective— that it is, so to speak, out of human control. It cannot be selective because between any two humans, or any two creatures, all Creation exists as a bond. Charity cannot be just human, any more than it can be just Jewish or just Samaritan. Once begun, wherever it begins, it cannot stop until it includes all Creation, for all creatures are parts of a whole upon which each is dependent, and it is a contradiction to love your neighbor and despise the great inheritance on which his life depends. Charity even for one person does not make sense except in terms of an effort to love all Creation in response to the Creator's love for it. (273)

Such charity, for Berry the inverse of heroic individualism, is inevitably social and communal. As "a practical virtue," enacted by the "true lover of material things" (274, 279), it is likewise sacramental. Experiencing the physical world sacramentally involves a tragic dimension, too, lying beyond the scope of moral duty. It draws one into the mystery of nature's pain as well as its glory. In this vein, though Berry typically invokes marriage as his defining sacrament of encounter with the world, he ends "The Gift of Good Land" with a poignant recollection of the Eucharist. He observes that we have a clear moral obligation to prevent air pollution and other forms of environmental degradation. And yet, he concludes,

> that is not to suggest that we can live harmlessly, or strictly at our own expense; we depend upon other creatures and survive by their deaths. To live, we must daily break the body and shed the blood of Creation. When we do this knowingly, lovingly, skillfully, reverently, it is a sacrament. When we do it ignorantly, greedily, clumsily, destructively, it is a desecration. In such desecration we condemn ourselves to spiritual and moral loneliness, and others to want. (281)

For Berry, then, making peace with Creation is not just an ethical obligation. If daily and consciously transacted in the spirit of Christ, it becomes a sacramental act of communion. Such communion with Creation acknowledges the violence endemic to natural processes. Berry distinguishes, though, between the tragic necessity of this violence, which is potentially sacramental, and the desecration caused by needless human carnage. Following the terrorist attacks of September 11, 2001, he has been an outspoken opponent of the attempt by U.S. government leaders to answer this atrocity by targeting other nations—especially Iraq—for retributive violence. In his view, the isolationist arrogance of the Bush administration's zeal for war reflects a broader inability to revere the earth itself as commons, gift, and sacrament.

A peaceably secure nation is one whose people have begun to grasp the all-inclusive charity of regarding "the world as a community of all the creatures which, to be possessed by any one, must be shared by all."[16] Or, as Berry wrote earlier in *What Are People For?* "the grace that is the health of creatures can only be held in common."[17] Thus, the U.S. government's new willingness to endorse preemptive military action denies common charity. In the years between the first Gulf War and the events of September 11, 2001, Berry insists, "we made no improvement in our charity toward the rest of the world." Gripped by fear, "we have ignored the teachings and the examples of Christ, Gandhi, Martin Luther King, and other peaceable leaders" in our foreign policy as well in home economics. Ironically, it is American politicians who "are not *from* anywhere," who cultivate no deep-seated relation to a "home place," who have sponsored the new fixation on "homeland" security. So, too, a national administration that "has adopted a sort of official Christianity" seeks to forget that "the Christian gospel is a summons to peace, calling for justice beyond anger, mercy beyond justice, forgiveness beyond mercy, love beyond forgiveness."[18]

For all the leftish tilt of Berry's rhetoric against war, corporatization, and globalization, the political stance of this Kentucky farmer is also supported by "conservative" traditions of social philosophy and moral theology. As Berry affirms in "The Gift of Good Land," to honor Creation is to share ultimately in *sacramentum*, a religious mystery. Such participation, which reaches beyond

acquisitive interests and partisan faith, inspires a self-abnegating charity mod-
eled here on nothing less than the bodily sacrifice of Jesus.

Annie Dillard's Interrogation of Creation

Although Annie Dillard has by now published at least a dozen books, *Pilgrim
at Tinker Creek* (1974), her meditation on nature in an ordinary exurban neighborhood near Virginia's Blue Ridge, remains her most celebrated achievement.
Were it not for *Pilgrim*, in fact, Dillard's other publications on diverse topics
would never have sufficed to solidify her current reputation as a leading nature
writer. But if the youthful *Pilgrim* retains its standing as the centerpiece of
Dillard's environmental writing, later essay collections such as *Holy the Firm*
(1977), *Teaching a Stone to Talk* (1982), and *For the Time Being* (1999) enlarge
appreciation of the passionately religious character of Dillard's response to
nature as divine Creation.

Readers immediately sense that *Pilgrim at Tinker Creek* strives to conduct
a latter-day dialogue with American Transcendental naturalists such as Emerson and Thoreau. Dillard's solitary musings in a green shade, which this book
explicitly likens to Thoreau's "meteorological journal of the mind,"[19] also rep-
licates the strongly localized attachment to place embodied in *Walden*. Dillard's
book, conceived further into the post-Christian era than *Walden*, shows deeper
involvement with the dynamics of religious doubt and with disturbing features
of nature. Paradoxically, though, Dillard also shows more willingness than
Thoreau to explore spiritual paths mapped by traditional exponents of Christian
orthodoxy. Thus, she adopts for herself the archaic Christian title of "pilgrim,"
rather than the more updated Thoreauvian identity of "saunterer" or "sojourner." Within the setting of present-day intellectual culture, Dillard later
enacted her own version of scandalous self-reliance—but scarcely one that
Thoreau would welcome—when she disclosed her formal conversion to Roman Catholicism.[20] Despite the author's eclectic invocation of spiritual
traditions ranging from Hasidic Judaism and Islam to Native American religions and Transcendentalism, the dominant shape of religious inquiry in *Pilgrim at Tinker Creek* is arguably more Christian than syncretistic. And as Dillard
implies at the outset of *Pilgrim*, through a trope that depicts her house as an
anchoritic hermitage clamped to the side of Tinker Creek, she finds the contemplative strain of early Christianity particularly appealing. By the end, she
also perceives a surprising consonance between the visions of medieval mystics
and findings of modern scientists.

As Dillard knows, the inward benefit of "meditating on the creatures" had
been taught both within and beyond Christian spiritual traditions well before
the flowering of nature Romanticism in the nineteenth century. In the thir-
teenth century, Bonaventure had envisioned an affirmative "way" to God
through the soul's pursuit of those traces of divinity scattered throughout Creation. And by the seventeenth century, meditation on the creatures—together

with meditation on the self and meditation on Scripture—had become an established practice in both Catholic and Protestant devotionalism.[21] Such reflections might, of course, merely enforce didactic lessons or evidence preconceived doctrines. But physical Creation might also serve as a second Book of Revelation. Thus, Thomas Traherne, in his *Centuries of Meditations*, expresses a joyous discovery that "this visible world" is indeed "the body of God," a "very Paradise" and "Temple of his glory." According to Traherne, human beings are not merely permitted but enjoined "to enjoy the world." And if we fix our souls properly through meditation on "the beauty of the hemisphere," we "need nothing but open eyes, to be ravished like the Cherubims."[22]

This theme of devout wonder, transposed to a modern key with scientific accompaniment, is replayed in seasonal variations throughout *Pilgrim*. But unlike Traherne, Dillard does not restrict her contemplative gaze to elevating images, to sights inspiring gratitude, as offered along the via affirmativa. She doesn't simply *ask* the creaturely world, as does Augustine in book 10, chapter 6, of the *Confessions*, what it can show her positively about God and final truth. She *interrogates* the creatures—and, by extension, their Creator. She does so in a spirit at once appreciative and fiercely adversarial. Her book combines praise and protest. Although *Pilgrim* ends with "Amen" and "twin silver trumpets of praise," it argues further upstream that if God exists, God has a good deal to answer for. Is the world shaped by evolution a random order of circumstances without meaning or direction? Or if this universe we inhabit is indeed God's Creation, do its troubling cruelties and oddities and excesses show the Creator to be some kind of monster? Or a jokester? Or an absentee Lord, who has since abandoned this earth to live somewhere else?

Yet when Dillard presses these questions in the opening chapters of *Pilgrim*, she situates her skeptical inquiry within the believing tradition most famously articulated in the Book of Job. Thus, in *Pilgrim*, she confronts the classic problem of evil with primary reference to nonhuman creatures and the physical world. This attention to a theodicy of landscape gives way in *For the Time Being* to a more fragmentary style of metaphysical questioning centered on the world's social horrors. What can theology make of the genocidal atrocities committed just within the last half-century, including the recent outrage that "in 1994 Rwandan Hutus killed eight thousand Tutsis in one hundred days?" Or "why did God let the Romans flay an eighty-five-year-old Torah scholar?"[23]

Yet for Dillard, the pain of pursuing such issues is integral to her spiritual journey. So, too, is discovering the deficiency of all our knowledge about God and the inner workings of Creation. *Pilgrim* maintains that interrogating the creatures must finally confirm our knowledge of ignorance even—or especially—in an age of theoretically advanced science. Accordingly, the spiritual masters have long insisted that whatever or whoever we try to name as "God" must remain ineffable, indeterminate, elusive beyond all human conception or description. Such awareness of mystery at the heart of things gives rise to that practice of mystical religion known traditionally as the via negativa, or negative way. Approaching ultimate reality through meditation on what it is *not*, this mode of spirituality supposes further that creaturely nature might reveal as much to human understanding by way of negation as by positive illumination. As the author explains in her 1999 afterword, the binary structure of *Pilgrim at Tinker Creek* embodies these two distinct but compatible ways of reflecting on reality:

> Neoplatonic Christianity described two routes to God: the *via positiva* and the *via negativa*. Philosophers on the *via positiva* assert that God is omnipotent, omniscient, etc; that God possesses all positive attributes. I found the *via negativa* more congenial. Its seasoned travelers (Gregory of Nyssa in the fourth century and Pseudo-Dionysius in the sixth) stressed God's unknowability. Anything we may say of God is untrue, as we can know only creaturely attributes, which do not apply to God. . . .
>
> The book's first half, the *via positiva*, accumulates the world's goodness and God's. . . . The *via positiva* culminates in "Intricacy." A shamefully feeble "Flood" chapter washes all that away, and the second half of the book starts down the *via negativa* with "Fecundity," the dark side of intricacy. This half culminates in "Northing" (it is, with the last, my favorite chapter), in which the visible world empties, leaf by leaf. "Northing" is the counterpart to "Seeing." (280)

If this substratum of mystical theology sounds terribly esoteric, the primary gaze of Dillard's meditation remains fixed on a commonplace world. Her space of valley, framed by Blue Ridge mountains and shared with neighborhood children, is watered by two minor currents. The unspectacular flow of Tinker Creek and Carvin's Creek holds her attention and ours throughout this spiritual "pilgrimage." Tinker Creek offers Dillard a familiar "anchor-hold" for beholding that "mystery of the continuous creation" (4) active throughout the whole of nature. From her chosen window on the world, the author looks at myriads of common creatures. She want to become mindful not only of sedges, grasses, and trees but also of rabbits, squirrels, domestic steers, mockingbirds, chickadees, starlings, carp, turtles, slugs, frogs, and snakes. She examines coots, frogs, one-celled beasts by microscope, and a goldfish by the name of Ellery Channing. She stalks muskrats, fish, a green heron. Beyond the setting of "this rather tamed valley" (13), she also thinks about sharks, barnacles, and an old tomcat she once owned. The scene she surveys from a tear-shaped island in Tinker Creek features the motions of small-scale wildlife commonly visible on the edges of domestic settlement:

> In summer's low water, flags and bulrushes grow along a series of shallow pools cooled by the lazy current. Water striders patrol the surface film, crayfish hump along the silt bottom eating filth, frogs shout and glare, and shiners and small bream hide among roots from the sulky green heron's eye. I come to this island every month

of the year. I walk around it, stopping and staring, or I straddle the sycamore log over the creek, curling my legs out of the water in winter, trying to read. (7)

Eschewing scenic grandeur, Dillard dwells particularly on the obscure, un- glamorous life of insects. One reason she does so is her desire to comprehend the full scope of evolutionary nature; and by sheer animal numbers, "theirs is the biggest wedge of the pie" (65). Another reason is that insects—even more than large predators—force us to confront what seems to be the heartlessly grotesque, profligate, and unchangeable ways of "nature." Dillard admits she is appalled by the spectacle of waste and superabundance revealed by ento- mology. Haunted by the seemingly perverse instincts of the giant water bug, praying mantis, and bee-eating wasp, she finds here no evidence of conven- tionally defined Providence. Indeed, she suffers an "unholy revulsion" at the fixed compulsions of "the eggy animal world" (64, 163). Apparently the whole scheme runs on death, chance, mindless instinct, and parasitic nibbling. The image in chapter 1 of the giant water bug imbibing a frog lingers in the mind. Striking with merciless stealth, the bug punctures, paralyzes, and sucks all liquified life from the frog, which empties to become a bag of skin. Dillard complains that "fish gotta swim and bird gotta fly; insects, it seems, gotta do one horrible thing after another." "I never ask why of a vulture or shark," she adds, "but I ask why of almost every insect I see" (64).

This metaphysical problem of reconciling images of nature's grace and godly beauty with signs of savagery and apparent demonism reaches a crisis point in chapter 10, "Fecundity." After that, Dillard's obstinate questionings descend to a calmer pitch. Though the problem of evil returns to trouble the more human-centered essays in theodicy pursued through *Holy the Firm* and *For the Time Being, Pilgrim at Tinker Creek* concludes on a note of acceptance.

In *Pilgrim*, it is largely through the marvel of seeing that Dillard sustains the via positiva project of making nature sacred. Her main vocation as Tinker Creek's pilgrim-in-residence is simply learning "to look well at the creek" (104). As Dillard explains in the pivotal chapter "Seeing," such receptivity demands spiritual training. Authentic seeing is "a discipline requiring a lifetime of ded- icated struggle; it marks the literature of saints and monks of every order East and West, under every rule and no rule, discalced and shod." Hence the "lover can see, and the knowledgeable." Deep seeing requires patience, preparation, stillness, a spirit of humility and expectancy. Nonetheless, "the literature of illumination" confirms that the finest episodes of seeing are received as pure gift: "the pearl of great price" is discovered, not earned, in rare moments of surprise (35, 20).

Dillard's supreme illustration of illuminative vision appears at the climax of "Seeing." Having read of a child, blind since birth, who receives vision following cataract surgery, the author is moved by the child's awestruck per- ception of common objects, epitomized by her newly sighted description of "the tree with the lights in it." Dillard searched everywhere for a revelation of new creation comparable to what this child had seen. But after years of looking, she stumbles upon her luminous tree in an unguarded moment:

> Then one day I was walking along Tinker Creek thinking of nothing at all and I saw the tree with the lights in it. I saw the backyard cedar where the mourning doves roost charged and transfigured, each cell buzzing with flame. I stood on the grass with the lights in it, grass that was wholly fire, utterly focused and utterly dreamed. It is less like seeing than like being for the first time seen, knocked breathless by a powerful glance. The flood of fire abated, but I'm still spending the power. (36)

She goes on to call this apparition a "vision," thereby construing it as an occasion of imaginative in-sight beyond physical sight. The epiphany leaves her reeling, brushed by a power that makes her feel like someone being seen for the first time, like a bell "lifted and struck." The numinous atmosphere of the experience is unmistakable. Besides recalling the enlightened reputation of sacred trees in Hebrew, Buddhist, Christian, and pre-Christian history, Dillard 's account features the classic, fire-and-light emblems of biblical theophany. The author later declares that "on that cedar tree shone, however briefly, the steady, inward flames of eternity" (81). Yet the immediate object of her attention is no magical or supernatural object. *What* Dillard looks upon is just a familiar "backyard cedar," seen in the light of her previous reading. And as *Pilgrim* repeatedly shows, our view of nature invariably reflects the multiple human pretexts through which we interpret it.[24] In Christian terms, Dillard's "vision" does not trace an ascent from the common world to a realm of supernal beauty. It represents instead the gracious transfiguration of the ordinary.[25] The contemplative discovery enacted here involves not a suspension but an intensification of normal sight.

Thus, to envision each cell of the cedar buzzing with flame is, in effect, to look beneath surfaces toward the creature's hidden life. It is to witness, in the light of modern science, the interfusion of matter and energy. It is to see nature as a wondrously animated, multilayered creation encompassing what the Nicene Creed describes as "all things," both "seen and unseen." Finally, it is to glimpse, without quite comprehending, the mystery of life itself.

The process of unknowing needed to see a tree transfigured also connects this positive epiphany, paradoxically, to the via negativa. Un-self-conscious seeing demands a lover's self-emptying gaze and attentiveness. Opening oneself to the grace of vision means denying the ego's anxiety in favor of "a healthy poverty and simplicity" (17). And to encounter a self-transcending presence in the physical world, the one who sees must negate his or her subjective mastery of sense-data to experience "being for the first time seen." Emerson had felt such an interpenetrative connection in ecstasy on the bare common. Dillard knows, however, that while the luminous moment "comes and goes," it "mostly goes" (36). The via negativa calls to mind what physics confirms: that all matter, from subatomic particles to stars, stands amid larger expanses of nothingness.

"Everywhere," we find, "darkness and the presence of the unseen appalls" (21). We are left to wonder whether divine darkness, or simply a void, surrounds the flame-lit cedar. And when the illumination fades, the gloomy enigma of evolution—an immensity of pain, cruelty, waste, and strife—remains.

How, then, does *Pilgrim* respond to this enigma? How does Dillard reconcile her conflicting impressions of nature as divine or senseless, gracious or savagely horrific?

Inevitably, the book supplies only partial and tentative answers to such metaphysical questions. Humans cannot "solve" the problem of metaphysical evil in rational terms. But one spiritual response that Dillard proposes is simply a resolve to live within the question. In the tradition of biblical Job, she sees a disposition of quizzical doubt bound up with habits of faith, just as she sees "power and beauty, grace tangled in a rapture with violence" (10). So if the problem of evil cannot be definitively solved, it can at least be reenvisioned.

Such is what it means to reaffirm the contemplative vision of God—and of nature—as authentic mystery rather than puzzle. And Dillard insists that not only ancient mystics but also modern physicists see inexhaustible mystery in the very nature of nature. After Werner Heisenberg articulated the Principle of Indeterminacy in 1927, we began to know "for sure that there is no knowing" and indeed no *way* of knowing concurrently the speed and location of a subatomic particle. This revelation of enduring uncertainty, later enlarged by chaos theory, overturned "our whole understanding of the universe." For Dillard, it means realizing as well that some "physicists are once again mystics," that "knowledge does not vanquish mystery, or obscure its distant lights" (205, 206, 244).

Pilgrim reinforces this via negativa mood of contemplation through its seasonal structure. Unlike *Walden*, which opens in temperate weather and traverses winter to end triumphantly with the return of spring, Dillard's book opens in January and reaches the winter solstice in its final chapter. In the penultimate chapter, "Northing," the author highlights her negative resolve to seek "a reduction, a shedding, a sloughing off" (255). Absorbing the cooler winds and "sere branches" of November, she describes the austere peace that comes with standing under that season's "wiped skies directly, naked, without intercessors" (263).

The path of unknowing offers further solace insofar as it reveals the intrinsic fallibility of all human judgments about cosmic pain. Realizing the contingency of our perspective on the world enables us to see how unqualified we humans are to deduce any kind of cosmic morality from the water bug's behavior. If "creation itself is blamelessly benevolently askew by its very free nature," we are driven to conclude "that it is only human feeling that is freakishly amiss" in such a case (180). Dillard pursues the inward route of meditative dispossession, reiterating her consent to live within the question:

> My rage and shock at the pain and death of individuals of my kind
> is the old, old mystery, as old as man, but forever fresh and com-
> pletely unanswerable. My reservations about the fecundity and waste

of life among other creatures is, however, mere squeamishness. After all, I'm not the one having the nightmares. It is true that many
of the creatures live and die abominably, but I am not called upon to
pass judgment. Nor am I called upon to live in that same way, and
those creatures who are, are mercifully unconscious. (181)

Above all, *Pilgrim* responds to what looks like nature's senseless savagery
by affirming the free-flowing extravagance of creation. Dillard thus disavows
the model of harmony and fixed design conventionally embraced by natural
theology. Instead of running like clockwork, as in that classically mechanical
paradigm of the Enlightenment, the world runs over with boundless energy.
Instead of closed harmony, we perceive ample dissonance and dynamism in
the open system proposed by post-Newtonian science. The new paradigm is
wilder, more organic and unpredictable. It is also less susceptible to moralized
interpretations predicated on the notion of divinely predetermined "purposes"
embedded in nature.

Dillard nonetheless sees enough to sense the presence of a Creator within
this new Creation. She thus favors a "panentheistic," rather than pantheistic,
theology that affirms God's transcendence as well as immanence in the world.[26]
And throughout her meditations, she calls to mind the divine quality of Tinker
Creek's free-flowing, superabundant stream. Here is clear evidence of what
grace must look like. Dillard declares flatly, in a chapter titled "The Present,"
that the creek "is, by definition, Christmas, the incarnation" (104). So for her,
the current becomes a visible incarnation of God's wildness, exuberance, and
extravagance. In *Pilgrim*, Dillard's urge to voice this extravagance sometimes
causes her to overwrite. But her main intent is to dramatize the breadth of
evolutionary freedom with which Creation has been endowed. As she remarks
in *For the Time Being*, God does not intervene directly to provoke rock slides
or to send people glaucoma.[27] God's free-flowing Creation mingles the gentle
current of a neighborhood creek with Melvillean apparitions of strife in
the raging sea. Nature runs wild because God, too, is an untamed lover of
freedom:

> The point of the dragonfly's terrible lip, the giant water bug, bird-
> song, or the beautiful dazzle and flash of sunlighted minnows, is
> not that it all fits together like clockwork—for it doesn't particularly,
> not even inside the goldfish bowl—but that it all flows so freely
> wild, like the creek, that it all surges in such a free, fringed tangle.
> Freedom is the world's water and weather, the world's nourishment
> freely given, its soil and sap: and the creator loves pizzazz. (139)

Dillard ends her meditative journey by registering assent to a universe
made "in earnest," as well as in high-spirited extravagance, "by a power that is
unfathomably secret, and holy, and fleet" (275). This power remains mysteriously engaged with the flow of evolution without determining its precise
course. Dillard's God loves not only "pizzazz," the energy that ceaselessly
shapes a wondrously gratuitous creation, but matter itself. The presiding deity

of Tinker Creek thus resembles the actively indwelling Spirit revered by Pierre Teilhard de Chardin, that luminous twentieth-century mystical theologian and scientist whose career occupies much of Dillard's attention in *For the Time Being*.

Paradise Regained in Suburbia: John Cheever's Fable of Beasley's Pond

Neither Wendell Berry's farm in Kentucky nor Annie Dillard's former anchorhold at Tinker Creek qualify as wilderness areas. But where, it is fair to ask, might the prospect of discovering outdoor spiritual renewal seem less likely than in the faceless suburbs of the United States? Surprisingly, though, John Cheever managed to make a postindustrial exurban community his primary setting for declaring the holiness of Creation in the last fiction he composed, *Oh What a Paradise It Seems* (1982).

On the surface, this short neglected novel takes the form of an environmental melodrama-cum-morality play. Cheever's tale of paradise lost and regained seems at first to follow a predictably didactic course. The plot concerns the fate of Beasley's Pond, located in the former milltown of Janice, not far from New York City.[28] Though scarcely pristine, the pond offers townspeople rare access to natural wonder, innocence, and recreation. It seems to them a spot of paradise indeed amid the banal anxieties of contemporary life. The story's almost-elderly main character, Lemuel Sears, likewise relishes the "divine" pleasure of skating across its glassy surface during a winter visit to the town, where his daughter resides. But unseen malefactors with underworld connections and political sanction have conspired to pollute the communally owned watershed for personal profit. The fantasy aura of this intervention recalls the preface to Rachel Carson's *Silent Spring*, in which "some evil spell had settled on the community." Beasley's Pond becomes the dumping ground for wastes, including large appliances, generated by a throwaway culture. This desecration is cloaked in patriotism, since corrupt town leaders have agreed to refashion the site into a memorial for forgotten war dead. In Cheever's fable of social corruption, the polluters even resort to murder in their efforts to preserve economic control. They kill two honest men, a lawyer and an environmentalist named Horace Chisholm. Ultimately, though, these greedy despoilers are defeated by green vigilantes—including Sears and the martyred environmentalist. The dumping stops. Through technical engineering, with support from a newly formed legal foundation, eutrophication is arrested at Beasley's Pond. Its toxified water is purified; its loveliness is restored.

Thus far, the story reads like a modern morality tale denouncing the pollution spread by desecrators of the American Eden.

Not far beneath the surface of this facile conflict, however, Cheever exposes several illusions that color the environmental imagination of his central character. One such fantasy is the pastoral innocence of the town itself, a quiet settlement whose many "gardens and orchards" are "irrigated ideally." Cheever first paints the quaint picture of a "little village by the waterfall where the mill, so many years ago, used to produce gingham" and where no fast-food franchises intrude.[29] Yet it is only by computer error, not civic resolve, that Janice has been temporarily unlinked from the fast-food chains. Full of nostalgia for an idealized past, Sears does not want to consider the unbucolic life that textile workers must have led in Janice, which derived its name from the wife of a former mill master. Nor is he aware at the outset that this apparently countrified village within commuting distance of New York will become the scene of rank corruption, petty strife, ecoterrorism, and a double homicide.

Thus, the subsurface narrative, like the subsurface of Beasley Pond, is darker and less tidy than the protest literature mood of the story's opening would allow. When Lemuel Sears manages ultimately to "save" the pond, if not his own soul and human dignity, he does so by questionable means. His reforming efforts are supported most effectually by the initiative of Betsy Logan, a vengefully aggrieved character who succeeds in blackmailing town leaders allied with the polluters by poisoning several jars of teriyaki sauce at the local grocery. And Sears applies so much technical engineering to effect the pond's rehabilitation that the result resembles an outdoor aquarium as much as a "natural" body of water.

Then too, Sears's character flaws plainly disqualify him for the role of environmental hero. Too pleased with his own restoration efforts, "Sears liked to think that the resurrection of Beasley's Pond had taught him some humility, but his humility was not very apparent" (97). Through much of the story, he comes across as naive, sexually insecure, oblivious to the absurdity of his male midlife longing to evade mortality by recovering an imagined past.

Sears seems particularly self-deceived about the fantasy of sexual rejuvenation that grows from his chance encounter in the city with an attractive younger woman named Renée Herndon. The "aged man" (5) never really comes to know his enigmatic lover. She underscores the point by reminding him, with hilarious persistence: " 'You don't understand the first thing about women' " (13). Yet Sears finds in Renée not only the solace of erotic pleasure but also the existential promise of rebirth implied by her name. From the first, he relishes "the smoothness of her naked back—its marked absence of declivity—so like a promised land." He imagines her physical features to be "a declaration of paradise, either mountainous or maritime, depending upon one's tastes" (12).

Plainly, then, the paradise that Sears projects onto Renée's body is merely a variant of the pastoral dream he identifies with the landscape near Beasley's Pond. Lovely as a painting, the pond offers Sears visible access to a purity and clarity that he feels painfully lacking in himself. He sees it, in fact, as a rare enclave of holiness in a hostile, dis-enchanted world. So it is telling that when Sears protests the pond's contamination in a letter to the town newspaper, he titles his remarks " 'Is Nothing Sacred?' " (91). Taking the impression of this pond, and the stream draining its wetlands, into his psyche seems to be his best hope of experiencing something that transcends the pettiness and lone-liness of his life, something equivalent in religious terms to a sacrament of divine origins:

> The illusion of eternal purity the stream possessed, its music and the greenery of its banks, reminded Sears of pictures he had seen of paradise. The sacred grove was no legitimate part of his thinking, but the whiteness of falling water, the variety of its sounds, the se-renity of the pools he saw corresponded to a memory as deep as any he possessed. He had on his knees in countless cavernous and ill-ventilated Episcopal churches praised the beginning of things. He had heard this described in Revelation as a sea of crystal and living creatures filled with eyes, but it seemed that he had never believed it to be anything but a fountainhead. . . . A trout stream in a forest, a traverse of potable water, seemed for Sears to be the bridge that spans the mysterious abyss between our spiritual and our carnal selves. How contemptible this made his panic about his own con-tamination. (84–85)

Or so it seems to Sears. In several respects, though, this spiritualization of the landscape runs contrary to the facts. Even while Sears fancies seeing an "eternal purity" in the stream, Horace Chisholm recites a long litany of poisons suffusing the Beasley watercourse. Chemically speaking, the polluted body of Beasley's Pond is no more Edenic or pristine than the local supermarket. In-deed Buy-Brite, the large food store in a shopping mall by the interstate, seems to offer Betsy Logan, along with other typically American consumers from Janice, "a paradise of groceries" (46).

The delusions that Sears harbors about Renée coincide with his masculin-ized image of Janice as a long-lost paradise. Though Renée seems to him a "promised land," she is by profession a realtor. So her real business is selling rather than preserving land. And far from realizing a "homecoming" (7) by wedding the Eve who personifies the garden of this suburban village, Sears ends up alone. Renée abandons him as abruptly and inexplicably as she once became his lover.

Much the same is true of Eduardo, the elevator operator with whom Sears finds himself sporadically involved in homoerotic relations. At one point Sears decides to drive north with the younger man to a pond near the Canadian wilds, far from Janice, that he thinks he remembers fishing years ago. But just as "what he felt for Eduardo seemed more like nostalgia than the adventur-ousness of traditional love" (68) so also his nostalgia for a nature sanctuary purer than Beasley's Pond turns out to be misplaced. Ironically, Sears and Eduardo cannot fish there because acidic waters have destroyed aquatic life throughout the whole region.

Cheever suggests that even Sears's motives for purifying Beasley's Pond are slightly tainted. More than a little self-serving energy drives this reform effort, since Sears thinks he has discovered "some sameness in the search for love and the search for potable water." Once the pond is restored, he expresses satisfaction that "the clearness of Beasley's Pond seemed to have scoured his consciousness of the belief that his own lewdness was a profound contamination" (99). Thus regarding his cleanup campaign as a blend of personal therapy and combat, he relishes the conflict it precipitates. We might suspect him of worrying less about preserving nonhuman life and health for its own sake, or about defending the public welfare of Janice's citizenry, than he does about fighting off anyone who would threaten *his* place in paradise. In one oddly revealing paragraph, Cheever voices the wish-fantasy of a narrator, presumably an alter ego of Sears, to shoot and kill some youthful "pretender" who might interrupt the green repose he enjoys while lying concealed in a stream bed redolent of mint. This homicidal narrator savors "the naturalness of the garden" (24) wherein he lies—but wants to share neither the place nor its fishing rights with anyone else.

Some such love of nature has been known to motivate the affluent environmentalism that flourishes in pockets of American suburbia. If we applaud the restoration of Beasley's Pond, we might also want to ask at what and whose expense it has been "saved." All those rusty appliances and bedsteads that ruined a picturesque scene at the pool must now be dumped somewhere else. But where? Material and energy from somewhere else must also be extracted to support the tubing, blowers, and compressors that maintain the pool's purity. To some degree, Sears's reconstructed pond reflects the larger suburban ideal of making nature utopian—in the literal sense of utopia as a place perfected so uniformly that it becomes nowhere in particular. Even the ecological expert Chisholm suffers from *anomie*, an affliction heightened by his association with this nomadic culture. "He seemed to be searching for the memory of some place," writes Cheever, "some evidence of the fact that he had once been able to put himself into a supremely creative touch with his world and his kind" (76).

In light of all this, one cannot read *What a Paradise* as expounding naive pastoralism. Thus far, anyway, the "nature" embraced by Sears looks more like a cultural construction—or a personal projection—than an inherently sacred presence. The essentialist dream of an earthly paradise looks like pure delusion. And thus far the story's main character, conceived by an author not known to have championed environmental causes, seems almost a caricature of the zealous but inwardly conflicted reformer. So is nothing sacred? If Cheever's irony and social satire tell the whole story, that's obviously the case. The question itself sounds ludicrous from the standpoint of deconstructive materialism, just as it does to most of those who hear Sears's editorial letter read at a Janice town meeting.

Yet a fully disillusioned reading fails to recognize some crucial elements of the story. For one thing, Cheever tells this tale with a ribald humor that conveys not only mockery of Sears but also deep compassion and love of life. It is hard not to smile at the foibles of this well-meaning businessman who shows himself to be, at worst, more befuddled than malicious. And as a willful, sexually troubled personality who knows he is nearing death, Sears bears no small resemblance to the author. Although Sears's motives are impure, his larger aspiration to do the right thing, to improve himself while preserving some communal remnant of uncultivated beauty, is unmistakable. Cheever verified in a late interview that he considered Sears "quite useful" since "he purifies a large body of water" and "there really is little one can do that's comparably useful today."[30] *Paradise* suggests that environmental reform, especially when it embodies place-centered affection, can be a worthy thing even when its results are problematic and its instigators impure. Acknowledging that tainted motives are at work in every human endeavor should therefore lead us to humility rather than cynicism.

Most remarkably, the penultimate paragraph of Cheever's dis-illusioning book ends up affirming through Lemuel Sears that beauty, redemption, and numinous nature all exist for real, though human imagination shares in their creation:

> The sky was clear that morning and there might still have been stars
> although he saw none. The thought of stars contributed to the
> power of his feeling. What moved him was a sense of those worlds
> around us, our knowledge however imperfect of their nature, our
> sense of their possessing some grain of our past and of our lives to
> come. It was that most powerful sense of our being alive on the
> planet. It was that most powerful sense of how singular, in the vast-
> ness of creation, is the richness of our opportunity. The sense of
> that hour was of an exquisite privilege, the great benefice of living
> here and renewing ourselves with love. What a paradise it seemed!
> (99–100)

And what a paradise this world *is*, Cheever concludes, for one who wills to believe and who thankfully reveres the palpable yet transcendent grandeur of Creation. For once, the writing displays a glowing lyricism devoid of irony. Exposing a second-level naïveté beyond Sears's first innocence,[31] the passage conveys genuine wonder at the inexhaustible vitality, beauty, and holiness of Creation. Its optimism is all the more striking—and poignant—in view of the author's personal condition at the time. Having suffered neurological seizures after battling his addiction to alcohol some years before, he was now dying of cancer. Yet love, renewal, "that most powerful sense of our being alive on the planet"—all of this rings true for him at the end. Like Dante's *Paradiso*, Cheever's *Paradise* concludes with a reach toward the stars.

Admittedly, Sears sees no stars in the morning sky. So his response to their presence is shaped by imagination. Yet there is more to his knowledge than meets the eye. Certainly, too, there is more stuff out there than we have ever constructed through human thought or action: the stars exist for real, and their being stands in space beyond our control. Looking skyward to contemplate those other worlds reminds us of the paradise we are gifted to inhabit on earth. And for Sears, the moment confirms his intuition that nature at large is not only vast, but created in love.

The paragraph's sudden enlargement of perspective opens us, then, toward an image of nature much larger than Beasley's Pond. This shift to a cosmic plane, like God's whirlwind discourse in the Book of Job, elevates the tenor of concern. "Can you bind the chains of the Pleiades," God asks, "or loose the cords of Orion?" (Job 38:31). If not, know that holiness is beyond your mastery. I think Cheever likewise intimates here that yes, *something* around us is sacred—even if it can't be readily defined or located. Something or someone is sacred, though our sense of this presence in the world must be mediated by imagination, itself a power arising for Coleridge from "the infinite I AM." A self-described churchgoer through most of his adult life, Cheever regularly attended Episcopal communion services because, as he once put it, "prayer seems to contain certain levels of gratitude and aspiration that I know no other way of expressing."[32] Susan Cheever, his daughter, has speculated: "I think he hoped to find at church some sense of redemption for the sins he had committed by thought, word, and deed against what he saw as the purity and innocence of the natural world—a world somehow represented by Christianity."[33]

So let's concede that the natural paradise Sears "seems" to find in a village pond ends up looking partly like a mental fabrication. As such, the place is partly illusion. But not fantasy—or fraud. For fiction, too, qualifies as an artful illusion. And Cheever, as a literary artist, surely knew that fiction contains its own truth. Sears should not be scorned as obtuse, after all, when he compares the scenic beauty of Beasley's Pond to a painting. For Cheever, "nature," like art, may be in some measure fictional—but the beauty of its imaginative reality remains, in human terms, essential. Even the remade Beasley's Pond is worth preserving, as an image of wilder nature and common site of renewal for Janice's citizens.

Up to a point, then, *Paradise* does discredit the idea of unspoiled nature, particularly as displayed in suburban ideals of American pastoralism. In the process, Cheever's dis-illusioning satire points up the need for activists to cultivate self-criticism, humor, and sensitivity about the ambiguities of environmental intervention. But this course of disillusionment stops short of ecological indifference. Above all, the book insists—by its closing pages, anyway—that we still live in a spiritually enchanted cosmos. Accordingly, we should not assume that debunking all forms of belief in paradise would improve our condition or that of the nonhuman world. This last Cheever novel, which the author once described as "really the first ecological romance,"[34] is also a compelling testament of faith.

The Undomesticated Ecology of
Marilynne Robinson's *Housekeeping*

Like *Paradise*, Marilynne Robinson's novel *Housekeeping* (1980) describes a town beside a lake whose presence dominates the story. But Robinson's book sustains a much darker mood than Cheever's tale of restoration. Set in an

FIGURE 9.1. Lake Pend Oreille near Sandpoint, Idaho, with railroad bridge visible toward the left. (Photo by Jay Mock.)

isolated town on a mountain-rimmed glacial lake of the Pacific Northwest, *Housekeeping* portrays a starkly unyielding landscape that recalls Robinson's birthplace in Sandpoint, Idaho (see fig. 9.1)[35] The cold, deep waters of Fingerbone Lake image not paradise but an abyss. Herein lies the fluidity of a chaos that threatens continually to overwhelm surrounding homes—and all human principles of order. In Robinson's account, the lake defines a nonhuman world that is elemental and unpredictable, capable of destroying as well as regenerating human life.

Ruth, the story's narrator, relates a grim family history. Her grandfather, who first drew the family west, perished in a dramatic train wreck that took place on the bridge crossing Fingerbone Lake. So the lake is a sink of bitter memories. It still covers not only his body and the sunken train but also the body of Ruth's mother, who drowned herself by driving a car into its depths. Ruth and her sister Lucille have been raised by a succession of relatives, none more eccentric than their aunt Sylvia. Responding to the suggestion forwarded in a letter, Sylvia arrives one day, unannounced, to assume management of the household.

But as her name implies, Sylvia is more at home in the woods, or by the lake, than she is in polite society. A free-spirited drifter, she offends townsfolk by her unconventional housekeeping. Even Ruth cannot help noticing that "our aunt was not a stable person."[36] For Sylvie, the outdoor environment flows unimpeded through house walls. "Wasps and bats and barn swallows" enjoy free rein here (85). The house shelters leaves, crickets, squirrels, sparrows, and some thirteen or fourteen cats. Stacks of cans, newspapers, and magazines fill the parlor. Worse still, Sylvie fails to guide the social development of the children under her care. As they approach adolescence, the girls become increasingly melancholy and alienated from their peers. They often skip school, preferring instead to wander by the lake. Once they spend a night alone in the woods. In time, Lucille becomes disenchanted with Sylvie's nonconformity and decides to move in with another family. Ruth, however, identifies all the more fiercely with her iconoclastic aunt. One night Sylvie leads Ruth on what the town regards as a scandalous adventure. They row off in a stolen boat, then wait to feel a train pass while they sing on the water, huddled against the bridge. After they return to town by hitching a ride on a freight car, town authorities are so distressed by Sylvie's itinerant disposition that they threaten to remove Ruth from her aunt's custody. Ruth and Sylvie decide to flee instead. "Now truly we were cast out to wander," Ruth explains, "and there was an end to housekeeping" (209).

The story approaches its apocalyptic climax when Ruth and Sylvie try to cover their escape from town by setting the house on fire. Desperate to evade their pursuers, they perform an unprecedented feat. In windy darkness, they walk across the railroad bridge, a passage so long and perilous it takes them all night. Ruth's narrative trails off with the disclosure that Ruth and Sylvie later lost touch with Lucille and became perpetual wanderers.

From the first, Robinson's language of "housekeeping" alerts us not only to feminist questions about womanly domesticity[37] but also to environmental themes. At base, Sylvie's approach to housekeeping reflects her sense of a universal "ecology" (that is, a great household) in which humans inhabit common space with the rest of Creation. Accordingly, Sylvie perceives no crucial divide between living space inside the house and the wilder world outdoors. She prefers to imagine their habitation as "sunk in the very element it is meant to exclude" (99). This point is dramatized in several ways. When lake waters pour into the house during one flood season, for example, Sylvie refuses to panic. She instead pulls Ruth through large waltz steps as "the house flowed around us" (64).

Ruth gradually develops a similar conviction of continuity between wild and domestic orders of being. For her, this sense of liminality is reinforced when she comes upon an abandoned homestead during her fateful trip with Sylvie. Viewing these disordered ruins in the light of her own unsettled life, she recognizes that "now there was neither threshold nor sill" (154) between herself and the place's former inhabitants. But the turning point in her awareness comes earlier, during the night she spends with Lucille in a driftwood hut by the woods.[38] Unlike Lucille,[39] who is unsettled by a darkness filled with cries of coyotes, owls, hawks, and loons, Ruth accepts the discovery "that all our human boundaries were overrun" (115). Ruth says she "simply let the darkness in the sky become coextensive with the darkness in my skull and bowels and bones" (116).

Sylvie, too, is drawn toward the contemplative boundlessness of darkness. At night, even indoors, she prefers to sit and to eat in the dark. This darkness belongs to the same realm of primal, formless mystery as the waters of Fingerbone Lake. "Looking out at the lake," Ruth says, "one can believe that the Flood had never ended" (172). Typically in American letters it is the male protagonist who pursues this formless freedom by transgressing civilization's boundaries. A character like Huck Finn can retain readers' approval even when he finally lights out for the territories, becoming a permanent dropout. American literary women rarely enact this form of rebellion. So Robinson's sympathetic portrayal of female drifters is arresting.

Its antisocial message can also be troubling, depending on how we interpret the novel's import as ecofiction. At the simplest level, this tale of a sadly dysfunctional family seems to endorse not only the obscuring of frontiers between settled and unsettled worlds but also a drastically individualistic repudiation of common life in community. Read in literalistic and prescriptive terms, the story shows that vagrancy—as contrasted with the inevitable pretensions of bourgeois housekeeping—represents the only authentic style of life in present-day America. Such, we may presume, was never Robinson's intent. Indeed, a whole nation of itinerants would pose its own threats to environmental stability.

The existential principle of dispossession at the core of Robinson's concern in *Housekeeping* ends up having little to do with our worldly occupation or residential address. It derives instead from the more ultimate sorrow "that every soul is put out of house," that "every spirit passing through the world fingers the tangible and mars the mutable, and finally has come to look and not to buy" (179, 73). Ultimately, we are all wanderers, children of Ishmael and of Cain. Though some of us may bear the sociological label of "unredeemed transient" (177), all of us live in exile from Eden. Meanwhile, time brings "a mourning that will not be comforted," which is "why the first event is known to have been an expulsion, and the last is hoped to be a reconciliation and return" (192). Cain, who was both killer and afflicted creator, left progeny "through a thousand generations, and all of them transients" (193). And "might we not all have been kinder and saner," Robinson has opined elsewhere, "if we had said that discontent is our natural condition, that we are the Ishmael of species, that while we belong in the world, we have no place in the world?"[40] We are to presume that there is a method, then, to Sylvie's holy madness, and that Ruth is progressing toward an essential truth as she feels herself "breaking the tethers of need, one by one" (204).

As several pivotal but unobtrusive biblical allusions in *Housekeeping* attest, Robinson's handling of this existential theme rests, in turn, on her underlying religious sense of the world. A self-described "contrarian" essayist,[41] Robinson sees things from the standpoint of a distinctive Christian orthodoxy, though she is careful not to frame her novel in overtly evangelical terms. And of course many spiritual traditions hold that a soul's realization of inner freedom and detachment aptly begins with its practice of material dispossession. So the Buddha left his father's palace to wander homeless in the forest, and Jesus says he "hath not where to lay his head" (Matthew 8.20). The biblical Book of Ruth, a mothering story that Robinson's novel parallels in several respects, dwells on the initially homeless state of its title character.[42] The gospels also describe Jesus' disciples going out from their home villages in pairs, not unlike the wandering twosome of Sylvie and Ruth, with the charge to take nothing but a staff for their journey (Mark 6:7–11).

William Bradford likewise found biblical corroboration for believing with the rest of his seventeenth-century brethren that they had no enduring home on earth. Hence "they knew they were pilgrims" (Hebrews 11:31–36) whether residing in England, Holland, or America, as did Anne Bradstreet while engaged in poetic "Contemplations" on the earth's scenic beauty. Bradstreet's Calvinist Christianity sharpened her conviction that one may love the world without becoming permanently attached to that which is by nature unenduring. Remarkably, Robinson's late-twentieth-century novel coincides thus far with the outlook of these seventeenth-century Puritans. Robinson has actually argued in defense of Puritanism, maintaining that it is also time to rehabilitate our image of John Calvin.[43] But *Housekeeping* also demonstrates that, whatever our doctrine, losing rather than keeping what we own is an inevitable fact of nature.

According to Christianity's theology of kenosis, the embodiment of God's self-emptying love, Christ enacts a supreme dispossession by casting off all prerogatives of divinity to accept a humiliating death.[44] So in effect, God, too, consents to be reimmersed in the threatening waters of primordial chaos at the point of Jesus' execution. Robinson, in the poetically theologized interlude with which she begins chapter 10 of *Housekeeping*, observes in this vein that "God Himself was pulled after us into the vortex we made when we fell, or so the story goes" (194). The remark follows several biblical references, earlier in the novel, that link Fingerbone Lake to images of the primordial sea as well as to Noah and the Great Flood. And it leads directly toward Robinson's depiction, in her final chapter, of a terrifying night passage across the lake.

Ruth confirms that the experience of crossing the bridge was decisive in rendering her thereafter "so unlike other people." Charged with mythic connotations, the episode makes this shadowy lake figure the great void, or a sea of being that encompasses all origins and destinies. Crossing the waters is thus a rite of passage intermingling sensations of birth, death, and baptism. Ruth also compares the event to the trauma of separating more than once from her mother, and to what she imagines to have been her own biological conception in darkness, after which she "walked forever through reachless oblivion" (214).

Ruth and Sylvie receive no luminous epiphany during their passage. Their pilgrimage discloses nothing equivalent to Annie Dillard's tree with lights in it. Ruth does feel that at one memorable moment on the bridge "something happened," that she and Sylvie may then have heard "some sound too loud to be heard, some word so true we did not understand it, but merely felt it pour through our nerves like darkness or water." Yet this revelation, such as it is, remains obscure and uncertain. The sense of ineffable presence in Ruth's testimony is embedded in via negativa sensations of the void:

> I believe it was the crossing of the bridge that changed me finally.
> The terrors of the crossing were considerable. Twice I stumbled and
> fell. And a wind came up from the north, so that the push of the
> wind and the pull of the current were the same, and it seemed as
> though they were not to be resisted. And then it was so dark. (215)

The ecospirituality of *Housekeeping* centers, then, on a vision of "nature" as holy and terrifying abyss. Fingerbone's railroad trestle bridges but does not domesticate the void. Of course the Fingerbone region, with its settlements and rail connections, amounts to something of a mixed or semibuilt landscape. Nor are the sites later traversed by Sylvie and Ruth in their wandering identifiable as wilderness preserves. Yet impressions of nature's unhoused, unfettered energy dominate this book. The nonhuman world cannot be construed here as a prelapsarian paradise.[45] It must be respected as more chthonic than Edenic. In the settings Robinson evokes most memorably, God's presence is felt, if at all, only obliquely, through the dark passageway of the via negativa. Preserving humanity's mediated access to this kind of existential knowledge would seem to require the preservation of actual wild places, whether or not they hold wilderness designation.[46] In any event, *Housekeeping* confirms that a turbulent lake in the Pacific Northwest, no less than a village green in New England, belongs indeed to the American commons.

10

Learning to Love Creation

The Religious Tenor of Contemporary Ecopoetry

Religious Features of "The Secular Pilgrimage"

Although "nature poetry" resists definition,[1] most of the current writing assigned to this category can be readily distinguished from its nineteenth-century antecedents. Particularly since World War I, confidence in the intelligibly providential design of all creaturely existence has faded. So has Transcendental faith in the emblematic spirituality of every natural fact. Although earlier writers had certainly reflected on humanity's social ills, injustices, and assaults on the earth, they had not found reason to image the accelerated extinction of species or planetary annihilation. As Denise Levertov remarks in a poem titled "A Hundred a Day" that begins "Dear 19th century," premoderns lived in an "unconscious sanctuary" from the knowledge that one hundred species of plants and animals could fall or be driven into extinction each day. Still comforted by "the illusion of endless time to reform, if not themselves, then the world," they were inclined to regard "Nature" as something "to be marveled at, praised and conquered, / a handsome heiress." Victorian biological debate "concerned / the origin and subsequent behaviour of species, not their demise."[2]

Predictably, modernist and contemporary poetry reflects the demise of such assumptions. Largely picturesque impressions of natural scenes have given way to grittier images of vegetable decay, animal gore and predation, or human destruction of landscapes and ecosystems. Excrement, vultures, microbes, roadkill—all of these find a place in works by poets such as Gary Snyder, Mary Oliver, or Maxine Kumin. *Garbage* (1993), a poetic collection by A. R. Ammons, graphically illustrates the shift.

Conditioned by reminders of relativity, newer nature poetry also highlights the ignorance, the highly compromised objectivity, with which human subjects must observe the nonhuman world. On the one hand, poets may insist that we are indeed part of nature, that we can—as Levertov suggests in "The Almost-Island"—retain awareness of nonhuman beings even in constructed settings. On the other hand, they are paradoxically disposed to demonstrate that the otherness, the discrete integrity of nonhumans must be respected, even reverenced. Humans, despite their anthropomorphic dreams, cannot really think like a bear or a woodchuck—much less a mountain. Nor can poets reliably express the voices of creatures other than their own kind. Some years ago, Robert Frost concluded in a well-known poem that only one "versed in country things" could believe wholeheartedly that phoebes did *not* grieve as humans do over scenes of architectural desolation. Levertov has likewise described nature as "A world / parallel to our own though overlapping." We may sojourn in this other realm, welcoming the "pure (almost pure) / response to that insouciant life" discerned in "animal voices" and in "cloud, bird, fox, the flow of light, the dancing / pilgrimage of water." Such encounters may even change us, "a little," as something in us "breaks free." But we are finally obliged to reenter "our own sphere," there "to evolve our destinies."[3]

Awareness of humanity's problematic, sometimes antagonistic relation to earth's environment was of course heightened by cultural movements evident in America by the late 1960s. *Turtle Island,* Gary Snyder's collection of poetry and seminal prose published in 1969, marks the emergence of an explicitly ecological poetic. Some of this new writing allied to environmentalism conveyed anger—not only against those deemed responsible for specific ecological crimes but often against Western civilization itself. For obvious reasons, protest poetry has remained an enduring subgenre of environmental literature. This poetry of witness ranges over a variety of occasions and settings. It includes works such as Gary Snyder's "Mother: Earth: Her Whales," Patiann Rogers's "Animals and People: 'The Human Heart in Conflict with Itself,' " and Wendell Berry's cantankerous "Mad Farmer" poems. Although Levertov may be better known for her antiwar poems, she has also written passionate statements of environmental resistance such as "It Should Be Visible" and "Protesting at the Nuclear Test Site," as well a poetic version of Rachel Carson's toxicity complaint titled "Silent Spring." Even Mary Oliver, who declines to write protest poems or to be identified politically as an "environmentalist," occasionally bemoans land abuse, as in her prose comment that "wilderness shrinks beneath our unkindnesses and our indifference."[4]

But I would argue that love, not rage, has inspired the larger and better share of present-day nature poetry. This love of earth typically involves embracing the particularity of visible things while honoring an invisible web of spiritual and biotic affinities. It means affirming humanity's felt relation to some larger life-presence that transcends scientific materialism and personal egotism. To that extent its tenor is broadly religious. This chapter highlights what I take to be a resurgent, unexpectedly resilient strain of spirituality in contemporary American poetry.

American literary tradition has perpetuated a countervailing antireligious impulse, too, from the Wasteland era to now. Prominent in the modernist sensibilities of Pound, early Eliot, and Stevens, this demystifying urge has also played an important role in the work of certain nature-based writers such as Ed Abbey and Robinson Jeffers. Yet an imposing magnitude of nature poetry published in the United States over the past two or three decades imagines prospects of faith and healing that transcend wasteland pessimism. In effect, this religious ecopoetic looks to incorporate, but to pass beyond, Jeffers's misanthropic philosophy of "inhumanism."[5] The faith it envisions may not be explicitly theistic, in Judeo-Christian terms. Nor, for that matter, recognizably pantheistic. The poet's religious viewpoint may grant the possibility of transcendence while quite rejecting supernaturalism. Thus, as a religious poet combining shamanistic and Buddhist beliefs, Gary Snyder avoids using diction associated with Western theism.[6] As religious poets primarily identified with Christian spirituality, Wendell Berry, Pattiann Rogers, and Denise Levertov do occasionally draw on that tradition's vocabulary of God, Holy Spirit, grace, redemption, and sacrament. Mary Oliver falls somewhere in between. In addition to the five poets selected for illustration in this chapter, several others— including William Everson, Joy Harjo, Galway Kinnell, and Richard Wilbur— could be discussed under the heading of spiritually infused ecopoetry.

Wendell Berry, in an essay devoted to assessing contemporary nature poetry, uses the term "secular pilgrimage" to describes the "peculiar aspiration" of poets such as A. R. Ammons, Denise Levertov, and Gary Snyder. In fact, Levertov was often disposed to invoke the figure of life as pilgrimage.[7] Berry understands the poets' shared sense of pilgrimage to be secular insofar as it remains grounded in an animated material world. Moreover, it ordinarily "takes place outside of, or without reference to, the institutions of religion, and it does not seek any institutional shrine or holy place; it is in search of the world." Yet Berry considers it "a pilgrimage nonetheless because it is a religious quest." As such, it seeks harmonious engagement with "the created world in which the Creator, the formative and quickening spirit, is still immanent and at work." Aspiring to heal "the schism in the modern consciousness," it journeys toward the recovery of worship, wholeness, and humility in the face of Creation's irreducible mystery.[8]

A novel feature of this ecological spirituality is its emphasis on *reciprocal* restoration. As Berry points out, conventional Christianity can lead souls to become obsessed with their personal salvation, while virtually ignoring the larger health of communities and the earth. Poets of the Romantic era, too, fixed attention on the human benefits of restoration offered by a vernal wood. The idea was to reform one's inner being, rather than anything in the material biosphere. It remained for the age of ecology to ripen awareness that self-integration and environmental restoration were synergistically related. Present-day poets who are enacting some version of the secular pilgrimage usually imagine their own progress toward healing to be bound up with the larger health of the planet.

As Mary Oliver puts it, "the pine tree, the leopard, the Platte River, and ourselves—we are at risk together, or we are on our way to a sustainable world together. We are each other's destiny." Oliver also confesses, with disarming frankness: "Now I think there is only one subject worth my attention and that is the recognition of the spiritual side of the world and, within this recognition, the condition of my own spiritual state." "For me," she writes, "the door to the woods is the door to the temple."[9] Pattiann Rogers has described the religious aspiration of her poetic no less openly:

> I want my poems that explore the essence of god and divinity to in-
> corporate the best of all that I am able to bring to any poem. In my
> inadequacy and ignorance, I hope they contain my grateful thanks,
> my ceaseless curiosity and steady faith, my compassion and rever-
> ence for the universe in all of its manifestations and creations.[10]

As these statements imply, ecopoetry seems best suited to support medi-tation rather than persuasion. It favors discovery over argument, thankful amazement over advocacy. Unlike environmental nonfiction, which readily conveys indignation and prophetic exhortation, lyrical poetry wants to sing. Reading itself can be construed as an oddly solitary, contemplative activity in the setting of present-day society. Reading poetry is even stranger. The me-dium's slow-paced rhythms demand patience, inwardness, and concentration— disciplines comparable to those traditionally applied to meditation. Thus, read-ing and writing poetry has an inherently meditative aspect worth considering in relation to the special case of earth-centered verse. In the preface to his *Sabbath Poems*, Wendell Berry points out that he composed his poems unhur-riedly, "in silence, in solitude, mainly out of doors," and he recommends that they be read, so far as possible, under similar conditions.[11] Berry also dem-onstrates that some forms of verse meditation, following the precedent of bib-lical psalms, amount to praise declarations. Mary Oliver likewise professes a resolve to "write praise poems that might serve as comforts, reminders, or even cautions if needed, to wayward minds and unawakened hearts."[12]

While ecopoetic meditation characteristically aims to integrate interiority with landscape by way of imagination, its outward focus differs from one writer to another—and, for that matter, from one poem to another. Berry's medita-tions often dwell on and among trees. Levertov's last poems frequently image blossoming flowers, and the distant peak of Mount Rainier. Gary Snyder char-acteristically sets the mind on "riprap," the stone cobble of horse trails, as well as on scat, rugged mountains, Ponderosa pine, and other creatures of the American West. Mary Oliver's reflections fix most memorably on predators— hawk, bear, and snapping turtle—commonly found in the Northeast. Ordinar-ily, too, Oliver prefers to concentrate attention by setting these images of non-human life within the frame of unpeopled landscapes. Pattiann Rogers, like A. R. Ammons, tries to incorporate spirituality into the cosmology of modern science. Fascinated by her previous academic studies in zoology and astronomy, she is also married to a physicist. Accordingly, her verse meditations encompass a universe of being, ranging from quasars, protozoa, and marsh wrens to astral radiation.

For each of these poets, pondering concretely sensate images of Creation leads toward discovery of a spirituality thoroughly embedded in the material world. As Mary Oliver puts it, "I am sensual in order to be spiritual."[13] Gary Snyder shows comparable devotion to sense experience in earthy poems such as "Song of the Taste" (from *Regarding Wave*) and "The Flowing" (from in *Mountains and Rivers Without End*). Echoing Psalm 34, Levertov titled a 1964 volume of her poetry "Oh Taste and See." Patiann Rogers, whose work frequently accents bodily or erotic physicality, wrote a poem titled "Rolling Naked in the Morning Dew." Fulfilling the spirit of Wendell Berry's previously cited remarks, such poetry embodies a theology of radical immanence. Those poets (including Berry, Rogers, and Levertov) who eventually accept an explicit theism repeatedly dramatize God's continuing, incarnational involvement in the process of creation. They emphasize not God's eternal sovereignty or providential wisdom but God's compassion, mystery, even vulnerability.

In this vein, Pattiann Rogers offers speculatively adventurous pieces with titles such as "Inside God's Eye" and "The Possible Suffering of a God During Creation." She concludes another poem by declaring, in aptly fractured syntax:

> God is a process, a raveled nexus
> forever tangling into and around the changing
> form of his own moment—pulse and skein,
> shifting mien, repeating cry
> of loss and delivery.[14]

Moreover, Rogers envisions human beings acting conjointly with God in the project of making nature sacred. As she explains in a prose commentary on her poem "The Dream of the Marsh Wren: Writing as Reciprocal Creation":

> And perhaps the divine, the sacred, the holy, only come into complete existence through our witness of them, our witness for them and to them. Perhaps reciprocal creation, as I observe it operating in my own writing—creating the poem which simultaneously creates me which simultaneously creates the poem coming into being—just as the marsh wren created by the marsh simultaneously creates and dreams the marsh of its creation and therefore creates itself—is the same phenomenon occurring in regard to divinity.[15]

Denise Levertov likewise suggested in 1984, at which time she described herself as "a Christian, though not a very orthodox one," that "there is a way of looking at Christian faith as involving the cooperation of man" and that "I think that's part of the meaning of Incarnation."[16] Influenced by her father's studies in Hasidic spirituality and her own exposure to the *Zohar*, Levertov came to appreciate the idea of a "divine spark" indwelling in Creation. Her father became an Anglican clergyman but retained a sense of Jewish ethnicity; her mother was descended from a noted Welsh mystic. Levertov's fascination with nature's holy strangeness thus owed something to a confluence of Jewish, Christian, and Welsh elements in her personal heritage.[17] But she was also struck by the idea of God's silence, the elusiveness of divine presence in an evolving world. This sentiment captured her imagination not only during her years of agnostic seeking but also during the latter part of her career, through the 1980s and 1990s, when clearer commitment eventually led her to acknowledge membership in the Roman Catholic Church. In the poem "Kin and Kin" (from *A Door in the Hive*, 1982) she expresses hope that within the larger process of evolution, humankind might choose to develop spiritually so as to improve its cognizance of kinship as well as "kindness" toward other species. The theme of immanence is particularly prominent in her poem "On the Mystery of the Incarnation," collected in the same volume. In a treatment laced with sardonic humor, Levertov reflects on how the doctrine of God's becoming human should be interpreted to stir not anthropocentric pride but chastened humility in the face of divine compassion.

Poetry of Sabbath Spaces

Wendell Berry's *Sabbath Poems*, a series written over nearly two decades, aptly illustrates the poet's own prose remarks about a religiously inspired "secular pilgrimage." If Gary Snyder's *Mountains and Rivers Without End* is the product of walking meditation through landscapes of Asia, Alaska, Australia, and California, Berry's poems move within much narrower bounds. Berry saunters exclusively through the fields and woods of his own farmland in Port Royal, Kentucky. In the course of this walking meditation, he centers his soul on familiar ground. So figuratively, at least, he is also practicing a kind of sedentary reflection equivalent to the zazen literally practiced by Gary Snyder. He begins his opus in 1979 by declaring that after a week's labor in the field, "I go among trees and sit still."[18] The sense of this line, recalling George Herbert in its rich simplicity, resonates throughout the series' many allusions to stillness, rest, and attentive waiting. When the poet reminds himself to "Be still" in his 1982 "Thrush song" poem (43), that formula recollects in broader context the traditions of contemplative practice surrounding Psalm 46:10: "Be still, and know that I am God."

Instead of attending church, Berry devotes himself to a meditative walk each Sunday morning. Clearly he prefers his own solitary ritual, for when "the bell calls in the town" to announce the start of service, "I hear, but understand / Contrarily, and walk into the woods" (9). Yet he understands his dissenting practice to be no less disciplined and worshipful than the devotions then taking place indoors. In fact, the series dramatizes Berry's resolution to remain faithful to Judaism's underlying rationale for Sabbath observance. Aspiring to recover the archaic meaning of Shabbat, a vision enlarged through earth-grounded meditation, these poems also develop a distinctively contemporary and personal spirituality of place. In a poem titled "The Farm," Berry even links his particular practices of crop rotation to biblical teaching concerning "A Sabbath for the land" (139).

The Jewish theologian Abraham Heschel points out that the Sabbath day signifies the wholeness and fulfillment of Creation. Its justification is not merely utilitarian, to provide intervals of respite for the sake of ensuring a productive work week. Or, as Heschel writes, "the Sabbath as a day of rest, as a day of abstaining from toil, is not for the purpose of recovering one's lost strength and becoming fit for the forthcoming labor." Rather, "the Sabbath is a day for the sake of life," an occasion when "we are called upon to share in what is eternal in time, to turn from the results of creation to the mystery of creation."[19] Mythically, the Sabbath day enacts the sacralization of time since it is a period set apart from humanity's normal schedule of labor, obligation, and anxiety. It is a time to transcend worries about what we are doing or becoming. It is time simply to be, to contemplate the joyous gift of Creation. Sabbath time thus calls to mind that perpetually fresh moment of divine Creation when, in biblical language prized by John Muir, the morning stars "sang together and all the sons of God shouted for joy" (Job 38:7).

Throughout the lyric meditations recorded in *A Timbered Choir*, Berry voices his intent to share in this song of Creation. His collection first sounds the theme with an epigraph from Isaiah 14:7: "The whole earth is at rest, and in quiet: they break forth into singing." The volume's opening poem and many subsequent verses then develop this motive of song and blissful harmony. Retiring from the scene of his weekday labor in the fields, Berry flees distraction by entering the woods. "Here where the world is being made" beyond human design (35), he concentrates his yearning for wholeness in the light of an "all-welcoming, / all-consecrating Sabbath" (88). But he must quiet the mind before he can embrace Creation's "blessed conviviality"(8) or hear earth's songs arise as "field and woods and all in them / Rejoin the primal Sabbath's hymn" (13). This hymn celebrates that spiritual ecology by which creatures are constituted "Members one of another, / Here in our holy room," an ecology whose invisible bonds unite

> Light, leaf, foot, hand, and wing,
> Such order as we know,
> One household, high and low,
> And all the earth shall sing. (52)

Although the meditations in *A Timbered Choir* move toward such a perfected image of harmony, they also recognize the divisions and failings common to actual experience. Throughout the series, Berry develops an oppositional rhetoric that invokes diverse polarities such as labor/rest, fields/woods, song/silence, light/dark, movement/stillness, way/place, and falling/rising. Yet the integrative aim of his meditation is to work through these dualities, accepting the apparent contraries as mutually enriching contributions to a larger process of renewal and exchange. Thus, the poet sees himself deriving much of his ability to sing effectively on Creation's behalf from his contrasting absorption of silence: "But on the days I am lucky / or blessed, I am silent" (182). And the creative rhythm of Berry's life depends on juxtaposing the day of contemplative rest with six days' active labor.

The poems record a corresponding spatial oscillation between fields and woods. Although the woods offer a distinctive place of "rest" in contrast to cultivated fields, they are not the only site open to blessedness and grace. Ultimately, *A Timbered Grace* aspires to pass beyond the most culturally entrenched polarities of cultivated/uncultivated and human/nonhuman. To make one's peace with "nature" is thus, in Berry's agricultural setting, to reinhabit one's home landscape so as to enjoy common kinship with its tamed and untamed inhabitants. Just as the "edge" environment of cultivated fields helps create ecologically diverse habitats for birds and other wildlife, so also this cleared terrain contributes spiritually as well as economically to the poet's quest for wholeness. "When field and woods agree," Berry writes, "they make a rhyme" recollecting "the whole / First Sabbath's song." The poet's vision of "A harmony between forest and field vocation" reintegrates "The world as it was given for love's sake" with "The world by love and loving work revealed / As given to our children and our Maker" (14–15). And just as the free movement of walking meditation remains bounded in place and time, so also the restricted space of cleared field images one approach to the sacred:

> Enclosing the field within bounds
> sets it apart from the boundless
> of which it was, and is, a part,
> and places it within care.
> The bounds of the field bind
> the mind to it. (17)

The poet shows special fondness for language that plays on the dialectical opposition between "falling" and "rising." Traditional Christian vocabulary often describes both human and nonhuman nature as "fallen"—that is, lowered through sin or infirmity beneath its Edenic ideal. Even the most stalwart oaks eventually tumble to earth. In this light, Berry laments with Saint Paul that all mortal creatures, still awaiting the perfect liberty of God's new Creation, must "groan in misery" (13). And that includes human beings, "For we are fallen like the trees, our peace / Broken" (74). Yet the nonhuman world also presents signs of achieved resurrection. For example, the poet welcomes "the resurrection / of bloodroot from the dark" (155). "What stood will stand, though all be fallen," he insists, and therefore "Let praise / Rise up out of the ground like grass" (13). In his "Thrush song" poem, he connects observations in the field to the gospel account of Jesus' postresurrection appearance in John 20:15, when he writes of how "A man who seems to be / a gardener rises out of the ground, / Stands like a tree, shakes off the dark"(43).

Berry also likes to ruminate on the ecological cycle of life by which "fallen" creatures, most obviously embodied by autumnal leaves, become regenerative through rather than despite their death and decay.[20] In the composting process, degeneration becomes organically wedded to regeneration. Where vegetative decay proceeds undisturbed, one can witness a transformation in which "centuries of leaves" contribute to a "mold of all that grew and fell" as "the timeless / Fell into time" (16). As the poet's consciousness of mortality becomes more acute within the unfolding series of poems, this circuit of death, decay, and new life becomes more prominent. Following the biological cycle of soil-building leads, in turn, to meditation on the richly spiritual ecology by which "Thus falling founds, / Unmaking makes the world" (57).

One way these poems challenge the human/nonhuman divide is by experimentally identifying with creatures of another species. Yet Berry applies this traditional technique somewhat unconventionally. Characteristically, he identifies with select traits of the organism while indicating respect for its separate sphere of being. Thus, in one 1980 poem he admires the way "The frog with lichened back and golden thigh / Sits still" on its leafy, lichened stem. He takes the reptile's "almost invisible" blending with its environment to be "Its sign of being at home / There in its given place, and well" (28). Without pretending to think or act like the frog in any other respect, he finds this single trait of adapting to one's habitat inspiring as he, too, seeks to make himself wholly at home on earth. But whereas the frog is already perfectly situated in *its* home, the poet meditates on the perpetual motion by which

> . . . I, through woods and fields, through fallen days
> Am passing to where I belong:
> At home, at ease, and well,
> In Sabbaths of this place. (28)

Like Anne Bradstreet centuries earlier, Berry regards his human songs of praise as poetically distinct from, yet spiritually harmonious with, those articulated by nature's other creatures. The divine grace of thrush music, for example, lies in its un-self-conscious fluidity. So thrush song differs from the poem's fixed impressions on a page, or the self's urge to locate a still center of being. Yet even such partial identification with nonhuman song serves to move the poet's imagination:

> Thrush song, stream song, holy love
> That flows through earthly forms and folds,
> The song of Heaven's Sabbath fleshed
> In throat and ear, in stream and stone,
> A grace living here as we live,
> Move my mind now to that which holds
> Things as they change. (43)

The full stop that interrupts the coursing rhythm of this verse-paragraph marks the point of human difference from nonhuman discourse. But that crucially conjunctive "as," in "as we live," also supplies a ligature between us and them. Connoting concurrent as well as analogous forms of experience, it effectively joins what Levertov had recognized as parallel worlds.

Some of the finest poems in *A Timbered Choir* embody Berry's long emotional association with trees. One such poem describes the process of gradual reforestation by which "great trees" appear in an undisturbed lot. The piece begins with language evocative of measured growth: "Slowly, slowly, they return / To the small woodland let alone." Instead of regarding these trees as a detached observer, the speaker internalizes the mystery of their silence, their apparently still yet dynamic life. The poet seeking Sabbath rest doubtless has reason to emulate the absolute calm with which they "stand in waiting all around / Uprisings of their native ground." Berry imagines these creatures not merely claiming but indeed hallowing this place made native both for them and him:

> Patient as stars, they build in air
> Tier after tier a timbered choir,
> Stout beams upholding weightless grace
> Of song, a blessing on this place. (83)

Unlike the "bare ruined choirs" of Shakespeare's famous sonnet, these expansive timbers do support birdsong while tracing spacious designs in air. Great trees, despite their solidity, also support vital processes involving light and energy, microorganisms, motile fluids, and the exchange of atmospheric gasses. For Berry, once again, the dynamic of this physical synergism reflects a divine economy of grace:

> Receiving sun and giving shade,
> Their life's a benefaction made,
> And is a benediction said
> Over the living and the dead. (83)

Again, too, Berry envisions the seasonal lapse of foliage as a fortunate fall. The energy captured in the trees' "brightened leaves" enables humans "To walk on radiance, amazed," and arouses the poet's closing benediction: "Oh light come down to earth, be praised."

For Berry, the discipline of composing Sabbath poems has evidently been a labor of love. In fact, he doubts he could have been a poet at all "except that I have been in love / alive in this mortal world" (182). But for all his love of words and native scenes, Berry believes that love leads ultimately "to life beyond words, silent / and secret" (182). Despite his semiorthodox theology, he evidently associates this love with religious trust that "the Presence that we come into with song / is here, shaping the seasons of His wild will" (73). It seems to me that some form of love, rather than ideology, likewise animates the finest ecological poetry produced by other current writers, though the love is bound in each case to an individually defined spirituality.

Love for "All of It"

While campaigns for environmental reform often appeal to humankind's sense of duty or fear of self-destruction, the poets we are considering typically invoke love. Mary Oliver, in her poem "Spring," announces this theme quite overtly when she describes a black bear's emergence from hibernation. Identifying the bear's own silent, primal, and sensuous awakening as "perfect love," the poet declares: "There is only one question: / how to love this world."[21] What does she mean? Is this love of earth anything but sentimental enthusiasm?

For Oliver, Snyder, and the rest, earth-love seems to involve, in the first place, simple familiarity with one's environment, attentiveness to its biotic and topographic details. Oliver's black bear, whose moving fists and tongue connect her un-self-consciously to the waking world, is evidently at home in the place where she finds herself. On many occasions, Gary Snyder has voiced an equivalent imperative for humans to know the animals, plants, and earth of the place they inhabit. For Snyder, recovering this elemental connection is a form of love that binds us together in solidarity with other members of earth's planetary community. It enables us to reverence even roadkill, as evidenced in "The Dead by the Side of the Road," and to renew allegiance to North America's archaic identity as "Turtle Island." In the prose section of *Turtle Island*, Snyder argues that members of the settler culture must commit themselves to "loving and protecting this soil, these trees, these wolves" if they would become genuine natives of the continent they inhabit (105).[22] And as he has said in an interview,

> What are we going to do with this planet? It's a problem of love; not the humanistic love of the West—but a love that extends to animals, rocks, dirt, all of it. Without this love, we can end, even without war, with an uninhabitable place.[23]

For all of these poets, such love sometimes reveals itself through sensuous immersion in the material world. At the same time, paradoxically, their earth-love contains an element of reserve that enforces respect for the inhuman autonomy of other creatures. Denise Levertov's poem "In Tonga," for example, concludes its description of "the sacred bats" who live on islands of the central Pacific by insisting that if these "alien" creatures "could think" in anything like human terms, "it would not be of us."[24] And though Patiann Rogers fancies in various poems what it might be like to be a horned toad, a red bird, or a marsh wren, she maintains an ironic, reverential distance between herself and the nonhuman figures she represents through imagination.

Mary Oliver, too, knows she will never become identical to that black bear in "Spring" whose aboriginally sensate, direct communion with her environment the poet dreams of emulating. Simply imagining the experience of this animal, which the poet never claims to observe directly, ties her spiritually to the "dazzling darkness" of her own animal origins. Yet the poet's life, with its words and "its music / and its glass cities," unfolds in a realm largely distinct from that of the bear's "wordlessness" and "perfect love."[25] The idea of reverencing alien, elusive animal presences likewise informs Wendell Berry's poem "To the Unseeable Animal," Denise Levertov's "Come into Animal Presence," and Gary Snyder's "Jackrabbit" and "The Bear Mother"(in *Mountains and Rivers Without End*). In *Turtle Island*, Snyder also calls to mind the vast ages preceding

236 MAKING NATURE SACRED

human settlement during which "persons" such as "ponderosa pine, manzanita, black oak, mountain yew," along with bear, deer, coyote, and gray squirrel, completed their own lives at home on this continent. A poem such as Snyder's "Toward Climax" likewise supports an expansive evolutionary vision. This poem invokes the principle of succession in its witness of respect for the self-regulating dynamic of forest ecosystems "at / Climax" whether or not they qualify technically as "Virgin."[26]

Another form of earth-love involves the poet's struggle to accept natural processes that seem cruel or absurdly profligate from the standpoint of humanistic values. In "Turtle," Mary Oliver displays compassion for the predator no less than for its prey. Having seen a snapping turtle stalk and devour a teal's "sweet" chick by the edge of a pond, she insists on the supreme importance of not denying "the great and cruel mystery of the world, / of which this is a part."[27] Accordingly, she says she once returned a snapper to pond water after rescuing it from a city street. In "Nature," she celebrates the owl's wild instinct of hunting by night, finding in this bloody ritual a "true gift" and inevitability of nature "which is the reason / we love it." The poem's unrelenting cadences and lack of end-stopped lines reinforce this theme. And though the poet is troubled at first by the imperfection of nibbled lilies that crowd the black waters of summer in "The Ponds," she finally asserts her will to believe in the transcendent prospect of floating "a little / above this difficult world." To love the world is to look beyond imperfection to an affirmation that she is indeed "looking / into the white fire of a great mystery."[28]

For Pattiann Rogers, as for Gary Snyder, fully accepting the nonhuman world means acknowledging, too, what science discloses about its inner life. And it means imagining how things might look from other, nonanthropocentric points of view. Such love of earth draws a poet's soul into the inscape of evolution. Rogers's sense of sympathetic identification with the pain of other beings extends even to God, as evidenced by her poem on "The Possible Suffering of a God During Creation." The great spiritual challenge is to accept not only one's own suffering—for Buddhists, the realization known as *dukkha*—but also the pain and imperfection of all things.

Earth-love, then, expands finally toward universal compassion. Compassion, literally a matter of feeling and suffering *with* the other, plays a conspicuous role in Christian redemptive theology. It is also integral to Buddhist spirituality, particularly in the Mahayana tradition's focus on a Buddha of compassion. The selfless ideal of the bodhisattva, for example, involves solicitude for the welfare of all sentient creatures. It is appropriate, then, that Gary Snyder begins his epic poem *Mountains and Rivers Without End* with this epigraph from the great Tibetan poet-saint Milarepa (1040–1123): "The notion of Emptiness engenders Compassion."

This thread of *sutra*, or aphoristic teaching, runs through the whole of Snyder's monumental work. It is echoed in the poem's last section, "Finding the Space in the Heart," and its spirit is invoked in several other sections (including "With This Flesh," "The Hump-Backed Flute Player" and "An Offering for Tārā") with reference to rivers and to Tārā, a female Buddha figure of compassion and wisdom. Snyder explains in a prose account of the poem's making that while his title had been derived from that of an actual East Asian scroll painting, his experiences in Japan and elsewhere opened further understanding of what mountains and rivers could mean: "I came to see the yogic implications of 'mountains' and 'rivers' as the play between the tough spirit of willed self-discipline and the generous and loving spirit of concern for all beings."[29]

Beginning with poetic meditation on the scroll's "created space" (5) of landscape, *Mountains and Rivers Without End* moves directly into the outer space of geographies experienced at disparate times on several continents. Though the action centers geographically on arid country of the Great Basin around Nevada (whose enclosed watershed, coincidentally, is "without end" at any ocean), it runs as well to scenes in Japan, the bedrock of New York City, and other places. The poem's Whitmanian imagination ranges to explore a multitude of circumstances, characters, registers of language, and moods. One finds here earthy, seemingly mundane descriptive catalogues of "things to do," sagebrush varieties, and highway happenings; one also finds refashionings of Asian and Native American mythology that must strike some readers as esoteric. The poet relates episodes of mental travel into art and fable, as well as lots of plain walking, driving, or kayaking with his mate. And he identifies experimentally with a vast array of selves and alien characters—including a female presence in "The Elwha River" and a nonhuman one in "The Mountain Spirit."

Mountains and Rivers Without End presses beyond all sorts of boundaries—spatial, temporal, and spiritual. The richness of its literary and thematic exposition cannot be captured through critical synopsis. But we can return briefly to one crucial concern: how does this poem imagine that emptiness leads to compassion and, in turn, to environmental reverence?

The emptiness in question is neither a physical vacuum nor equivalent to Western nihilism. The void named by *sunyata* is instead a spiritual reality—a boundless suchness that is dynamic, undivided, and undiscoverable through analytic reasoning.[30] Snyder's poetry illustrates how embracing this emptiness dissolves familiar antimonies of inner versus outer, art versus life, and the Emersonian ME versus NOT ME. To enter this void means knowing that "there is no place we are / but maybe here" (131), or, as the Mountain Spirit whispers, that

> All art and song
> is sacred to the real.
> As such. (146)

Above all, the emptiness of *Mountains and Rivers* signifies openness to the unbounded flow of planetary space. Only as the craving ego is pushed aside can space appear for compassion. And such space, which unfurls gradually like a handscroll, is potentially ubiquitous. "The Blue Sky" shows it extending, in a sense beyond Zen, to open heavens of the healing Buddha's Pure Land. Love, a going out of oneself, aims to encircle the world and overleap all boundaries between self and environment. Snyder explains in an essay collected in *The Practice of the Wild* that true love of the land extends beyond wilderness terrain and that "*Sacred* refers to that which takes us (not only human beings) out of our little selves into the whole mountains-and-rivers mandala universe."[31] Accordingly, in the poem "Earth Verse" he characterizes the spirit of ecopoetry as "Wide enough to keep you looking / Open enough to keep you moving" (148). But unlike Whitman, Snyder often mutes the first-person voice in favor of detached imagistic representation, as in his "Walking the New York Bedrock" with its surge of physical impressions. Preoccupation with "our little selves" must, after all, preclude our embracing the present moment, the present place. So the spiritually charged exercise of walking around a place, as enacted by Snyder and Allen Ginsberg in "The Circumambulation of Mt. Tamalpais," offers an antidote to solipsism. As Snyder and Allen take a day to walk around this ridge in Marin County, California, joking and chanting along the way, they are at once blessing and being blessed by the land. This encircling action also embodies the notion of a world in flux. The walkers are themselves moving, ever changing, as is their environment. To know emptiness is to know that we can grasp nothing permanently, a point that is pressed home by the larger poem's incantatory refrain

> *Walking on walking,*
>   *under foot earth turns*
> *Streams and mountains never stay the same.* (152)

Snyder's poem also illustrates how the free flow of compassion extends to healing. One notable instance can be found in the portrayal of Kokop'ele, an enigmatic wanderer represented in "The Hump-backed Flute Player." With his image inscribed in rocks throughout the Southwest and Mexico, he is primarily a Native American figure, but in Snyder's treatment he recalls Asian pilgrims as well. Kokop'ele's hump is a pack—perhaps linking him historically to traders wandering up from the south. But in Snyder's presentation, the flute player carries no items of commercial trade but "emptiness," or "mind only." Furthermore, the poet links his spirit to that of Wovoka, otherwise known as Jack Wilson, a Paiute prophet of Ghost Dance religion who dreamed of reuniting Indians in an order free of white oppression. We learn that Black Coyote "saw the whole world," including "the bottomless sky," in the "empty hat" of Wovoka (81).

The poem's composite pilgrim thus combines healing powers of the Buddhist saint and conjuring shaman. But Kokop'ele, unlike the exploitative agents of settler culture, who have left only "ghost bison, ghost bears, ghost bighorn" (80) to roam the Great Basin, carries no intrusive structures onto the land. He travels light, leaving no marks of his passage. Moreover, Snyder speculates in a note that Kokop'ele's pack might have held seeds. This circumstance would display restorative compassion in yet another way since "as a possible emblem of genetic diversity his work is not over" but involves "guardianship and preservation, not just of plants and animals, but of peoples and cultures as well" (Snyder's prose note, 160).

And as a musician, Kokop'ele, like the poet, is a bearer of intangible beauty. The poet, as he lies by a cave in Arizona's Canyon de Chelly, absorbs the emptiness of the flute player's compassion. This self-dispossession—combined, it seems with the spirit of Tārā, or "she who saves"(80)—inspires him in turn to re-create the Basin's mountain music of bristlecone pine and pinyon pine.

Such particularities of place reference help present-day readers of the poem recover their own sense of what Snyder calls "the ancient, sacred turtle island landscape" ("The Making of *MRWE*," 155). The poem abounds in illustrations of the land's "wideness" and of "the foolish loving spaces / full of heart" (152). Paradoxically, though, *Mountains and Rivers* also defies localization, since its attention never rests in a single place. Within its own planetary context, then, this imposing work recalls Thoreau's project, in the final chapter of *Walden*, to define the geography of the sacred in terms that transcend the literalism of mapped space.

Beyond Humanism toward Reverence: The Beauty of Unknowing

During the final years of her life, Denise Levertov moved to Seattle, where Gary Snyder as a child had discovered East Asian landscape painting in the city museum. As Levertov remarks wryly in a poem titled "Settling," the damp, gray weather common in the Pacific Northwest reminded her of London, where she was born. In her new setting, the natural feature that seized her imagination most insistently was Mount Rainier, looming on the southern horizon within sight of the house she had purchased. Several of the place-centered poems she wrote during the last phase of her career, between the time she moved to Seattle in 1989 and her death in 1997, amount to an extended meditation on this mythic prominence (see fig. 10.1).

That Mount Rainier should have become the focal point of Levertov's final musings about numinous nature seems fitting. Often shrouded in clouds, the snow-capped peak, otherwise known as Tacoma, had long been revered as "the mountain" by native peoples inhabiting the region's lowlands.[32] Glacial ice mantles this tallest volcano of the Cascade Range. Although Rainier is currently inactive, no one knows when it will erupt again. So an apprehension of future apocalypse surrounds the mountain, as does a recollection of earth's origins embedded in glacial and volcanic geology. In her poem "Against Intrusion," Levertov captures the threateningly sublime majesty of this mountain that, "forbearing—so far—from volcanic rage, / blesses the city it is poised above."[33] Gary Snyder, too, discloses that "being able to see Mount Rainier far off to the east on a clear day" became a key element of his childhood perception of the world when he lived on a small farm north of Seattle.[34]

On the one hand, Rainier makes a striking impression throughout the greater Seattle-Tacoma region. On the other hand, seeing it can become so habitual that one fails to remain seriously mindful of its presence. In "Wit-

FIGURE 10.1. Mount Rainier and Mowich Canyon. (Photo from the Library of Congress.)

ness," Levertov admits that just as the mountain is often hidden from her in clouds, so also she has sometimes been "hidden from the mountain" when she has forgotten to go look at it because of "inattention, apathy, fatigue" (*Life*, 71). More often, though, Levertov dedicates herself to absorbing the sense of Rainier at regular intervals. The persistence of her gaze centers her attention, unifies her imaginative powers. She will do all she can to know "a mountain's vast presence, seen or unseen"("Settling," *Life*, 58). This sense of welcoming the capaciousness of Creation echoes the invocation of "all things, seen and unseen" in Christianity's Nicene Creed. For Levertov, though, the mountain brings the image of Creation to focus. And her impulse "to reconfirm / that witnessing presence" ("Witness") again and again helps to place her, spiritually as well as physically, in the discrete environment she has now chosen to inhabit.

Thus, the process of conceiving these mountain poems, comprising more than a dozen meditative portraits of Rainier in diverse settings, required both aesthetic and spiritual discipline. It is profitable to read these pieces in conjunction with one another to appreciate how Levertov tried to enter the mountain's mystery of an ever-shifting identity amid sameness. She writes about the peak's appearance in successive seasons, under changing light and atmospheric conditions. She knows, too, that her own views of this stationary object remain in flux. The mountain's appearance is invariably colored by its surroundings, as well as by the observer's variable moods. Sometimes it strikes her as a "massive presence," "obdurate" and inertly indifferent; sometimes as an "animal mountain," panting with discomfort as snows melt in "dark streaks" across its folds ("Presence," "The Mountain Assailed"). At times it presents a "luminous" reality; at other times it seems merely a mirage. In "Elusive," Levertov highlights the mountain's uncertain ocular status through haze, as it "comes and goes / on the horizon" with "a rhythm elusive as that of a sea-wave" (*Life*, 59). So whatever Rainier finally means to her, theologically or otherwise, she understands to be the product of a phenomenological equation involving her inward soul as well as outward geography.

By sketching the same object with variant shading in poem after poem, Levertov displays a technique of concentrated mindfulness often practiced by visual artists. One thinks of Claude Monet's famous canvasses exploring diverse views of Rouen Cathedral, or Georgia O'Keefe's multiple renderings of Cerro Pedernal Mountain near Abiquiu, New Mexico. Simon Schama's book *Landscape and Memory*, which the poet reports she was reading with pleasure in 1990, describes how ancient Chinese Buddhist and Taoist paintings image mountains as sacred objects of meditation that defy human mastery.[35] In "Pentimento," a poem whose title refers to the reappearance of previously obscured design in a painting, Levertov describes one visual impression of the mountain's form as "a draft / the artist may return to" (*Life*, 66).

Yet her intensely reiterated scrutiny of Rainier only confirms that she can never grasp its totality. Her photographs fail utterly to represent what is presumably there. Like Matsuo Basho, the seventeenth-century Zen poet who takes to heart the elusive, half-hidden magic of Mount Fuji,[36] Levertov is captivated above all by Rainier's revelation of the unknown and unknowable. This sacred aspect of the mountain is best exposed in "Open Secret," a poem that dwells on the apophatic or negating dimension of Levertov's vision. Particularly because she wills to look on Rainier only from afar, she knows that its denser features must elude her gaze. She nonetheless find this absence, like the mountain's disappearance under cloud, spiritually enlarging. "Its vanishings / are needful, as silence is to music," she points out in "Against Intrusion." There is mystical rather than gnostic truth in the mountain's revelation of such unknowing. And in "Open Secret," she explains why she is reluctant to visit Rainier's meadows or touch its snow:

> This one is not, I think, to be known
> by close scrutiny, by touch of foot or hand
> or entire outstretched body; not by any
> familiarity of behavior, any acquaintance
> with its geology or the scarring roads
> humans have carved in its flanks.
> This mountain's power
> lies in the open secret of its remote
> apparition.... (*Life*, 70)

Much of the time, Levertov's mountain evidently resembles a god. Rainier qualifies as an archaic nature deity in its majesty, in its capacity to channel fearfully elemental powers of creation and destruction. At the same time, Levertov teases out resemblances between this singular peak and the One God of Abrahamic religion. Her symbology of Rainier thus mediates between strict

242 MAKING NATURE SACRED

monotheism and certain polytheistic or animistic impulses that she likewise found attractive, and that Trinitarian Christianity strives to incorporate.[37] Thus, in "Morning Mist," she compares the mountain's periodic "absences" to Christianity's sense of "Deus absconditus," the hidden God whom biblical theophanies typically portray as veiled in cloud. She perceives yet another image of God in the all-enveloping peace cast by the mountain's "white stillness / resting everywhere" and lending "to all things / an hour of Sabbath" (*Life*, 60) In a late, posthumously collected poem titled "The mountain's daily speech is silence," she compares Rainier's stillness not only to the quiet maintained in monasteries between liturgical offices but also to "the silence God maintains / throughout the layered centuries."[38] Moreover, her impression of Rainier sometimes suggests a personal presence affiliated with the Judeo-Christian conception of divine personhood. Yet the deity shadowed in Levertov's mountain poems, like the deity imaged by other contemporary poets, also remains vulnerable and mutable rather than impassively omnipotent.

Above all, the Rainier poems enact reverence for a physically embodied, transhuman presence that urges us to admit human limitation even if we live in a technologically advanced place like Seattle. As such, these poems reflect a contemporary approach to sacred nature that links urban civilization to its bioregional environment. Levertov's evocation of the sacred is contemporary, too, insofar as the presence she describes is phenomenologically interactive, not completely derived from an intrinsic power of place. So whatever enchantment the mountain creates must depend, at least in part, on someone's willingness to engage its mystery, to invest her own soul and imagination in the scene. The mountain's "witnessing presence" presupposes the presence of a human witness.

And though Rainier might *resemble* a god or God, Levertov recognized that it was *not*, in itself, either one of these. This last apophatic principle also helps clarify what "making nature sacred" might mean in present-day terms. Levertov's postmythical sensibility ensures that Mount Rainier cannot serve as her idol. It cannot be, or contain, the poet's god. But it can and does function as a religious icon, an object through which humans look to discover forms of presence beyond themselves. Levertov develops this point in several poems, particularly in one titled "Looking Through." Here the weather's atmospheric coloring on a late summer day allows her to imagine that "the whole great mass of mountain" is "transparent" (*Life*, 68), a notion consonant with Eastern Orthodoxy's view of sacred iconography as well as with Emerson's philosophy.

Viewed at closer range, Mount Rainier may not look godly at all. In "Against Intrusion," Levertov says she has friends who have already climbed there, been there, done that. She will not follow suit. Those "scarring roads" leading toward the peak scarcely inspire worship; and it would be hard not to notice that parts of Rainier National Park have become yet another overcrowded shrine to American tourism. No wonder Levertov prefers to keep her distance, living on close terms with a mountain she will encounter only from miles away.

Levertov's deciding to leave the mountain alone is, in itself, an exceedingly modest token of restraint and respect. Yet the poet knows that, for her at least, this place cannot be made or kept sacred without her inward consent. Today it seems plainer than ever that the reverence motivating such consent is an acquired virtue. It can scarcely be taken for granted. To ensure sustainable life on the planet, individuals and whole societies must deliberately choose to restrain instincts of conquest that have commonly driven the long march of human civilization. In a poem called "Tragic Error," Levertov laments the misreading of biblical texts that has thus far sanctioned humanity's voracious consumption of God's earth. "Surely," she writes, our charge was "to love the earth, / to *dress and keep it* like Eden's garden." And our proper "dominion" was to have been "those cells of earth's body that could / perceive and imagine" (*Life*, 12).

Amending this error will require a change of heart, a drastic renewal of reverence such as Albert Schweitzer had only begun to imagine. Environmental reverence, like any other virtue, must be instilled through deliberate training and exercise. First of all, though, the virtue's beauty must be imagined and articulated persuasively enough to seem appealing. That vocation is one Levertov has shared with a worthy company of green-spirited writers throughout the tradition of American letters.

Afterword

When John Cheever's character of Lemuel Sears asks "Is nothing sacred?" he means the question rhetorically, to deride those who would tolerate ruining a lovely pond for profit. And yet, in the current cultural climate, the question must also be entertained in earnest. It is no longer clear to what extent society at large recognizes any space, time, or being as authentically sacred—that is, as inviolately preserved from ordinary human manipulation. In contemporary America, even the indoor architecture of worship sites may not be constructed or apprehended as sacred space. Many newly built or renovated churches are staged to resemble talk-show settings rather than temples of the numinous. So it is perhaps symptomatic of our time that the elderly, reclusive artist whom John Updike makes the central consciousness in his recent novel *Seek My Face* (2002) should feel an indefinable loss over what she takes to be evidence of God's absence or nonexistence in the world. Postmodern secularism no longer construes this shift as a momentous existential drama involving "the death of God." It presumes instead a quiet evaporation of all thoughts about signifying presence. If a hermeneutic of suspicion becomes all in all, nothing indeed can be sacred. Moreover, our aggressively consumerist culture has the effect not of assailing but rather of trivializing godliness, rendering pursuit of the numinous irrelevant. By now, Victorian and modernist hopes that humanity's spiritual hunger could be satisfied by replacing religion with art have faded as well.

Yet the very title of Updike's novel, based on the Psalmist's resolve to seek the face of the Lord (Psalm 27:8), testifies to the insatiability of this hunger even in the new millennium. It is telling that a decidedly worldly character named Hope, the narrative focal point of

Updike's story, says she has aspired to paint holiness—and has never lost her longing to find or to help create something like holiness. The closing chapters of my book attest that humankind's current hope for saving wholeness, its faith in a life beyond itself, rests as much as ever on engagement with the nonhuman world. Receptivity to some prospect of earth-centered transcendence remains important across a startling range of current U.S. literatures.

Still, I think Bill McKibben is right to argue that humankind's ability to imagine anything numinous in nature may be severely—perhaps even fatally—impaired by environmental degradation.[1] Once we construct the physical world so thoroughly that we can no longer see, to rephrase Wordsworth, anything in nature that is *not* ours,[2] religion itself is endangered along with countless biotic species. McKibben contends that, deep ecology notwithstanding, we need continuing access to real-life "nature" for the sake of our own physical and spiritual survival—and, it so happens, for religion's sake as well.

Conversely, we may also need religion—especially spirited, radically incarnational religion—for nature's sake. To be sure, faith-sponsored calls for conversion to sustainable living seem comparatively rare. They also seem to have little immediate impact. A recent Christian evangelical campaign to conserve fossil fuel, launched under the provocative slogan "What would Jesus drive?" has not yet moved Americans to abandon their SUVs. But an extensive survey of American nature writing confirms that Henry Thoreau, John Muir, Gary Snyder, and most other American writers who have given eloquent voice to the environmental imagination write from the soul. In so doing, they have also stimulated major reforms in environmental policy—albeit, in some cases, indirectly or unwittingly. The imaginative hopes of these visionaries spring from their passionate spirituality, a re-creative impulse that is religious to the core, whatever its relation to traditional orthodoxies. Figures as theologically disparate as Henry Thoreau, John Muir, Wendell Berry, Mary Oliver, and Annie Dillard share not only a passionate interest in wild creatures and places but a conviction that God, too, must be less tame and respectable than has been piously rumored. This other-than-safely-human Maker of all things, visible and invisible, may even be, as Berry claims, "the wildest being in existence."

Notes

INTRODUCTION

1. Ernest Hemingway, *The Sun Also Rises* (New York: Scribner's, 1926, 1954), p. 245.

2. Nathaniel Hawthorne, *The Marble Faun*, in *The Centenary Edition of the Works of Nathaniel Hawthorne*, ed. William Charvat et al. (Columbus: Ohio State University Press, 1968), 4:3.

3. J. Hector St. John de Crèvecoeur, *Letters from an American Farmer and Sketches of Eighteenth-Century America* (New York: Penguin, 1981), p. 76.

4. Thomas Cole, "Essay on American Scenery," in *American Art, 1700–1960: Sources and Documents*, ed. John W. McCoubrey (Englewood Cliffs, N.J.: Prentice-Hall, 1965), pp. 102, 100.

5. One informed and frequently cited account of the word's manifold meanings appears in Raymond Williams, *Keywords: A Vocabulary of Culture and Society* (New York: Oxford University Press, 1976), pp. 184–189.

6. By "strangeness" I mean a quality of otherness surpassing human understanding. Nature itself is thus understood to bear a power of "defamiliarisation," or making things strange, comparable to that which the Russian Formalist Victor Shklovsky attributed to art. See Raman Selden, *A Reader's Guide to Contemporary Literary Theory* (New York: Harvester Wheatsheaf, 1985; 2nd ed. 1989), pp. 10–11.

7. Perry Miller, *Nature's Nation* (Cambridge: Harvard University Press, 1967), p. 203. Among the many noteworthy books in this vein are Henry Nash Smith, *Virgin Land: The American West as Symbol and Myth* (Cambridge: Harvard University Press, 1950), R.W.B. Lewis, *The American Adam: Innocence, Tragedy and Tradition in the Nineteenth Century* (Chicago: University of Chicago Press, 1955), Leo Marx, *The Machine in the Garden: Technology and the Pastoral Ideal in America* (New York: Oxford University Press, 1964), Roderick Nash, *Wilderness and the American Mind* (New Haven: Yale University Press, 1967), and Peter N. Carroll, *Puritanism and the Wilderness* (New York: Columbia University Press, 1969).

8. Cheryll Glotfelty, "Introduction: Literary Studies in an Age of Environmental Crisis" (pp. xviii–xix), and William Howarth, "Some Principles of Ecocritism" (p. 78), in Cheryll Glotfelty and Harold Fromm, eds., *The Ecocriticism Reader: Landmarks in Literary Ecology* (Athens: University of Georgia Press, 1996). Glotfelty (p. xxviii) points out that the term "ecocriticism" was coined by William Rueckert in 1978.

9. Lawrence Buell, *The Environmental Imagination: Thoreau, Nature Writing, and the Formation of American Culture* (Cambridge: Harvard University Press, 1995). Buell followed up this study with *Writing for an Endangered World: Literature, Culture, and Environment in the U.S. and Beyond* (Cambridge: Harvard University Press, 2001). Other signs of an ecocritical turn include the publication of John Elder's two-volume edition of biographical-critical essays titled *American Nature Writers* (New York: Scribner's, 1996), Glotfelty's and Fromm's *The Ecocriticism Reader*, John Elder's *Imagining the Earth: Poetry and the Vision of Nature* (Athens: University of Georgia Press, 1996), and several anthologies of primary sources. The subfield can also claim now its own professional association and a journal, *ISLE: Interdisciplinary Studies in Literature and Environment*, published at the University of Nevada at Reno.

10. Jay Parini, "The Greening of the Humanities," *New York Times Magazine* (October 29, 1995), pp. 52–53.

11. Catherine L. Albanese, *Nature Religion in America: From the Algonkian Indians to the New Age* (Chicago: University of Chicago Press, 1990), p. 7. Aside from Albanese's book, historically centered investigations parallel to my concern can be found in Roderick Nash's previously cited *Wilderness and the American Mind*, in Nash's later study *The Rights of Nature: A History of Environmental Ethics* (Madison: University of Wisconsin Press, 1989) (especially chapter 4, "The Greening of Religion"), and in Barbara Novak's *Nature and Culture: American Landscape and Painting 1825–1875* (New York: Oxford University Press, rev. ed. 1995).

12. Exceptions can nonetheless be found; and one should note that in *American Pastoral* (1997), Philip Roth offers a brilliant novelistic critique of values rooted in myths of rural virtue and stability. Andrew Furman discusses the dearth of Jewish environmental literature in "No Trees Please, We're Jewish," *ISLE* 72 (summer 2000): 115–136.

13. Clyde A. Holbrook, *Jonathan Edwards, the Valley and Nature: An Interpretive Essay* (Lewisburg, Penn: Bucknell University Press, 1987), p. 33.

14. R. W. Emerson, *Nature* in *Collected Works of Ralph Waldo Emerson*, ed. Robert Spiller and Alfred R. Ferguson (Cambridge: Harvard University Press, 1971), 1:10.

15. Belden C. Lane, *Landscapes of the Sacred: Geography and Narrative in American Spirituality* (Baltimore: Johns Hopkins University Press, 1988; 2nd ed. 2001), esp. pp. 5, 11, 15, 23, 39, 41–42; Paul Ricoeur, *The Symbolism of Evil* (New York: Harper and Row, 1967), pp. 351–357, cited p. 352. Likewise pertinent to the problem of theorizing a phenomenology of the sacred are "Manifestation and Proclamation" and "The 'Sacred Text' and the Community," in Ricoeur, *Figuring the Sacred*, ed. Mark I. Wallace (Minneapolis: Fortress Press, 1995), pp. 48–72.

16. Lane, *Landscapes of the Sacred*, p. 19.

17. John Muir, *My First Summer in the Sierra*, in *John Muir: Nature Writings*, ed. William Cronon (New York: Library of America, 1997), p. 160.

18. See Bill McKibben, *The End of Nature* (New York: Random House, 1989), and Carolyn Merchant, *The Death of Nature: Women, Ecology, and the Scientific Revolution* (San Francisco: Harper and Row, 1980).

19. Edward Hoagland, series editorial preface to Penguin Nature Classics, in

William Bartram's *Travels* (New York: Penguin Books, 1988) p. vi; Rachel Carson is cited in Paul Brooks, *The House of Life: Rachel Carson at Work: With Selections From Her Writings Published and Unpublished* (Boston: Houghton Mifflin, 1972), p. 315.

20. Barry Lopez, *Arctic Dreams: Imagination and Desire in a Northern Landscape* (New York, Random House, 1986), p. xxii.

CHAPTER I

1. Cited in *Seventeenth-Century American Poetry*, ed. Harrison T. Meserole (New York: Norton, 1972), p. 397. We do know, at least, that Tillam became denominationally affiliated with Baptists and ended up settling in Germany.

2. Henry Thoreau, "Walking," in *Excursions* (Boston: Ticknor and Fields, 1863; rpt. Gloucester, Mass.: Peter Smith, 1975), pp. 161–162, 190; on the nature characteristics of Algonkian religion, see Catherine L. Albanese, *Nature Religion in America: From the Algonkian Indians to the New Age* (Chicago: University of Chicago Press, 1990), pp. 16–33.

3. William Wood, *New England's Prospect*, ed. Alden T. Vaughan (Amherst: University of Massachusetts Press, 1977), pp. 15, 20.

4. Robert Frost, "The Gift Outright," in *Collected Poems, Prose, and Plays* (New York: Library Classics of the United States, 1995), p. 316.

5. Stowe's remark appears in *Life and Letters of Harriet Beecher Stowe*, ed. Annie Fields (Boston: Houghton Mifflin, 1897), p. 351. In *Providence Island, 1630–1641: The Other Puritan Colony* (New York: Cambridge University Press, 1993), Karen Kupperman discusses an actual case of short-lived Puritan colonization in the tropical West Indies, off the coast of Nicaragua. The environmental circumstance of Providence Island clearly affected its reliance on plantation slavery and privateering but did not substantially alter the conversion theology of its leaders.

6. Wood, *New England's Prospect*, pp. 31–32; see also John Canup's remarks on weather and on the trope of cultural transplantion in *Out of the Wilderness: The Emergence of an American Identity in Colonial New England* (Middletown, Conn.: Wesleyan University Press, 1990), pp. 4–28.

7. William Bradford, *Of Plymouth Plantation, 1620–1647*, ed. Samuel Eliot Morison (New York: Random House, 1952), pp. 25, 62–63. Subsequent references in my text are to this edition. The Pilgrim-Puritan conceit of North America as "unpeopled" coexisted uneasily with the contrary migration rationale of evangelizing native peoples. On the colonizers' image of New England as empty for occupation, see also William Cronon, *Changes in the Land: Indians, Colonists, and the Ecology of New England* (New York: Farrar, Straus and Giroux, 1983), p. 90; and Joseph A. Conforti, *Imagining New England: Explorations of Regional Identity from the Pilgrims to the Mid–Twentieth Century* (Chapel Hill: University of North Carolina Press, 2001), p. 20. The term "Pilgrim" is conventionally applied to "saints" (by no means the total population) of Plymouth Colony, often in contrast to the "Puritans" (nonseparating Congregationalists) who settled elsewhere in southern New England. But despite minor differences in ecclesiology, these two groups held equivalent beliefs in theology; so I have sometimes used the term "Puritan" with broader reference to both.

8. *Mourt's Relation: A Relation or Journal of the English Plantation Settled at Plymouth in New England, by Certain English Adventureres both Merchants and Others*, ed. Dwight B. Heath (1622; New York: Corinth Books, 1963), p. 15. Edward Winslow is usually thought to have been the principal author of this anonymous work, to which

Bradford may also have contributed. If Bradford himself composed this first narrative section, as some believe, the contrasting rhetorical aims of the two accounts become all the more arresting.

9. Two prominent treatments of this wilderness paradox can be found in Roderick Nash, *Wilderness and the American Mind*, rev. ed. (New Haven: Yale University Press, 1973), and Peter N. Carroll, *Puritanism and the Wilderness: The Intellectual Significance of the New England Frontier 1629–1700* (New York: Columbia University Press, 1969).

10. From *The Planters Plea* (1630) as cited in Conforti, *Imagining New England*, p. 21.

11. Discerning accounts of Bradford's work as providential history are supplied by Robert Daly, "William Bradford's Vision of History," *American Literature* 44 (1973): 557–569, and by David Levin, "William Bradford: The Value of Puritan Historiography," in *Major Writers of Early American Literature*, ed. Everett Emerson (Madison: University of Wisconsin Press, 1972), pp. 11–31; David Read, in "Silent Partners: Historical Representation in William Bradford's *Of Plymouth Plantation*," *Early American Literature* 33 (1998): 291–314, challenges the view that Bradford was trying to write providential history in the Second Book.

12. See, for example, "General Considerations for the Plantation in New-England," in *Chronicles of the First Planters of the Colony of Massachusetts Bay: 1623–1636*, ed. Alexander Young (1846; New York: Da Capo Press, 1970), pp. 275–277.

13. Cecelia Tichi, *New World, New Earth: Environmental Reform in American Literature from the Puritans Through Whitman* (New Haven: Yale University Press, 1979), esp. pp. 1–36.

14. See, for example, Cronon, *Changes in the Land*, pp. 63, 69.

15. George F. Willison, *Saints and Strangers* (New York: Reynal and Hitchcock, 1945), p. 392. The biblical passage invoked here is Psalm 24:1.

16. Lynn White, Jr., "The Historical Roots of Our Ecologic Crisis," *Science* 155 (1967): 1203–1207. White's often-reprinted essay has provoked many published responses, including my remarks in "The Uses of Wilderness: A Christian Perspective," *Anglican Theological Review* 62 (1980): 256–265; and James Barr's informed exegetical commentary, "Man and Nature: The Ecological Controversy and the Old Testament," in *Ecology and Religion in History*, ed. David and Eileen Spring (New York: Harper and Row, 1974), pp. 48–75. One noteworthy discussion of how shifting European views of science affected attitudes toward nature is Carolyn Merchant, *The Death of Nature: Women, Ecology, and the Scientific Revolution* (San Francisco: Harper and Row, 1980).

17. *Changes in the Land*, pp. 127–156.

18. See, for example, Yi-Fu Tuan, "Our Treatment of the Environment in Ideal and Actuality," *American Scientist* 58 (1970): 248; Yi-Fu Tuan, "Discrepancies Between Environmental Attitude and Behaviour: Examples from Europe and China," *Canadian Geographer* 12 (1968): 176–191, reprinted in Spring, *Ecology and Religion in History*, pp. 91–113; and René Dubos, *A God Within* (New York: Scribner's, 1972).

19. Andrew Delbanco, *The Puritan Ordeal* (Cambridge: Harvard University Press, 1989), p. 42.

20. See Peter N. Carroll, *Puritanism and the Wilderness*, pp. 215–217. In *Out of the Wilderness* (pp. 180–183), John Canup observes, however, that these warnings were prompted at least partly by fears of too much "heathenizing" contact with wild peoples of the forest, while Delbanco (*Puritan Ordeal*, pp. 76–77) points out that communitarian ideals were compromised by land speculation and bids to enlarged personal landholding, often on the part of founding gentry.

21. This point is emphasized by several recent scholars, including Conforti in *Imagining New England*, pp. 11–34.

22. *Letters from New England: The Massachusetts Bay Colony, 1629–1638*, ed. Everett Emerson (Amherst: University of Massachusetts Press, 1976), pp. 21, 22, 30.

23. Cotton Mather, *Magnalia Christi Americana*, books 1 and 2, ed. Kenneth B. Murdock with Elizabeth W. Miller (Cambridge: Harvard University Press, 1977), pp. 117, 118, 122.

24. On this church building's significance in relation to Cotton's identity and career, see Delbanco, *Puritan Ordeal*, p. 119.

25. Despite their rejection of sacred buildings, Puritans were also disposed to image the whole of New England as a temple edifice. Edward Johnson, for example, affirms as much in his *Wonder-Working Providence of Sions Saviour in New-England*, ed. Edward J. Gallagher (1654; rpt. Delmar, N.Y.: Scholars' Facsimiles and Reprints, 1974), p. 200: "so they came over this boysterous billow-boyling Ocean, a few poor scattered stones newly raked out of the heaps of rubbish, and thou Lord Christ hast now so far exalted them, as to lay them sure in thy Sion, a building, to be the wonder of the world, orderly are they placed in five and forty several Churches, and that in a Wilderness, where civility scarce ever took place."

26. *Mourt's Relation*, p. 89.

27. *Magnalia Christi Americana*, pp. 121, 55, 123, 130, 118.

28. Cecelia Tichi, *New World, New Earth*, pp. 37–66; Johnson, *Wonder-Working Providence*, pp. 26, 3, 81, 32–34.

29. Thomas Jefferson, *Notes on the State of Virginia*, in *The Portable Thomas Jefferson*, ed. Merrill D. Peterson (New York: Viking Press, 1975), p. 217.

30. John Seelye, *Prophetic Waters: The River in Early American Life and Literature* (New York: Oxford University Press, 1977), p. 166; Nathaniel Hawthorne, "The May-Pole of Merry Mount," in *Twice-Told Tales*, in *The Centenary Edition of the Works of Nathaniel Hawthorne*, ed. William Charvat et al. (Columbus: Ohio State University Press, 1963–87), 9:54.

31. Thomas Morton, *New English Canaan: Text, Notes, Biography and Criticism*, ed. Jack Dempsey (Scituate, Mass.: Digital Scanning, 2000), pp. 14, 171, 37, 22. Subsequent references are to this edition.

32. *Book of Common Prayer* (Cambridge, England: John Baskerville, Printer to the University of Cambridge, 1762), p. D4. See also Jack Dempsey's remarks in the commentary section of Dempsey, *New English Canaan*, pp. 32–33.

33. Jack Dempsey, in the critical and biographical remarks attached to his edition of Morton, makes a plausible case for dismissing these shadowy charges, though I find some of Dempsey's claims for Morton—e.g., that he deserves recognition as "the continent's first poet in English" (xxxii)—extravagant.

34. That conventional European tropes of a feminized landscape took on new force and meaning in America, thereby replacing benign pastoralism with presumptions of violation and inevitable despoilation, has been emphasized by feminist critics, particularly Annette Kolodny in *The Lay of the Land: Metaphor as Experience in American Life and Letters* (Chapel Hill: University of North Carolina Press, 1984).

35. As commentators such as Jack Dempsey and Richard Slotkin (in *Regeneration Through Violence: The Mythology of the American Frontier, 1600–1860* [Middletown, Conn.: Wesleyan University Press], 1973, p. 59), have observed, Morton also *revises* biblical usage in describing his "New English Canaan" to manifest sympathy for the non-Hebrew, pagan Canaanites of ancient Palestine. This emphasis indeed characterizes several passages in his work. Typically, though, Morton wants to have it both

ways. As his reference to "the Israelites' Canaan" indicates, he nonetheless tries frequently to appropriate the honored status of "Israel" for New England and freely adapts biblical imagery, as when he compares himself to the troubled prophet Jonah, to suit his own rhetorical purposes.

CHAPTER 2

1. David D. Hall, *Worlds of Wonder, Days of Judgment: Popular Religious Belief in Early New England* (Cambridge: Harvard University Press, 1990), pp. 71, 75, 76.

2. *The Scarlet Letter*, in *The Centenary Edition of the Works of Nathaniel Hawthorne*, ed. William Charvat et al. (Columbus: Ohio State University Press, 1963–87), 1:155.

3. "The Great Bones Dug up at Claverack," in *Edward Taylor's Minor Poetry*, in *The Unpublished Writings of Edward Taylor*, ed. Thomas M. and Virginia L. Davis (Boston: Hall, 1981), 3:211, 213.

4. Lawrence Lan Sluder, "God in the Background: Edward Taylor as Naturalist," *Early American Literature* 7 (1973): 265–171.

5. In *Gracious Laughter: The Meditative Wit of Edward Taylor* (Columbia: University of Missouri Press, 1989), I summarize these traditions and scholarship pertaining to them (pp. 53–54, 59, 78, 181); I also discuss Taylor's related insect poems (192–199). See also Barbara Kiefer Lewalski, *Protestant Poetics and the Seventeenth-Century Religious Lyric* (Princeton: Princeton University Press, 1979), pp. 147–169 and esp. pp. 150–151 and 162–169.

6. *Edward Taylor's "Church Records" and Related Sermons*, in *Unpublished Writings of Edward Taylor*, 1:179.

7. *The Poems of Edward Taylor*, ed. Donald E. Stanford (New Haven: Yale University Press, 1960), p. 471.

8. Meditation 9, second series, in *The Poems of Edward Taylor*, p. 94.

9. Cited in *The Works of Anne Bradstreet*, ed. Jeannine Hensley (Cambridge: Harvard University Press, 1967) p. 241. Subsequent references to Bradstreet's verse and prose, identified parenthetically by page number, are to this edition.

10. The fullest case for this poem's anticipation of Romanticism can be found in Alvin H. Rosenfeld, "Anne Bradstreet's 'Contemplations': Patterns of Form and Meaning," *New England Quarterly* 43 (1970): 79–96.

11. I discuss these forms of meditation more fully in *Gracious Laughter*, pp. 50–62.

12. Richard Baxter, *The Saints' Everlasting Rest*, cited in *The Doubleday Devotional Classics*, ed. E. Glenn Hinson (New York: Doubleday, 1978), 1:139. On Bradstreet's relation to meditative and emblem traditions, see also Ann Stanford, *The Worldly Puritan: An Introduction to Her Poetry* (New York: Burt Franklin, 1974), pp. 93–106. Broader treatments of Puritan meditation relevant to Bradstreet's case include Louis L. Martz's important foreword to *The Poems of Edward Taylor*, Lewalski, *Protestant Poetics*, and Charles E. Hambrick-Stowe, *The Practice of Piety: Puritan Devotional Disciplines in Seventeenth-Century New England* (Chapel Hill: University of North Carolina Press, 1982), esp. pp. 163–164, 273.

13. Though Bradstreet elsewhere images God as a monarch, her emphasis in "Contemplations" accords more nearly with what the theologian John Macquarrie has described as "the organic model," in contrast to the "the monarchical model," of divine relation to the creation. See Macquarrie, "Creation and Environment," in *Ecology*

and Religion in History, ed. David and Eileen Spring (New York: Harper and Row, 1974), pp. 48–75.

14. Higginson cited in *Letters from New England: The Massachusetts Bay Colony, 1629–1638,* ed. Everett Emerson (Amherst: University of Massachusetts Press, 1976), p. 35; Josselyn cited in *John Josselyn, Colonial Traveler: A Critical Edition of "Two Voyages to New-England,"* ed. Paul J. Lindholdt (Hanover, N.H.: University Press of New England, 1988), p. 71. Lindholdt attaches Josselyn's "New-England Nightingale" to the painted bunting, *Passerina ciris* (pp. 71–72, n. 145), but this identification strikes me as questionable since the bunting's normal breeding range falls well south of New England; William Bartram, *Travels Through North & South Carolina, Georgia, East & West Florida* (New York: Penguin Books, 1996), p. 247.

15. The mythological portrayal of Philomela, as rape victim and daughter of King Atticus, is doubtless relevant to Bradstreet's gender identification. In *The Nightingale's Burden: Women Poets in American Culture Before 1900* (Bloomington: Indiana University Press, 1982), Cheryl Walker explores further thematic and self-representational implications of Bradstreet's feminization of this bird.

16. See also Ann Stanford, "Anne Bradstreet's Emblematic Garden," in *Critical Essays on Anne Bradstreet,* ed. Pattie Cowell and Ann Stanford (Boston: Hall, 1983), p. 251. Of the two candidates that Ann Stanford proposes, wood thrush or mockingbird, the first strikes me as most plausible. See also John Josselyn's thrush references in *John Josselyn, Colonial Traveler,* p. 71.

17. Robert Daly, "Anne Bradstreet and the Practice of Weaned Affections," in *God's Altar: The World and the Flesh in Puritan Poetry* (Berkeley: University of California Press, 1978), pp. 82–127, considers the poet's broader poetic response to Puritan demands that believers must love earthly creatures neither too little nor too much.

18. Geographic information about this region and about Bradstreet's residence in North Andover can be found in Elizabeth Wade White, *Anne Bradstreet: The Tenth Muse* (New York: Oxford University Press, 1971), pp. 222–227, and 326–329; Stanford, *The Worldly Puritan,* p. 78; Sarah Loring Bailey, *Historical Sketches of Andover, Massachusetts* (Boston: Houghton Mifflin, 1880), pp. 2, 12, 126–131; and Edward G. Roddy, review of *The Valley and Its Peoples—An Illustrated History of the Lower Merrimack,* by Paul Hudon, in *Essex Institute Historical Collections* 119 (1983): 264–267.

19. Josselyn in *John Josselyn, Colonial Traveler,* pp. 118–119.

20. William Wood in *New England's Prospect,* ed. Alden T. Vaughan (Amherst: University of Massachusetts Press, 1977), p. 64; William Hammond in *Letters from New England,* p. 111.

21. Bartram, *Travels,* pp. 145, 11, 65. James Dickey's remarks appear in the introduction (p. xi). Subsequent references are to this edition.

22. As Thomas P. Slaughter indicates in *The Natures of John and William Bartram* (New York: Knopf, 1996), pp. 62–66 and 178, William's beliefs about the continuously cohesive ordering of creation resembled his father's and were doubtless influenced by John. John, in turn, had drawn on works such as Thomas Burnet, *The Sacred Theory of the Earth,* and John Ray, *The Wisdom of God Manifested in the Works of Creation,* to develop his disdain for the Cartesian view of animals as machines lacking soul and genuine emotion (pp. 60–61). And as Michael Branch points out in "Indexing American Possibilities: The Natural History Writing of Bartram, Wilson, and Audubon," in *The Ecocriticism Reader: Landmarks in Literary Ecology,* ed. Cheryll Glotfelty and Harold Fromm (Athens: University of Georgia Press, 1996), pp. 288–289, unpublished remarks of William Bartram challenge anthropocentric arrogance even more pointedly than what he published in his *Travels.*

23. The paleontologist Richard Fortey comments on the blurring of distinctions between plant and animal kingdoms in *Life: A Natural History of the First Four Billion Years of Life on Earth* (New York: Vintage Random House, 1997), pp. 69–75.

24. See Slaughter, *Natures of John and William Bartram*, pp. 14–15. Slaughter points out that John, a formidably self-possessed personality, continued to attend weekly meeting even after his censure.

25. Slaughter, *Natures of John and William Bartram*, pp. xvi, 4, 66, 138, 144. In "The Quaker Background of William Bartram's View of Nature," *Journal of the History of Ideas*, 46 (1985): 435–448, Larry R. Clarke suggests that William's spiritual path often took him "closer to traditional Quakerism" (444) than his father's more rationalistic and fiercely anticlerical religious mood would dictate.

26. In "William Bartram," in *American Nature Writers*, ed. John Elder (New York: Scribner's, 1996), 1:67, Philip G. Terrie remarks, for example, on Bartram's perceptions concerning the ecological place of insects with regard to the food chain.

27. Slaughter, *Natures of John and William Bartram*, p. xvii.

28. Slaughter, *Natures of John and William Bartram*, pp. 20, 43–44, 155–60, and 204–206. On Bartram's later disavowal of slavery, see also N. Bryllion Fagin, *William Bartram: Interpreter of the American Landscape* (Baltimore: Johns Hopkins University Press, 1933), pp. 16–17.

29. *Travels*, pp. 257, 224–225. Bartram nonetheless recounts, a few pages earlier, the story of his killing a rattlesnake that threatened a Seminole encampment.

30. *The Journal of John Woolman*, in *The Journal and Major Essays of John Woolman*, ed. Phillips P. Moulton (New York: Oxford University Press, 1971), pp. 24–25.

31. *The Journal of John Woolman*, p. 28. For further examples of Woolman's enduring concern for animals, as reflected in the *Journal* and elsewhere, see Margaret E. Stewart, "John Woolman's 'Kindness Beyond Expression': Collective Identity *vs.* Individualism and White Supremacy," *Early American Literature* 26 (1991): 260 and 273–274 n. 2.

32. Fagin, *William Bartram*, pp. 128, 134–139, 165, draws on John Livingston Lowe's classic account (*The Road to Xanadu*, 1927) to discuss Coleridge's reliance on Bartram in composing *The Rime of the Ancient Mariner*. In a letter to Thomas Poole of February 6, 1797, cited in *Collected Letters of Samuel Taylor Coleridge*, ed. Earl Leslie Griggs (Oxford: Clarendon Press, 1956), 1:302, Coleridge wrote: "I should almost despair of that Man, who could peruse the Life of John Woolman without an amelioration of heart." Coleridge later followed this remark, which precedes his composition of *The Rime*, with another laudatory reference to the *Journal*.

CHAPTER 3

1. Clyde A. Holbrook, *Jonathan Edwards, The Valley and Nature: An Interpretive Essay* (Lewisburg: Bucknell University Press, 1987), pp. 24, 107, 17. In *Jonathan Edwards* (New York: Dell, 1949), Perry Miller expressed the opinion that "No poet was more sensitive to the beauty of nature than Edwards" (p. 290).

2. Perry Miller, "From Edwards to Emerson," in *Errand into the Wilderness* (Cambridge: Harvard University Press, 1956), pp.184–203; see also Mason I. Lowance, Jr., *The Language of Canaan: Metaphor and Symbol in New England from the Puritans to the Transcendentalists* (Cambridge: Harvard University Press, 1980), pp. 249–295; Conrad Cherry, *Nature and Religious Imagination: From Edwards to Bushnell* (Philadelphia: Fortress Press, 1980), pp. 14–44; Wallace E. Anderson, introduction to "Images of Divine Things" and "Types," in Jonathan Edwards, *Typological Writings*, in *The Works of Jona-*

than Edwards, gen. ed. Harry S. Stout (New Haven: Yale University Press, 1993), 11:3–33; and Stephen H. Daniel, *The Philosophy of Jonathan Edwards: A Study in Divine Semiotics* (Bloomington: Indiana University Press, 1994), pp. 41–65.

3. "Images of Divine Things" (1728), in *Typological Writings*, in *The Works of Jonathan Edwards*, 11:106.

4. For elaboration of these terms, as derived from moral philosophers such G. E. Moore, see Roger N. Hancock, *Twentieth-Century Ethics* (New York: Columbia University Press, 1974), pp. 18–40; J. Baird Callicott, "The Conceptual Foundations of the Land Ethic," in *Environmental Ethics: Divergence and Convergence*, ed. Susan J. Armstrong and Richard G. Botzler (New York: McGraw-Hill, 1993), pp. 386–399; Roderick Frazier Nash, *The Rights of Nature: A History of Environmental Ethics* (Madison: University of Wisconsin Press, 1989), pp. 69–70; and Paul W. Taylor, *Respect for Nature: A Theory of Environmental Ethics* (Princeton: Princeton University Press, 1986), pp. 59–98.

5. George Marsden, "Jonathan Edwards, American Augustine," *Books and Culture* 6 (November/December 1999): 11.

6. Aldo Leopold, *A Sand County Almanac* (1949; New York: Oxford University Press, rpt. 1966), pp. xvii–xix. Subsequent references in my text are to this edition. It seems to me curiously wrongheaded that here and elsewhere (e.g., p. 240) Leopold should identify the Abrahamic legacy with absolutely possessive, private, and exploitative property owning since the primary biblical understanding seems to be rather that Abraham's land is a sacred trust offered to the community on morally contingent grounds.

7. This is not the place to rehearse the complicated publishing history of Leopold's book, which is summarized by Peter A. Fritzell in "Aldo Leopold," in *American Nature Writers*, ed. John Elder (New York: Scribner's, 1996), 1:525–547. It may suffice here simply to acknowledge that the stylistic character and final form of Leopold's posthumously published book was much influenced by others even though it reflects emotions authentically attributable to its author.

8. Albert Schweitzer, *Out of My Life and Thought: An Autobiography*, trans. C. T. Campion (New York: Holt, 1949), pp. 158–159.

9. See Roderick Frazier Nash, *The Rights of Nature*, pp. 60–71, together with Nash's earlier commentary in *Wilderness and the American Mind* (New Haven: Yale University Press, 1967), pp. 194–196.

10. "Personal Narrative," in *A Jonathan Edwards Reader*, ed. John E. Smith, Harry S. Stout, and Kenneth P. Minkema (New Haven: Yale University Press, 1995), pp. 281, 285, 284, 286, 289.

11. "Personal Narrative," p. 285.

12. John Updike, "The Future of Faith: Confessions of a Churchgoer," *New Yorker* (November 29, 1999): 91.

13. "Personal Narrative," p. 285.

14. "Personal Narrative," p. 288.

15. "Beauty of the World," in *A Jonathan Edwards Reader*, p. 14.

16. "Images of Divine Things," in *Works of Jonathan Edwards*, 11:66, 127, 67.

17. "Images of Divine Things," in *Works of Jonathan Edwards*, 11:53, 72–73, 81.

18. See Roland André Delattre, *Beauty and Sensibility in the Thought of Jonathan Edwards: An Essay in Aesthetics and Theological Ethics* (New Haven: Yale University Press, 1968), pp. 133–137.

19. Jürgen Moltmann, *God in Creation: a New Theology of Creation and the Spirit of God* (San Francisco: HarperSanFrancisco, 1991), pp. 2, 15, 98, 103. Although Ed-

wards's Trinitarian references are less obvious in *The End* and *True Virtue* than they are in some other writings (including the "Miscellanies" and "An Essay on the Trinity") they underlie his vision of God and of the world as conjoined communities of being. See also Paul Ramsey's editorial notes in *Ethical Writings*, in *The Works of Jonathan Edwards* (New Haven: Yale University Press, 1989), 8:432 n.4 and 530 n.6; Robert W. Jenson's account of how Edwards sought to renew Christian doctrine of "The Triune God," in *America's Theologian: A Recommendation of Jonathan Edwards* (New York: Oxford University Press, 1988), pp. 91–98; and Norman Fiering's remarks in *Jonathan Edwards's Moral Thought and Its British Context* (Chapel Hill: University of North Carolina Press, 1981), pp. 82–84.

20. Cherry, *Nature and Religious Imagination*, p. 50. Cherry is drawing, in turn, on notions formulated by Arthur O. Lovejoy. That Edwards showed less concern for graded distinctions among creatures than between all creatures and God has likewise been emphasized by Michael J. McClymond in *Encounters with God: An Approach to the Theology of Jonathan Edwards* (New York: Oxford University Press, 1998), pp. 30–31.

21. *Concerning the End for Which God Created the World*, in *Ethical Writings*, in *The Works of Jonathan Edwards*, 8:419. Subsequent references are to this edition.

22. Despite lingering suspicions that Edwards's Calvinism must discourage favorable estimations of the material world, it has been argued that, according to John Calvin's actual theology, all creatures participate in God's glory. See Belden C. Lane, "Spirituality as the Performance of Desire: Calvin on the World as a Theatre of God's Glory," *Spiritus: A Journal of Christian Spirituality* 1 (2001): 1–30. Moltmann (*God in Creation*, pp. 11–12) likewise credits Calvin with having recalled attention to the Holy Spirit as the fountain of life and agent of divine immanence in creation.

23. *The Nature of True Virtue*, in *Ethical Writings*, in *The Works of Jonathan Edwards*, 8:540. Subsequent references are to this edition.

24. This point is confirmed, though not elaborated, by Fiering in *Jonathan Edwards's Moral Thought and Its British Context*, p. 326.

25. For a contextualized summary of limitations in Edwards's general view of animal life, see Holbrook, *Jonathan Edwards, The Valley and Nature*, pp. 26–27. Holbrook is also correct to point out that one strand of argument in *True Virtue* and *The End* is strangely at odds with gospel Christianity since the idea of "proportionality sometimes leads the author to suggest that we should love most those creatures who already possess the most being and benevolence." In *Encounters with God* (pp. 62–64), McClymond addresses the concern that Edwards's principle of "proportionate regard" seems to forbid saints from loving depraved persons and perhaps any creatures at all, since their finite worth must be deemed incomparable to that of an infinitely worthy God.

CHAPTER 4

1. The significance of Thoreau's writings beyond literary circles is evidenced, for example, by David R. Foster's use of them to discuss New England ecological history and forestry in *Thoreau's Country: Journey Through a Transformed Landscape* (Cambridge: Harvard University Press, 1999).

2. *Walden*, ed. J. Lyndon Shanley, in *The Writings of Henry D. Thoreau* (Princeton: Princeton University Press, 1971), p. 192. David E. Whisnant, in "The Sacred and the Profane in *Walden*," *Centennial Review* 14 (1970): 277, points out that Thoreau's la-

ment echoes the cry of the Psalmist in Psalm 137: "How shall we sing the Lord's song in a strange land?"

3. See Alan D. Hodder, *Emerson's Rhetoric of Revelation: Nature, The Reader, and the Apocalypse Within* (University Park: Pennsylvania State University Press, 1989), pp. 12–22; and Roger Lundin, "Natural Experience: Emerson, Protestantism, and the Emergence of Pragmatism," *Religion and Literature* 32 (2000): 38–39.

4. William Paley, *Natural Theology; or Evidences of the Existence and Attributes of the Deity, Collected from the Appearances of Nature*, 3rd ed., 2 vols. (Oxford: for J. Vincent, 1836), 1:16, 55; 2:206.

5. The classic scholarly account of this phenomenon, as embodied in British and Continental literatures, is M. H. Abrams, *Natural Supernaturalism: Tradition and Revolution in Romantic Literature* (New York: Norton, 1971).

6. Lydia Maria Child, *"Hobomok" and Other Writings on Indians*, ed. Carolyn L. Karcher (New Brunswick: Rutgers University Press, 1986), p. 76.

7. *The Poetical Works of William Cullen Bryant*, ed. Henry C. Sturges (1903; New York: AMS Press, 1969), p. 79. Subsequent references in my text are to this edition.

8. Bryant joined no church until 1858, when he was baptized as a Unitarian, but never identified strongly with the doctrinal stance of any church. See Charles II. Brown, *William Cullen Bryant* (New York: Scribner's, 1971), p. 333.

9. Brown, *William Cullen Bryant*, pp. 92–93.

10. James Fenimore Cooper, *The Pioneers, or the Sources of the Susquehanna: A Descriptive Tale*, ed. James Franklin Beard, Lance Schachterle, and Kenneth M. Andersen, Jr., in *The Writings of James Fenimore Cooper* (Albany: State University of New York Press, 1980), p. 456. Subsequent references are to this edition.

11. James Fenimore Cooper, *The Deerslayer or The First War-Path*, ed. James Franklin Beard, Lance Schachterle, Kent Ljungquist, and James Kilby, in *The Writings of James Fenimore Cooper* (Albany: State University of New York Press, 1987), p. 17. Subsequent references are to this edition.

12. A vintage reading of the episode is that offered by R.W.B. Lewis in *The American Adam: Innocence, Tragedy, and Tradition in the Nineteenth Century* (Chicago: University of Chicago Press, 1955), pp. 98–105.

13. Richard Slotkin, *Regeneration Through Violence: The Mythology of the American Frontier, 1600–1860* (Middletown, Conn.: Wesleyan University Press, 1973), p. 484.

14. Natty, too, sometimes justifies preemptive attacks against human beings with the argument that "This is nat'ral law, 'to do lest you should be done by' " (*Deerslayer*, 494), but his ethical viewpoint on the matter is not firmly consistent.

15. His outward plainness perhaps recollects that of Isaiah's Suffering Servant, who had "no form nor comeliness; and when we shall see him, there is no beauty that we should desire him" (Isaiah 53:2).

16. In *The Prairie*, Cooper's hero likewise dies, by his own account, as "a christian man."

17. See John T. Frederick's searching discussion in *The Darkened Sky: Nineteenth-Century American Novelists and Religion* (Notre Dame, Ind.: University of Notre Dame Press, 1989), pp. 1–26. Frederick concludes that "from a first position essentially deistic, he moved—influenced in significant degree by his European experiences— through prolonged and sometimes painful self-examination to the positive conviction expressed by his ultimate religious action" (1).

18. Donald A. Ringe, *James Fenimore Cooper*, updated ed. (Boston: Hall, 1988), preface, n.p. Though all five romances show Natty maintaining a liberal expectation

that human salvation is possible for Indians as well as whites, in *Deerslayer* he gives a christological reason for this hope when he reminds Chingachgook that " 'there's been a great deed of salvation done that, by God's help, enables all men to find a pardon for their wickednesses' " (457).

19. Real-life precedent for such excess is described by the author's daughter, Susan Fenimore Cooper, in her *Rural Hours* (Syracuse, N.Y.: Syracuse University Press, 1968), when she describes huge catches of Otsego bass "in former years" (p. 258).

20. There are, however, some excellent article-length commentaries on the subject, including William Rossi, "Emerson, Nature, and Natural Science," in *A Historical Guide to Ralph Waldo Emerson*, ed. Joel Myerson (New York: Oxford University Press, 2000), pp. 101–150; and Michael P. Branch's entry "Ralph Waldo Emerson," in *American Nature Writers*, ed. John Elder (New York: Scribner's, 1996), 1:287–307.

21. "Know then, that the world exists for you. For you is the phenomenon perfect." R. W. Emerson, *Nature*, ed. Robert Spiller and Alfred Ferguson in *Collected Works of Ralph Waldo Emerson* (Cambridge: Harvard University Press, 1971), 1:44–45. Subsequent references are to this edition.

22. Cited in Lundin, "Natural Experience," 32.

23. For a more encompassing analysis of Emerson's response to biblical teachings on self-denial, and to the Christian principle of kenosis set forth in Philippians 2: 7, see pp. 33–68 in Hodder, *Emerson's Rhetoric of Revelation*.

24. See Robert D. Richardson, Jr., *Emerson: The Mind on Fire* (Berkeley: University of California Press, 1995), pp. 138–142.

25. See Lundin, "Natural Experience," 38–39.

26. Roy M. Robbins, *Our Landed Heritage: The Public Domain, 1776–1970* (1942; 2nd ed., rev., Lincoln: University of Nebraska Press, 1976), pp. 59–71. Robbins reports that "in 1836, twenty million acres sold for the all-time high of fifty-four million dollars" and that from 1830 to 1836 "the value of real estate throughout the country rose 150 per cent" (59–60).

27. Cited in Robbins, *Our Landed Heritage*, pp. 68–69. I am grateful to Kurt Heidinger for directing me to the relevant material in Robbins. For further comment on the history of public lands, see also Bernard Shanks, *This Land Is Your Land: The Struggle to Save America's Public Lands* (San Francisco: Sierra Club Books, 1984).

28. Foster, *Thoreau's Country*, p. 8.

29. See Diana Muir, *Reflections in Bullough's Pond: Economy and Ecosystem in New England* (Hanover, N.H.: University Press of New England, 2000), esp. pp. 136, 143.

30. David Lowenthal, *George Perkins Marsh: Apostle of Conservation* (Seattle: University of Washington Press, 2000), pp. 4–7.

31. Lemuel Shattuck, *A History of the Town of Concord* (Boston: Russel, Odiorne, 1835), p. 41.

32. See Robert A. Gross, *The Minutemen and Their World* (New York: Hill and Wang, 1976), pp. 76–89.

33. Shattuck, *History of Concord*, p. 213.

34. Robert Sattelmeyer, "Depopulation, Deforestation, and the Actual Walden Pond," in *Thoreau's Sense of Place: Essays in American Environmental Writing*, ed. Richard J. Schneider (Iowa City: University of Iowa Press, 2000), p. 241.

35. R. W. Emerson, "Farming," in *Society and Solitude*, in *The Complete Works of Ralph Waldo Emerson* (Boston: Houghton Mifflin, 1904), 7:151.

36. *Poems*, in *The Complete Works of Ralph Waldo Emerson*, 9:35, 37.

37. "The Method of Nature" (1841), in *The Collected Works of Ralph Waldo Emerson*, 1:135.

38. *The Journals and Miscellaneous Notebooks of Ralph Waldo Emerson*, ed. Alfred Ferguson (Cambridge: Harvard University Press, 1964), 4:335, 355; see also Gay Wilson Allen, *Waldo Emerson: A Biography* (New York: Viking Press, 1981), pp. 245, 250.

39. "The Divinity School Address," in *The Collected Works of Ralph Waldo Emerson*, 1:92.

40. Entry for August 1836 in *The Journals and Miscellaneous Notebooks of Ralph Waldo Emerson*, 5:189.

41. See Lundin, "Natural Experience," 34–42.

42. "Experience," in *Essays, Second Series* (1844), in *The Collected Works of Ralph of Ralph Waldo Emerson*, 3:37.

43. George Perkins Marsh, *Man and Nature*, ed. David Lowenthal (Cambridge: Harvard University Press, 1965), p. 43.

44. Jaroslav Pelikan, preface to Ralph Waldo Emerson, *Nature* (Boston: Beacon Press, 1985), p. vii.

45. The most obvious point of reference for that tradition is the episode of healing by the pool of Siloam presented in John 9.

46. "The Adirondacs," *Poems*, in *The Complete Works of Ralph Waldo Emerson*, 9: 182–183, 185. Subsequent references are to this edition.

47. The success on this occasion turned out to be only temporary, however, since the cable link between Ireland and Newfoundland failed after three months; a lasting connection was not achieved until 1866. Additional information concerning the biographical and historical circumstances of the poem is provided by Joseph Jones, "Thought's New-Found Path and the Wilderness: 'The Adirondacs,' " in *Emerson: Prospect and Retrospect*, ed. Joel Porte (Cambridge: Harvard University Press, 1982), pp. 105–119; and by Ronald A. Sudol, " 'The Adirondacs' and Technology," in *Emerson Centenary Essays*, ed. Joel Myerson (Carbondale: Southern Illinois University Press, 1982), pp. 173–179.

48. Jane Eblen Keller, *Adirondack Wilderness: A Story of Man and Nature* (Syracuse, N.Y.: Syracuse University Press, 1980), pp. 82–83, 96–97; and Paul Schneider, *The Adirondacks: A History of America's First Wilderness* (New York: Holt, 1997), pp. 202–203. Bill McKibben describes the twentieth-century recovery of the Adirondack ecosystem in *Hope, Human and Wild: True Stories of Living Lightly on the Earth* (St. Paul, Minn.: Hungry Mind Press, 1995), pp. 7–55.

49. Richardson, *Emerson: The Mind on Fire*, pp. 206–208.

50. Gay Wilson Allen, *The Solitary Singer: A Critical Biography of Walt Whitman* (New York: New York University Press, 1967), p. 116.

CHAPTER 5

1. "The Old Manse," in *The Centenary Edition of the Works of Nathaniel Hawthorne*, ed. William Charvat et al. (Columbus: Ohio State University Press, 1974), 10: 25. References hereafter are to this edition.

2. I am thinking here of sketches such as "Earth's Holocaust," "The Hall of Fantasy," and "The Christmas Banquet," as well as of better known tales such as "The Birth-mark" and "Rappaccini's Daughter."

3. "Esthetique du Mal," in *Poems by Wallace Stevens*, selected by Samuel French Morse (New York: Random House, 1959), p. 124.

4. Vera Norwood presents an informative cultural survey of women's gardens and garden literature in *Made from this Earth: American Women and Nature* (Chapel Hill: University of North Carolina Press, 1993), pp. 98–142; see also Norwood's more detailed account of Celia Thaxter in *American Nature Writers*, ed. John Elder (New York: Scribner's, 1996), 2:905–917.

5. Norwood, *Made from this Earth*, p. 110.

6. Catharine E. Beecher and Harriet Beecher Stowe, *The American Woman's Home* (1869; rpt., Hartford: Stowe-Day Foundation, 1975), pp. 21–22, 24–25, 294. This work draws heavily on Beecher's antebellum *Treatise on Domestic Economy* (1841).

7. Celia Thaxter, *An Island Garden* (Boston: Houghton Mifflin, 1894), pp. 93, 24. Subsequent references are to this edition.

8. See Perry D. Westbrook, "Controversy with Nature: Celia Thaxter," in *Acres of Flint: Sarah Orne Jewett and Her Contemporaries* (Metuchen, N.J.: Scarecrow Press, 1981), pp. 105–127; and Rosamond Thaxter. *Sandpiper: The Life and Letters of Celia Thaxter* (Portsmouth, N.H.: E. Randall, 1963), pp. 163–168.

9. Cited in *The Essential Margaret Fuller*, ed. Jeffrey Steele (New Brunswick: Rutgers University Press, 1992), pp. 31–32.

10. I discuss this dimension more fully in *American Madonna: Images of the Divine Woman in Literary Culture* (New York: Oxford University Press, 1997), esp. p. 42.

11. "The Magnolia of Lake Pontchartrain," in *The Essential Margaret Fuller*, p. 48.

12. *The Essential Margaret Fuller*, p. 11.

13. *The Essential Margaret Fuller*, pp. 192, 222, 177.

14. "Leila" and "To Sarah" (poem), in *The Essential Margaret Fuller*, pp. 53, 54, 232.

15. *The Essential Margaret Fuller*, pp. 50, 51.

16. Walt Whitman, "Crossing Brooklyn Ferry," in *Leaves of Grass*, ed. Bradley Sculley and Harold W. Blodgett (New York: Norton, 1973), pp. 163, 164, 160, 165. Unless otherwise indicated, subsequent Whitman references are to this edition.

17. Accounts of Whitman's religious ideas and attitudes can be found in Gay Wilson Allen, *The New Walt Whitman Handbook* (New York: New York University Press, 1975), esp. pp. 161–205; David Kuebrich, *Minor Prophecy: Walt Whitman's New American Religion* (Bloomington: Indiana University Press, 1989); Alfred Kazin, *God and the American Writer* (New York: Knopf, 1997), pp. 107–119; George B. Hutchinson, *The Ecstatic Whitman: Literary Shamanism and the Crisis of the Union* (Columbus: Ohio State University Press, 1986); and George L. Sixbey, "Chanting the Square Deific—A Study in Whitman's Religion," *American Literature* 9 (1973): 171–195.

18. Allen, *New Walt Whitman Handbook*, p. 88; Roy Harvey Pearce, introduction to *Leaves of Grass by Walt Whitman, 1860 Facsimile Edition* (Ithaca: Cornell University Press, 1961), pp. xix, xxviii.

19. Implications of the poet's pervasive body language have frequently been discussed by Whitman critics, including Jon Rosenblatt, "Whitman's Body, Whitman's Language" in *Walt Whitman: Here and Now*, ed. Joann P. Krieg (Westport, Conn.: Greenwood Press, 1985), and Harold Aspiz, *Walt Whitman and the Body Beautiful* (Urbana: University of Illinois Press, 1980). In *The Body of God: An Ecological Theology* (Minneapolis: Fortress Press, 1993), the contemporary theologian Sallie McFague discusses the relation of body metaphors to an organic model of the world and to Christian beliefs in the bodily incarnation of God.

20. In this case, since Whitman made the reference to deity—God comes a loving bedfellow"—explicit in the 1855 version, I am citing here that version as printed in *Leaves of Grass*, facsimile (New York: Eakins Press, 1966), p. 15.

21. I have argued this case more fully in "Whitman's ReVision of Emersonian Ecstasy in 'Song of Myself,' " in Krieg, *Walt Whitman*, pp. 173–183.

22. R. W. Emerson, *Nature*, in *Collected Works of Ralph Waldo Emerson*, ed. Robert Spiller and Alfred Ferguson (Cambridge: Harvard University Press, 1971), 1:10.

23. *Nature*, in *The Collected Works of Ralph Waldo Emerson*, 1:10.

24. That Whitman's championing of faith, praise, and spirituality were more nearly extensions of a Romantically exalted self than apprehensions of God as sacred Other has been observed by several critics. See, for example, Kazin, *God and the American Writer*, pp. 15, 110–111, 113; James Dougherty, *Walt Whitman and the Citizen's Eye* (Baton Rouge: Louisiana State University Press, 1993), pp. 200–201; and Roger Lundin, "Interpreting Orphans: Hermeneutics in the Cartesian Tradition," in Roger Lundin, Clarence Walhout, and Anthony C. Thiselton, *The Promise of Hermeneutics* (Grand Rapids, Mich.: Eerdmans, 1999), pp. 19–20.

25. See note 38 hereafter.

26. Emerson, *Nature*, 1:11. Melville first heard Emerson lecture in 1849; he owned volumes of his essays, and it is evident that he read his works—probably including *Nature*—with intense interest, though we lack definitive evidence of his encountering the specific text. See Jay Leyda, *The Melville Log: A Documentary Life of Herman Melville, 1819–1891* (New York: Harcourt, Brace, 1951), 1:292, 2:640; and Merton M. Sealts, Jr., "Melville and Emerson's Rainbow," in *Critical Essays on Moby-Dick*, ed. Brian Higgins and Hershel Parker (New York: Hall, 1992), pp. 349–354.

27. Herman Melville, *Moby-Dick* (1851), ed. Harrison Hayford and Hershel Parker (New York: Norton, 2002), p. 136. All subsequent references to *Moby-Dick* are to this edition, as are references to other Melville writings that are conveniently gathered here.

28. The circumstance of actual cannibalism, as Owen Chase's *Narrative* (1821) disclosed its practice by supposedly civilized survivors of the wrecked whaleship *Essex*, inevitably influenced Melville's treatment of this theme. See Melville's manuscript notes in *Moby-Dick*, p. 573; Hershel Parker, *Herman Melville: A Biography*, vol. 1, *1819–1851* (Baltimore: Johns Hopkins University Press, 1996), pp. 196–199; Nathaniel Philbrick, *In the Heart of the Sea: The Tragedy of the Whaleship Essex* (New York: Viking, 2000); and, by way of heavily theorized discussion, Geoffrey Sanborn, *The Sign of the Cannibal: Melville and the Making of a Postcolonial Reader* (Durham, N.C.: Duke University Press, 1998), esp. pp. 202–207.

29. See, for example, T. Walter Herbert, *Moby-Dick and Calvinism: A World Dismantled* (New Brunswick: Rutgers University Press, 1977); and Thomas Werge, "*Moby-Dick* and the Calvinist Tradition," *Studies in the Novel* 1 (1969): 484–506. Readers have long realized that Melville reveals more about himself than about his ostensible subject when he describes the "great power of blackness" in Hawthorne, deriving its "force from its appeals to that Calvinistic sense of Innate Depravity and Original Sin, from whose visitations, in some shape or other, no deeply thinking mind is always and wholly free" ("Hawthorne and His Mosses," cited in *Moby-Dick*, p. 521). The same is doubtless true of Melville's characterization of Hawthorne as a heroically honest religious iconoclast who "says NO! in thunder" (*Moby-Dick*, p. 537).

30. Melville, letters to Hawthorne of November 17, 1851, and April 16?, 1851, cited in *Moby-Dick*, pp. 545 and 537.

31. Kazin, *God and the American Writer* (New York: Knopf, 1997), pp. 14 and 86–106.

32. See Lawrence Buell, "*Moby-Dick* as Sacred Text," in *New Essays on Moby-Dick*,

ed. Richard H. Brodhead (New York: Cambridge University Press, 1986), pp. 53–72. Accounts of Melville's religious attitudes include Kazin, *God and the American Writer*, pp. 14, 46, 88–106; William Braswell, *Melville's Religious Thought* (Durham, N.C.: Duke University Press, 1942); Herbert, *Moby-Dick and Calvinism: A World Dismantled*; Nathalia Wright, *Melville's Use of the Bible* (New York: Octagon Books, 1949); and Rowland A. Sherrill, "Melville and Religion," in *A Companion to Melville Studies*, ed. John Bryant (New York: Greenwood Press, 1986), pp. 481–513.

33. Albert Camus, *The Rebel*, trans. Anthony Bower (New York: Random House, 1956), p. 24.

34. Lawrence Thompson, *Melville's Quarrel with God* (Princeton: Princeton University Press, 1952).

35. Lawrence Buell, *Writing for an Endangered World: Literature, Culture, and Environment in the U.S. and Beyond* (Cambridge: Harvard University Press, 2001), pp. 208–209.

36. Buell, *Writing for an Endangered World*, p. 210.

37. This association is ably described, with proper qualifications, by Milton R. Stern in *The Fine Hammered Steel of Herman Melville* (Urbana: University of Illinois Press, 1968), pp. 1–28.

38. The best account I have read of cosmic orphanhood as a defining image of modernity is Roger Lundin's "Interpreting Orphans," in *The Promise of Hermeneutics*, pp. 1–64. Lundin's analysis " 'The Shadow of Absence": Orphans and the Interpretive Quest,' " includes a very revealing assessment of *Moby-Dick* (pp. 42–49) in the context of Melville's cultural milieu and as informed by hermeneutical theorists. With the benefit of such analysis, one can more fully appreciate the pain Ahab suffers of "abandonment and divine indifference" (p. 48).

39. Hawthorne, *The English Notebooks*, ed. Randall Stewart (New York: Modern Language Assoc. of America, 1941), pp. 432–433.

40. C. S. Lewis, *Reflections on the Psalms* (New York: Harcourt, Brace and World, 1958), pp. 81, 82–83.

41. Melville's preoccupation with the *deus absconditus* drew on several cultural precedents, including those found in Calvinist and in Jewish biblical traditions. The first of these is highlighted by Werge in *"Moby-Dick* and the Calvinist Tradition," 486; the second is addressed by Stan Goldman, "The Hiddenness and Silence of God," in *Melville's Protest Theism: The Hidden and Silent God in "Clarel"* (Dekalb: Northern Illinois University Press, 1993), pp. 12–46. It is scarcely coincidental that God's silence and inscrutability are major themes in the biblical books of Job and Ecclesiastes, two texts recognizably central to Melville's alllusive imagination in *Moby-Dick*.

42. In this light, Melville's unpious view of Milton's religious attitudes, as indicated in marginalia to a prefatory "Life of Milton" he was reading around 1849, seems less peculiar than it might otherwise. "I doubt not that darker doubts crossed Milton's soul, than ever disturbed Voltair. And he was more of what is called an Infidel"; cited in Parker, *Herman Melville: A Biography*, p. 618.

43. Eric Gorski, "Evangelical Theologians Reject 'Open Theism,' "*Christian Century* 118 (December 12, 2001), pp. 10–11. Introduced in 1994 with the publication by five evangelical scholars of *The Openness of God*, "open theism" suggests that traditional doctrines of "God's immutability, impassability and foreknowledge demand reconsideration" and that, as Gorski puts it, "God does not fully know the future because people have been given the freedom to help shape it through their decisions."

44. For a cogent reading of the biblical text in this light, see Robert Gordis, "Job

and Ecology (and the Significance of Job 40:15)," *Hebrew Annual Review* 9 (1985): 189–201.

45. See Henry A. Pochmann, *German Culture in America: Philosophical and Literature Influences, 1600–1900* (Madison: University of Wisconsin Press, 1957), pp. 436–439.

CHAPTER 6

1. Brochure from Walden Forever Wild, Inc. issued from P.O. Box 275 in Concord. The group's quarterly newsletter, "Voice of Walden," has had an editorial office in Storrs, Connecticut. Mary Sherwood, a forester who championed preservation of the Walden plot and had formerly lived in Concord, was ninety-five when she died in July 2001. In *The Environmental Imagination: Thoreau, Nature Writing, and the Formation of American Culture* (Cambridge: Harvard University Press, 1995), Lawrence Buell comments extensively on the process of Thoreau's extraliterary canonization (pp. 311–369) and observes that he is now widely recognized as "the patron saint of American environmental writing" (p. 115).

2. See, for example, Buell, *The Environmental Imagination*, especially p. 117; and Walter Harding, *The Days of Henry Thoreau: A Biography* (1962; rpt. New York: Dover, 1982), pp. 290–293. Some of Thoreau's later natural history writings, including "The Dispersion of Seeds" and "Wild Fruits" (edited by Bradley P. Dean in 1993 under the title *Faith in a Seed*), are indeed highly scientific and largely but not entirely secular in orientation, as discussed by Ronald Wesley Hoag, "Thoreau's Later Natural History Writings," in *The Cambridge Companion to Henry David Thoreau*, ed. Joel Myerson (New York: Cambridge University Press, 1995), pp. 152–170.

3. "Walking," in *Excursions* (Boston: Ticknor and Fields, 1863; rpt. Gloucester, Mass.: Peter Smith, 1975), pp. 161, 214.

4. *Walden*, ed. J. Lyndon Shanley, in *The Writings of Henry D. Thoreau* (Princeton: Princeton University Press, 1971), pp. 4, 155. Hereafter abbreviated in citations as *W*.

5. William J. Wolf, *Thoreau: Mystic, Prophet, Ecologist* (Philadelphia: United Church Press, 1974), p. 93. In addition to Wolf's book, other general assessments of Thoreau's religious beliefs can be found in Walter Harding and Michael Meyer, *The New Thoreau Handbook* (New York: New York University Press, 1980), pp. 130–132; Catherine L. Albanese, *Nature Religion in American: From the Algonkian Indians to the New Age* (Chicago: University of Chicago Press, 1990), pp. 87–93; Alexander C. Kern, "Church, Scripture, Nature, and Ethics in Henry Thoreau's Religious Thought," in *Literature and Ideas in America: Essays in Memory of Harry Hayden Clark* (Columbus: Ohio University Press, 1975), pp. 79–95; and Edward Wagenknecht, *Henry David Thoreau: What Manner of Man?* (Amherst: University of Massachusetts Press, 1981), pp. 155–172. Relevant but more specialized commentaries linked to specific Thoreauvian texts include John B. Pickard, "The Religion of 'Higher Laws,' " *Emerson Society Quarterly* 39 (1965): 68–72; Reginald L. Cook, "Ancient Rites at Walden," *Emerson Society Quarterly* 39 (1965): 52–56; and Jonathan Bishop, "The Experience of the Sacred in Thoreau's *Week*," *English Literary History* 33 (1966): 66–91. See also *The Crossroads of American History and Literature* (University Park: Pennsylvania State University Press, 1996), pp. 228–233 and 246–249, for Philip F. Gura's illuminating remarks about Thoreau's religious responses to foxfire and other signs of " 'certain *transcendentia*' " in the creaturely world during his travels in Maine. Thoreau's eclectic and largely self-fashioned interest in Asian religions, which I do not attempt to analyze

here, has been ably discussed elsewhere—by Arthur Christy, *The Orient in American Transcendentalism: A Study of Emerson, Thoreau, and Alcott* (New York: Farrar, Straus and Giroux, 1972), pp. 185–233; and by Arthur Versluis, *American Transcendentalism and Asian Religions* (New York: Oxford University Press, 1993), pp. 79–99. Another noteworthy account of Thoreau's religious imagination, Alan D. Hodder, *Thoreau's Ecstatic Witness* (New Haven: Yale University Press, 2001), appeared while my own study was assuming its final shape. I regard Hodder's approach as different from yet fundamentally compatible with mine. Hodder emphasizes Thoreau's responses to Orientalism (142, 174–217), his religious appreciation of "ecstasy" (that is, "experiences of inspiration and euphoria in the natural world," 21), and his lifelong "spiritual biography" (xiv) as reflected in the journal and *A Week* as well as in *Walden*. My treatment is more concerned with close reading of certain sections of *Walden* (particularly the sand foliage passage), with the influence of biblical Christianity and hermeneutics on Thoreau's religious outlook, and with the author's sense of place and internalization of developmental science. It should be apparent, however, that I share Hodder's insistence on "the intensely religious character" of Thoreau's "personal transactions with nature" and "the emphatically religious character of so much of his life and writing," even though he was "no friend of organized religion" (300, 20, 3).

6. In the "Sunday" chapter of *A Week on the Concord and Merrimack Rivers*, Thoreau inveighs with some passion against anthropomorphic images sponsored by Jewish and Christian theism. But this earlier polemic against divine "personality," which corresponds to Emerson's Transcendental principle that the "soul knows no persons," gives way to a less consistent, more complex theological language in *Walden*.

7. *The Writings of Henry D. Thoreau: Journal*, ed. John C. Broderick, Robert Sattelmeyer, Mark Patterson, and William Ross (Princeton: Princeton University Press, 1981), 3:61; hereafter abbreviated and cited parenthetically as *PJ*.

8. Mircea Eliade's classic study *The Sacred and the Profane: The Nature of Religion* (New York: Harcourt, 1959), likewise defines the sacred as "the opposite of the profane" (p. 10). At least one previous commentator has confirmed Eliade's pertinence to *Walden*, particularly with reference to the "book's persistent dialectic between the sacred and the profane" (268). See David E. Whisnant, "The Sacred and the Profane in *Walden*," *Centennial Review* 14 (1970): 267–283.

9. Eliade, *Sacred and Profane*, pp. 37, 39.

10. R. W. Emerson, *Nature*, in *The Collected Works of Ralph Waldo Emerson*, ed. Robert E. Spiller (Cambridge: Harvard University Press, 1971), 1:7.

11. Despite Thoreau's somewhat facetious reference to the Bible as "an old book" (*W* 5), sacramental language linked to Christian imagery is surprisingly abundant in his writing. In 1845, for example, he reported feeling that through his fruit and nut diet, "eating became a sacrament—a method of communion" and of "sitting at the communion table of the world" (*PJ* 2:165). As discussed by R. W. Lewis in *The American Adam: Innocence, Tragedy, and Tradition in the Nineteenth Century* (Chicago: University of Chicago Press, 1955), pp. 20–27, Thoreau significantly revised Saint Paul's understanding of sacred mystery in formulating "his own sacramental system" (22). But Lewis interprets Thoreau's nature-centered ritualism as a total inversion of Paul's emphasis on overcoming "nature" and the "natural man." I consider the relation to be more complicated and problematic—not only because of major linguistic shifts in meaning from Paul's first-century "natural man" (1 Corinthians 2:14 in KJV) to Thoreau's nineteenth-century "nature" but also because of the highly ambivalent anthropology Thoreau manifests in "Higher Laws." The tendency to confuse premodern references to "nature," as a philosophic term unrelated to outdoor landscapes, with biota

in the modern sense persists in many current discussions of environmental issues. In Paul's typical usage, for example, the "natural" or "unspiritual" is best understood as antithetical not to culture or civilization but to "spiritual" persons and things.

12. On Emerson's circumstance as proprietor, see *The Variorum Walden and the Variorum Civil Disobedience*, ed. Walter Harding (New York: Simon and Schuster, 1968), p. 268 n. 132, together with Harding's remarks in *The Days of Henry Thoreau*, pp. 179–80, 191, 216.

13. For elaborative commentary on the pond's connection to sacred cosmology, see Whisnant, "Sacred and Profane in *Walden*," pp. 277–280.

14. "Walking," p. 185; Aldo Leopold, *A Sand County Almanac* (New York: Oxford University Press, 1966), p. 141.

15. William Cronon, ed., *Uncommon Ground: Toward Reinventing Nature* (New York: Norton, 1995), esp. pp. 69, 71, 74–75.

16. On the intellectual history of sublime landscapes, see, for example, Cronon, *Uncommon Ground*, p. 73, and Barbara Novak, *Nature and Culture: American Landscape Painting, 1825–1875* (New York: Oxford University Press, 1980). The more depressing and intimidating aspect of Thoreau's response to Katahdin does not, however, entirely fit conventional notions of the sublime.

17. Thoreau's personal claims to have become a yogi remained tentative and qualified. Yet two elements of Hindu religious tradition strike me as particularly relevant to the Thoreavian faith highlighted in my subsequent discussion: (1) a sense of physical creation as continuous process, emanating directly from God; (2) a perception of the yogi's vocation as cocreator with God. As Robert Kuhn McGregor observes in *A Wider View of the Universe: Henry Thoreau's Study of Nature* (Urbana: University of Illinois Press, 1997), Thoreau would have encountered the dynamic principle associated with the first point from his early reading of "The Laws of Menu" (98). And in a journal entry for 1851, Thoreau asserts that "the Yogin, absorbed in contemplation, contributes for his part to creation. . . . Divine forms traverse him without tearing him, and united to the nature which is proper to him, he goes he acts, as animating original matter" (*PJ* 3:216).

18. Eliade, *Sacred and Profane*, pp. 24–26.

19. Sherman Paul, *The Shores of America: Thoreau's Inward Exploration* (Urbana: University of Illinois Press, 1958), esp. pp. 306–307. More recently, several commentators have emphasized the unpristine character of Thoreau's physical environment at Walden and have analyzed more closely the marginal social circumstances (as regards race and class) of his human neighbors. See, for example, Robert Sattelmeyer, "Depopulation, Deforestation, and the Actual Walden Pond," in *Thoreau's Sense of Place: Essays in American Environmental Writing*, ed. Richard J. Schneider (Iowa City: University of Iowa Press, 2000), pp. 235–243; Robert Kuhn McGregor, *A Wider View of the Universe*, esp. pp. 7–31; and David R. Foster, *Thoreau's Country: Journey Through a Transformed Landscape* (Cambridge: Harvard University Press, 1999).

20. See Buell, *The Environmental Imagination*, pp. 31–52.

21. See Philip Van Doren Stern's remarks in *The Annotated Walden* (New York: Potter, 1970), p. 45.

22. In *The Roots of Walden and the Tree of Life* (Nashville: Vanderbilt University Press, 1990), Gordon V. Boudreau surveys the enormous quantity and range of commentary that this section of *Walden* has elicited. As Boudreau observes, "in the latter half of the twentieth century the sand foliage passages have become a critical proving ground for Freudian and Eriksonian critics" (2). For historically based analysis focused on philological implications of the passage, see Philip F. Gura, *The Wisdom of*

Words: Language, Theology, and Literature in the New England Renaissance (Middletown, Conn.: Wesleyan University Press, 1981), pp. 132–137. Though the section's religious import has rarely been emphasized, Boudreau's book offers useful suggestions toward constructing such a reading.

23. See Wagenknecht, *What Manner of Man*, pp. 170–172; and Wolf, *Thoreau*, pp. 151–162 and 172–175. Although Horace Greeley's influential (and disparaging) description of *Walden's* philosophy as pantheistic might seem to be confirmed by the explicit homage to Pan that Thoreau had recorded in *A Week*, Wolf (157) points out the etymological fallacy involved in this linkage. Hodder presents another view of the matter in *Thoreau's Ecstatic Witness*, pp. 143–144.

24. Cited in Foster, *Thoreau's Country*, p. 5.

25. Ken Wilber, *A Brief History of Everything* (Boston: Shambala, 1996).

26. See William Rossi, "Thoreau's Transcendental Ecocentrism," in Schneider, *Thoreau's Sense of Place*, pp. 29–40; and Robert Sattelmeyer, *Thoreau's Reading: A Study in Intellectual History* (Princeton: Princeton University Press, 1988), pp. 82–87.

27. Charles Lyell, *Principles of Geology*, vol. 1 (1830–33; rpt. Chicago: University of Chicago Press, 1990), p. 79. See also Laura Dassow Wells, *Seeing New Worlds: Henry David Thoreau and Nineteenth-Century Science* (Madison: University of Wisconsin Press, 1995), pp. 42–44. In addition to Wells (76–130), Ning Yu offers useful analysis of how Thoreau responded to Humboldt's holistic understanding of science in "The Hydrological Cycle on Katahdin: Thoreau and the New Geography," *ESQ: A Journal of the American Renaissance* 40 (1994): 1–25.

28. In this regard, Coleridge's prose writings offered Thoreau the rare example of evolutionary perception on both planes. In *Confessions of an Inquiring Spirit* and *Aids to Reflection*, Coleridge unfolded his hermeneutics of biblical interpretation, while less prominently in these works but directly in *Hints Towards A More Comprehensive Theory of Life* he reflected on the language of God presented scientifically by an ascending scale of natural process that reaches from inanimate matter to human consciousness.

29. For Thoreau's exposure to this work, see Robert Sattelmeyer, *Thoreau's Reading*, pp. 86–87; and for a recent assessment of Chambers, Janet Browne, "Anonymous Author Who Left *Vestiges*," *Times Literary Supplement* (July 13, 2001), 6–7.

30. Robert Chambers, *Vestiges of the Natural History of Creation and Other Evolutionary Writings*, ed. James A. Secord (Chicago: University of Chicago Press, 1994), pp. 185, 153, 196, 203, 197, 21.

31. Boudreau, *Roots of* Walden, p. 128.

32. See Barbara Packer, "Origin and Authority: Emerson and the Higher Criticism," in *Reconstructing American Literary History*, ed. Sacvan Bercovitch (Cambridge: Harvard University Press, 1986), pp. 6–92; and Richard A. Grusin, *Transcendentalist Hermeneutics: Institutional Authority and the Higher Criticism of the Bible* (Durham, N.C.: Duke University Press, 1991), pp. 1–7 and 81–114.

33. Emerson, *Nature*, 1: 29.

34. In *Thoreau as Romantic Naturalist: His Shifting Stance Toward Nature* (Ithaca: Cornell University Press, 1974), James McIntosh emphasizes Thoreau's disinclination to follow "the logic of Emerson's subordination of nature, even while he remains aware of this logic with a part of his mind" (p. 9).

35. In recasting Champollion as an interpreter of nature's rather than of ancient Egypt's hieroglyphics, Thoreau may have been influenced by Lyell. In his *Principles of Geology*, vol. 1 (p. 76), Lyell mentions Champollion by way of reminding his readers that prior contextual knowledge (in this case, knowledge of geological history and an-

thropology) is needed to interpret rightly signs presented by the physical world. Further examples of Thoreau's disposition to correlate written texts with biotic signs can be found in several journal entries preceding the publication of *Walden*: *PJ* 1: 47–48, 1: 131, 2: 163, 2: 178, 3: 62, 4: 28, and 4: 392.

36. See Robert Sattelmeyer and Richard A. Hocks, "Thoreau and Coleridge's *Theory of Life*," in *Studies in the American Renaissance*, ed. Joel Myerson (Charlottesville: University Press of Virginia, 1985), pp. 269–284; and Boudreau, *Roots of Walden*, p. 33. As Sattelmeyer and Hocks point out, Thoreau copied out substantial extracts from this work soon after its posthumous publication in 1848. In *Thoreau's Reading*, Sattelmeyer discusses Thoreau's "marked interest" (30) in other Coleridge prose works—*Aids to Reflection, The Statesman's Manual*, and *Confessions of an Inquiring Spirit*—that he encountered between January and April 1841.

37. *Confessions of an Inquiring Spirit*, in *The Collected Works of Samuel Taylor Coleridge: Shorter Works and Fragments*, part 2, ed. H. J. Jackson and J. R. de J. Jackson (Princeton: Princeton University Press, 1995), 11: 1156, 1121, 1168.

38. The solitary bias of Thoreau's religious perspective, particularly as evidenced in *A Week*, is persuasively defined by Bishop in "The Experience of the Sacred," 83–85.

39. The irony of Thoreau's citation here from the Calvinist-inflected Shorter Catechism is multilayered. Although plainly satirizing what he takes to be the oversimple assurances of this version of Christian orthodoxy, he is even more disdainful of unreflective believers—that is, those who have "*somewhat hastily*" reached their doctrinal conclusions on the basis of authority, without benefit of existential inquiry or experience. Curiously, though, Thoreau's book *does* end up affirming, in its own unorthodox but serious religious terms, that "it is the chief end of man to 'glorify God and enjoy him forever.'" Doubtless Thoreau would insist that *Walden* demonstrates more authentic *enjoyment* of God than does the Westminster catechism. For fuller contextual elucidation of the citation and its relation to *The New England Primer*, see Sargent Bush, Jr., "The End and Means in *Walden*: Thoreau's Use of the Catechism," *ESQ: A Journal of the American Renaissance* 31 (1985): 1–10.

40. Writing to William Sotheby in 1802, Coleridge declares: "Nature has her proper interest; & he will know what it is, who believes & feels, that every Thing has a Life of it's own, & that we are all one Life." Cited in *English Romantic Writers*, ed. David Perkins (New York: Harcourt, Brace and World, 1967), p. 526.

41. "Meditation 8 (First Series)," in *The Poems of Edward Taylor*, ed. Donald E. Stanford (New Haven: Yale University Press, 1960), p. 18. Karl Keller discusses Taylor's varied use of excremental and erotic imagery in *The Example of Edward Taylor* (Amherst: University of Massachusetts Press, 1975), pp. 91–220. Biblical examples of language (as rendered by KJV) in which divine mercy is associated with bowels include Isaiah 63: 15, Philippians 1: 8 and 2: 1, Colossians 3: 12, and 1 John 3: 17.

42. "Formation of a More Comprehensive Theory of Life," in *Selected Poetry and Prose of Coleridge*, ed. Donald A. Stauffer (New York: Random House, 1951), p. 578.

43. See Robert D. Richardson, Jr., "Thoreau and Science," in *American Literature and Science*, ed. Robert J. Scholnick (Lexington: University Press of Kentucky, 1992), pp. 110–127. Richardson (110) quotes here from Thoreau's *Journal*.

44. Mary Oliver, *New and Selected Poems* (Boston: Beacon Press, 1992), p. 239.

CHAPTER 7

1. On the character and chronology of Darwinism's influence on American culture, see Stow Persons, *The Impact of Darwinian Thought on American Life and Culture*

(Austin: University of Texas Press, 1959); Richard Hofstadter, *Social Darwinism in American Thought* (Boston: Beacon Press, 1955); Peter J. Bowler, *The Non-Darwinian Revolution: Reinterpreting a Historical Myth* (Baltimore: Johns Hopkins University Press, 1988); Jon H. Roberts, *Darwinism and the Divine in America: Protestant Intellectuals and Organic Evolution, 1859–1900* (Madison: University of Wisconsin Press, 1988); and Ronald L. Numbers, *Darwinism Comes to America* (Cambridge: Harvard University Press, 1988). Although Bowler and Numbers differ on some points of their assessments (see Numbers, pp. 22, 40), they agree that American culture was particularly slow to accept Darwin's theory of natural selection even when the general principle of organic evolution gained favor. Numbers (42) also doubts that evolution was apt to precipitate any immediate religious crisis in the lives of scientific naturalists. Although Bowler minimizes the late nineteenth-century "cultural impact" (3) of materialist conceptions of nature and Darwinian natural selection, he does not attempt to discuss literary expression as an element of culture.

2. Numbers, *Darwinism Comes to America*, pp. 26–29. Drawing on James Moore's scholarship, Numbers points out (41) that Darwin was apparently led to disavow Christianity not so much because of evolution but because of his responses to the deaths of his daughter and father.

3. For an account of how religious attitudes varied with respect to evolution among scientific naturalists of the period, see Numbers, *Darwinism Comes to America*, pp. 24–48; for a revealing summary of attitudes adopted by other leading intellectuals, see Perry Miller's editor's introduction to *American Thought: Civil War to World War I* (New York: Holt, Rinehart and Winston, 1954), pp. xxi–xxxix, and Roberts, *Darwinism and the Divine in America*, p. ix.

4. Roberts, *Darwinism and the Divine in America*, pp. xiv, 91–231.

5. Herman Melville, "Misgivings" (in *Battle-Pieces*), in *The Poems of Herman Melville*, ed. Douglas Robillard (Kent, Ohio: Kent State University Press, 2000), p. 53; Emily Dickinson, "Those Dying then" (dated around 1882, no. 1551 in Thomas Johnson's numbering), in *The Poems of Emily Dickinson: Variorum Edition*, ed. R. W. Franklin (Cambridge: Harvard University Press, 1998), 3: 1386.

6. I am referring here to a cultural fable, insofar as Darwin's own, more nuanced exposition in *Origins* does not focus so much on combative struggle but recognizes that adaptive survival also depends largely on reproduction and food supply.

7. Roberts, *Darwinism and the Divine in America*, p. ix.

8. Émile Zola, *The Experimental Novel and Other Essays*, trans. Belle M. Sherman (New York: Haskell House, 1964), pp. 23, 26–27, 29.

9. That "creation" should be seen as biblically aligned toward future redemption has been a persistent theme of the theologian Jürgen Moltmann, particularly in his *God in Creation: A New Theology of Creation and the Spirit of God*, trans. Margaret Kohl (San Francisco: HarperSanFrancisco: 1991). Taking account of both scientific and religious issues, the astrophysicist Arnold Benz has more recently offered stimulating reflection along the same trajectory in *The Future of the Universe, Chance, Chaos, God?* (New York: Continuum, 2000).

10. Lawrence Buell, *The Environmental Imagination: Thoreau, Nature Writing, and the Formation of American Culture* (Cambridge: Harvard University Press, 1995), pp. 280–308.

11. Annie Dillard, *A Pilgrim at Tinker Creek* (New York: Harper and Row, 1974; 1999), p. 206.

12. John Muir, "The Story of My Boyhood and Youth," in *John Muir: Nature Writings*, ed. William Cronon (New York: Library of America, 1997), p 7.

13. Accounts of the origin and character of Campbellite religious communities in relation to the Disciples of Christ and to Daniel Muir's beliefs can be found in Steven J. Holmes, *The Young John Muir: An Environmental Biography* (Madison: University of Wisconsin Press, 1999), pp. 58–61; and Donald Worster, *The Wealth of Nature: Environmental History and the Ecological Imagination* (New York: Oxford University Press, 1993), pp. 191–194.

14. John P. O'Grady, *Pilgrims to the Wild: Everett Ruess, Henry Thoreau, John Muir, Clarence King, Mary Austin* (Salt Lake City: University of Utah Press, 1993), p. 48.

15. John Muir, *A Thousand-Mile Walk to the Gulf*, ed. William Frederic Badè (1916; rpt. San Francisco: Sierra Club Books, 1991), pp. 1, 77.

16. John Muir, *Letters to a Friend: Written to Mrs. Ezra S. Carr, 1866–1879* (Boston: Houghton Mifflin, 1915), p. 32.

17. John Muir, *John of the Mountains: the Unpublished Journals of John Muir*, ed. Linnie Marsh Wolfe (Boston: Houghton Mifflin, 1938), p. 47.

18. *My First Summer in the Sierra* (pp. 295, 197, 301) and *The Mountains of California* (p. 499), in *John Muir: Nature Writings*. Subsequent references to *My First Summer* and *The Mountains* are to this edition.

19. Holmes surveys some of the previously expressed views of Muir's religious identity in *The Young John Muir*, p. 7.

20. Muir, *Letters to a Friend*, pp. 178, 126.

21. Muir, *John of the Mountains*, pp. 58, 88.

22. Muir, *Letters to a Friend*, p. 1.

23. See Mark Stoll, "God and John Muir: A Psychological Interpretation of John Muir's Journey from the Campbellites to the 'Range of Light,' " together with Dennis Williams, "John Muir, Christian Mysticism, and the Spiritual Value of Nature," in *John Muir: Life and Work*, ed. Sally M. Miller (Albuquerque: University of New Mexico Press, 1990), pp. 64–81, 83–99; Frederick Turner, *Rediscovering America: John Muir in His Time and Ours* (New York: Viking Books, 1985), pp. 67–71; and Robert L. Dorman, *A Word for Nature: Four Pioneering Environmental Advocates, 1845–1913* (Chapel Hill: University of North Carolina Press, 1998), pp. 112–122.

24. This point has been previously noted by Williams, "John Muir, Christian Mysticism, and the Spiritual Value of Nature," p. 87; and by Michael P. Cohen, *The Pathless Way: John Muir and American Wilderness* (Madison: University of Wisconsin Press, 1984), p. 53.

25. Roderick Frazier Nash, *The Rights of Nature: A History of Environmental Ethics* (Madison: University of Wisconsin Press, 1989), pp. 42–43.

26. John Muir, *Life and Letters of John Muir*, ed. William Frederic Badè (Boston: Houghton Mifflin, 1924), 1: 3.

27. In *John of the Mountains*, for example, Muir regards the beauty apparent even in dead flowers of "silky white-leaved Eriogonum" as demonstrating "the love and tenderness of God" (80). See also Cohen, *The Pathless Way*, p. 163.

28. *John Muir: Nature Writings*, p. 595.

29. As cited by Dennis Williams (88) from a letter written by Muir in December 1872, the expression refers to Muir's gratitude at seeing "Spirit Light" bathe California's "holy mountains" after experiencing temporary blindness as a result of his factory accident.

30. The expression recalls Paul's language in 1 Corinthians 15:28, "that God may be all in all."

31. In *The Young John Muir* (143 n.12), Holmes also remarks on the Pauline over-

tones of Muir's ocular trauma and apparently sudden "conversion." Several commentators have noted the further irony that in embracing a life devoted to the antimechanistic recovery of wild nature, Muir left behind a promising future as an inventor of machines.

32. Cohen (*The Pathless Way*, 11) has pointed out Jeane Carr's comparison of Muir to Saint Francis, while Worster (*The Wealth of Nature*, 184–202) highlights Muir's legacy of reforming Protestantism.

33. *A Thousand-Mile Walk to the Gulf*, 80.

34. The relevant biblical reference here is to Isaiah 35: 5, echoed as well in Matthew 11: 5 and Luke 7: 22.

35. See Cohen's pertinent remarks about language of the 1964 Wilderness Act in *The Pathless Way*, pp. 86–87, 189–190.

36. Later incorporated into Badè's posthumously published edition of *A Thousand-Mile Walk to the Gulf*, these remarks appear here in the form originally represented in Muir's journal, as cited in *John Muir: Nature Writings*, pp. 865–866.

37. Entry for May 3–4, 1838, in *The Writings of Henry D. Thoreau: Journal*, ed. John C. Broderick, et. al (Princeton: Princeton University Press, 1981), 1:44–45.

38. Dorman, *A Word for Nature*, pp, 220–221.

39. "Lines Composed a Few Miles Above Tintern Abbey," *William Wordsworth: Selected Poems and Prefaces*, ed. Jack Stillinger (Boston: Houghton Mifflin, 1965), p. 110.

40. Gary Snyder, "Is Nature Real?" in *The Gary Snyder Reader: Prose, Poetry, and Translations 1952–1998* (Washington, D.C.: Counterpoint, 1999), p. 388.

41. Lawrence Buell, *Writing for an Endangered World: Literature, Culture, and Environment in the U.S. and Beyond* (Cambridge: Harvard University Press, 2001), pp. 9–18.

42. See Turner, *Rediscovering America*, pp. 191, 259–263; and Cohen, *The Pathless Way*, pp. 184–190.

43. Mary Austin, *Earth Horizon: Autobiography* (New York: Literary Guild, 1932), pp. 188, 298, 276, 198. On the Austin-Muir connection, see also Carol E. Dickson, " 'Recounting' the Land: Mary Austin and Early Twentieth-Century Narratives of Nature," in *Such News of the Land: U.S. Women Nature Writers*, ed. Thomas S. Edwards and Elizabeth A. DeWolfe (Hanover, N.H.: University Press of New England, 2001), p. 256 n. 6. On the teleological and mystical character of Austin's "naturist" philosophy, as allied with her vocabulary of "the Soul Maker" and "the Friend of the Soul of Man," see T. M. Pearce, *Mary Hunter Austin* (New York: Twayne, 1965), pp. 121–124.

44. Mary Austin, *The Land of Little Rain* (Boston: Houghton Mifflin, 1903), p. 279. Subsequent references are to this edition. Relevant information about circumstances of the book's publication and of Austin's life can be found in Augusta Fink, *I-Mary: A Biography of Mary Austin* (Tucson: University of Arizona Press, 1983); and Esther Lanigan Stineman, *Mary Austin: Song of A Maverick* (New Haven: Yale University Press, 1989).

45. Stineman, *Mary Austin*, p. 22.

46. Stineman, *Mary Austin*, p. 18; Austin, *Earth Horizon*, pp. 51–52, 74, 125. Mark Hoyer has discussed Austin's syncretistic blend of Native American and Christian religion in a book-length treatment, briefly summarized in "Ritual Drama/Dramatic Ritual: Austin's 'Indian Plays,' " in *Exploring Lost Borders: Critical Essays on Mary Austin*, ed. Melody Graulich and Elizabeth Klimasmith (Reno: University of Nevada Press, 1999), pp. 41–43.

47. Stineman, *Mary Austin*, pp. 44–45.

48. Fink, *I-Mary*, pp. 141–142, 219; Austin, *Earth Horizon*, p. 274.

49. *Earth Horizon*, pp. 341–342, 52, 116, 126, 268.

50. The citation here from Austin's correspondence and information about Austin's experience in Italy come from Fink, *I-Mary*, pp. 144, 187.

51. Edward Abbey, *Desert Solitaire: A Season in the Wilderness* (New York: Random House, 1968), p. 6.

52. *Black Elk Speaks: Being the Life Story of a Holy Man of the Oglala Sioux*, as told through John G. Neihardt (Lincoln: University of Nebraska Press, 1979), p. 43. Subsequent references are to this edition.

53. See Raymond J. DeMaillie, "John G. Neihardt's Lakota Legacy," in *A Sender of Words: Essays in Memory of John G. Neihardt*, ed. Vine Deloria, Jr. (Salt Lake City: Howe, 1984), p. 123; and Ross Enochs, "Black Elk and the Jesuits," in *The Black Elk Reader*, ed. Clyde Holler (Syracuse: Syracuse University Press, 2000), p. 287.

54. Deloria comments on the book's major significance for Native Americans in his introduction to the Nebraska edition of *Black Elk Speaks*, p. xiii; see also Frances W. Kaye's remarks about the book's effect on AIM Leaders and the Red Power movement in "What Is Cultural Appropriation, Anyway? The Ethics of Reading *Black Elk Speaks*," in *The Black Elk Reader*, p. 158.

55. From a 1971 interview, cited in Blair Whitney, *John G. Neihardt* (Boston: Hall, 1976), p. 91.

56. Lucile F. Aly, *John G. Neihardt: A Critical Biography* (Amsterdam: Rodopi, 1977), p. 12.

57. Whitney, *John G. Neihardt*, p. 90.

58. Edited and recorded by Joseph Epes Brown, *The Sacred Pipe: Black Elks's Account of the Seven Rites of the Oglala Sioux* (Norman: University of Oklahoma Press, 1953); this source includes some explicit mention of the holy man's Christian faith in contrast with the silence of *Black Elk Speaks* on this point.

59. Joel W. Martin, *The Land Looks After Us: A History of Native American Religion* (New York: Oxford University Press, 1999), pp. 96–98. On the basis of extensive interviews with Black Elk's daughter and others who knew the holy man, Michael F. Steltenkamp presents the fullest case for his wholehearted acceptance of Christianity and his undespairing accommodation to cultural change in *Black Elk: Holy Man of the Oglala* (Norman: University of Oklahoma Press, 1993). This position has been challenged, however, most sharply by Julian Rice in *Black Elk's Story: Distinguishing Its Lakota Purpose* (Albuquerque: University of New Mexico Press, 1991); Rice also impugns Neihardt's outlook (implausibly, it seems to me) as both Christian and racist.

60. I do not mean to cast doubt on the essential authenticity of Neihardt's account, as a cultural translation and as representation of many salient features of Black Elk's experience. Still, certain omissions and revisions appear inevitably in any such translation. For example, Neihardt's readers were and are apt to regard Native Americans who adopt Christianity as having unambiguously compromised their genuine Indian heritage with "white man's religion," whereas the Plains peoples' adoption of European-introduced horses poses no such challenge to the popular image of genuine Indian ways.

61. John Fire/Lame Deer and Richard Erdoes, *Lame Deer: Seeker of Visions* (New York: Simon and Schuster, 1972). On this theme, though certainly not on all representations of Lakotan belief and practice, the testimony attributed to Lame Deer (see chapter 6, "The Circle and the Square," pp. 108–118) in a later generation coincides with that of Black Elk.

62. Letter of E.D. (July 1862) to Thomas Higginson, in *Emily Dickinson: Selected*

Letters (Cambridge: Harvard University Press, 1971), p. 176; poem no. 1263 (no. 1129 in Thomas Johnson's numbering), in *The Poems of Emily Dickinson*, ed. R. W. Franklin, 2:1089; R. W. Emerson, "Uriel," in *Poems*, in *The Complete Works of Ralph Waldo Emerson* (Boston: Houghton Mifflin, 1904), 9:14.

63. Cited in Whitney, *John G. Neihardt*, p. 91.

64. "The Second Coming," in *The Collected Poems of W. B. Yeats* (Toronto: Macmillan, 1956), p. 184.

65. A older but still cogent commentary on this theme's relevance to another literary context can be found in Robert B. Heilman, " 'The Birthmark' ": Science as Religion," *South Atlantic Quarterly* 48 (1949): 575–583.

66. Rachel Carson, from an introductory essay (1956) and from address to women journalists (1954), both cited in *Lost Woods: The Discovered Writing of Rachel Carson*, ed. Linda Lear (Boston: Beacon Press, 1998), pp. 167, 163; Rachel Carson to Dorothy Freeman (February 1, 1958), in *Always, Rachel: The Letters of Rachel Carson and Dorothy Freeman, 1952–1964*, ed. Martha Freeman (Boston: Beacon Press, 1995, pp. 248–249.

67. *Lost Woods*, p. 160; Lear, *Rachel Carson: Witness for Nature* (New York: Holt, 1997).

68. Rachel Carson, *The Sense of Wonder* (New York: Harper and Row, 1965; 2d ed.: HarperCollins, 1998), pp. 100, 55, 101.

69. Cited in Lear, *Rachel Carson*, p. 227.

70. Lear, *Rachel Carson*, pp. 10, 15–17, 24–27, 32–33, 228, 338, 384, 402, 438–440, 444, 479, 482.

71. *Always, Rachel: The Letters of Rachel Carson and Dorothy Freeman*, pp. 247, 241.

72. *The Sense of Wonder*, p. 91; *The Sea Around Us* (New York: Oxford University Press, 1951; new ed. 1989), pp. 57–74, 46, 131–132.

73. *The Edge of the Sea* (Boston: Houghton Mifflin, 1955), pp. 1–2.

74. See, for example, Carson's 1963 lecture remarks in "The Pollution of Our Environment," in *Lost Woods*, pp. 230–232; and her remarks pertaining to the "unseen world" and the "ecology of the world within our bodies," in *Silent Spring* (Boston: Houghton Mifflin, 1962), p. 189.

75. Later, highly publicized warnings about the atmospheric effects of excess carbon dioxide and methane emissions include those presented by Bill McKibben in *The End of Nature* (New York: Random House, 1989), 9–22.

76. *The Sea Around Us*, pp. 15, xi–xiii; *Silent Spring*, p. 127. In chapter 14 of *Silent Spring* (pp. 219–243), the author comments explicitly on the perilous spread of chemical carcinogens.

77. *Silent Spring*, pp. 1, 2, 6.

78. *The Edge of the Sea*, pp. 1–2.

79. *The Edge of the Sea*, pp. 2–4.

80. *The Edge of the Sea*, p. 5.

81. *Always, Rachel: The Letters of Rachel Carson and Dorothy Freeman*, pp. 67–68.

82. Remarks concerning Albert Schweitzer's philosophy of Reverence for Life, made on January 7, 1963, upon Carson's receiving the Schweitzer Medal of the Animal Welfare Institute and cited in Paul Brooks, *The House of Life: Rachel Carson at Work with Selections from her Writings Published and Unpublished* (Boston: Houghton Mifflin, 1972), p. 315.

83. *The Edge of the Sea*, pp. 7, 250.

84. *Silent Spring*, p. 99.

85. *Always, Rachel: The Letters of Rachel Carson and Dorothy Freeman*, pp. 186–187, 9; *The Edge of the Sea*, p. 100.

86. Loren Eiseley, "The Star Thrower," in *The Star Thrower* (New York: Times Books, 1978), pp. 180, 182.

87. "The Star Thrower" first appeared in Eiseley's book *The Unexpected Universe*. Anthony Lioi presents a useful account of the work's origin, context, and significance in "Coasts Demanding Shipwreck: Love and the Philosophy of Science in Loren Eiseley's 'The Star Thrower,' " *ISLE: Interdisciplinary Studies in Literature and Environment* 6 (1999): 41–61.

88. *Always, Rachel: The Letters of Rachel Carson and Dorothy Freeman*, pp. 329, 355, 358, 414, 459.

89. Mary A. McCay, *Rachel Carson* (New York: Twayne MacMillan, 1993), p. 95.

90. Lear, *Rachel Carson*, pp. 463–465; *Always, Rachel: The Letters of Rachel Carson and Dorothy Freeman*, pp. 482, 485, 488.

CHAPTER 8

1. Barry Lopez, *Arctic Dreams: Imagination and Desire in a Northern Landscape* (New York: Scribner's, 1986), p. xxii. Subsequent citations are to this edition.

2. See David Lionel Smith, "African Americans, Writing, and Nature," in *American Nature Writers*, ed. John Elder (New York: Scribner's, 1996), 2:1003–1012. In *Ride Out the Wilderness: Geography and Identity in Afro-American Literature* (Urbana: University of Illinois Press, 1987), Melvin Dixon remarks on the proclivity of slave songs and slaves narratives to image "wilderness," typically associated with southern woods or swamps, "as a place of refuge beyond the restricted world of the plantation" (3).

3. Harriet Beecher Stowe, *Dred: A Tale of the Great Dismal Swamp* (New York: Penguin Books, 2000), p. 211. See also Herbert Aptheker, "Maroons Within the Present Limits of the United States," in *Maroon Societies: Rebel Slave Communities in the United States*, ed. Richard Price (Baltimore: Johns Hopkins University Press, 1973; 2nd ed. 1979), pp. 149–167; John W. Blassingame, *The Slave Community: Plantation Life in the Antebellum South* (New York: Oxford University Press, 1972); and Manning Marable, *Blackwater: Historical Studies in Race, Class Consciousness, and Revolution* (Dayton, Ohio: Black Praxis Press, 1981).

4. Victor Turner and Edith Turner, *Image and Pilgrimage in Christian Culture* (New York: Columbia University Press, 1978), pp. 34–35. This theme is elaborated by Belden C. Lane in *The Solace of Fierce Landscapes: Exploring Desert and Mountain Spirituality* (New York: Oxford University Press, 1998), pp. 38, 43, 240 n. 7.

5. *The Confessions of Nat Turner*, ed. Kenneth S. Greenberg (Boston: St. Martin's Press, 1996), pp. 46–48.

6. Frederick Douglass, *My Bondage and My Freedom*, in *Frederick Douglass: Autobiographies*, ed. Henry Louis Gates, Jr. (New York: Library of America, 1994), pp. 278–281.

7. *The Life and Adventures of Henry Bibb: An American Slave*, with an introduction by Charles J. Heglar (Madison: University of Wisconsin Press, 2001), pp. 15, 18, 121–124, 131.

8. Literary references to this area appear in writings by Longfellow, Stowe, Melville, and others. Extensive commentary on its history and geophysical character is available in *The Great Dismal Swamp*, ed. Paul W. Kirk, Jr. (Charlottesville: University Press of Virginia, 1979).

9. Stowe, *Dred*, pp. 198, 238, 239, 274.

10. William C. Nell, *The Colored Patriots of the American Revolution* (New York: Arno Press, 1968), pp. 227–229. Nell credits Edmund Jackson, whose article appeared in the periodical "Liberty Bell" for 1853, as his source.

11. William Wells Brown, *Clotel or, The President's Daughter* (New York: Modern Library, 2000), p. 177.

12. See Albert J. Raboteau, *Slave Religion: The 'Invisible Institution' in the Antebellum South* (New York: Oxford University Press, 1978), and Gayraud S. Wilmore, *Black Religion and Black Radicalism* (Maryknoll, N.Y.: Orbis Books, 1973; 3rd ed., 1998). Peter Randolph is cited in Marble, *Blackwater*, p. 27.

13. W. E. B. Du Bois, *The Quest of the Silver Fleece: A Novel* (A. C. McLurg, 1911; rpt., New York: Arno Press, 1969), pp. 294, 78, 371. Subsequent page references are to this edition.

14. Later passages present Zora's postconversion faith in less orthodox terms. In chapter 33, for example, she urges dispossessed swampdwellers to "free yourselves" (370) instead of relying on divine grace. She also challenges the preacher at a revival meeting; and Du Bois then says of her earlier conversion experience in Washington: "There she found God after a searching that had seared her soul; but He had simply pointed the Way, and the way was human" (372). It is well known that Du Bois himself became highly critical of Christian institutions, from which he severed all personal connection after the age of thirty, because he deplored the churches' role in supporting racial oppression and African-American passivity. But while Du Bois grieved to see that "the Church of Christ fought the Communism of Christianity," he never disavowed religion altogether or denied the formative value of spirituality and interiority in African-American experience. See "My Character" (1125), in *W. E. B. Du Bois: Writings*, ed. Nathan Huggins (New York: Library of America, 1986). Beyond "My Character," Du Bois offers revealing general or autobiographical statements about religion in *The Souls of Black Folk* and *Dusk of Dawn* (all in *Writings*). Those familiar with Du Bois as self-described agnostic and communist may also be surprised to read the articulations of devotional feeling preserved in his *Prayers for Dark People*, ed. Herbert Aptheker (Amherst: University of Massachusetts Press, 1980). Manning Marable analyzes the complexity of Du Bois's religious attitudes in "The Black Faith of W. E. B. Du Bois: Sociocultural and Political Dimensions of Black Religion," in *Down by the Riverside: Readings in African American Religion*, ed. Larry G. Murphy (New York: New York University Press, 2000), pp. 122–131.

15. *Souls of Black Folk*, p. 505, in *W. E. B. Du Bois: Writings*.

16. In *Souls of Black Folk* (pp. 384–385), Du Bois voices frustration that the U.S. government's postwar promises of agricultural land grants to freedmen, including "the vision of 'forty acres and a mule,'" were never realized. Accordingly, African Americans throughout the rural South found themselves "bound by law and custom to an economic slavery" (390) that endured into the twentieth century.

17. Aside from religion, these initially unseen depths of landscape may involve imaginative textures and embedded features of cultural history, as discussed by Kent C. Ryden in *Mapping the Invisible Landscape: Folklore, Writing, and the Sense of Place* (Iowa City: University of Iowa Press, 1993). Yet for Lopez and many other American writers, discovering "a fundamental strangeness in the landscape itself" that is seen but suggestive of things unseen also reveals "something sacred" (12, 274). In *Seeking Awareness in American Nature Writing: Henry Thoreau, Annie Dillard, Edward Abbey, Wendell Berry, Barry Lopez* (Salt Lake City: University of Utah Press, 1992), Scott Slovic describes Lopez's technique of "particularizing the exotic" (145–150) in *Arctic Dreams*.

18. Lopez (pp. 278–279) here credits the formulations of the geographer Yi-Fu Tuan. See especially Yi-Fu Tuan, *Space and Place: The Perspective of Experience* (Minneapolis: University of Minnesota Press, 1977); Belden C. Lane develops a parallel distinction between the Greek words *topos* (simple location) and *chora* (a site drawing energy and imagination) in *Landscapes of the Sacred: Geography and Narrative in American Spirituality* (Baltimore: Johns Hopkins University Press, 1988; rev. ed. 2001), pp. 38–41.

19. In *Reverence: Renewing a Forgotten Virtue* (New York: Oxford University Press, 2001), Paul Woodruff discusses reverence as an ancient civil virtue that admits human limitation and displays a capacity to respect someone or something—including nonhuman creatures (22–25)—outside the self. It is germane to the case at hand that Woodruff perceives reverence to be not so much a matter of belief as of disposition. Commonly expressed through some form of outward ceremony, it need not be associated with a defined religious faith or with religion at all.

20. Cited in Nicholas O'Connell, "Religion and the Environment: On Sacred Ground," *Sierra* 83 (November/December 1998): 58–60.

21. The chief biblical statement of kenosis is Philippians 2:5–11.

22. Cited in William Johnston, *The Inner Eye of Love: Mysticism and Religion* (San Francisco: Harper and Row, 1978), p. 37.

23. Kallistos Ware, *The Orthodox Way* (Crestwood, N.Y.: St. Vladimir's Seminary Press, 1995), p. 15. I am indebted for this reference to an unpublished essay by Ralph C. Wood of Baylor University. Belden C. Lane, in *The Solace of Fierce Landscapes*, comments at length on the nexus between severe physical settings and spiritual traditions of negative way theology.

24. From Andrew Harvey, *A Journey in Ladakh*, as cited in Lane, *Solace of Fierce Landscapes*, p. 54.

25. Barry Lopez, *About This Life: Journeys on the Threshold of Memory* (New York: Knopf, 1998), pp. 66–72.

26. Lopez graduated from Notre Dame in 1966. Since the interval of his study there happens to have overlapped with my own (1964–1968), I know that selections from Descartes's philosophic writing were assigned at this time in the Collegiate Seminar course required of all undergraduates. For Lopez's most fully elaborated statements on the sensibility of animals, see "Renegotiating the Contracts" in *This Incomparable Lande: A Book of American Nature Writing*, ed. Thomas J. Lyon (New York: Viking Penguin, 1989), pp. 381–388; and *Of Wolves and Men* (New York: Scribner's, 1978).

27. Cited in O'Connell, "Religion and the Environment," p. 60.

28. In *About This Life*, Lopez discloses: "If I were asked what I want to accomplish as a writer, I would say it's to contribute to a literature of hope" (14).

29. See, for example, comments by Belden Lane (*Solace of Fierce Landscapes*, p. 85) about his reluctance to look at a snow leopard caged in the St. Louis Zoo.

30. Matthiessen's prolific output, now represented by more than two dozen book titles, also includes works of social criticism focused on topics such as the unionizing initiatives of Cesar Chavez, the economic struggle of Long Island fishermen, and the failure of U.S. government interactions with Native Americans.

31. Matthiessen displays this engagement in several of his books, including *In the Spirit of Crazy Horse* (1983) and *Indian Country* (1984). In *About This Life* (9), Lopez tells of first meeting Matthiessen, "a writer I would later come to admire and get to know," early in life when the older man was running a charter boat off Montauk Point, Long Island.

32. William Dowie, *Peter Matthiessen* (Boston: Twayne, 1991), pp. 105–116; Peter Matthiessen, *Nine-Headed Dragon River: Zen Journals 1969–1985* (Boston: Shambhala, 1986), pp. 9, xii, 10–11. Linking Matthiessen's Zen practice of meditation to Aldo Leopold's discovery of ecological awareness, McKay Jenkins, " 'Thinking Like a Mountain': Death and Deep Ecology in the Work of Peter Matthiessen," in *Reading Under the Sign of Nature: New Essays in Ecocriticism*, ed. John Tallmadge and Henry Harrington (Salt Lake City: University of Utah Press, 2000), discloses that Matthiessen "recently received transmission as a *roshi*, the highest achievement for a Zen practitioner" and "continues to teach in his own small wooden zendo on Long Island near the Atlantic Ocean" (271).

33. Wendy Smith, "PW Interviews: Peter Matthiessen," *Publishers Weekly* 9 (May 9, 1986): 241.

34. Paul Rea, "Causes and Creativity: An Interview with Peter Matthiessen," *Re Arts and Letters: A Liberal Arts Forum* 15 (Fall 1989): 29.

35. Peter Matthiessen, *The Snow Leopard* (New York: Viking Books, 1978), p. 43. Subsequent citations are to this edition.

36. Cited in Anonymous, "Peter Matthiessen," in *World Authors: 1950–1970*, ed. John Wakeman (New York: Wilson, 1975), p. 957.

37. Michael Heim, "The Mystic and the Myth: Thoughts on *The Snow Leopard*," *Studia Mystica* 4 (Summer 1981): 6.

38. Lawrence Buell, *The Environmental Imagination: Thoreau, Nature Writing, and the Formation of American Culture* (Cambridge: Harvard University Press, 1995), p. 16.

39. Kay Bonetti, "An Interview with Peter Matthiessen," *Missouri Review* 12 (1989): 120.

40. Peter Matthiessen, *Lost Man's River* (New York: Random House, 1997), p. 118. Hereafter abbreviated as *LMR*.

41. Peter Matthiessen, *Killing Mr. Watson* (New York: Random House, 1990), p. 15. Hereafter abbreviated as *KMW*.

42. In Matthiessen's *Bone by Bone* (New York: Random House, 1999) (hereafter abbreviated as *B*) Watson confirms his denial both of God's existence (169) and of any cosmic meaning or purpose. Nature, he insists, is "simply *there*, oblivious, indifferent" (168). In *KMW*, a neighbor testifies that "*nothing mattered*" for Watson: "It didn't *matter* that our mortal days were bloodsoaked, cruel, and empty, with nothing at the end but disease and darkness" (212).

43. John Cooley, "Matthiessen's Voyages on the River Styx: Deathly Waters, Endangered Peoples," in *Earthly Words: Essays on Contemporary American Nature and Environmental Writers* (Ann Arbor: University of Michigan Press, 1994), p. 185.

44. Cited in Deborah Houy, "A Moment with Peter Matthiessen," *Buzzworm* 5 (March 1993): 28.

45. Pico Iyer, "Laureate of the Wild," *Time* (January 11, 1993): 42.

CHAPTER 9

1. Gary Snyder, "The Place, the Region, and the Commons," in *The Practice of the Wild* (San Francisco: North Point Press, 1990), pp. 30–31, 28.

2. Andrew J. Angyal provides an informative biographical account in *Wendell Berry* (New York: Twayne-Simon & Schuster Macmillan, 1995). Berry's best-known autobiographical statements—including "The Rise," "The Long-Legged House," "A Native Hill," and "The Making of a Marginal Farm"—are available in his *Recollected Essays: 1965–1980* (San Francisco: North Point Press, 1981). My former graduate stu-

dent John Jacobs Holden has explored the prophetic character of Berry's writing in "The Land as Sacrament: Wendell Berry's Prophetic Vision" (Ph.D. diss., University of Connecticut, 1998).

3. My pairing of these terms reflects a disapproval widely shared by Berry's post-agricultural readers. For Berry himself, however, tobacco growing is a complex issue quite unlike the morally abhorrent legacy of slavery. See also Angyal's commentary (pp. 41–46) on slavery and racism; and Wendell Berry, "The Problem of Tobacco," in *Sex, Economy, Freedom and Community* (New York: Pantheon Books, 1992), pp. 53–68.

4. *Recollected Essays*, p. ix.

5. Wendell Berry, "God and Country," in *What Are People For? Essays by Wendell Berry* (New York: North Point Press, 1990), p. 96; *Sex, Economy*, p. 115

6. "God and Country," in *What Are People For?* p. 95; "Christianity and the Survival of Creation," in *Sex, Economy*, pp. 97, 101, 96.

7. *Sex, Economy*, p. 100.

8. "Word and Flesh," in *What Are People For?* p. 200.

9. Berry, "The Making of a Marginal Farm," in *Recollected Essays*, p. 333. Subsequent references are to this edition.

10. One of Berry's poetry collections, *The Country of Marriage* (New York: Harcourt Brace Jovanovich, 1973), bears this title. Berry's essays, too, often explore parallels between his marital state and physically committed relation to the land.

11. Berry alludes to one of Merton's essays in *A Continuous Harmony: Essays Cultural and Agricultural* (New York: Harcourt Brace Jovanovich, 1970), p. 16.

12. "The Conservation of Nature and the Preservation of Humanity," in *Another Turn of the Crank: Essays by Wendell Berry* (Washington, D.C.: Counterpoint, 1995), pp. 67–69.

13. Such is the main argument in Berry, *Life Is a Miracle: An Essay Against Modern Superstition* (Washington, D.C.: Counterpoint, 2000). To my mind, though, parts of this book are weakened by a polemical rhetoric that is negatively, narrowly, and personally directed (or misdirected) against the sociobiologist E. O. Wilson.

14. All citations in this paragraph come from "The Conservation of Nature and the Preservation of Humanity," pp. 78, 76–77.

15. "The Gift of Good Land," in *The Gift of Good Land: Further Essays Cultural and Agricultural* (San Francisco: North Point Press, 1981), 267. Subsequent references are to this edition.

16. Wendell Berry, "A Citizen's Response to the National Security Strategy of the United States of America, *Orion* 22 (March/April 2003): 23.

17. *What Are People For?* p. 9.

18. "A Citizen's Response," 27; Wendell Berry, "Thoughts in the Presence of Fear," in *In the Presence of Fear: Three Essays for a Changed World* (Great Barrington, Mass.: Orion Society, 2001), p. 7; "A Citizen's Response," pp. 21, 26. See also Berry's remarks about the destruction of the World Trade Center in "Two Minds," *Progressive* 66 (November 2002): 21–29.

19. Annie Dillard, *Pilgrim at Tinker Creek* (New York: HarperCollins, 1974; with afterword 1999), p. 13. Subsequent references are to this edition.

20. Raised in a Presbyterian family but disavowing church membership in adolescence, Dillard studied theology with great interest during her student years at Hollins College. She admits that she enjoyed scandalizing her academic colleagues at Wesleyan University when she eventually became a Roman Catholic, a shift readers might already expect from her remarks in *Teaching a Stone to Talk*. "There was no way I could shock my community more profoundly than by becoming a Catholic," she has

said, "and it succeeded beyond my wildest dreams." Yet she denies that this profession marks a radical shift in her beliefs, observing that despite her enduring attraction to Hasidisim and other spiritual teachings, "I've been a *Christian* writer from the moment I started writing." For her religion is not, in any case, "about giving intellectual assent" to "a checklist of dogmas." Interview remarks cited in Ray Kelleher, "Pilgrim at Planet Earth," *Notre Dame* (Winter 1998–99): 26. Other commentary about Dillard's religious background in relation to *Pilgrim* can be found in James I. McClintock, "Annie Dillard: Ritualist," in *Nature's Kindred Spirits* (Madison: University of Wisconsin Press, 1994), pp. 88–108; Linda L. Smith, *Annie Dillard* (New York: Hall, 1991), pp. 1–41; and Don Scheese, "Annie Dillard," in *American Nature Writers*, ed. John Elder (New York: Scribner's, 1996), 1:213–219.

21. See Barbara Lewalski, *Protestant Poetics and the Seventeenth-Century Religious Lyric* (Princeton: Princeton University Press, 1979), pp. 151–152, 162–165; Helen White, *English Devotional Literature, 1600–1640* (Madison: University of Wisconsin Studies in Language and Literature, 1931), esp. pp. 154, 179–180, 212–213; and Louis L. Martz, *The Poetry of Meditation: A Study in English Religious Literature of the Seventeenth Century* (New Haven: Yale University Press, 1954; 2nd ed. 1962).

22. Thomas Traherne, *Centuries* (Oxford: Clarendon Press, 1960), pp. 65, 10, 5, 18. Although Traherne left his work untitled, the theme of meditation figures prominently throughout sections of his manuscript.

23. Annie Dillard, *For the Time Being* (New York: Knopf, 1999), pp. 58, 29.

24. Accordingly, it does not strike me as terribly important to know whether episodes like the water bug's assault on the frog were based on Dillard's immediate observation or on her reading. Such things do happen, in any case. The author stirred controversy when she admitted, in remarks circulated through the Association for Literature and the Environment website, that she had embellished or even fabricated some of the field observations she included in *Pilgrim*. But it seems to me pointless, a case of misplaced literalism, to worry about whether all the events described in this book "really" took place in the way they are narrated. *Pilgrim*, like *Walden*, is a work of creative nonfiction that inevitably blends recollected facts of personal experience with imaginative artistry.

25. The New Testament episode (recorded in the synoptic gospels, including Matthew 17) in which three disciples see Jesus transfigured with light on a high mountain in Galilee provides a revealing religious context for understanding Dillard's account of the transfigured cedar. In the last section of *Holy the Firm*, Dillard likewise associates her perception of a translucent, "transfigured" world to gospel narrations of Jesus' baptism by John in the Jordan River.

26. In *For the Time Being* (p. 137), Dillard describes panentheism in connection with Jewish mystical theology. See also Smith, *Annie Dillard*, pp. 16–17.

27. *For the Time Being*, p. 167.

28. Particularly insofar as Janice's large old homes had never been torn down for the sake of town renewal, the settlement resembles Cheever's own place of residence in Ossining, New York. Cheever comments on this Westchester County town in a 1976 interview with Shirley Silverberg. See *Conversations with John Cheever*, ed. Scott Donaldson (Jackson: University Press of Mississippi Press, 1987), pp. 86–89. I am grateful to Karen Renner for pointing out these remarks, as well as the reactions Cheever recorded (in *The Journals of John Cheever*, ed. Robert Gottlieb [New York: Knopf, 1991], pp. 371, 392) to local reports of toxic waste and water pollution.

29. John Cheever, *Oh What a Paradise It Seems* (New York: Random House, 1982), p. 3. Subsequent references are to this edition.

30. Interview (1982) with Joshua Gilder, in *Conversations with John Cheever*, p. 228.

31. For explanation of this terminology, with reference to Paul Ricoeur's theory, see my introduction.

32. Interview with Joshua Gilder, in *Conversations with John Cheever*, p. 231; see also pp. 218–219.

33. Susan Cheever, *Home Before Dark* (Boston: Houghton Mifflin, 1984), p. 167.

34. Interview with Joshua Gilder in *Conversations with John Cheever*, p. 226.

35. The town of Sandpoint is situated on Lake Pend Oreille, a body of water traversed by a railroad bridge comparable to that described in Robinson's novel.

36. Marilynne Robinson, *Housekeeping* (New York: Farrar, Straus and Giroux, 1980), p. 82. Subsequent references are to this edition.

37. Not surprisingly, in view of Robinson's almost exclusive focus on womanly interactions, this aspect of the novel has been underscored in critical commentaries. But I do not believe that Robinson's feminism carries as much rejection of Christian tradition as has been argued, for example, by Sonia Gernes, "Transcendent Women: Uses of the Mystical in Margaret Atwood's *Cat's Eye* and Marilynne Robinson's *Housekeeping*," *Religion and Literature* 23 (Autumn 1991): 143–165.

38. For a useful reading of *Housekeeping* that includes an effective elaboration of this point, see Nicholas O'Connell, "Contemporary Ecofiction," in *American Nature Writers*, ed. John Elder (New York: Scribner's, 1996), 2:1050–1054.

39. Gary Williams, "Resurrecting Carthage: *Housekeeping* and Cultural History," *English Language Notes* 29 (December 1991): 70–78, points out (74) that the etymology of Lucille's name suggests lucidity and light in contrast to the darkness preferred by Sylvie and Ruth.

40. Marilynne Robinson, *The Death of Adam: Essays on Modern Thought* (Boston: Houghton Mifflin, 1998), p. 165.

41. *The Death of Adam*, p. 1.

42. See Maggie Galehouse, "Their Own Private Idaho: Transience in Marilynne Robinson's *Housekeeping*," *Contemporary Literature* 41 (Spring 2000): 181, 121–122.

43. *The Death of Adam*, pp. 10–24 and 150–173, 227–244. In the same volume (pp. 227–244), Robinson describes her own denominational background as Presbyterian with a subsequent shift to Congregationalism.

44. The classic biblical expression of kenosis appears in Philippians 2:5–11.

45. Paul, in Romans 8:21–22, suggests that not only humanity but creation, too, awaits final redemption: "The whole creation groaneth and travaileth in pain" to be delivered. *Housekeeping* endorses this sentiment in several ways, as when Ruth remarks during flood season that "the lake still thundered and groaned, the flood waters still brimmed and simmered" (70).

46. This sociopolitical issue is not, of course, properly addressed in Robinson's fiction even though Robinson, unlike Cheever or Dillard, has been publicly identified with environmental advocacy through her book-length critique of nuclear power practices in Britain. Still, in *The End of Nature* and in *The Comforting Whirlwind: God, Job, and the Scale of Creation* (Grand Rapids, Mich.: Eerdmans, 1994), pp. 81–92, Bill McKibben presses the point that eliminating wild places might radically alter the spiritual sensibility of humankind. In "Wilderness," an essay included in *The Death of Adam*, Robinson argues that preserving the beauty of less settled landscapes should not be pursued single-mindedly, at the expense of an overall environmental reform that must be centered in civilization.

CHAPTER 10

1. Wendell Berry, acknowledging that in broadest terms most poetry could be called "nature poetry," has argued for applying the term more restrictively to verse reflecting a "sustained attentiveness to nature." It is written by those who have "turned to the natural world, not as a source of imagery, but as subject and inspiration," those for whom that world is "a primary interest." See the essay "A Secular Pilgrimage" in Wendell Berry, *A Continuous Harmony: Essays Cultural and Agricultural* (New York: Harcourt Brace Jovanovich, 1970), pp. 3–4. David W. Gilcrest attempts to distinguish among nature poetry, environmental poetry, and ecological poetry in *Greening The Lyre: Environmental Poetics and Ethics* (Reno: University of Nevada Press, 2002). Other notable statements about modern and contemporary American nature poetry can be found in John Elder, *Imagining the Earth: Poetry and the Vision of Nature* (Athens: University of Georgia Press, 1985; 2nd ed. 1996); and Christopher Merrill, "The Forms of American Nature Poetry," in *American Nature Writers*, ed. John Elder (New York: Scribner's, 1996), 2:1079–1097.

2. Denise Levertov, "A Hundred a Day," in *This Great Unknowing: Last Poems* (New York: New Directions, 1999), p. 13.

3. Levertov, "Sojourns in the Parallel World," previously in *The Sands of the Well* (1996) but cited here in Levertov's thematically unified collection *The Life Around Us: Selected Poems on Nature* (New York: New Directions, 1997), pp. 75–76.

4. Mary Oliver, *Winter Hours: Prose, Prose Poems, and Poems* (Boston: Houghton Mifflin, 1999), p. 101.

5. See John Elder, *Imagining the Earth* (pp. 1–23, 161–162, 210) for useful reflections on Robinson Jeffers as well as on imaginative portrayals of healing by various modern and nineteenth-century poets.

6. Useful accounts of Snyder's quest to combine Asian values (centered on study of Zen and other forms of Buddhism) with insights derived from Native American shamanism can be found in James I. Mclintock, *Nature's Kindred Spirits* (Madison: University of Wisconsin Press, 1994) pp. 109–128; Elder's *Imagining the Earth*, pp. 40–74; and Patrick Murphy, "Gary Snyder," in *American Nature Writers*, 2:829–846.

7. Berry, "A Secular Pilgrimage," in *A Continuous Harmony*, pp. 3–35. See Levertov's remarks in interview with Jewel Spears Brooker, *Conversations with Denise Levertov*, ed. Jewel Spears Brooker (Jackson: University Press of Mississippi, 1998), p. 188–189; together with Denise Lynch, "Denise Levertov in Pilgrimage," in *Denise Levertov: Selected Criticism*, ed. Albert Gelpi (Ann Arbor: University of Michigan Press, 1993), pp. 288–302; and Paul A. Lacey, "Wanderer and Pilgrim; Poet and Person," in *Denise Levertov: New Perspectives*, ed. Anne Colclough Little and Susie Paul (West Cornwall, Conn.: Locust Hill Press, 2000), pp. 241–252.

8. Berry, "A Secular Pilgrimage," pp. 6, 15.

9. *Winter Hours*, pp. 102, 98.

10. Patiann Rogers, *The Dream of the Marsh Wren: Writing as Reciprocal Creation* (Minneapolis: Milkweed Editions, 1999), p. 92.

11. Wendell Berry, *A Timbered Choir: The Sabbath Poems 1979–1997* (Washington, D.C.: Counterpoint, 1998), p. xvii.

12. *Winter Hours*, p. 102.

13. *Winter Hours*, p. 100.

14. Patiann Rogers, "Fractal: Repetition of Form over a Variety of Scales," in *Song of the World Becoming: New and Collected Poems 1981–2001* (Minneapolis: Milkweed Editions, 2001), p. 465.

15. *The Dream of the Marsh Wren*, p. 91.

16. Levertov interview with Lorrie Smith, in *Conversations with Denise Levertov*, p. 141.

17. For information about Levertov's family and religious background, together with discussion of the shifts in belief she experienced at various stages of her career, see other interview remarks by Levertov in *Conversations with Denise Levertov*, pp. 49–50, 60–61, 89–90, 111, 125–126, 140–141, 158–159, and 176–180; James Dougherty, "Presence, Silence, and the Holy in Denise Levertov's Poems," unpublished essay; Mark C. Long, "Affinities of Faith and Place in the Poetry of Denise Levertov," *ISLE: Interdisciplinary Studies in Literature and Environment* 62 (Summer 1999): 31–40; Edward Zlotkowski, "Levertov and Christianity: A Journey Toward Renewal," *Christianity and Literature* 41 (Summer 1992): 443–470; and Zlotkowski's continuation of the previous essay in "Levertov's Christianity: Work That Enfaiths," *Christianity and Literature* 42 (Autumn 1992): 97–116. Two revealing essays by Levertov bearing on her religious views ("Some Affinities of Content" and "Work that Enfaiths") are collected in her *New and Selected Essays* (New York: New Directions, 1992).

18. *A Timbered Choir: The Sabbath Poems 1979–1997*, p. 5. Subsequent references are to this edition.

19. Abraham Heschel, *The Sabbath: Its Meaning for Modern Man* (New York: Farrar, Straus and Giroux, 1951), pp. 14, 10.

20. In *Imagining the Earth* (pp. 24–39 and 207–209), Elder provides searching commentary on this theme of regenerative decay within the broader context of modern poetry and culture

21. Mary Oliver, "Spring," cited in *New and Selected Poems* (Boston: Beacon Press, 1992), p. 70.

22. Gary Snyder, *Turtle Island* (New York: New Directions, 1974), p. 105.

23. Gary Snyder, *The Real Work: Interviews and Talks 1964–1979*, ed. William Scott McLean (New York: New Directions, 1980), p. 4.

24. Denise Levertov, *A Door in the Hive* (New York: New Directions, 1989), p. 59.

25. *New and Selected Poems*, p. 71.

26. Gary Snyder, "What Happened Here Before" and "Toward Climax," in *Turtle Island*, pp. 79, 85.

27. Mary Oliver, "Turtle," in *House of Light* (Boston: Beacon Press, 1990), p. 22.

28. Mary Oliver, "Nature" and "The Ponds," in *New and Selected Poems*, pp. 90, 93.

29. *Mountains and Rivers Without End* (Washington, D.C: Counterpoint, 1996), p. 155. Subsequent references are to this edition.

30. See Masao Abe's remarks on "dynamic sunyata" and on Mahayana Buddhism's sense of *karuna* (compassion), in *Divine Emptiness and Historical Fullness: A Buddhist-Jewish-Christian Conversation with Masao Abe*, ed. Christopher Ives (Valley Forge, Penn.: Trinity Press International, 1995), pp. 50–90, 188–89.

31. Gary Snyder, "Good, Wild, Sacred," in *The Practice of the Wild* (San Francisco: North Point Press, 1990), p. 93.

32. Ruth Kirk, *Exploring Mount Rainier* (Seattle: University of Washington Press, 1968), pp. 39–41. In *The Mountain That Was 'God'* (New York: Putnam, 1911), John H. Williams gave an influential though probably exaggerated account of Rainier's deification by coastal Indians (pp. 25–41). I am indebted to James Dougherty's unpublished essay, previously cited, for making me aware of Levertov's religious fascination with Mount Rainier in the late poems.

33. "Against Intrusion," in *The Life Around Us*, p. 72. The *Life* volume includes fifteen poems focused on Mount Rainier. Eleven of these had appeared in *Evening*

Train (1992) and four in *Sands of the Well* (1996). Four more mountain poems were printed posthumously in *This Great Unknowing* (1999).

34. Gary Snyder, interviewed in *The Real Work*, p. 93.

35. Simon Schama, *Landscape and Memory* (New York: Knopf, 1995), pp. 406–411. I am grateful to my colleague Donna Hollenberg, who is writing a biography of Levertov, for informing me of the poet's comments about *Landscape and Memory* as recorded in an unpublished and undated letter to James Laughlin. In "Some Affinities of Content," collected in *New and Selected Essays*, Levertov also suggests that in spiritually animated poetry of the Pacific Northwest, "the strong influence of Chinese and Japanese poetry and of Buddhism on a people dwelling in a landscape which, with its mists and snowy mountains, often seems to resemble one of these great scroll paintings of Asian art, comes into play . . . and gives rise to a more or less conscious desire to immerse the self in that large whole" (6).

36. See Belden C. Lane, *The Solace of Fierce Landscapes: Exploring Desert and Mountain Spirituality* (New York: Oxford University Press, 1998), p. 103

37. In "Levertov's Christianity: Work That Enfaiths" (98–99, 104–105), Zlotkowski analyzes the poet's references, particularly in poems written during the 1980s, to nature spirits that she calls "earth-gods." The theologian Jürgen Moltmann discusses ways Trinitarian doctrine might accommodate truthful elements of pantheistic and polytheistic responses to nature in his *God in Creation: A New Theology of Creation and the Spirit of God* (San Francisco: HarperSanFrincisco, 1985), pp. 2, 15–16, 98, 103.

38. "The mountain's daily speech is silence," in *This Great Unknowing*, p. 42.

AFTERWORD

1. As I have previously noted, McKibben presents the most widely publicized version of this argument in *The End of Nature* (New York: Random House, 1989). But he elaborates the case most fully in *The Comforting Whirlwind: God, Job, and The Scale of Creation* (Grand Rapids, Mich.: Eerdmans, 1994). There he argues that religious readings of the natural environment are not only possible but essential—for the future of religion as well as of civilization. It is also worth knowing about the more hopeful aspect of McKibben's ecological vision, as articulated in *Hope, Human and Wild: True Stories of Living Lightly on the Earth* (St. Paul, Minn.: Hungry Mind Press, 1995).

2. I have in mind here the line in Wordsworth's sonnet "The World Is Too Much with Us" that reads "Little we see in Nature that is ours."

Index

McKibben, Bill, 10, 246, 248n.18, 259n.48, 272n.75
McPhee, John, 175
Meditation, practice of and relation to environmental literature, 13–14, 38–40, 112, 132–133, 207–214, 228, 230–234, 237, 240–241
  on the creatures, 38, 40–43, 207–208
Melville, Herman, 8, 10, 69, 103, 115, 116–125, 140, 144, 168, 213
  critical skepticism of, 121–122, 125
  and critique of idyllic naturalism, 116–117
  as exponent of nonhuman creation's freedom and uncontrollable dynamism, 124–125, 262n.43
  and inscrutability of God and Creation, 120–123
  and problem of metaphysical evil (theodicy), 117
  works: Battle-Pieces, 144; Moby-Dick, 8, 10, 116–125; Pierre, 121, 122
Merrimack River, 46–48, 127
Merton, Thomas, 203
Methodism and Methodist Church, 159, 179
Milarepa, 236
Miller, Perry, 5, 35, 55
Milton, John, 124
Moltmann, Jürgen, 64, 268n.9
Monet, Claude, 241
Morrison, Toni, 7, 176
Morton, Thomas, 6, 27–33
Mourt's Relation, 18, 20, 26
Muir, Daniel, 148–149
Muir, John, 10, 30, 89, 144, 145, 146, 147–158, 172–173, 246
  conception of God, 148, 150–151, 154, 155–156
  disposition to retain selected elements of biblical Christianity, 150, 151, 153, 154–156
  dynamic refashioning of conventional temple imagery, 153–155
  as exponent of earth-centered revelation through rugged landscapes, 149–150, 152
  mystical character of, 149, 151, 269n.24
  Protestant character of, 150, 151–152

rejection of human-centered religion, 149–150, 155
  and resistance to his father's Campbellite Christianity, 148–151
  revision of Darwinism, 151
  scientific background, 148, 151, 154
  works: "God's First Temples: How Shall We Preserve Our Forests," 153; The Mountains of California, 151, 152, 154; My First Summer in the Sierra, 152–157; "The Story of My Boyhood and Youth," 148; A Thousand-Mile Walk to the Gulf, 148, 155; Unpublished Journals, 149, 150
Muir Woods, 173

Nash, Roderick, 255n.4
Native American views of nature, 6, 15, 30, 32, 145–146, 159–160, 161–165, 188, 239
Natural Theology (William Paley), 61, 73–74
Nature, problem of defining, 4, 10, 17
Naturalist Buys an Old Farm, A (Edwin Way Teale), 199
Negative Way (apophatic) theology and mysticism, 13, 44, 122–123, 125, 128, 186, 208–209, 211–212, 224, 241
Neihardt, John G., 146, 162–165
Nell, William C., 178
Nelson, Marilyn, 200
New Englands Prospect (William Wood), 16, 17
New English Canaan (Thomas Morton), 27–33
Nicene Creed, 36, 168, 211, 240
Norris, Kathleen, 7, 200

O'Connor, Flannery, 82
Oh What A Paradise It Seems (Cheever), 214–219, 245
O'Keefe, Georgia, 241
Oliver, Mary, 13, 142, 200, 225, 227–229, 235–236, 246
  reverence for otherness of nonhuman creatures in "Spring," 235
  struggle to accept predatory nature in "Nature," "The Ponds," and "Turtle," 236
Otsego Lake, 86, 87–88

CPSIA information can be obtained at www.ICGtesting.com
Printed in the USA
LVOW04s0426190815

450683LV00006B/44/P